NET PUBLICATIONS

24/08

PETER DRAGICEVICH
JOLYON ATTWOOLL

SYDNEY
C I T Y   G U I D E

INTRODUCING SYDNEY

Swimming in Sydney doesn't always mean surf and sand: take a dip at Bondi Icebergs (p175), a local institution

Sydney doesn't care what you think of him; he knows he's fabulous. He's got it all – he's sporty, arty, sexy, successful, confident, good-looking and damn interesting.

His Australian siblings won't admit to being jealous, but who wouldn't be? You'd hate him too, if he wasn't so completely charming. He's got a sunny disposition, but can be rather dry. Sure, he's got his rough edges and his problems, but he keeps them all well hidden behind his dazzling façade. He's a bit Manly and a lot Darling (Harbour, Point, -hurst, -ton).

What's more, Sydney is easy. He's an easy city to visit – easy to get around, easy to strike good weather, easy to have a good time. There are no bushels hiding Sydney's talents – he knows what he's got and shows it off. The same can be said for his inhabitants. The stereotypical Sydneysider isn't demure. What's the point of a shirt if you've got abs you could wash clothes on?

The Sydney experience can be so many different things. It's the smell of frangipanis on a balmy summer night. It's knocking back a cold beer at a beachside pub. It's catching a show at the Opera House. It's the sound of a 10-year-old girl screaming 'smash him' as a rugby league player takes down an opponent. It's stumbling across an Aboriginal rock carving on a harbour headland. It's washing the salt from your hair after a day's body-surfing and body-watching at Bondi.

Most attractions are laid out around the metropolis' greatest natural asset, that glittering harbour. Jump on a ferry and Sydney's your oyster – the harbour prises the city's two halves far enough apart to reveal an excess of pearls.

CITY LIFE

Sydney is home to nearly 4.3 million people – the biggest city in Oceania, but not even scraping into the top 50 in the world. That doesn't disqualify it from being one of the planet's great cities.

Sydneysiders tend to be casual, forthright, irreverent, curious and friendly. The best things in life here are free – the beaches, the mountains, the parks and the much-loved harbour. The weather's reasonably moderate – although it can get stinking hot in the height of summer and chilly (but never freezing) in winter.

Water is a hot topic of conversation. When will the drought lift? Will we ever be able to wash our cars with a hose again? When it rains heavily, why does it only ever seem to put sewage into the harbour and not water into the dams?

State politics is another quagmire. Breakdowns in the political machine, along with the odd allegation of corruption, add to the feeling that Sydney's convict shackles haven't been completely shaken off. Most Sydneysiders would be happy with a transport system that didn't break down or cost a fortune in tolls, and a better public health system. The election in 2007 engendered a mix of apathy and despair. Many felt that the Labor party that has been governing NSW since 1995 didn't deserve to win, but were even more disillusioned with the opposition. Even returning Premier Morris Iemma implied in his acceptance speech that his return to power was in part due to Liberal Prime Minister John Howard's unpopular federal workplace reforms.

Other touchy subjects include race relations and immigration (see p119). The majority of Australia's immigrants make a beeline to this pot of gold, where a third of the population was born overseas. The city's mixture of pragmatic egalitarianism and natural indifference has made for a generally accepting environment. Most locals are happy to live in a cosmopolitan place with international cuisines to enjoy. But for others, attitudes harden to those who speak a different language or arrive as a refugee. The term 'un-Australian' is continually bandied about by politicians and the media at any perceived departure from traditional behaviour.

In the end, however, Sydney's relentlessly cheery attitude tends to bowl over any obstacle. A glorious display of fireworks over the harbour and a general back-thumping over how great the city is does wonders for everyone's spirits, and inadvertently slaps a quick band-aid over any ill that dares to rear its ugly head.

Sydney is a foodie at heart, offering flavoursome dishes based on fresh local produce (p136)

HIGHLIGHTS

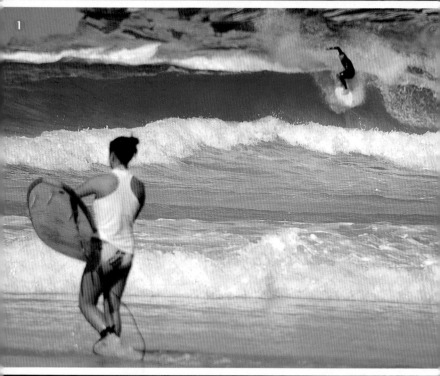

1

BEACHES

From placid harbour beaches to the raging surf of the coast, Sydney is spoilt for choice. Dramatic sandstone cliffs are broken by beautiful bays, glittering with golden sand and bronzed bodies.

2

1 Bondi Beach
Catch a wave or join the beautiful people on Sydney's most iconic golden sands (p93)

2 Camp Cove
Soak up the city views at family-friendly bays hugging the harbour (p117)

3 Manly
Meander along Manly's sun-drenched promenade (p109)

4 Mahon Pool
Splash about in this idyllic ocean pool (p97)

SYDNEY HARBOUR

Cutting a glistening, glamorous path through the city, the harbour is Sydney's great love affair. Entering through the heads, it's easy to visualise the landscape that greeted the First Fleet in the scrubby cliffs of Sydney Harbour National Park.

❶ Sydney Ferries
Traverse the harbour on the city's most thrilling public transport (p217)

❷ Sydney Opera House
Witness this wonder of modern architecture, fascinating both inside and out (p57)

❸ Sydney Harbour Bridge
Sydneysiders love their bridge, the city's second-most-famous icon (p52)

❹ The Gap
Explore native bush, secluded beaches and indigenous rock engravings (p116)

❺ Sydney Harbour National Park
Amble along the walking tracks and admire the greenery of this scenic park (p106)

1 **Lord Nelson Brewery Hotel**
Knock one back at Sydney's oldest continually licensed premises (p155)

2 **Historic streets**
Wander the network of once-dangerous narrow lanes (p52)

3 **The Rocks Market**
Enjoy street performances while wandering the stalls (p124)

4 **Observatory Hill**
An ideal place to gaze at the stars or enjoy peaceful views (p53)

THE ROCKS

Australia's convict history began here with a squalid canvas shanty town on a rocky shore. Its raucous reputation continues in its atmospheric laneways lined with historic buildings, with more than its fair share of pubs.

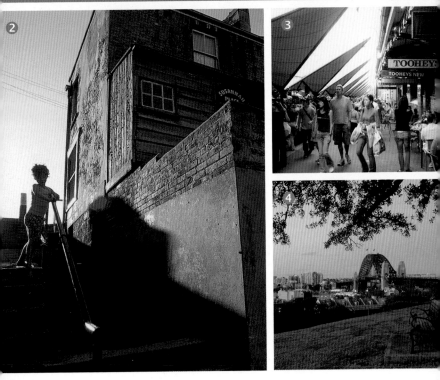

PARKS & GARDENS

Sydney's an outdoorsy city, with lots of green space to play in. Throw together a picnic and find a shady Moreton Bay fig to shelter under, or grab a Frisbee, bike or footy ball and get active.

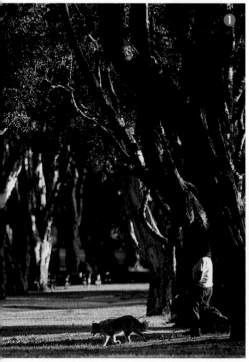

❶ Centennial Park
Do as the locals do and stretch your legs in the city's largest park (p83)

❷ Royal Botanic Gardens
Hang out with the wildlife in this harbourside paradise (p57)

❸ Hyde Park
Fresh air and peaceful surrounds make for a relaxing escape from the bustling city (p66)

NIGHTLIFE

Sydney sizzles at night, particularly during balmy summer ones. Whether you're catching a show at the Opera House, propping up a bar or cutting up a dance floor, you'll find plenty to keep you entertained.

① Theatre
Dive into the vibrant local thespian scene, starting with a visit to the State Theatre (p68)

② Pubs & Bars
Choose between dozens of atmospheric local boozers and of chic cocktail lounges, such as classy Orbit (p156)

③ Clubs
Party up large to cutting-edge beats in Sydney's clubs (p154)

3 1833 05389 1609

❶ Sydney Gay & Lesbian Mardi Gras
Be dazzled by the glamour and humour of this world-famous festival (p17)

❷ New Year's Eve Fireworks
See in the New Year with one of the world's greatest spectacles (p19)

❸ Rugby League Grand Final
Witness one of the international game's most prestigious annual challenges (p18)

EVENTS

No-one's ever accused Sydney of shying away from a celebration. Every week it seems that someone is letting off fireworks somewhere. The annual calendar is crammed with events that attract visitors from far and wide.

SYDNEY VIEWS

Showing off is what Sydney does best, so you may as well take a good hard look. Although it's a fairly flat city, there are spots that offer breathtaking views of the harbour and beyond.

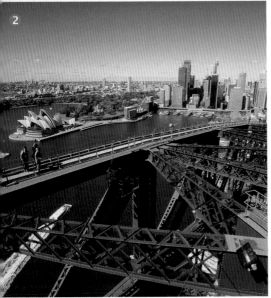

❶ Sydney Tower
Watch the city turn into Toytown from 250m above (p68)

❷ BridgeClimb
Enjoy spectacular views from the top of the Harbour Bridge (p226)

❸ Doyles Palace Hotel, Watsons Bay
Check out the harbour action over a jug of sangria (p166)

CONTENTS

Continued from previous page.

Peter Dragicevich

Throughout the '90s Peter's pilgrimages to the Emerald City became more and more frequent, until he finally threw in the towel and took up residence in 1998. For the best part of the next decade he would call Sydney's central suburbs home, while managing the city's most popular gay and lesbian newspaper and then a stable of glossy food, fashion and photography magazines. This is the sixth book he's co-authored for Lonely Planet.

PETER'S TOP SYDNEY DAY

It's a lazy, sunny Sunday morning so I head up to Challis Ave in Potts Point to meet some friends for brunch. By some minor miracle I manage to nab a table outside Spring Espresso and I'm onto my second flat white before Kerri and Carly arrive. Carly commences an elaborate charade of discreet pointing and whispering before I realise that David Wenham is sitting at the next table.

After brunch we decide to go for a stroll, so we head down McElhone Stairs to glistening Woolloomooloo Bay and then up into The Domain. The Archibald Prize is on, so we drop into the Art Gallery to check out the weird and wonderful portraits and argue over favourites. The girls are keen to continue down to the Royal Botanic Gardens, but I've promised David and Barry that I'll join them at North Bondi so I head for the bus instead.

The beach is pumping. The boys have already claimed a patch of sand so I join them and spend the afternoon people-watching and bodysurfing. By late afternoon we're parched, so we head back to the flat to shower before decamping to the Green Park Hotel in Darlinghurst to rehydrate.

I've arranged to meet Jo for a cheap and cheerful dinner at Chu Bay in Surry Hills before the Grinderman gig at the Gaelic Club, so I farewell the boys and head on my way. The food and the show are both brilliant, but I'm not ready for the day to end just yet. Wandering back up to Oxford St, I have the feeling that it's going to be a messy night.

Jolyon Attwooll

Born in Sydney's King George V Memorial hospital, Jolyon spent his primary school years in Australia before upping sticks to England. This project was perfectly timed: during a recent Ashes series Jolyon *almost* supported the English cricket team, an urge that thankfully subsided after time with his Sydneysider friends.

Jolyon wrote the Excursions chapter, the history and architecture sections of the Background chapter, as well as most of the walking tours in the Neighbourhoods chapter.

Sydney may be easy, but it's also extremely popular. Planning ahead for accommodation is definitely recommended as occupancy rates run exceptionally high in summer and around key events. Booking well ahead will secure a cheaper deal in most of the bigger hotels – and often a better room.

It may seem silly, but serious foodies should consider booking top restaurants beforehand as well. Tetsuya's (p141), Sydney's most famous, books up months in advance. Likewise, if you're planning to attend big-name shows, theatre or concerts, it will pay to book ahead (see p168).

Anything else can be easily sorted out once you arrive.

WHEN TO GO

Anytime in Sydney is a good time, but don't be fooled into thinking that it's eternally sunny and hot. The city may enjoy more than 300 clear days annually, but lying around beaches isn't an option in the winter. That said, the months of July through September offer plenty of crisp sunny days and the best of the sports season. By October it's starting to warm up, and November and early December are usually stunning.

The absolute peak season straddles the New Year, when accommodation is at its priciest. It's also when the temperature gets unpleasantly hot and bushfires can blanket the city in haze and soot. These cons need to be weighed against the major pro of witnessing the incredible New Year's Eve fireworks over the harbour. February and early March is Mardi Gras time, although the sizzle is sometimes tempered by heavy rain. In May and June Sydney heads indoors for fashion, film and art, braving the outdoors only for the annual clash of titans, the rugby league State of Origin.

FESTIVALS

Sydney loves to celebrate, and any excuse will do. Events range from the bare breasts and buttocks of the Mardi Gras parade to the resolutely highbrow Sydney Biennale.

January

SYDNEY FESTIVAL
☎ 8248 6500; www.sydneyfestival.org.au
This cultural festival is a big deal on the Sydney calendar, attracting about a million people to 300 performances held over three weeks. A wide range of events are scheduled, from art exhibits and street theatre to huge, free concerts in The Domain. Any performance at the Opera House forecourt is worth looking into.

FLICKERFEST
☎ 9365 6888; www.flickerfest.com.au; Bondi Pavilion
Around a thousand entries compete for a slot in this 10-day international short film festival.

AUSTRALIA DAY
www.australiaday.com.au
Australia's 'birthday' (the day the First Fleet landed) is 26 January, and Sydneysiders celebrate with picnics, barbecues, fireworks on the harbour and, increasingly, much nationalistic flag-waving. In less mood to celebrate are the Aboriginal community, who refer to it as Invasion Day or Survival Day. A Survival Day Concert takes place at Woomera Reserve in La Perouse. It's an alcohol-free event and runs from about 10am until sunset.

FERRYTHON
www.sydneyfestival.org.au
Part of the Sydney Festival, this mad contest is held on Australia Day (26 January) and sees four 'first fleet' catamarans, decorated with balloons and streamers, race from Circular Quay around Shark Island and back to the Harbour Bridge.

BIG DAY OUT
www.bigdayout.com; Sydney Showgrounds
The biggest day on the calendar for music fans, this touring one-day alternative music festival hits Sydney on Australia Day weekend. It features a line-up of cutting-edge artists from all over the world, including some huge names and plenty of Australian acts. It's traditionally had a friendly, grungy, laid-back vibe, although recent years have

seen some loutish behaviour. Tickets go on sale in October and are snapped up quickly.

February

CHINESE NEW YEAR
www.sydneychinesenewyear.com.au
Kung hei fat choy! Depending on the phase of the moon, this three-week celebration centred on Chinatown arrives with a bang (literally) in either January or February, featuring fireworks, a parade, dragon dancers, dragon boat races and oodles of noodles.

TROPFEST
www.tropfest.com; The Domain
The world's largest short-film festival is viewed from picnic blankets in The Domain on the last Sunday in February. A compulsory prop appears in each entry (to discourage cheating and inspire creativity). World-famous movie stars are roped in for the judging – in previous years they've included Guy Pearce, Salma Hayek, Russell Crowe, Sam Neill, Samuel L Jackson, Keanu Reaves and Nicole Kidman. It's a big deal.

SYDNEY GAY & LESBIAN MARDI GRAS
www.mardigras.org.au
This world-famous festival (p182) runs for a month, culminating in a spectacular (straight-friendly) parade along Oxford St (first Saturday in March) and the bacchanalian Mardi Gras party.

March & April

ST PATRICK'S DAY
On 17 March a large part of Sydney's population, swelled by every backpacker in town, adds an 'O' to their surname (if they don't have one already) and gets blotto on Guinness in The Rocks. Rowdy festivities start early in the morning and continue until well into the next. Wearing green and funny hats is de rigueur – full marks if you can score a 'who's your Paddy' T-shirt from one of the pubs.

GOLDEN SLIPPER FESTIVAL
☎ 9930 4000; www.theraces.com.au; Rosehill Gardens
A month-long horse-racing carnival culminates in the world's richest race for two-year-olds (with a purse of $3.5 million) on the Saturday before Good Friday.

ROYAL EASTER SHOW
www.eastershow.com.au; Sydney Showground
Ostensibly an agricultural show, this wonderful Sydney tradition is a two-week fiesta of carnival rides, showbags and sugary treats. The crowds are massive. Bring the kids.

THE GREAT ESCAPE
www.thegreatescape.net.au; Newington Armoury
Sydney's answer to Glastonbury, this three-day music festival featuring big-name local and international artists is a relative newcomer to the city's calendar but already a firm favourite. Bring a tent.

EASTER CARNIVAL
www.ajc.org.au; Royal Randwick Racecourse
This is Sydney's biggest horseracing carnival, spanning four glamorous race days, culminating with the Sydney Cup. There's a lively atmosphere, getting decidedly raucous on Derby Day, when the lawn party attracts former reality TV contestants, arrogant princesses in big hats and drunken blokes in ill-fitted suits.

May

AUSTRALIAN FASHION WEEK
www.afw.com.au
Where the gaunt, pert and pubescent tread the catwalk in Circular Quay wearing local designer duds. Expect plenty of skin, impracticality and mundane bitchy gossip, plus the usual round of 'Australian fashion has come of age' PR speak.

SYDNEY WRITERS' FESTIVAL
☎ 9252 7729; www.swf.org.au
This excellent, week-long event is held in late May in Walsh Bay, bringing together local and international writing talent to discuss a broad range of literary topics.

June & July

STATE OF ORIGIN SERIES
www.australianrugbyleague.com.au
Rugby league fanatics consider this gripping series of three matches between Queensland (the Maroons, or Cane Toads) and New South Wales (the Blues, or Cockroaches) the pinnacle of the game. Scheduled anytime from late May to July, either one or two games are played in Sydney depending on who won the series the previous year. It's

ADVANCE PLANNING

Three months prior: book accommodation (p188); book a table at Tetsuya's (p141); make sure your passport, visa and travel insurance are in order. One month prior: book any other top restaurants; check to see if your visit coincides with any major events (p16, opposite) and book tickets (p168). A week prior: top up your credit cards; pay bills; check the Sydney news sites (opposite); who's looking after the cat? As you leave the house: tickets, money, passports!

worth catching for its dazzling displays of speed, tactics and bloody-nosed aggression. The fans go crazy.

SYDNEY FILM FESTIVAL
www.sydneyfilmfestival.org
Held in part at the magnificent State Theatre, this excellent, highly regarded film festival screens art-house gems from Australia and around the world. It starts in early June and runs for two weeks.

BIENNALE OF SYDNEY
www.biennaleofsydney.com.au
In even-numbered years this two-month international arts festival showcases the bold, the brilliant and the downright mind-boggling. It's held around a number of city venues, including the Art Gallery of NSW.

YULEFEST
www.katoomba-nsw.com/yulefest.html
The Blue Mountains in July is about as close to the Northern Hemisphere Christmas as Sydney gets. 'Tis the season when local hotels and restaurants cash in with traditional holiday beverages, roaring fires, a carol or two and Christmas dinner with all the trimmings. The Winter Magic Festival (www.wintermagic.com.au) is held in Katoomba on the weekend closest to the winter solstice. It includes a parade where participants wear rather more clothes than you'll see in the Sydney Gay & Lesbian Mardi Gras parade.

August
CITY2SURF RUN
http://city2surf.sunherald.com.au
On the second Sunday in August some 60,000 runners pound the 14km from Hyde Park to Bondi Beach; some are deadly

serious, some are in costume, and everyone gets their name and finishing position published in the paper. The all-time record to beat is 40.04 minutes, set by Steve Moneghetti in 1991.

September & October
FESTIVAL OF THE WINDS
www.aks.org.au
Held on the second weekend in September, this festival brings spectacular kites shaped like animals and aliens to Bondi Beach. The kids will love it.

QUEERDOC
☎ 9332 4938; www.queerscreen.com.au; Chauvel Cinema & Dendy Newtown
Running over two weeks in mid-September, this is the only queer documentary festival in the world. The organisers also put on the Mardi Gras Film Festival in February and one-off screenings throughout the year.

MANLY INTERNATIONAL JAZZ FESTIVAL
www.manly.nsw.gov.au/manlyjazz
This enjoyable event takes place on the Labour Day long weekend (early October). The music ranges from traditional and big band to fusion, bop and contemporary.

SLEAZE BALL
www.mardigras.org.au; Hordern Pavilion & RHI
The Mardi Gras party is so fabulous that once a year isn't enough, with its sluttier spin-off taking place on the Saturday of the Labour Day long weekend. Proceeds go towards staging the annual parade.

RUGBY LEAGUE GRAND FINAL
www.nrl.com.au; Telstra Stadium
The culmination of the rugby league season is an atmospheric clash, held on the Sunday of the Labour Day long weekend. There's a carnival atmosphere, big-name entertainment and a fired-up crowd. It makes for great Sleaze Ball recovery.

November
SCULPTURE BY THE SEA
www.sculpturebythesea.com
This outdoor sculpture exhibition utilises the spectacular Bondi to Tamarama cliff top to display stunning artworks from local and international artists. It's free, open 24 hours and great for starting debates.

December

HOMEBAKE
www.homebake.com.au; The Domain
Held on the first Saturday in December, this one-day music fest is a showcase of the best Australian and New Zealand bands.

CHRISTMAS PARTY
The international family of travellers have traditionally descended on Bondi Beach on Christmas Day. Because of out-of-control scenes in the past, alcohol has been banned on the beach and an organised party is staged at the Pavilion instead. It changes every year; previous years have seen a pricey Gatecrasher dance party.

SYDNEY TO HOBART YACHT RACE
www.rolexsydneyhobart.com
On 26 December Sydney Harbour is crowded with boats farewelling the international yachts competing in this race, a gruelling 628-nautical-mile course.

NEW YEAR'S EVE
Join hundreds of thousands of revellers pouring into harbourside vantage points (make sure you can see the bridge) for magnificent fireworks. And yes, they really are worth the hassle of nabbing a spot hours beforehand.

COSTS & MONEY
Sydney is not a cheap place to visit. If you bed down in dorms, eat takeaway and use public transport you'll still get little change out of $60 per day. Sharing a double room at a budget hotel and sitting down for a nice evening meal will kick this up to about $100 per person. Bank on $140 per person for a few more comforts (a shared three-star hotel room and three decent meals). At the upper end, the sky's the limit.

Most accommodation options have cheaper rates for stays of longer than a week and you can reduce your daily transport budget with weekly bus/train/ferry passes. If travelling with kids, look out for family rates on transport and attractions. And while some sights are downright pricey, there's plenty to do for free (see p56).

INTERNET RESOURCES
There are dozens of websites offering the latest on upcoming events in the city. See also the ticketing sites on p168.

www.smh.com.au Good for upcoming events, restaurant and bar reviews, and to take the pulse of the city.

www.cityofsydney.nsw.gov.au Visitor information, disabled access, parking, history and downloadable walking tours.

www.visitnsw.com.au Neighbourhood by neighbourhood visitors' guide.

www.sydney.citysearch.com.au What's on listings.

www.eatability.com.au User-generated dining and bar reviews.

www.inthemix.com.au What's on in the dance music and club scene.

www.hht.net.au Exhibition and visitor information on 12 museums and historic houses.

www.art-almanac.com.au Extensive commercial and public gallery listings.

SUSTAINABLE SYDNEY
Given Sydney's relative isolation, a sustainable alternative to air travel may not be possible. If you're heading on to other Australian destinations, consider using trains and buses but remember that the distances are vast.

There's really no need to hire a car in Sydney. The bus, train and ferry services will get you everywhere you want to go with less hassle. Consider hiring a bike (p217) to explore the eastern beaches, Centennial Parklands and the inner west.

By the time this book is published it's hoped that the drought that has gripped Sydney and much of Australia will have lessened, but this is unlikely to fix the city's water problems. Mandatory water restrictions are in place for

---

HOW MUCH?

Litre of unleaded petrol $1.30

Short train trip $2.40

Short taxi ride $10

Schooner of Tooheys New $4

Litre of bottled water $2.50

Flat white coffee $3

Harry's Café de Wheels pie $3.50

Souvenir T-shirt $15

Movie ticket $16

Hostel dorm bed $25

residents, who are forbidden to use hoses to water their gardens or clean their cars. You can do your bit by being conscious of your water usage while in the city. Don't run taps unnecessarily – for instance, when brushing your teeth. Cut down on your shower time. Don't make your hotel wash your towels after every use. Use half flush on the loo.

Other small things you can do for the environment while in Sydney include saying no to plastic bags in shops, refilling water bottles from the tap and disposing of cigarette butts in the bin. If you stamp butts out on the street, they end up in the harbour with the next big rainfall. The same goes for other litter.

HISTORY
ABORIGINAL SETTLEMENT

Australia was the last great landmass to be claimed by Europeans, but the first inhabitants of this country were here for tens of thousands of years before the First Fleet stomped a foot down under. Australian Aboriginal society has the longest continuous cultural history in the world, its origins dating to at least the last ice age. Although mystery shrouds many aspects of Australian prehistory, it is thought that the first humans probably came here across the sea from Southeast Asia more than 50,000 years ago.

Archaeological evidence suggests that descendants of these first settlers colonised the continent within a few thousand years. They were the first people in the world to make polished, edge-ground, stone tools; to cremate their dead; and to engrave and paint representations of themselves and the animals they hunted.

Aborigines were traditionally tribal people, living in extended family groups. Knowledge and skills obtained over millennia enabled them to use their environment extensively and in a sustainable manner. Their intimate knowledge of animal behaviour and plant harvesting ensured that food shortages were rare.

The simplicity of the Aborigines' technology contrasted with their sophisticated cultural life. Religion, history, law and art were integrated in complex ceremonies, which not only depicted ancestral beings who created the land and its people, but also prescribed codes of behaviour. Aborigines continue to perform traditional ceremonies in many parts of Australia.

When the British arrived at Sydney Cove in 1788 there were probably somewhere between 500,000 and one million Aborigines in Australia, and between 200 and 250 distinct regional languages. Governor Arthur Phillip estimated that around 1500 Aborigines lived around Sydney at first contact, although figures are unreliable.

The coastal people around Sydney were known as the Eora (which literally means 'from this place'). Cadigal people lived in the Sydney area, but their population was soon ravaged by smallpox introduced by the European settlers. Three main languages were used by Aborigines in the area, encompassing several dialects and subgroups. Although there was considerable overlap, Ku-ring-gai was generally spoken on the northern shore, Dharawal along the coast south of Botany Bay, and Dharug and its dialects on the plains at the foot of the Blue Mountains.

top picks

WEBSITES TO UNRAVEL SYDNEY'S PAST

- www.cityofsydney.nsw.gov.au/barani
  Great background from the city council on the story of Sydney's Aboriginal population.
- www.dictionaryofsydney.org
  A major online project to document all aspects of Sydney.
- http://firstfleet.uow.edu.au
  A comprehensive, absorbing University of Wollongong project to tell the First Fleet story.
- www.nla.gov.au/oz/histsite.html
  National Library Of Australia resources.

TIMELINE

40,000 BC	AD 1770	1788
The Eora people live in Sydney, hunting and painting rock art, split into separate tribes including the Dharug-speaking Cadigal band in Sydney Cove	Captain James Cook lands at Botany Bay and claims Australia for the British Crown; he writes of the indigenous population: 'all they seem'd to want was us to be gone'	The First Fleet drops anchor in Botany Bay, followed by la Pérouse five days later; the English decide Botany Bay is unsuitable and head to Port Jackson, pitching their tents in Sydney Cove

As Aboriginal society was based on tribal family groups, a coordinated response to the European colonisers wasn't possible. Without any 'legal right' to the lands they once lived on, Aborigines became dispossessed. Some were driven away by force, some were killed, many were shifted onto government reserves and missions, and thousands succumbed to foreign diseases introduced by the Europeans.

Communities that had survived for millennia before the arrival of the settlers were changed – sometimes shattered – forever.

THE EUROPEANS COME KNOCKING

When the American War of Independence disrupted the transportation of convicts to North America, Britain lost its main dumping ground for undesirables and needed somewhere else to chuck them. Joseph Banks, who had been Captain James Cook's scientific leader during the expedition in 1770, piped up with the suggestion that Botany Bay would be a fine new site for criminals.

TALES OF FIRST CONTACT: PEMULWUY

Aboriginal resistance to European colonisation was a subject long glossed over in Australian history books, although it began pretty much at first contact. Dutch sailors in the early 17th century had violent run-ins on the west coast, and after Captain Cook came ashore in 1770 and had a rock chucked at him, he wrote of the locals 'all they seem'd to want was us to be gone'.

Pemulwuy, a member of the Bidjigal group of Dharug speakers from near Botany Bay, very much wanted the British to be gone. He was around 20 years old when Cook visited, and pushing 40 by the time Arthur Phillip and the new arrivals from the First and Second Fleets had begun killing and kidnapping his countrymen and generally acting like they owned the place.

Pemulwuy branded himself as a troublemaker in 1790 by spearing to death Governor Phillip's game shooter. The shooter, John McIntyre, was a convict who reportedly brutalised Aboriginal people, but this didn't stop Phillip from threatening a bloody revenge. He sent out the first-ever punitive force against the locals, at first with orders to kill 10 Bidjigals and bring their heads back to Sydney in sacks. Phillip soon relented and issued milder orders to capture six for possible hanging.

The mission was an utter flop in any case, and Pemulwuy's 12 years as leader of the struggle against the British began in earnest. At first he limited his guerrilla campaign to small, sporadic raids on farms, stealing livestock and crops, but eventually worked up to leading attacks by groups of more than a hundred men – a huge number, by Aboriginal standards of the time.

During his lifetime Pemulwuy survived being shot, as well as having his skull fractured in a rumble with the enormous 'Black Caesar', a bushranger of African descent. He thoroughly cemented his reputation in 1797 in a bloody battle against soldiers and settlers at Parramatta. During the fracas, Pemulwuy took seven pellets of buckshot to the head and body and went down. Bleeding severely and near death, he was captured and placed in hospital. Within weeks he managed to escape, while still wearing the leg irons he'd been shackled with.

Pemulwuy's luck ran out in 1802, when he was ambushed and shot dead. It's not entirely clear by whom, but there *was* a price on Pemulwuy's head – which was cut off, pickled in alcohol and sent to England. (A similar fate befell Yagan, an Aboriginal resistance leader in southwestern Australia, some 30 years later.) Pemulwuy's son Tedbury carried on the fight until 1805.

For further reading on Pemulwuy, check out *Pemulwuy: The Rainbow Warrior*, by Eric Willmot.

1791	1842	1900
It's estimated that only three Cadigal people survive; many were wiped out by smallpox that arrived with the First Fleet, which the Cadigal had no natural immunity to	Convict transportation effectively ceases in New South Wales; over the course of the previous half century 150,000 people had been dumped in the colony	Bubonic plague kills 103 people in Sydney's overcrowded and unhygienic slums; as a result, large areas of substandard housing are cleared and rebuilt

TALES OF FIRST CONTACT: BENNELONG

Pemulwuy's story (opposite) is in stark contrast to that of another Aborigine who became famous for his association with the British settlers. Bennelong was born around 1764 into the Wangal tribe, the westerly neighbours of the Cadigal who lived in the area around central Sydney. He was captured in 1789, and brought to Governor Arthur Phillip, who was hoping to use Bennelong to understand the local Aborigines' customs and language. Bennelong took to life with the white settlers, developing a taste for alcohol, food and learning to speak the language of his new masters. Eventually he escaped, but had returned by 1791 when reassured that he would not be held against his will. He developed a strong friendship with Governor Phillip, who had a brick hut built for him on what is now Bennelong Point. In 1792, Bennelong went on a 'civilising' trip to England, and returned in 1795 with a changed dress sense and altered behaviour. Described as good natured, and stoutly made, Bennelong ultimately was no longer accepted by his countrymen and never really found happiness with his white friends either. He died a broken, dispossessed man in 1813, probably as a result of his affection for the bottle.

The First Fleet landed at Botany Bay in January 1788. This motley group comprised 11 ships carrying 730 male and female convicts, 400 sailors, four companies of marines, and enough livestock and booze to last two years. Captain Arthur Phillip, eager to be the colony's first governor, didn't take to Botany Bay's meagre natural supplies. He weighed anchor after only a few days and sailed 25km north to the harbour Cook had named Port Jackson (now known as Sydney Harbour), where he discovered a crucial source of fresh water in what is now Sydney Cove. The day was 26 January 1788, now celebrated as Australia Day.

The settlers liked Sydney Cove much better and from here the town of Sydney grew. Word spread, and the Second Fleet came around in 1790 with more convicts and supplies. A year later, following the landing of the Third Fleet, Sydney's population had swollen to around 4000. The early days of the colony weren't for softies and the threat of starvation hung over the settlement for at least 16 years.

Convicts were put to work on farms, roads and government building projects, but Governor Phillip was convinced that the colony wouldn't progress if it relied solely on convict blood and sweat. He believed prosperity depended on attracting free settlers, to whom convicts would be assigned as labourers, and on the granting of land to officers, soldiers and worthy emancipists (convicts who had served their time). In 1791 James Ruse was the first former convict to be granted land by Governor Phillip. He was given 12 hectares as reward for his successful work in agriculture (see p119).

When Governor Phillip had had enough, Francis Grose took over. Grose granted land to officers of the New South Wales Corps, nicknamed the Rum Corps. With so much money, land and cheap labour in their hot little hands, this military leadership made huge profits at the expense of small farmers. They began paying for labour and local products in rum. Meeting little resistance, they managed to upset, defy, outmanoeuvre and outlast three governors, including William Bligh, the unlucky leader of the infamous *Bounty*.

The Rum Rebellion was the final straw for the British government, and in 1809 it decided to punish its unruly child. Lieutenant Colonel Lachlan Macquarie was dispatched with his own regiment and ordered the New South Wales Corps to return to London to get their knuckles rapped. Having broken the stranglehold of the Rum Corps, Governor Macquarie began laying the groundwork for social reforms.

1902	1908	1932
Women are granted the right to vote; this same right is not extended to the indigenous Aborigines until almost 70 years later	South Sydney wins the first Rugby League premiership, beating Eastern Suburbs (now Sydney City Roosters) and starting a rivalry between the clubs that survives today	Sydney's second-most-famous icon, the Harbour Bridge, opens; the structure is immediately loved dearly by Sydneysiders for both aesthetic and practical reasons

WILD COLONIAL BOYS

In 1800 Sydney Cove was still the only European settlement on the Australian mainland. Inroads were only made into the vast interior of the continent in the ensuing 40 years.

In 1851 the discovery of large gold deposits near Bathurst, 200km west of Sydney, caused an exodus of hopeful miners from the city and forced the government to abandon the law of ownership of gold discoveries. Instead, it introduced a compulsory digger's licence fee of 30 shillings a month. Controversially, the fee was payable whether the miner found gold or not, to ensure the country earned revenue from the incredible wealth being unearthed.

Another massive gold rush in Victoria shortly afterwards kept Sydney (the capital of NSW) of secondary size and importance to Melbourne (the capital of the southern colony of Victoria). This lasted from the 1850s until the economic depression of the 1890s... and so the Sydney–Melbourne rivalry began (see p39).

MOVING INTO THE 20TH CENTURY

The Commonwealth of Australia came into being on 1 January 1901, and NSW became a state of the new Australian nation. However, Australia's legal ties with, loyalty to and dependency on Britain remained strong. When WWI broke out in Europe, Australian troops were sent to fight in the trenches of France, at Gallipoli in Turkey and in the Middle East. Although almost 60,000 of the 330,000 troops perished in the war, for Australia this was a first test of physical stamina and strength – and they held their own. A renewed patriotism cemented the country's confidence in itself. But, in the wake of so much slaughter, many Australians also questioned their relationship with their old colonial rulers – ties between Britain and Australia were never quite the same.

If Australia was now notionally independent, the same sadly could not be said for its indigenous peoples. From 1910 to the end of the 1960s, a sinister policy of 'cultural assimilation' allowed Aborigine children (usually of mixed race) to be removed from their families. Around 100,000 children were separated from their mothers and fathers in this way – 'the stolen generation' – causing untold stress and damage to the nation's indigenous community. The 2002 movie *Rabbit Proof Fence* is a moving portrayal of this shameful episode in Australia's past.

Meanwhile, Australia's economy continued to grow in the 1920s until the Great Depression hit the country hard. By 1932, however, Australia was starting to recover as a result of rises in wool prices and a revival of manufacturing. With the opening of the Harbour Bridge in the same year, Sydney's building industry revived and its northern suburbs began to develop.

In the years before WWII, Australia became increasingly fearful of the threat to national security posed by expansionist Japan. When war broke out, Australian troops again fought beside the British in Europe. Only after the Japanese bombed Pearl Harbor did Australia's own national security begin to take priority. A boom with a net barrage was stretched across the entrance channels of Sydney Harbour and gun fortifications were set up on the rocky headlands.

Sydney escaped WWII comparatively unscathed, although on 31 May 1942 several Japanese midget submarines were destroyed after becoming trapped in the harbour boom. A week later, another Japanese submarine entered the harbour, sank a small supply vessel and lobbed a few shells into the suburbs of Bondi and Rose Bay.

Ultimately, US victory in the Battle of the Coral Sea helped protect Australia from a Japanese invasion and pushed along Australia's shift of allegiance from mother Britain to the USA.

1959	1984	1994
Construction of the much-admired Sydney Opera House commences; it won't be opened until 1973, after a long and eventful period of construction	Homosexuality is decriminalised in NSW; however, an equal age of consent with heterosexuals will not be achieved until almost 20 years later in 2003	Four people die in a series of horrific bushfires circling Sydney; the Woods Royal Commission, investigating police corruption, commences

THE CHINESE IN SYDNEY & AUSTRALIA

Colourful Sydney and many other large cities have come to realise the benefits of having a multicultural society, but Australia hasn't always been so racially tolerant (and still has a way to go, in fact).

Chinese immigrants started to come to Australia around 1840, when convict shipments were decreasing and labouring jobs became more freely available. Initially Chinese immigrants were considered a solution to the labour shortages, but as gold rush greed came on racial intolerance grew. The tireless Chinese were seen as competitive threats, and state entry restrictions were in place from the early 19th century into much of the 20th century. In 1861 the NSW Government put in place the now shameful 'White Australia Policy', aimed at reducing the influx of Chinese immigrants. This included a refusal of naturalisation, restricted work permits and acts such as the 1861 *Chinese Immigration Regulation and Restriction Act* (a tax on Chinese immigrants). As a result of this policy (and the fact many Chinese returned to China after the gold rush), the Chinese population remained low.

Sydney's Chinese community eventually gravitated to Dixon St, and soon this area became a bustling commercial centre known for its opium dens and gambling. While the opium dens are long gone, you'll still find plenty of action in the area (now called Chinatown), along with plenty of Australians of Chinese descent. For the traveller, this translates into some really tasty and great-value food. One of the country's most renowned chefs, Kylie Kwong, is from the largest Chinese family in Australia and a proud Sydneysider. She describes herself as '29th-generation Kwong and fifth-generation Australian'.

The aftermath of WWII, along with postwar immigration programs, made Australia more appealing to migrants from Britain, Germany, Italy, Poland, Greece and Ireland, among other places. Australia experienced new growth and prosperity, and Sydney's population spurted. The city's borders rapidly spread west.

Despite the influx of these new immigrants and a strong trade-union movement, Australia came to accept the US view that communism threatened the increasingly Americanised Australian way of life. In 1965 the Liberal Party government sent troops to serve in the Vietnam War, even when Britain did not.

During these Vietnam War years the face of Sydney changed as American GIs flooded the city for rest and recreation (R&R). Kings Cross became an entertaining playground for US troops on leave, sealing its sleazy reputation as a den of drinking and bordellos. Meanwhile, civil unrest over the issue of conscription eventually helped bring about the election of the Australian Labor Party (ALP) in 1972, the first time in 23 years that it had been in power.

Aborigines took part in this vote, only the second time they were able to participate in an Australian general election. It wasn't until 1967 that a national referendum was held on whether to allow Aboriginal people the right to vote. More than 90% of white Australians voted in favour.

THE TRANSITION TO THE NEW MILLENNIUM

The Sydney basking in the afterglow of the magnificent 2000 Olympic Games is quite different from the city of the mid-1970s. Many Sydneysiders were feeling shackled by old British ties, especially in the wake of the shock ousting of Labor Party Prime Minister Gough Whitlam in 1975. The controversy was all about the man who sacked him, Governor General John Kerr. As the British monarch's representative, Kerr was not an Australian-elected official and highlighted the influence the former colonial rulers still wielded.

2000	2003	2007
Sydney stages a dazzling Olympic Games, at which Australia wins 16 gold medals, placing the country fourth after the US, Russia and China	Linda Burney, a member of the 'stolen generation' who first met her father at age 28, becomes the first indigenous member of the New South Wales state parliament	Morris Iemma is re-elected as New South Wales State Premier, after taking on the reins following Bob Carr's retirement in 2005

During Whitlam's shortened reign, the Australian government had withdrawn Australian troops from Vietnam and abolished national service. Another legacy of Whitlam's more tolerant government was the waves of immigrants that settled in Sydney, often defining a certain area – the Vietnamese in Cabramatta and the Chinese in Ashfield, for example.

A booming 1980s economy saw Sydney skyscrapers shoot up, while the Bicentennial celebrations in 1988 also boosted the city's confidence. A subsequent bust in 1989 left a number of holes in the city centre, but with the announcement of the 2000 Olympic Games Sydney renewed itself and put on a great show for the world. Sydney was left with a glowing image and a vigorous tourist trade.

Indigenous issues over the last couple of decades have been somewhat more fraught, both in Sydney and further afield. In 1992, a landmark High Court case overturned the principle of *terra nullius* (the idea that Australia was uninhabited when the First Fleet arrived). A later court case provoked the Wik decision, which declared that pastoral leases do not necessarily extinguish native title. In other words, Aborigines may still be able to claim some of their ancestral land. The implications of this ruling are still being resolved.

More recently, pressure piled on the Australian Prime Minister John Howard to apologise for historic, systematic ill treatment of Australia's original inhabitants. This intensified after the publication of the damning *Bringing them Home* report, which graphically detailed the harm done to the 'stolen generation' (see p24). In May 2000, a quarter of a million people (Aboriginal and non-Aboriginal) marched across Sydney Harbour Bridge in support of National Sorry Day. However, Howard steadfastly refused to budge, arguing that the government should not be obliged to apologise for the actions of previous administrations. Perhaps a change in leader may bring a change in heart, but, at the time of writing, sorry still seems to be the hardest word…

On a state politics level, Sydneysiders are often cynical – surprisingly perhaps, given such a thriving city and a lifestyle that is the envy of many. In July 2005, Labor's Bob Carr, NSW's longest continually serving premier, resigned suddenly after 10 years in office. Carr had overseen one of Sydney's biggest ever infrastructure projects for the Olympic Games, but still faced sharp criticism for congestion, poor public transport and problems with the public health service. These are issues still faced by Morris Iemma, previously NSW's health minister and also of the Labor Party, and Carr's replacement as state premier.

The election of the colourful Clover Moore as Lord Mayor in 2004 perhaps reflected a general frustration with state politics. As an independent pollie (politician), she came with none of the baggage of her rivals from Australia's main political parties. She also embraces many of the issues for which Sydney is famed – such as a sustainable environment and gay rights.

ARTS

While it's not about to match New York City or London for sheer volume of theatres, galleries or performance venues, Sydney nevertheless lays claim to a very healthy and robust arts scene – what else could you expect from a major city with an opera house as its most popular symbol? And as opposed to taking the sniffy, superior attitude so prevalent in many artsy societies, Sydney has a laid-back, open-minded view of its artistic pursuits – perhaps a fortunate consequence of relaxing sand, surf and sea elements being so close by. Also influencing the city's arts scene is a constant pursuit of identity, with its many multicultural facets constantly chiming in. Does this cultural mix work out for the best? You bet it does.

Sydney's blessed environment offers another pleasant bonus for art lovers. Outdoor events are a common theme, especially when the weather turns warm and sultry. Don't be surprised to see sculptures by the sea, hear an author read at an alfresco luncheon, watch cinema in the park under the stars or witness modern dance outside the Opera House on Circular Quay's promenade.

You won't find yourself waiting for cultural events to fall into your lap, either – Sydney's sociable 'get out and be seen' nature keeps gallery openings, theatrical first nights, film screenings and book readings firmly entrenched in many local diaries (see p16 for festivals and events). So whether you're staying just a few days or a few months, be sure to take full advantage of what Sydney's arts scene has to offer – it won't disappoint.

CINEMA & TV

Australia saw some of the world's earliest attempts at cinematography. In 1896, just one year after the Lumiere brothers opened the world's first cinema in Paris, Maurice Sestier (one of the Lumieres' photographers) came to Sydney and made the country's first films. Sestier also opened Australia's first cinema in Sydney during this time – Salon Lumiere on Pitt St – and on 17 October premiered the landmark *Passengers Alighting from Ferry 'Brighton' at Manly*.

One of the most successful of the early Australian feature films was *The Sentimental Bloke* (1919), which premiered in Melbourne but included scenes shot in Manly, the Sydney Royal Botanic Gardens and Woolloomooloo.

The cavalry epic *Forty Thousand Horsemen* (1940), directed by the great filmmaker Charles Chauvel, was a highlight of locally produced and financed films of the 1930s to 1950s (which were often based on Australian history or literature). Chauvel also made the country's first colour movie, the Aboriginal-themed *Jedda* (1955), which was also the first Australian flick to make an appearance at the Cannes film festival. The final scenes were reshot in the Blue Mountains after original footage was lost in a plane crash.

Government intervention in the form of both state and federal subsidies (as well as tax breaks) reshaped the future of the country's film industry from 1969 through the 1970s, with the Australian Film Commission (AFC) being created in 1975. An ongoing 'renaissance' of Australian cinema was thus established, and today Sydney is a major centre for feature-film making.

One director who gained fame during this period and continues to be successful in Hollywood is Sydney-born Peter Weir, who oversaw films like *Gallipoli* (1981), *Dead Poets Society* (1989) and, more recently, *Master and Commander* (2003).

The 1990s saw films that cemented Australia's reputation as a producer of quirky

top picks

SYDNEY FILMS

- *Finding Nemo* (2003) An excellent animated feature that follows the adventures of a wild clownfish who finds himself captive in a Sydney aquarium. Directed by Andrew Stanton.
- *Lantana* (2001) Touted as a 'mystery for grownups', this is an extraordinary ensemble piece and deeply moving meditation on life, love, truth and grief. Directed by Ray Lawrence.
- *Looking for Alibrandi* (2000) A charming story of what it's like to grow up Italian in modern Sydney. Directed by Kate Woods.
- *The Matrix* (1999-2003) A trio of futuristic mind-bending flicks with plenty of martial-arts action, slick costumes and dark themes. Filmed in Sydney's streets and soundstages. Directed by Andy and Larry Wachowski.
- *The Adventures of Priscilla, Queen of the Desert* (1994) A side-splitting comedy starring Hugo Weaving, Terence Stamp and Guy Pearce as Sydney drag queens on a road trip to Alice Springs. Directed by Stephan Elliott.
- *Muriel's Wedding* (1994) Both hilarious and genuinely affecting, following Toni Collette as she makes the transition from Porpoise Spit's Muriel to Darling Point's Mariel. Directed by PJ Hogan.
- *Strictly Ballroom* (1992) A breakthrough Aussie comedy set in the surreal world of competitive ballroom dancing. Directed by Baz Luhrmann.
- *Puberty Blues* (1981) Shows southern Sydney's 1970s surf culture at its most 'perf'. Directed by Bruce Beresford.
- *Two Hands* (1999) A humorous look at Sydney's surprisingly daggy criminal underworld, starring a young Heath Ledger. Directed by Gregor Jordan.
- *The Sum Of Us* (1994) A touching father-son tale in which Russell Crowe jogs around Sydney in his footy shorts as the gay lead. Directed by Geoff Burton and Kevin Dowling Lucas.

BACKGROUND ARTS

comedies about local misfits: *Strictly Ballroom* (with locations in Pyrmont and Marrickville), *Muriel's Wedding* (Parramatta, Oxford St, Darling Point and Ryde) and *The Adventures of Priscilla, Queen of the Desert* (Erskineville). Actors who got their cinematic start around this time include Guy Pearce, Hugo Weaving, David Wenham, Russell Crowe, Cate Blanchett, Heath Ledger, Toni Collette and Rachel Griffiths.

Sydney's flashest film studio, Fox Studios, was once the site of Sydney's much-loved Royal Easter Show. It's now the multimillion-dollar centre of a revitalised and flourishing local industry, and many movies financed with overseas money have been shot and produced here. These include big-budget extravaganzas like the trilogy *The Matrix* (featuring numerous Sydney skyscrapers), *Mission Impossible 2* (Elizabeth Bay and Sydney Harbour) and the *Star Wars* prequels. Sydneysider Baz Luhrmann's *Moulin Rouge* was also made here, and starred Sydney's favourite celebrity and Oscar-winner Nicole Kidman.

Films with Aboriginal themes had mixed success in the past, but have recently gained ground. Sydneysider Phillip Noyce's *Rabbit Proof Fence* (2002) broke open Australian cinematic racial barriers to become the year's most successful film. David Gulpilil, the most well-known Aboriginal actor, has charmed audiences in *Walkabout* (1971), *The Last Wave* (1977), *Crocodile Dundee* (1986), *Rabbit Proof Fence* and *The Tracker* (2002). For more information on other local film festivals and cinemas, see p16 and p169.

Sydney's three commercial TV stations (channels seven, nine and 10) serve up a steady diet of reality TV dross, soap operas, American comedy imports, sensationalistic news, plenty of sports and enough home/garden makeover shows to make you wonder if Australians ever leave their domiciles to savour all that beautiful weather. One local production that has added to this sunny perception of Oz is *Home and Away,* which is often filmed at Palm Beach on Sydney's Northern Beaches.

ABC (channel two) is the national broadcaster and specialises in BBC-related programs (along with more local news and current affairs) that appeal to a wide sector of Australian society. SBS, the multicultural broadcaster, is the thinking person's TV station and a national gem: its 6.30pm news bulletin is easily the best in the country. For more on TV, see p228.

PAINTING

Traditional European arts didn't quite mesh with the strange and beguiling Australian landscape. The first European landscape painters used colours and features that didn't authentically represent this new land, and today they wouldn't be regarded as typically 'Australian'. This was mainly due to the fact that European aesthetic standards were being applied to a non-European landscape. Some early painters, however, made an effort to approach the Australian landscape on its own terms.

In the early 19th century John Glover (a convict) was an early adopter of the Australian landscape painting style, using warm earth tones and accurate depictions of gum trees and distant mountains in his work. Colonial artists such as Conrad Martens (a friend of Charles Darwin) painted Turneresque landscapes of Sydney Harbour in the 1850s, startling current Sydneysiders used to seeing a foreshore dominated by exclusive housing rather than miles of bush.

ABORIGINAL ART

Aboriginal art is one of the oldest forms of creativity in the world, dating back more than 50,000 years. It has always been an integral part of Aboriginal life, forming a connection between the past and the present, the supernatural and the earthly, the people and the land. This art is a reflection of Aboriginal people's ancestral Dreaming, or the 'Creation', when the earth's physical features were formed by the struggles between powerful supernatural ancestors. Ceremonies, rituals and sacred paintings are all based on the Dreaming.

Aboriginal art is widely varied and includes dot paintings from the central deserts, bark paintings and weavings from Arnhem Land, woodcarving and silk-screen printing from the Tiwi Islands, and batik printing and woodcarving from central Australia. Warmun artists are known for their ochres, while the Wangkatjunkga community is famous for abstract paintings. Many great young artists are based out of Lockhart River in north Queensland.

Dot and canvas paintings especially have become very popular in the last 25 years, which has given Aboriginal artists both a means with which to preserve their ancient Dreaming values and a way to share this rich cultural heritage with the wider community in Australia. Modern materials like glass, fibre and aluminium have also been incorporated by recent Aboriginal artists, encompassing traditional themes with contemporary expression.

The best way to support Aboriginal artists is to buy their art at a reputable store that guarantees authenticity (and has the papers to prove it) and from Aboriginal-owned galleries and outlets. Some top Aboriginal artists include Mabel Juli, Eubena Nampitjin, Rosella Namok, Gloria Petyarre, Kathleen Petyarre, Minnie Pwerle, Jimmy Pike, Paddy Japaljarri Stewart, Rover Thomas, Mick Namarari Tjapaltjarri and Judy Napangardi Watson. See the Shopping chapter (p122) for some store recommendations.

CONTEMPORARY ART

The first significant art movement in Australia, the Heidelberg School, emerged around the 1890s. Using impressionistic techniques and favouring outdoor painting, the school represented a major break with prevailing British and Germanic tastes. Painters such as Tom Roberts and Arthur Streeton were the first to render Australian light and colour in this naturalistic fashion. Originally from Melbourne, they came to Sydney and established an artists' camp at Little Sirius Cove in Mosman in 1891, which became a focal point for Sydney artists. Roberts and Streeton depicted what are now considered typically Australian scenes of sheepshearers, pioneers and bushrangers. Their paintings were powerful stimulants to the development of an enduring national mythology.

Frederick McCubbin was also associated with the Heidelberg School and became the first significant white artist born in Australia. His impressionistic work was influenced by his association with Roberts, and his most famous work *Lost* was inspired by a young girl lost in the bush for three weeks.

top picks

GALLERIES

- Art Gallery of NSW (p66) Everything from classic to modern and local to international, plus an exceptional collection of Aboriginal and Torres Strait Islander works.
- Object Gallery (p89) Gorgeous crafts and contemporary household designs on display at this new Surry Hills centre.
- Museum of Contemporary Art (p53) Marvellous temporary exhibitions complement the permanent works at this large modern art museum. Great café also.
- Australian Centre for Photography (p85) Offers a constant roster of interesting photographic exhibitions.
- Sherman Contemporary Art Foundation (p86) Temporary exhibitions of contemporary Australian, Asian and Pacific work.

At the beginning of the 20th century Australian painters began to flirt with modernism, which originally started in Sydney. French-influenced Nora Simpson kick-started the innovative movement, which experimented with cubism and expressionism. Grace Cossington Smith and Margaret Preston were other highly regarded early modernists, both based in Sydney.

In the 1940s there began a flowering of symbolic surrealism in the work of such painters as Sidney Nolan, Arthur Boyd, Albert Tucker and Russell Drysdale. This movement used a spontaneous and transcendent approach to the visual arts, and added another dimension to the Australian creative process through the level of mythology.

In the 1960s Australian art drew on a wide range of cultures and abstract trends. This eclecticism is best represented by the work of Sydney artist Brett Whiteley, who died in 1992 and was an internationally celebrated *enfant terrible* (though it doesn't take much to get called that in these parts). He painted bold, colourful canvases, often with distorted figures, as well as landscapes of Sydney Harbour and Lavender Bay. His studio, containing many of his works, has been preserved as a gallery in Surry Hills (see p89).

Drawing on popular cultural images for much of his work, Martin Sharp first rose to prominence in the 1960s as cofounder of the satirical magazine *Oz*. In the 1970s he helped restore the 'face' at Luna Park, but is especially famous for his theatrical posters and record covers (including Cream's *Disraeli Gears* and *Wheels Of Fire*).

On the design front, Australia's most successful export has been the work of Marc Newson. His aerodynamic Lockheed Lounge (1985-86) has been snapped up by savvy furniture collectors and design buffs the world over. A graduate of the Sydney College of the Arts, he has long resided overseas.

Performance art can be found at galleries such as Artspace (p80) in Woolloomooloo – and some of it is certainly not for the faint-hearted. In 2003 Mike Parr performed a piece at Artspace titled *Democratic Torture,* in which people could deliver electric shocks to him via the internet; he's also nailed himself to a wall here in *Malevich: A Political Arm*.

Photographic exhibitions are always on at the Australian Centre for Photography (p85) in Woollahra. Finally, some of Sydney's quirkiest and most idiosyncratic art can be found in the fashion choices of locals – artist Reg Mombasa's work regularly pops up in the designs of surfwear label Mambo (see p131).

SYDNEY SCULPTURE WALK

One thing that makes Sydney such a pleasant city to stroll around is the Sydney Sculpture Walk, an excellent collection of 10 intriguing artworks created by local and overseas artists. They're dotted around central Sydney, mostly in its parks and gardens.

In the Royal Botanic Gardens you'll stumble upon Bronwyn Oliver's sculptures, *Magnolia* and *Palm*, which depict over-sized seedlike matter. Nearby in Farm Cove, Brenda Croft pays tribute to the area's indigenous clans with *Wuganmagulya*. Look down for this – it's a mix of coloured concrete and tile work in the footpath. More traditional is Fiona Hall's *Folly for Mrs Macquarie*, a beautifully symbolic birdcagelike gazebo. It's on Lawn 62 of the Botanic Gardens.

In The Domain is Debra Phillips' *Viva Voce* at Speaker's Corner, a fitting tribute to the soapboxers. Nearby is the large-scale *Veil of Trees* by Janet Laurence and Jisuk Han, which features clear glass, opaque steel and 100 eucalyptus trees native to the area. Also in The Domain is a sandstone spiral entitled *Memory is Creation Without End*, by Kimio Tsuchiya, which uses its surrounding space beautifully.

The Archaeology of Bathing by Robyn Backen evokes the elements of the former Woolloomooloo baths of the 1830s. The site was used for bathing by the indigenous Cadigal people. Close by is Nigel Helyer's *Dual Nature*, which includes water- and land-based elements, some of which feature the effective use of soundscapes.

Lynne Robert-Goodwin's *Tank Stream – Into the Head of the Cove* does stream-spotters a great favour by placing five illuminated markers at street level to highlight the route of the Tank Stream, which runs under central Sydney. Last but not least, *Passage* by Anne Graham marks out the borders and some of the features of two Georgian-era houses that once stood in what we now call Martin Place.

Other modern artists of note include Sandy Bruch, Ian Fairweather, Keith Looby, Ian Grant, Judy Cassab, Lindy Lee and John Olsen.

SCULPTURE

Sydney's first sculptors of public art were the members of the indigenous Eora nation. Figures of animals and humans were engraved into the area's rock outcroppings, offering a tiny insight into the Dreamtime, social systems and occupational patterns. Although Sydney claims more engraving sites than any other city in Australia, many have been covered by modern construction. You can still see some engravings in Bondi (p95), Sydney Harbour National Park (p106) and Ku-ring-gai Chase National Park (p112). For more on Aboriginal art, see p28.

Sydney is no slouch when it comes to exhibiting sculpture in its public spaces. Exceptional pieces to keep an eye out for include *Edge of Trees* (Janet Laurence and Fiona Foley) in front of the Museum of Sydney; *Touchstones* (Kan Yasuda) in the Aurora Place plaza at Phillip and Bent Sts; *Three Wheeler* (Tim Prentice) in the reception of Aurora Place; and *Canoe* (Richard Goodwin) at 30 Hickson Rd. Clusters of interesting pieces can also be seen in the Royal Botanic Gardens, The Domain and Martin Place. For a self-guided sculpture walk in these areas, see above. Sydney Architecture Walks (p35) offers guided tours of public art and its place within Sydney's landscape.

Some of Sydney's buildings have incorporated sculptural pieces, such as the Art Gallery of NSW (p66), whose façade features four bronze relief panels by different sculptors. The Opera House shows obvious sculptural influences in its design.

The world's largest outdoor sculpture exhibition is Sculpture by the Sea (p18), which takes place in November on the stunningly gorgeous seaside walk between Bondi and Tamarama beaches. Don't miss it if you're in the area during this time.

MUSIC

Sydney offers the traveller everything from world-class opera and intimate jazz to urban indigenous hip-hop and live electronic beats. Rock gigs take place every night of the week in the city's pubs and theatres, and the city attracts plenty of big-name touring artists.

Rock, Pop & Dance

Australia loves its pop stars and is currently churning them out at a rate of knots in reality TV shows. It's enough to make you feel a little sad for the current crop of perky *Neighbours* and *Home & Away* stars who are missing out on the opportunity to be the next Kylie. Pop acts that have proven to be more than a flash in the pan include Delta Goodrem, Natalie Imbruglia, Paulini and Human Nature (a Sydney-based boy band who have been having hits for over 10 years). The best purveyor of credible local pop is Sydney producer paulmac, whose melodic tunes have crossed over from underground dance clubs to commercial radio.

For the best part of the last decade, dance music has ruled supreme in the local bar and club scene. You'll find a bit of everything being played around town, from drum'n'bass to electro. Big-name DJs include Kid Kenobi, Ajax, Sveta and the brilliant Stephen Allkins, who has released two excellent albums under the moniker [Love] Tattoo.

Following the international trend, guitar music is starting to have a renaissance. In the '70s and '80s, Australia turned out a swag of pub rockers; INXS, Midnight Oil and Men at Work hit the charts worldwide. The most obvious heirs to this tradition are Melbourne's Jet. Sydneysiders to listen out for include indie kids The Cops, rowdy punks Frenzal Rhomb, grungy rockers The Vines, folksy singer-songwriter Alex Lloyd, and the jangly guitar of The Whitlams and Eskimo Joe. Local grunge gods Silverchair launched their album *Young Modern* in Sydney in 2007 to much acclaim.

Not fitting neatly into any category is the amazingly talented Paul Capsis, whose husky, soulful vocals need to be heard to be believed. He can channel anyone from Janis Joplin to Billy Holiday at will.

For details on where to catch live music and DJs, see the Drinking & Nightlife chapter (p154).

Indigenous

Songs are an incredibly important part of traditional Aboriginal culture. Aboriginal mythology tells of the Dreamtime or Dreaming, the time when totemic spirits created the world with song. These spirits left emblems behind, and connecting them are songlines or invisible pathways that tell the story of this creation. For Aborigines these integral songs also function as totems, maps and a guiding system of land tenure.

Most recently traditional Aboriginal music has been hybridised with modern sounds to create a musical fusion that blends didgeridoo notes with dance beats, reggae, rock, blues, country and pop. Contemporary indigenous artists include Yothu Yindi, who combine traditional Aboriginal sounds with a dance beat, and Torres Strait Island pop singer Christine Anu. Hip-hop has proven enormously popular with indigenous and Islander youth, spawning vital acts such as MC Wire who hails from the NSW north coast.

Folk

The early European settlers' ballads and songs about the bush comprise a uniquely Australian folklore, and mark the first attempt to adapt European cultural forms to the Australian environment. These creative efforts evolved from convict ditties, campfire yarns, and English, Scottish and Irish folk songs. Part poetry and part music-hall romp, they paint an evocative picture of life in the bush in the

top picks

A SYDNEY PLAYLIST

- Darlinghurst Nights (The Go-Betweens, 2005) Sad Darlinghurst memories get an airing.
- Sydney Song (Eskimo Joe, 2001) Ode to Sydney wannabes.
- Never Had So Much Fun (Frenzal Rhomb, 1999) Local punks advise against drinking the water.
- You Gotta Love this City (The Whitlams, 1999) Or any other song from this album – 'God drinks at the Sando', 'Blow up the Pokies' etc.
- Purple Sneakers (You Am I, 1995) 'Had a scratch only you could itch, underneath the Glebe Point Bridge'.
- My Drug Buddy (The Lemonheads, 1992) Evan Dando gets wasted on Newtown's King St.
- Darling It Hurts (Paul Kelly, 1986) Ode to a Darlinghurst street worker.
- Reckless (Australian Crawl, 1983) Glacial '80s pop to listen to 'as the Manly ferry cuts its way to Circular Quay'.
- Power & the Passion (Midnight Oil, 1982) Peter Garrett, now a federal MP, vents about Sydney 'wasting away in paradise' and a great line about 'underarms and football clubs'.
- Bliss (Th' Dudes, 1979) Kiwi rockers score speed in Coogee and falafels in Kings Cross.
- Section 5 (Bus to Bondi) (Midnight Oil, 1979) Garrett proves his green credentials taking public transport.
- Khe Sahn (Cold Chisel, 1978) Classic Aussie rock about a Vietnam vet's return.

19th century. You can sometimes hear these old songs at venues in The Rocks area. *Waltzing Matilda* is the most famous example.

Classical

Classical music can be heard at the Sydney Opera House, at nearby universities and at various city venues like the exceptional City Recital Hall. Opera Australia, Australia's national opera company, keeps itself busy giving around 250 performances per year. It's based at the Sydney Opera House for seven months of the year (and in Melbourne the rest of the time). Some notable Australian opera singers you may be able to catch performing include Amelia Farrugia, Cheryl Barker, David Hobson and Joan Carden.

See p168 for more detailed listings of various companies and venues.

THEATRE

Sydney provides something for all mainstream tastes, from imported blockbuster musicals at major venues like the State Theatre to solid, crowd-friendly productions in well-built theatres in the city. While there are a few small theatre companies staging more experimental, exciting works in inner-city suburbs, Sydney's theatrical tastes tend towards, well, the unadventurous end of the spectrum, and sometimes appear to be riding the wave from its 1970s glory days.

While the bulk of Australian actors live and work in Sydney, Australia's geographic isolation and a lingering sense of the 'cultural cringe' mean that truly local theatre gigs are few and far between, and not particularly well paid. Thus, many actors prefer to get as much film and TV work as they can, or better yet, go overseas. The National Institute of Dramatic Art (NIDA) in Kensington is a breeding ground for new talent, and stages performances of students' work. For more details on theatre venues, see p172.

The city's biggest name in theatre is the popular Sydney Theatre Company (STC), at Miller's Point. Established in 1978, it provides a balanced program of modern, classical, local and foreign drama and attracts solid talent across the board. The company is still radiant from the opening of its state-of-the-art Sydney Theatre in 2004. However that achievement has lately been overshadowed by the announcement that it's scored Cate Blanchett along with her husband, playwright Andrew Upton, as its new artistic directors.

There are also many smaller theatre companies presenting genuinely innovative work: Sydney's much-loved Company B at the Belvoir St Theatre; Griffin at the Stables; Tamarama Rock Surfers at the Old Fitzroy, and various local independent companies at the Darlinghurst Theatre. The independent scene also supports 'boutique' companies like Pact Youth Theatre and the Sidetrack Performance group, which emphasise multicultural issues.

In 2006, Griffin's staging of Australian author Timothy Conigrave's memoir *Holding The Man*, adapted by Tommy Murphy, took Sydney by storm – returning in 2007 for another sell-out season before touring the country. It won the NSW Premier's Award for a new theatre work and is in the process of being staged by international theatre companies.

Sydney-based writers and directors of note include the acclaimed John Bell, who often takes the reins (when he's not appearing on stage) of his Bell Shakespeare Company; Neil Armfield, the prolific artistic director of Company B; Kate Gaul, who is known for interpreting new works; Adam Cook, who took on the challenging task of adapting and directing Patrick White's *The Aunt's Story* for the stage in 2001; and the political Stephen Sewell, who wrote the multi-award-winning play *Myth, Propaganda and Disaster in Nazi Germany and Contemporary America*.

Stage performers to keep an eye out for in local productions include Deborah Mailman, Jackie Weaver, Marcus Graham, John Howard (not that one), Robyn Nevin and Barry Otto.

Sydney is still recovering from the deaths of two of its brightest theatre stars in recent years: former STC founder Richard Wherrett (1940–2001), who might have been Australia's most successful and controversial theatrical director; and the much-loved playwright and teacher Nick Enright (1950-2003), whose legacy includes the musical *The Boy from Oz* and the Oscar-nominated screenplay *Lorenzo's Oil*. Both men contributed to the flourishing of the Sydney theatrical scene from the 1970s onwards.

LITERATURE & NONFICTION

Australia's literary history could be said to have started with the convict colony in Sydney in the late 18th century. New adventures and landscapes inspired the colonists to tell stories and eventually to record them with the written word. By the mid-19th century the Australian storytelling tradition was becoming established, and though many early works have been lost, some – like Marcus Clarke's *For the Term of his Natural Life* (1870) – managed to survive.

In the late 19th century a more formal Australian literary movement began to develop with *The Bulletin*, an influential publication that promoted an egalitarian and unionist school of thought (and survives to this day). Well-known contributing authors of the time included Henry Lawson (1867–1922), who wrote short stories about the Australian bush, and AB 'Banjo' Paterson (1864–1941), famous for his poems – especially *Waltzing Matilda* and *The Man from Snowy River*.

Miles Franklin (1879–1954) wrote *My Brilliant Career* (1901), considered the first authentic Australian novel. After coming out it caused a sensation, especially when it was revealed that Miles was a woman. Another gender bender was Ethel Florence Lindesay Richardson, who worked under the pseudonym of Henry Handel Richardson and is now regarded as one of Australia's most important early-20th-century writers.

Multi-award-winning Australian writers of international stature include Patrick White (the only Australian ever to have won the Nobel Prize in Literature, in 1973), Thomas Keneally (Booker Prize–winner 1982) and Peter Carey (Booker Prize–winner 1988 and 2001), as well as Commonwealth Writers Award–winners David Malouf, Murray Bail, Alex Miller, Tim Winton, Richard Flanagan and Kate Grenville. Other reliable reads include Neil Drinnan, Graeme Aitken, Peter Robb, Kate Jennings, Robert Dessaix and John Birmingham. For poetry look out for the

SYDNEY IN PRINT

- *The Secret River*, Kate Grenville (2005) The book that won Grenville the Commonwealth Prize and a Booker nomination, it's a powerful story of convict life set in the early 19th century in Sydney and the Hawkesbury River.
- *Sydney Architecture*, Paul McGillick and Patrick Bingham-Hall (2005) One for the coffee table, beautiful photographs and interesting text showcase over 100 of Sydney's most stunning buildings.
- *The Girl From Botany Bay*, Carolly Erickson (2004) A history in the style of a novel, telling the fascinating story of Mary Bryant, a First Fleet convict who escaped in a small boat, making it all the way to Indonesia before being recaptured.
- *30 Days in Sydney*, Peter Carey (2001) A rich and nostalgic account of Peter Carey's return to Sydney after 10 years of living in New York City. His emotions and experiences read like a diary, with full descriptions and a theme covering the four elements of earth, air, fire and water. A skilled observer and historian.
- *Quill*, Neal Drinnan (2001) A sassy and moving tale of gay love, life and death in Sydney, with party scenes that many Sydneysiders will relate to.
- *In the Gutter… Looking At the Stars* ed Mandy Sayer and Louis Nowra (2000) Absolutely spellbinding, this compilation of writings about Kings Cross paints a vivid portrait of the area's rich and varied history, decade by decade.
- *Leviathan*, John Birmingham (1999) A gritty history written in the tone of an unauthorised biography exploring Sydney's seamier side. You won't want to put it down.
- *Vanity Fierce*, Graeme Aitken (1998) Taking on the seeming shallowness of Darlinghurst gay life, this witty novel makes many a wry observation and wise crack.
- *The Cross*, Mandy Sayer (1995) Based on the life and disappearance of Juanita Nelson – an unsolved mystery still – this novel has Kings Cross as a central character and is an illuminating treatment of a nasty period in Sydney's history (the 1970s), when organised crime and property development led to murder.
- *The Playmaker*, Thomas Keneally (1987) The inverse of Carolly Erickson's book, this is a novel in the style of a history, with Mary Bryant making another appearance – this time as an actor in the first play ever staged in the new continent. It's hard-going at first, but worth the effort.
- *Voss*, Patrick White (1957) Nobel Prize–winner White contrasts the harsh and unforgiving outback with colonial life in Sydney in this modern masterpiece. It tells the story of German obsessive explorer Voss, who plans to cross Australia from coast to coast. In the 1980s *Voss* was transformed into an opera, with a libretto by David Malouf.
- *The Harp In The South*, Ruth Park (1948) A gripping and touching account of an impoverished family's life in Surry Hills when the suburb was a crowded slum.

ARTISTIC AWARDS

The New South Wales (NSW) Premier's Awards is an annual prize-giving bonanza that rewards the best local literary works in a variety of genres, including children's, young adults', fiction, translation, theatre and poetry, with $15,000 going to each winner. Winners are announced in May at Parliament House, as part of the Sydney Writers' Festival (p17). Learn more at www.arts.nsw.gov.au.

The Archibald Prize is a high-profile annual competition that attracts Australian artists not so much for the prizes (from $10,000 to $35,000), but for the exposure they gain. Prizes are given in different genres, which include portrait, landscape, mural/subject and photography. Winners are announced in April. The Archibald never fails to stimulate debates and controversies; for more information see www.thearchibaldprize.com.au.

works of Samuel Wagan Watson, Jaya Savige, John Tranter, Dorothy Porter and Jill Jones, among others.

One worthy literary journal that regularly showcases excellent Australian writing talent is *Heat,* which is edited by Sydney-raised Ivor Indyk and features poetry, fiction and nonfiction. It's available at many bookshops around Sydney and is published regularly by Giramondo.

See p17 for details on the annual Sydney Writers' Festival.

ARCHITECTURE
LANDSCAPE & HISTORY

Ever since Captain Arthur Phillip supped from the Tank Stream, water has shaped modern Sydney's settlement and development. The Tank Stream now runs in brick culverts beneath the city streets, but in the early days following the arrival of the First Fleet it defined the city. Phillip used the stream to separate convicts on the rocky west from the officers on the gentler eastern slopes. In effect, he used the landscape to hem convicts in by the sea on one side and soldiers on another. Following this pattern, government institutions were concentrated to the east of the stream, while industry set up shop on the western side of the city. In this way, social differences were articulated in the layout of the settlement and set a pattern that continued as the city grew. This class distinction had a lasting effect, which can still be seen in Sydney 220 years later.

According to scientist and author Dr Tim Flannery, many Aboriginal campsites used to lie near fresh water on the north-facing shore – and the settlers took their cue from the original inhabitants. Topographically, it makes sense. The area catches the winter sun, and is relatively sheltered from the chilling southerly and the bullying westerly winds. The northeasterly breeze, meanwhile, comes straight through the mouth of the harbour, delivering warm winter and cool summer breezes.

In one of history's great coincidences, Frenchman Jean Compte de la Pérouse arrived at Botany Bay days after the First Fleet. That event and fierce competition from other colonial powers meant there was a perceived threat of invasion from the outset. As a consequence, the navy appropriated much of the harbour foreshore. This was a fortunate twist of events – much of the land was not built upon, in effect conserving these regions as wildernesses while the rest of Sydney sprang up around them. Six key harbour sites, including the North Head and Cockatoo Island, have now been returned to the people of Sydney under the control of the Harbour Trust. See www.harbourtrust.gov.au for more information.

AN ANTIPODEAN BRITAIN

The men and women that arrived in the First Fleet were staggeringly ill prepared for the realities of building in their new, raw environment. British powers-that-be had not thought to include any architect on board. Design and construction duties largely fell to the one bricklayer among the new arrivals, James Bloodsworth. A convict transportee, he found himself in such a key role more by chance than by design. Inevitably, the early builders looked to the 'mother' country for inspiration, but shoddy workmanship, poor tools and a temporary feel to the colony conspired against long-term success.

Perhaps the most significant change to this ad-hoc, unplanned approach was the arrival of new governor Lachlan Macquarie in 1810. Both he and his wife viewed good architecture as an essential component of a thriving, healthy society. The arrival of several architects, including the immensely important Francis Greenway, a convict transported for forgery, helped transform Sydney's city landscape. The prevailing Georgian architecture of Britain was echoed in many of the buildings that sprang up at this time – adapted to local materials and skills.

As the 19th century progressed, the colony's architects still looked to Britain for inspiration, but broader European influences were seen, from the neoclassical Sydney Town Hall (see p68) to the early-Gothic-style spires of St Mary's Cathedral (see p67).

Australia became a fully fledged country in its own right at the beginning of the 20th century – and an increasing architectural autonomy reflected this new independence. Architects questioned the more traditional approaches and sought different ways to adapt buildings to Sydney's extraordinary landscape and location – particularly in the residential areas. In the city centre, meanwhile, the scrapping of height restrictions in the 1950s sparked Sydney's love-in with the skyscraper. Modernism was an influential movement with architects such as Harry Seidler looking to make best use of Sydney's sunny climate and harbour views – and embracing a much more diverse international attitude. Of course, the legacy of early British influence is still clear from a walk around central Sydney. Today's buildings, however, are much more sensitive to the environment rather than being influenced from afar.

UTILITARIAN

From the arrival of the first white settlers, Sydney has relied on its harbour. All sorts of cargo (including human) has been unloaded on its shores, feeding and sustaining the city. Some of the most interesting central buildings are the utilitarian wharves and warehouse structures that still line parts of the western shore. Many sprouted up after the arrival of the bubonic plague at the wharves in 1900 (which killed 103 Sydneysiders in eight months). This was used as the excuse by the government to resume control of the old, privately owned wharves and clean up The Rocks slums. The new industrial buildings reflected a turn to utilitarian simplicity, in contrast to the previous obsession with neoclassical forms. The 'containerisation' of shipping in the 1960s and 1970s made many of these sites redundant almost overnight.

Now, Sydneysiders' obsession for harbourside living is also putting many of these historic sites at risk. However, some have been transformed through some inspired redevelopment, with once dilapidated sheds becoming top-notch cafés, restaurants and apartments. The Woolloomooloo (p80) and Walsh Bay finger wharves (p56) are the most dramatic examples of the new uses for these old structures. One of the city's big architectural challenges is to retain the richness of a working harbour and adapt these industrial sites to a successful, working role of the city today.

MODERN

Between the two world wars, Australia looked to the US for architectural inspiration and a building boom took place. Martin Place (Map pp62–3), with its granite-bedecked Art Deco temples to commerce and big business, is a well-preserved example. Similarly lavish buildings began to dot the eastern suburban skyline, giving a stylish look to many suburbs, despite some hideous modern incursions.

The opening of the Sydney Harbour Bridge in 1932 was also a seminal moment for the city's architecture, opening up the densely forested north shore to development. Much of this shoreline retains its rural character to this day, reflecting the architects' determination to engage with Sydney's rugged natural charms. Some good news in the 1950s and

THE INSIDE STORY OF SYDNEY'S ARCHITECTURE

For a fresh, enthusiastic and expert insight into the building of Sydney, there's no better way than to take a stroll with an architect. The passionate building buffs at Sydney Architecture Walks (☎ 8239 2211; www.sydneyarchitecture.org; tours adult/child $25/20; ☼ 10:30am Wed, Sat & Sun) will open your eyes to Sydney's architecture, old and new. Those who are into the Sydney Opera House will love the Utzon walk. Other routes take in contemporary Sydney (with particular focus on Aurora Place), the harbour edge (with special emphasis on the Walsh Bay Finger Wharves) and consider architecture's relationship to the city's landscape. Strolls last two hours, and leave rain or shine from the Museum of Sydney (p66).

1960s came via the 'Sydney School', which pioneered a distinctively Australian architecture, characterised by the appreciation of native landscapes and natural materials and the avoidance of conventional and historic language. Further steps were taken as 'new Australians' like Harry Seidler and Hugh Buhrich brought to the local architectural scene a sensitivity to place, infused with Bauhaus and modernist-inspired concepts.

Since the early 1960s, central Sydney has become a mini-Manhattan of tall buildings vying for harbour views, thanks to the lifting in the late 1950s of the 150ft (46m) height limit. Best early modernist examples are Harry Seidler's Australia Square (p61) and MLC buildings. Plans for an almost total redevelopment of the city's historic districts were afoot in the 1960s as the irascible Askin Liberal Government (who kicked Sydney Opera House designer Jørn Utzon out of Sydney) deemed many Victorian and early-20th-century buildings undesirable in the race to construct an 'all new' metropolis. Thankfully, the 'green bans' campaign and plenty of vociferous local protests managed to save large chunks of The Rocks and areas such as Kings Cross, Paddington and Woolloomooloo.

Many buildings from the 1970s and 1980s are forgettable, but there are striking exceptions such as the Capita Centre on Castlereagh St and Governors Phillip and Macquarie Towers (p66) on Phillip St.

CONTEMPORARY

The spate of skyscraper-building that hit central Sydney following the lifting of height restrictions has defined the skyline. For a while, the city's older buildings were in danger of being neglected. That changed for the bicentennial celebrations of 1988 when cultural heritage soared up the agenda. As well as the refurbishment of Macquarie St and Circular Quay, developers turned their eye towards Darling Harbour. Although some critics accuse the end result of tackiness, few can question how completely the mostly disused industrial area was transformed.

The enthusiasm for retaining Sydney's historic character continues unabated. Many old buildings were earmarked for a new use, and some were done to surprising effect. Historic buildings like The Mint (p64) and the Sydney Conservatorium of Music (p59) on Macquarie St, the Customs House (p58) at Circular Quay and the Walsh Bay Finger Wharves (p56) are great examples of how thoughtful and sympathetic contemporary work can inject new life and energy into an area.

The other defining event that placed Sydney's architecture firmly on the international radar was, of course, the 2000 Olympic Games. Many of the buildings and infrastructure

SYDNEY OPERA HOUSE

Frank Lloyd Wright called it a 'circus tent' and Mies van der Rohe thought it the work of the devil, yet Danish architect Jørn Utzon bequeathed Sydney one of the 20th century's defining architectural moments.

Utzon was 38 when he entered the Opera House competition and, remarkably, had only realised a few small houses. Working from navigational maps of the site and memories of his travels to the great pre-Columbian platforms in Mexico, Utzon achieved the unimaginable. His great architectural gesture – billowing white clouds hovering above a heavy stone platform – tapped into the essence of Sydney, almost as if building and site had grown out of the same founding principles.

Eight years on, having realised his designs for the platform, concrete shells and ceramic skin, Utzon found himself with a new client, NSW Premier and Liberal Party scoundrel Robert Askin. By April 1966, owed hundreds of thousands of dollars in unpaid fees, Utzon was unceremoniously forced to leave his building half-finished. He says now that the six years he spent developing his House's interiors and glass walls, of which there is nothing to show, were the most productive of his working life.

Now in his nineties, Utzon is again working on his Opera House, this time through his architect son Jan Utzon and Sydney architect Richard Johnson. Attempts at reconciliation began in the 1990s, and Utzon agreed to be taken as a consultant. The majority of the new work concerns the interiors, most notably the design of a completely new acoustic interior for the Opera Shell. Utzon senior, however, has never returned to the country where his most famous work stands – and it is now unlikely he ever will.

developed around Homebush Bay, where the Games were largely held, were simply world class. Meanwhile, some of the most innovative contemporary work in Sydney often happens far from the public gaze in the realm of the single-family house. Here, enlightened clients can bankroll the creative ambition of their architects. Leading figures include Richard Leplastrier, Glenn Murcutt, Peter Stutchbury, Neil Durbach, Camilla Block and Richard Francis-Jones.

WHAT TO SEE

Modern Sydney began life in Sydney Cove – and the area immediately around it has been the hub of the city ever since. It's no surprise that central Sydney gives the best insight into how the city's architecture has matured from shaky, poorly crafted imitation to confident autonomy. For a self-guided journey around some of Sydney's key city centre buildings, see p69.

If the CBD is ideal for tracing the development of institutional and financial building styles, The Rocks is the place to head for the social background behind Sydney's architecture. See The Rocks walking tour (p59) for some of the essential sights. Millers Point (Map p54) also reveals some impressive social housing policies and the area's strong industrial maritime heritage.

For the best glimpse of inner-city Sydney residential development, make your way to Potts Point and Elizabeth Bay (Map p78). The backstreets of this dense suburb include superb Art Deco apartments, modern housing, coffee shops, boutique eateries and surprising harbour glimpses.

Outside of the city centre, places of architectural note are more sporadically located. Castlecrag Estate (Map pp50–1) is the classic example of considered North Shore development. Walter Burley Griffin and his wife built the estate from local sandstone in the 1930s, shaping the architecture in response to the dramatic, leafy topography of the area.

GREEN BUILDINGS

Environmental concerns have rocketed up the agenda in Sydney over the past decade – and that applies to its architecture, too. The Olympic Games didn't quite get the ball rolling, but they certainly quickened the momentum. There are several developments around Olympic Park that highlight the 'sustainable' agenda of the Games. In fact, one is probably the first thing you will see when you arrive in the area, the Olympic Park Rail Station, which is admired for its natural light and ventilation and striking, shell-like design. The modernist blocks of Newington Apartments (Bruce Eeles), originally the Olympic Village, also emphasise natural light as well as energy conservation and water recycling. While you are there, try to catch the sleek grace of Peter Stutchbury's Archery Pavilion.

Since the Olympics, 30 The Bond (Map p54) on Hickson Rd has become the benchmark for Sydney's green buildings. Its adjustable façade, chilled beam air-conditioning and large amounts of natural light make it the most energy efficient building in Sydney. Its developers were the first to pledge to achieving a five-star Australian Building Greenhouse rating.

Of course, sustainable building is not limited to big financial and infrastructure developments – 'green' residential projects are also coming on apace. It's not just new buildings either. Concerns about the environment have even led one resident to convert a 19th-century terraced house into the city's first sustainable home (p38).

ECONOMY

Sydney is Australia's chief commercial, financial and industrial centre and is responsible for about a quarter of Australia's economic activity. It's the headquarters of the nation's biggest businesses and banks. The Sydney economy is comparable to that of Singapore and larger than the whole of New Zealand. The city's economic growth is consistently above the national average and unemployment rates lower.

The Australian economy has been strong in recent years, but in 2007 things were heating up even more, driven by high export prices for commodities. Business and consumer confidence are running high, economic growth is strong (4% predicted) and unemployment is at a 32-year low. All of this has added to inflationary pressure, which is likely to result in interest rate hikes – bad news for mortgage holders and, if the strong dollar increases even further as a result, bad news for exporters and international tourists.

Sydney's two harbours and busy airport make it an important transport hub; most of Australia's foreign trade is conducted in Sydney and NSW. Its industry includes shipyards, oil refineries, textile mills, foundries, electronics and chemical plants. It's true that Sydney is obsessed by property. Property and business services employ the most people (14.8%), followed by the retail trade (13.9%) and manufacturing (12.6%), which was the biggest employer 10 years ago.

Housing prices remain high; Sydney has the 8th most expensive property by sq metre of any city in the world. While owning your own house is increasingly unaffordable, a rental shortage is contributing to a higher cost of living for the lower paid.

A 2007 international study rated Sydney as having the 9th best quality of living of any city in the world. This should be cause for celebration, but most Sydneysiders already believe their city is number one. Any joy in beating Melbourne (in 12th spot) is diminished by being ranked four spots lower than Auckland.

More joy can be taken from being ranked the 14th biggest hub of the new worldwide economy in a 2007 report commissioned by MasterCard Worldwide – confirming Sydney's place as the economic powerhouse of Australasia (Auckland didn't even make the list) and the fifth most important commercial centre in the Asia-Pacific region.

SYDNEY'S SUSTAINABLE HOUSE

It seems like an everyday 19th-century terrace house from the outside, one of hundreds in the inner-city suburb of Chippendale. In many ways it is. But there are signs that this is not quite as run of the mill as it first appears. The doorbell for example – you'll hear no electronic chime here. You simply pull on a string leading through the brick front to a bell on the other side. Welcome, then, to Sydney's original sustainable house.

Its owner, Michael Mobb, was getting his hands dirty for a more sustainable lifestyle way before it became the in-vogue media topic. Back in 1996, he and his wife were planning a kitchen and bathroom renovation. But that work turned into something a whole lot more ambitious and life-changing: they decided to switch their house into a fully sustainable home, with all their energy and water needs supplied on site.

'People thought I was really weird,' Michael remembers. 'Back then, people thought it was a nice idea but a bit bohemian. Now it's become mainstream – everyone likes to say they've got a solar panel on their roof.'

Like the string doorbell, many of the innovations in the house are disarmingly simple. All the fittings – from the rainwater filter on the drainpipe to the stainless-steel benches that magnify the sunlight and stop the need for electric light during the day – are available from normal tradespeople. And Michael is at pains to stress how ordinary the home is: 'If my kids have got friends over, there's no need to train them how to use the water or energy system – it's very straightforward'.

But the simplicity has not stopped the overhaul from having a huge effect. The average Sydneysider uses 274L of water a day. By using rainwater and recycling waste water efficiently, Michael's household of four uses just 220L a day – combined. The same dramatic decrease occurred with energy consumption. The house used to burn 24 kilowatts of electricity; now it uses just six. Indeed, by using the power generated by rooftop solar panels, the house exports more energy to the national grid than it uses. And when we walk into the house, Michael proudly shows off a new arrival that he hopes will cut his current power use even further – a large, super energy-efficient fridge. 'The one before was my biggest mistake,' he says. 'If I had put a grate under the fridge, the cool air could have increased efficiency by up to 25%'.

In fact, these mistakes are part of the reason he likes to share his experience. 'It shows people they can make a difference just by the way they put their fridge in the kitchen – if I put the information out there, people might develop better, simpler ideas, so it could become more affordable'.

So why set out to convert something as tricky as a 19th-century terraced house? 'The first act of defeat would have been to go and do this in an untouched bush setting – it would have been like running away', Michael says. 'Here, the message is much clearer, the fact that I did it 10 minutes from the centre of the city'.

More information on Sydney's sustainable house is available at www.sustainablehouse.com.au.

A TALE OF TWO CITIES

Athens and Sparta, Paris and Milan, Springfield and Shelbyville – their struggles pale beside the epic 150-year rivalry between Sydney and Melbourne. Australia's biggest city, Sydney is also its oldest, having begun in 1788 as a convict colony. Melbourne, currently in the number-two slot, was founded in 1835. Sixteen years later prospectors struck gold in Victoria, and the ensuing rush rocketed Melbourne ahead of Sydney in both wealth and population. The Sydney-Melbourne Rivalry (SMR) had begun.

Competition flared when Melbourne became Australia's temporary capital following nationhood in 1901. Purpose-built Canberra didn't replace Melbourne until 1927, by which time a driven Sydney had begun catching up financially, having already retaken the lead in human numbers.

These days, the SMR plays out for the most part as friendly chaffing, though discussions can get heated. Melburnians will point to Sydney's convict origins, its high housing prices and what they see as a lack of culture, while talking up their own city's multi-ethnicity, great pubs and lively arts scene. Sydneysiders will often either feign ignorance of any rivalry, or maintain that it's one-sided, an invention of envious Melburnians deluded enough to compare their boring burgh with the obviously superior Sydney.

If you should get caught in the middle between such types, don't pour oil on the waters by saying the two cities are nearing parity in their cultural diversity and culinary sophistication. Just put on your most innocent face and ask, 'Hey, does Canberra really suck as much as they say?'

ENVIRONMENT & PLANNING

THE LAND

Sydney lies on Australia's populous east coast, about 870km north of Melbourne by road and almost 1000km south of Brisbane. Standing on the cliffs near Bondi you get a sense of the vast sandstone shelf that forms this edge of the continent, sliced off by the waves below and carved like cheese by ancient waterways into harbours and inlets.

The city is centred on the harbour of Port Jackson, but Greater Sydney sprawls over 1800 sq km and has grown to encompass Botany Bay in the south, the foothills of the Blue Mountains in the west and the fringes of the national parks to the north.

FAUNA

Sydney's bird life is plentiful, spectacular and makes one hell of a din. The biggest show-offs are the sulphur-crested cockatoos, with their raucous squawks, sumptuous white plumage and yellow crowns. You'll also spot rainbow lorikeets, kookaburras, galahs, Australian white ibises (usually with their heads in the bins in Hyde Park), pelicans (by the fish market) and, if you're very lucky, lyrebirds (in Ku-Ring-Gai Chase National Park).

Possums are common and there's a large colony of grey-haired flying foxes at the Royal Botanic Gardens (p57), but you'll need to head to the national parks to spot wallabies and other native mammals. There's a small population of koalas at Avalon on the Northern Beaches.

Water dragons and blue-tongued lizards can sometimes be seen. Sydney is home to one of the deadliest snakes in the world, the eastern brown snake, although you'll rarely find it in urban areas. Other slithery locals include the common death adder, the diamond python and the red-bellied black snake.

On the other hand, spiders are quite likely to make an appearance. The large brown huntsman spiders (15cm) are scary looking but big softies. The ones to watch out for are the venomous redbacks and funnel-webs. You'll spot plenty of St Andrews Cross spiders in their elaborate webs all over Sydney.

GREEN SYDNEY

Sydney's residents are a reasonably environmentally sensitive bunch; when you start with such a glorious setting, you have a lot of incentive to keep things nice. Many households and businesses recycle paper, glass and plastic. Parks and bushland in and around Sydney act as animal and plant habitats, recreation reserves and the city's 'lungs'.

Sydney's glorious beaches are fairly clean but can become polluted after heavy rainfalls, when city runoff and sewage overflow streams into the city's harbour and coastal waters. Millions have been spent installing litter and pollution traps, but it's still best not to swim at harbour beaches for three days after heavy rain and avoid the ocean for a day. You can drink tap water without fear, however.

There is controversy around plans to build a desalination plant to overcome Sydney's falling dam levels during the ongoing drought. A desalination plant is an extremely energy-intensive way to provide drinking water, and the energy required is most likely to be provided by burning fossil fuels – adding to the already high greenhouse emissions.

Sydney's love affair with the car and the city's high humidity mean that air pollution can sometimes be bad, but it's nothing compared to Los Angeles, Bangkok or Buenos Aires. Those seriously affected by allergies and asthma, however, should check the daily air pollution levels in newspaper weather sections. Australia is on the edge of the giant hole in the ozone, making sun block a necessity.

URBAN PLANNING & DEVELOPMENT

Despite Sydney's overall beauty, this modern city was originally built with very little urban planning, confounded by a history of ruthless developers and corruption. It's taken public outcry and union 'green bans' to save many parks and historic areas (such as Potts Point and The Rocks) from the wrecking ball.

Circular Quay is a prime example of muddy vision; it's been the victim of more architectural abortions and near-sighted planning initiatives than is decent for what should be the city's showcase. On the plus side, recent redevelopments around Woolloomooloo and Walsh Bays have been handled sensitively.

THE LIFE AQUATIC

The movie *Finding Nemo* features a crew of cool-dude turtles surfing the East Australian Current. One suspects that they would get on mighty fine with Grant Willis, the senior aquarist at Sydney Aquarium (p71). This handsome 35-year-old bloke from Bronte with an applied science degree in coastal management seems like he'd be more comfortable on a surfboard than in a stuffy scientific laboratory. Lucky for Willis (and the turtles), he's the man in charge of rehabilitating marine creatures that come into the aquarium's care.

Injured turtles, penguins, seals and other critters that are picked up by the National Parks and Wildlife Service come to the aquarium to convalesce after being fixed up by Taronga Zoo's vets before being returned to the wild. They've also recently released five penguins born at the aquarium into the Sydney Harbour colony.

Willis has long been passionate about Sydney's marine life; he had his own fish tank when he was 10 and learned to dive at 16. He suggests Gordons Bay near Clovelly (p97) as a great spot to get among it – 'you'll see blue groupers, seahorses and 80% of what you'll see snorkelling around Sydney'. His pick of the beaches is Whale Beach (p112): 'It's quieter and harder to access, and there's no sewage runoff.'

He's not a fan of shark nets, which he describes as 'random killing machines', destroying turtles and dugongs without offering much protection to swimmers. Should visitors be worried about sharks?

'Mate, you're statistically more likely to have too many beers and get bowled over. There are more people killed by falling coconuts than shark attacks,' he says, adding that there have been no shark fatalities in Sydney since the 1960s. 'Drowning is more of a problem. Pay attention to the surf clubs and swim between the flags'.

One development that has him excited is the increase in the number of Humpbacks and Southern Right Whales along the coast. They're getting closer to shore and more confident – one even swam into Darling Harbour recently. From June to November there are plenty of tour operators that will get you close to these amazing creatures (see p225). Willis doesn't think the attention causes the whales any great concern: 'If you annoy them, chances are they'll just dive down and piss off'.

So what can visitors do to keep Australia's marine environment healthy? According to Willis, a great first step is to dispose of your rubbish properly. Cigarette butts stubbed out on the street end up in the harbour with the next big downpour. Don't collect shellfish and, if fishing, respect catch limits and don't use small fish as bait.

For information on the Sydney Aquarium Conservation Foundation, see www.sydneyaquarium.com.au/NonProfit /NON050.asp. For tips on choosing sustainable seafood, see p138.

WHEN THE CRITTERS TURN NASTY

Australia is famous for harbouring the lion's share of the world's most poisonous creatures. You might hear that eight out of 10 of the world's most poisonous snakes live in Australia, or that an innocent-looking cone snail could kill you with one prick, or that there are crocodiles that hunt out in the ocean – and of course all of these would be true. But don't panic yet; the chances of you running into any of these critters, especially in central Sydney, are pretty slim.

Although there are venomous snakes in Sydney's national parks, few are aggressive, and unless you have the misfortune to tread on one you're unlikely to be bitten. Snake bites don't cause instantaneous death and antivenins are usually available. Keep the victim calm and still, wrap the bitten limb tightly, as you would for a sprained ankle, then attach a splint to immobilise it. Then seek medical help, with the dead snake for identification, if possible.

There are a few nasty spiders around, including the funnel-web and the redback. The funnel-web bite is treated in the same way as a snake bite. For redback bites, apply ice and seek medical attention. Again, these are not creatures you're likely to find snuggling up to you in bed; these spiders like to hang around gardens and wood piles, not in hotel rooms or under restaurant chairs.

Other waterside critters to watch for include the stone fish (with poisonous spines) and the deadly blue-ringed octopus (they're small and hang around in rock pools – signs will be posted if there's a danger). Another threat is the small bluebottle jellyfish, which you can often find washed up on the shores of Sydney's beaches (don't touch it!). In the water they look like bright blue sacs with trailing tentacles up to 2m long. Stings aren't fatal but do cause severe pain and leave red welts. Remove any part still attached to the skin with tweezers or a gloved hand and apply ice and an anaesthetic cream. In extreme cases, go see the doc!

Sydney just keeps getting bigger, stretching its boundaries to house a growing population. From the original colony at The Rocks, things developed outwards in ever-expanding circles, and now the city is reaching its limits to the north and south (abutting national parks) and to the west (edging the Blue Mountains). This only leaves the agricultural southwest and northwest corridors open for expansion, and development plans into these areas will no doubt become politically controversial.

To the anger of many residents, the state government has continually passed roading projects on to private developers, adding to the hefty number of tolls for motorists to live with. In 2005 an outcry greeted the opening of the Cross City Tunnel, a 2km-long underground stretch of toll road that connects East Sydney and Darling Harbour. Not only had the good burghers of Sydney had to endure endless disturbance during its construction, existing public roads were altered to force people to use the pricey private toll road. People voted with their feet (or should that be wheels) and boycotted the tunnel, leaving the city traffic worse than before. The city was forced to back down and reopen the roads it had blocked. Ironically, it now faces a major lawsuit from the company that built the tunnel, blaming the city for its insolvency.

MEDIA

Packer and Murdoch: two media dynasties that engender a mix of fear, respect and loathing throughout the world. Their influence is felt no more strongly than in their own country. Australia's media ownership is one of the most concentrated in the world, with most daily newspapers owned by two organisations.

Kerry Packer was Australia's richest man before his death in 2005. His enormous media empire Publishing & Broadcasting Ltd (PBL) owns Channel 9 (TV) and Australian Consolidated Press. All in all PBL owns 60% of all magazines sold in Australia, including the Sydney-based *Bulletin* (news and current affairs), *Woman's Day* (celebrity gossip and

top picks

MEDIA WEBSITES

Sydney Morning Herald (www.smh.com.au) Newspaper.

The Australian (www.theaustralian.news.com.au) Newspaper.

The Chaser (www.chaser.com.au) Satirical newspaper.

ABC (www.abc.com.au) TV and radio.

SBS (www20.sbs.com.au) TV and radio.

local battler tales), *Australian Gourmet Traveller* (lovingly detailed food and wine escapes) and *Cleo* (fashion and orgasms for young women).

Rupert Murdoch's News Corporation owns Sydney's *Daily Telegraph, The Australian,* Sky News, Fox News, Foxtel, Fox Sports, 20th Century Fox, the NRL, and dozens of magazines and local newspapers.

Another media heavyweight is John Fairfax Holdings, publishers of the *Sydney Morning Herald* (daily broadsheet), the *Australian Financial Review* (financial news), *Business Review Weekly* (business) and the *Sun-Herald* (Sunday tabloid).

The Australian media relies heavily on foreign newspapers, especially British and American ones, for its international coverage. Bylines attributing news stories to the *Guardian, New York Times, Washington Post, Daily Telegraph* and *The Times* (of London) are fairly common. Having said that, foreign correspondents such as *the Sydney Morning Herald*'s Paul McGeough provide excellent independent coverage of, for example, the happenings in Iraq.

FASHION

Sydney's fashion scene caters to body-conscious locals keen to step out of their doorways as sleek and svelte as their wallets and thrice-weekly workouts can possibly make them. It's Sydney's climate that proves the major determining factor in wardrobe decisions. While there are plenty of over-the-shoulder glances towards Europe and the States for fashion ideas, no one's going to go crazy and start wearing floor-length fur coats to Puccini at the Opera House. Hot Sydney designers and fashion show darlings (see Australian Fashion Week, p17) include Sass & Bide (p128), Silence is Golden and Lee Mathews.

The city's fashion scene began to stretch its wings back in the 1970s, when stalwart designers such as Prue Acton, George Gross, Trent Nathan and Carla Zampatti won nods of approval from well-dressed locals who'd previously relied on foreign labels to fill their wardrobes. Australian designers, after all, were better placed to judge the needs of Australians when it came to getting dressed in a city where humidity and strong sunlight combine to create a tropical vibe for much of the year.

This laid-back ethos extends to the office, where pantyhose are not compulsory business attire for most women. While some ultra-conservative law firms or financial institutions may frown on women wearing trousers, this is not the norm. Men in the big city firms don't have it quite so easy: you'll still spot herds of auditors crossing the streets in dark suits and ties in the height of summer. Many offices adopt the practice of 'casual Friday', but then, some seem to have a policy of 'casual Monday to Friday'. If you're conducting business here, you may want to dress up, but be prepared to remove your jacket or tie early on in the day.

While local designers may sometimes seem too imitative to truly warrant their job description of 'designer', the one area where they are head and shoulders above the rest is swimwear. This is the country that invented the Speedo, after all. Australian designers' use of colour, cut and fabric make a trip to the beach that much more exciting. Labels to look out for include Zimmermann Swim, Tiger Lily and Expozay, which you'll find in department stores, surf shops and boutiques throughout the city.

One fashion personality who could sum up the Sydney experience is South African–born, New Zealand–raised Collette Dinnigan. A broken limb saw her housebound, with plenty of free time to start creating fastidiously detailed and sexy lingerie. Word spread, and after being besieged with requests Dinnigan decided to establish her namesake label in 1990. Enraptured women (and more than a few men) have flocked to her stores for her creations, which have come to include beautifully beaded and embroidered dresses and separates – and not just for stick figures either. The rich and famous have also discovered this treasure; join the ranks of Jade Jagger, Angelina Jolie and Halle Berry by donning one of Dinnigan's famous frocks. See p127 for details on her Sydney store.

SPORT

Sydneysiders – like most Aussies – are mad about sport, whether it's watching it, playing it or betting on it. In fact you'll often get the feeling that they would prefer physical activity to mental activity any day of the week. It's even been suggested that Australians would rather succeed in

GO RABBITOHS!

For a rugby league team that needed friends in high places, South Sydney (also known as Souths or the Rabbitohs) certainly managed to pull a few bunnies out of the hat. Try these names on for size: Ray Martin (host of *A Current Affair*), Andrew Denton (host of *Enough Rope*), Russell Crowe *(Gladiator)* and Tom Cruise (Australia's favourite ex-son-in-law).

Despite holding the record for more first-grade rugby league premierships than any other club (although the last one was in 1971), South Sydney was relegated to the scrap heap in the late 1990s. This was thanks to Super League and the business interests of the very rich, who had the local competition reduced from 17 teams to 14 in 1998. However, the Souths' passionate supporters did not appreciate this 'redundancy' and weren't going to go quietly. In June 2001, 80,000 green-and-red-clad supporters paraded from Redfern Oval through the streets of Sydney to the Town Hall at a 'Save the Game' rally. On 6 July 2001 the Federal Court of Australia gave the bunnies back their footy-playing rights and the number of teams in the comp was raised to 15.

While the Rabbitohs aren't usually at the top of the NRL ladder, it's good to know they're here to stay, and that a slice of local history is continuing. Since Russell Crowe (a lifelong fan) bought the club in 2006 their run of bad luck (and playing) seems to have ended. For current bunny stats see www.souths.com.au.

sports than in business. This national obsession makes for exciting times at the local pub and certainly contributed to Sydney's overwhelmingly successful 2000 Olympic Games.

There's plenty to see if you arrive in footy season (March to October). Footy in Sydney rightly means rugby league, but the term is also used for Aussie rules, rugby union and soccer. Rugby league (www.nrl.com.au) is especially popular in NSW, and Sydney is considered one of the world capitals for the code. The main Sydney teams in the premiership competition are Sydney City Roosters, South Sydney Rabbitohs, West Tigers, Canterbury Bulldogs, Cronulla Sharks, Parramatta Eels, Northern Sea Eagles, Penrith Panthers and St George Dragons.

Rugby union (www.rugby.com.au) is represented in Sydney by the Waratahs, and test matches by Australia's Wallabies against New Zealand's All Blacks provoke plenty of passion. Australian Football League (or Aussie rules football; www.afl.com.au) is growing in popularity since Sydney's beloved Swans won the 2005 premiership. Soccer is the poor cousin to the other codes, but had a boost with Australia's first ever qualification for the FIFA World Cup in 2006.

But there's more to Sydney than these macho pursuits; netball, swimming, basketball, cricket, tennis, hockey and surfing all have their avid fans. Surf life-saving competitions are popular – not unexpected considering the relationship between Australia and its massive coastline.

As for participation in sport, well, there's lots of that, too. Netball, swimming, tennis and golf are all well liked, and it's not unusual for workmates to band together and form their own league or 'comp' against workers from rival organisations. And, of course, gambling is another event that encourages personal involvement, with plenty of horse and greyhound racing venues (along with pokies at the pub) to feed the monster.

See p174 for more details.

NEIGHBOURHOODS

top picks

- **Sydney Opera House** (p57)
  Sydney's emblem and an architectural triumph.
- **Royal Botanic Gardens** (p57)
  A magnificent harbourside park with picture-postcard
  views.
- **Sydney Harbour Bridge** (p52)
  It's 75 years on and Sydney still loves the old coat hanger.
- **Bondi Beach** (p93)
  Australia's most famous beach lives up to its reputation.
- **Taronga Zoo** (p106)
  Captivity seems a small price to pay for digs this good.
- **Art Gallery of NSW** (p66)
  A rich introduction to Australia's artistic heritage.
- **Powerhouse Museum** (p74)
  A fascinating museum with plenty of buttons to push.
- **Sydney Aquarium** (p71)
  The thrills of Australia's marine life, spectacularly displayed.
- **Queen Victoria Building** (p68)
  Enchanting Victorian grandeur.
- **South Head** (p116)
  Beaches, harbour views and ocean-battered ramparts.

NEIGHBOURHOODS

Modern Sydney is a large, sprawling metropolis covering 1800 sq km bounded by the Pacific Ocean to the east, the wall of the Blue Mountains to the west and two large waterways to the north and south – the Hawkesbury River/Broken Bay and Botany Bay. Cutting through its centre is the great jagged tentacle of Port Jackson, better known by its sexier name Sydney Harbour.

It's hard to believe that only 220 years ago the Sydney penal colony was a ramshackle collection of tents around Sydney Cove (present-day Circular Quay). This remains the heart of the city, although geographical and demographical pedants are quick to point out that Parramatta is a more accurate contender.

'Dozens of suburbs, some with more spice and charm than others, unite to form the multifaceted personality of the city'.

The class divide of the First Fleet saw the convicts and marines pitch their tents to the west of Sydney Cove and the officers and gentlemen to the east. This socioeconomic pattern is echoed in the layout of the city today; the west is a vast expanse of working to middle-class suburbia, while Sydney's richest inhabitants clamour for a harbour view in the leafy Eastern Suburbs.

Sydney was not a planned city. The first streets were essentially Aboriginal paths and bullock trails, and its layout is complicated by hills and the numerous inlets of the harbour. The harbour divides the city into northern and southern halves, connected by the prominent Sydney Harbour Bridge and the not-so-prominent Harbour Tunnel. The south side holds most places of interest to visitors.

Dozens of suburbs, some with more spice and charm than others, unite to form the multifaceted personality of the city. We've broken down the most interesting into nine neighbourhoods.

Central Sydney is split into The Rocks and Circular Quay (effectively the Sydney of the First Fleet), the City Centre and the entertainment precinct of Darling Harbour and Chinatown. Most of the city's traditional tourist attractions are here, including a wealth of museums, parks and historic buildings.

Unsurprisingly, the ring of densely populated inner-city residential suburbs is the liveliest and the best place to take the pulse of the city. The first belt of suburbs to the east, from Darlinghurst to Potts Point (including Kings Cross), is where Sydney comes to indulge itself. The next set, from Paddington to Double Bay, is rather more genteel – focusing on fashion and the finer things in life. Heading south from Surry Hills to Alexandria is a groovier, grittier prospect with a distinct gourmet streak.

The inner city casts off its suit and relaxes at the Eastern Beaches, from Bondi to Coogee. The Inner West never wore a suit in the first place, outdoing the Eastern Suburbs with reserves of cool and plenty of chutzpah. The student-saturated neighbourhoods of Newtown and Glebe offer an invigorating alternative to Sydney's stereotypical glitziness.

Across the harbour the mostly staid North Shore is a world apart. Of most interest to travellers are the upmarket neighbourhoods of the Lower North Shore and the laid-back beach resort of Manly. A sparkling band of golden-sand bays is collectively known as the Northern Beaches. These stretch to Broken Bay and the Ku-ring-gai Chase National Park on Sydney's northern fringe.

Of course there are sights dotted around other parts of Sydney as well. You'll find a wealth of colonial history out west in Parramatta and some noteworthy parks, beaches and historic buildings in the wealthy harbourside suburbs heading east from Rose Bay to Watsons Bay. The city's suburbs now stretch south to incorporate Botany Bay, Captain Cook's landing point and the British government's planned location for Sydney. Cronulla, to the south, is one of Sydney's finest beaches. You'll find the highlights covered in the catch-all Other Neighbourhoods section of this chapter (p116).

Not one for modesty, most of Sydney's sights are openly exposed to anyone content to wander her streets, parks and beaches.

ITINERARY BUILDER

Sydney's not a hard city to explore, but to really get under its skin you'll want to look beyond the obvious. Some suburbs are famous for a particular thing – such as eating in Surry Hills, shopping in Paddington or partying in Kings Cross – but this tool should help you find a range of treats in all of the featured neighbourhoods.

AREA	ACTIVITIES	Sightseeing	Museums & Galleries	Outdoors
	The Rocks & Circular Quay	Sydney Opera House (p57) Sydney Observatory (p53) Customs House (p58)	Museum of Contemporary Art (p53) The Rocks Discovery Museum (p56) Susannah Place Museum (p55)	Royal Botanic Gardens (p57) Oz Jet Boating (p225) Walsh Bay Walk (p56)
	City Centre	St Mary's Cathedral (p67) St James' Church (p67) Martin Place (p65 & p65)	Art Gallery of NSW (p66) Hyde Park Barracks Museum (p67) Museum of Sydney (p66)	Hyde Park (p66) The Domain (p66) Andrew 'Boy' Charlton Pool (p175)
	Darling Harbour & Chinatown	Sydney Aquarium (p71) Sydney Wildlife World (p73) Dixon St (p75)	Australian National Maritime Museum (p71) Powerhouse Museum (p74) Australia's Outback Gallery (p125)	Chinese Garden of Friendship (p74) Sydney By Sail (p178) Tumbalong Park (p73)
	Darlinghurst to Potts Point	Elizabeth Bay House (p80) St John's Church (p80) Finger Wharf (p80)	Sydney Jewish Museum (p77) Australian Museum (p77) National Art School Gallery (p77)	Fitzroy Gardens (p80) Green Park (p79) Embarkation Park (p82)
	Eastern Suburbs	Bondi Beach (p93) South Head (p116) Bronte Beach (p96)	Vaucluse House (p116) Australian Centre for Photography (p85) Sherman Contemporary Art Foundation (p86)	Centennial Park (p83) Coogee Ocean Pools (p96) Neilsen Park (p116)
	Inner West & South Sydney	Sydney Fish Market (p103) University of Sydney (p99) Anzac Bridge (p103)	Nicholson Museum (p102) 2 Danks St (p91) Object Gallery (p89)	Camperdown Cemetery (p99) Victoria Park (p102) Sydney Park (p99)
	North Shore	Taronga Zoo (p106) Luna Park (p107) Sydney Harbour Bridge (p52)	Manly Quarantine Station (p111) Mary MacKillop Place (p107) Nutcote (p107)	Sydney Harbour National Park (p106) Manly Scenic Walkway (p110) Northern Beaches (p112)

HOW TO USE THIS TABLE

The table below allows you to plan a day's worth of activities in any area of the city. Simply select which area you wish to explore, and then mix and match from the corresponding listings to build your day. The first item in each cell represents a well-known highlight of the area while the other items are more off-the-beaten track gems.

Shopping	Eating	Drinking & Nightlife
Australian Wine Centre (p123) The Rocks Market (p124) Puppet Shop at The Rocks (p123)	Guillaume at Bennelong (p140) Café Sydney (p140) The Gumnut Teagarden (p140)	Lord Nelson Brewery Hotel (p155) Hero of Waterloo (p156) Blu Horizon Bar (p155)
Queen Victoria Building (p125) David Jones (p124) Strand Arcade (p125)	Tetsuya's (p141) Casa Asturiana (p141) Bar Quattro (p141)	Marble Bar (p158) Orbit (p156) Arthouse Hotel (p157)
Paddy's Markets (p124) Market City (p126) Gavala Aboriginal Art Centre (p125)	Zaaffran (p141) Marigold Restaurant (p142) Xic Lo (p142)	Home (p158) The Loft (p158) Cargo Bar (p158)
Central Station (p127) The Bookshop Darlinghurst (p183) House of Priscilla (p126)	Fratelli Paradiso (p143) Don Don (p142) La Buvette (p143)	Gazebo Wine Garden (p160) Green Park Hotel (p159) Beauchamp Hotel (p159)
Westfield Bondi Junction (p132) Paddington Markets (p86) Queen St, Woollahra (p87)	Bistro Moncur (p144) Jed's Foodstore (p148) Caffe Salina (p148)	Doyles Palace Hotel (p166) Light Brigade Hotel (p161) Fringe Bar (p161)
Better Read Than Dead (p132) Glebe Markets (p124) Wheels & Doll Baby (p130)	Spice I Am (p145) Bistrode (p145) Chu Bay (p145)	Bank Hotel (p164) The Dolphin (p162) A.B. Hotel (p165)
Kirribilli Markets (p124) The Corso, Manly (p106) Pure Wholefoods (p151)	Bathers' Pavilion (p150) Ripples (p150) Bottom Of The Harbour (p151)	Greenwood Hotel (p166) Manly Wharf Hotel (p166) Steyne Hotel (p166)

GREATER SYDNEY

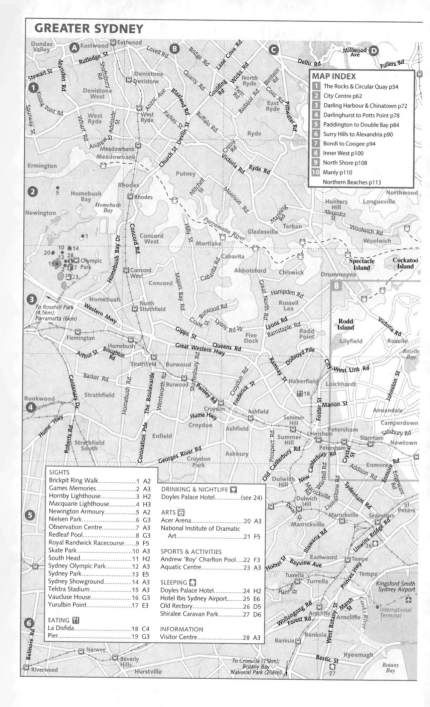

MAP INDEX

SIGHTS

Brickpit Ring Walk....................1 A2
Games Memories.....................2 A3
Hornby Lighthouse..................3 H2
Macquarie Lighthouse..............4 H3
Newington Armoury..................5 A2
Nielsen Park..........................6 G3
Observation Centre..................7 A3
Redleaf Pool..........................8 G3
Royal Randwick Racecourse......9 F5
Skate Park...........................10 A3
South Head..........................11 H2
Sydney Olympic Park..............12 A3
Sydney Park.........................13 E5
Sydney Showground...............14 A3
Telstra Stadium.....................15 A3
Vaucluse House.....................16 A3
Yurulbin Point.......................17 E3

EATING

La Disfida............................18 C4
Pier...................................19 G3

DRINKING & NIGHTLIFE

Doyles Palace Hotel..............(see 24)

ARTS

Acer Arena...........................20 A3
National Institute of Dramatic
   Art.................................21 F5

SPORTS & ACTIVITIES

Andrew 'Boy' Charlton Pool....22 F3
Aquatic Centre......................23 A3

SLEEPING

Doyles Palace Hotel...............24 H2
Hotel Ibis Sydney Airport........25 E6
Old Rectory.........................26 D5
Shiralee Caravan Park............27 D6

INFORMATION

Visitor Centre.......................28 A3

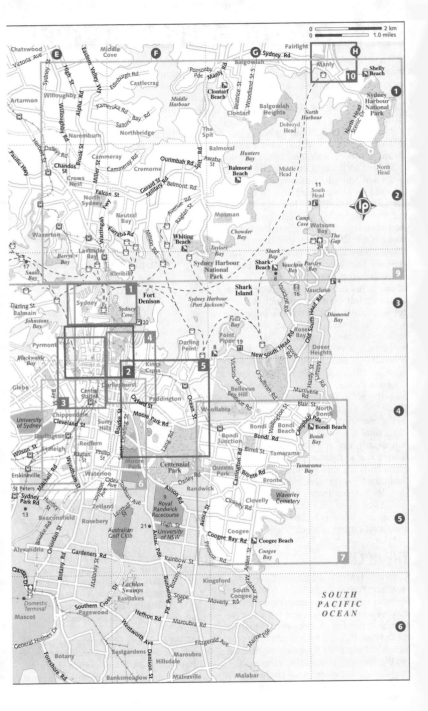

Drinking & Nightlife p155; Eating p139; Shopping p123; Sleeping p188

When the First Fleet sailed into the harbour in 1788, this is where they pitched their tents, making it the birthplace of modern Australia. Governor Phillip christened this bay Sydney Cove, after the British home secretary who planned the convict colony. The convicts were allocated the rocky spur of land to the west (The Rocks), while the governor and other officials claimed the east.

At some stage you'll end up here – you haven't really been to Sydney if you don't. Sure it's touristy and overpriced, but it remains the vibrant heart of the city, brimming with things to do and see, along with some of the swankiest hotels and restaurants.

Today The Rocks is unrecognisable as the squalid and overcrowded place it was soon after settlement, when the area was packed with convicts, ex-convicts, whalers and sailors – and brothels and inns to entertain them. In the 1820s the nouveau riche started building houses on the upper slopes, their sewage flowing to the slums below. Unsurprisingly, bubonic plague broke out in 1900, leading to the razing of whole streets. The construction of the Sydney Harbour Bridge (below) two decades later resulted in further demolition. Redevelopment in the 1970s turned what remained into a charming but sanitised precinct of narrow cobbled streets and fine colonial buildings.

Circular Quay's promenade serves as a backdrop for buskers and the departure point for harbour ferries. Built with convict labour between 1837 and 1844, it was originally (and more accurately) called Semi Circular Quay and was the main port of Sydney. In the 1850s it was extended further, covering the Tank Stream, which ran through the middle. Its two points are now crowned by the weight of Sydney's iconography – the Harbour Bridge and the Sydney Opera House (p57). Heading east the Royal Botanic Gardens (p57) begin the city's green fringe.

The star attraction is undoubtedly Sydney Harbour itself – stretching from the heads 20km until it morphs into the Parramatta River. It has shaped the local psyche for millennia, and today it's both a working port and the city's sparkling playground. Its waters, beaches, islands and shorefront parks offer all the swimming, sailing, picnicking, walking and real estate fantasies you could wish for. The most scenic section is from the city to the heads. If the budget doesn't stretch to a private yacht you'll still see plenty of this egalitarian mistress from the harbour ferries.

The sun doesn't always shine and wet-weather days are a good excuse to delve deeper into Sydney's sophisticated side – there are historic sites to explore, galleries and museums to peruse, and native critters to meet.

top picks

THE ROCKS & CIRCULAR QUAY

- Sydney Opera House (p57)
- Royal Botanic Gardens (p57)
- Sydney Observatory (opposite)
- Sydney Harbour Bridge (left)
- Museum of Contemporary Art (opposite)

THE ROCKS

SYDNEY HARBOUR BRIDGE Map p54

🚇 Milsons Point or Circular Quay

Sydney's second-most-famous icon, this massive steel bridge is visible from a surprising number of spots around the city. Nicknamed 'the coat hanger', it crosses the harbour at one of its narrowest points, linking the southern and northern shores. It's the largest and heaviest (but not longest) steel arch in the world. Sydneysiders hold it dear to their hearts – partly because of its sheer size, simplicity and symmetry, and partly because of its function in uniting the city. It's always the centrepiece of Sydney's frequent and spectacular harbour fireworks, and its 75th birthday in 2007 saw 250,000 people join the celebrations by walking across it.

The two halves of the mighty arch were built out simultaneously from each shore. After nine years of work, when the ends of the arches were only centimetres apart and ready to be bolted together, gale force winds of over 100km/h (62mph) set them swaying. But the bridge survived and the arch was soon completed. It cost $20 million, a bargain in today's money, and took until 1988 to pay off. Giving it a new coat of paint takes four years and 80,000 litres.

You can climb almost 200 stairs to the top of the southeastern Pylon Lookout (☎ 9240 1100; www.pylonlookout.com.au; enter Bridge Stairs, Cumberland St, The Rocks; adult/under 13/under 8 $9/3.50/free; ⏰ 10am-5pm); it has awesome views and a good museum with exhibits explaining how the bridge was built. The pylons may look as though they're shouldering the weight but they're largely decorative – right down to their granite facing.

Cars, trains, cyclists, joggers and pedestrians all use the bridge. The cycleway is on the western side, the pedestrian footpath on the eastern. The best way to experience the bridge is on foot; you don't get much of a view when crossing by car. Driving south there's a $3 toll.

The adventurous and vertigo-free can climb to the apex of the bridge itself on the hugely popular BridgeClimb (p226).

MUSEUM OF CONTEMPORARY ART Map p54

☎ 9245 2467; www.mca.com.au; 140 George St, The Rocks; admission free; ⏰ 10am-5pm; ⛴ Circular Quay

A slice of Gotham City on West Circular Quay, the stately Art Deco MCA has a fine collection of modern art (sculpture, painting, installation and moving image) from Australia and around the world and temporary exhibitions (prices vary) from the art world's superheroes. You'll often find Aboriginal art featured prominently. It's also home to the excellent MCA Store and a classy café.

SYDNEY OBSERVATORY Map p54

☎ 9921 3485; www.sydneyobservatory.com.au; Watson Rd, Observatory Hill; admission free; ⏰ 10am-5pm; ⛴ Circular Quay

The historically and architecturally interesting Sydney Observatory (1858) occupies a commanding position atop beautiful Observatory Hill, overlooking Millers Point and the harbour. Surrounded by huge Moreton Bay figs, this is the most peaceful park in the inner city. It was the site of the colony's first windmill (1796), which was used to grind wheat until its canvas sails were stolen and the structure eventually collapsed.

The observatory-cum-museum features an interesting exhibition about astronomy in Australia, covering Aboriginal sky stories and the technology and science of astronomy. There are interactive displays and videos, and a great variety of vintage apparatus, ranging from chronometers to telescopes large and small.

During the day, the only way to visit the copper dome and its big telescope is with a ticket to the virtual reality 3-D Space Theatre (adult/child $7/5; ⏰ 2.30pm & 3.30pm daily, extra screenings 11am & noon Sat & Sun). Night viewings (adult/child $15/10, bookings essential) include the exhibition, stargazing through the telescopes and a 3-D screening.

GARRISON CHURCH Map p54

☎ 9247 1268; www.thegarrisonchurch.org.au; 62 Lower Fort St, Millers Point; admission free; ⏰ 9am-5pm; ⛴ Circular Quay

Also known as Holy Trinity (1843), this lovely sandstone Anglican church at the west end of the Argyle Cut was the colony's

TRANSPORT: THE ROCKS & CIRCULAR QUAY

Train The best option to avoid city traffic. Circular Quay is one of the City Circle stations.

Ferry Circular Quay is the main ferry hub. Useful destinations include Manly, Taronga Zoo, Double Bay, Rose Bay, Watsons Bay, Mosman, Cremorne, Kirribilli, Balmain, Darling Harbour, Sydney Olympic Park and Parramatta.

Bus Circular Quay is the major terminus for routes including: 301-303 to Surry Hills and Waterloo; 309-10 to Redfern and Alexandria; 311 to Railway Square via Woolloomooloo, Potts Point, Kings Cross and Darlinghurst; 324-5 to Watsons Bay via Kings Cross and Double Bay; 373 to Coogee; 380 to Watsons Bay via Bondi; 389 to North Bondi via Woollahra; 422-3 and 426-8 to Newtown; 435-8 and 440 to Leichhardt. Other routes commence from the corner of Argyle and Lower Fort Sts in The Rocks including: 339 to Clovelly; 431 to Glebe Point; and 432-4 to Balmain via Glebe.

Parking Try Wilsons Parking, Sydney Opera House (enter from Macquarie St; one hour $9).

THE ROCKS & CIRCULAR QUAY

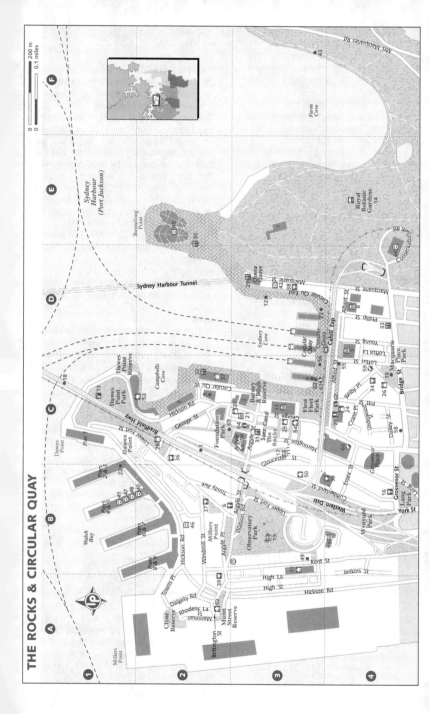

THE ROCKS & CIRCULAR QUAY

first military church. It's a charming place, lined with regimental flags, and it's also wheelchair accessible. The first prime minister of Australia, Edmund Barton, received his primary school education in the school house, which is now the parish hall; the sandstone walls are nearly 80cm thick.

ST PATRICK'S CHURCH Map p54

☎ 9247 3525; www.stpatschurchhill.org; 20 Grosvenor St, The Rocks; admission free; ☿ 9am-5pm; ⊛ Wynyard

This sumptuous sandstone church (1844) was built on land donated by William Davis, an Irishman transported for his role in the uprisings of 1798. His home (on the site of the chapel-turned-café) may have been the first Catholic chapel in Australia; it was used for clandestine devotions and secretly housed a consecrated host left when the colony's only priest was deported in 1818. An elaborate brass altar, spectacular stained glass windows and colourful statues (look for St Patrick, St Joan of Arc and St Michael complete with dragon) stand in colourful contrast to the Protestant churches of the same period.

SUSANNAH PLACE MUSEUM Map p54

☎ 9241 1893; www.hht.net.au/museums/sp/; 58-64 Gloucester St, The Rocks; adult/child/family $8/4/17; ☿ 10am-5pm Sat & Sun Feb-Dec, 10am-5pm Jan; ⊛ Circular Quay

Welcome to 19th-century working-class life. Visits to this row of tiny 1844 terrace houses start with a video in the dilapidated parlour of the first home before heading through the neighbouring two. In the backyard, see how generations of Rocks women cooked and laundered their clothes in a wood-fired copper (near the dunny). The curators wear period dress and run the cuter-than-cute corner shop that sells wares from the period.

SH ERVIN GALLERY Map p54

☎ 9258 0173; www.nsw.nationaltrust.org .au/properties/gallery/default.asp; Watson Rd, Observatory Hill; adult/child/under 12 $6/4/free; ☿ 11am-5pm Tue-Sun; ⊛ Circular Quay

This small gallery is located in the old Fort St School (1856), close to the Sydney Observatory. It houses temporary exhibitions of Australian art, and every year it hosts the

top picks

FOR FREE

- Any of Sydney's beautiful beaches and parks
- Art Gallery of NSW (p66)
- State Library of NSW (p61)
- Museum of Contemporary Art (p53)
- Victoria Barracks (p83)
- Australian National Maritime Museum (p71)
- Customs House (p58)
- Camperdown Cemetery (p99)
- Sydney Observatory (p53)
- Nicholson Museum (p102)

extremely popular Salon des Refusés show, for rejected Archibald and Wynne Prize contenders. Disabled access is good.

WALSH BAY Map p54
Hickson Rd; 🚇 Circular Quay
This waterfront between Millers Point and Dawes Point was Sydney's busiest before container shipping and the construction of new port facilities at Botany Bay. The last decade has seen these attractive Federation-era wharves, no longer the preserve of crusty seadogs, gentrified beyond belief into luxury hotels, apartments and restaurants. The self-guided Walsh Bay Walk starts at Pier 2 and leads you through 11 well-labelled stops, with fascinating plaques and clear directions to point you on your way. Pier 4 houses the Wharf Theatre (p169), home to the renowned Sydney Theatre Company (p172), Sydney Dance Company (p171) and Bangarra Dance Theatre (p171).

CADMAN'S COTTAGE Map p54
☎ 9247 5033; 110 George St, The Rocks; 🕐 9.30am-4.30pm Mon-Fri, 10am-4.30pm Sat & Sun; 🚇 Circular Quay
The oldest surviving house in the inner city, this cottage was built in 1816 as the coxswains' barracks. When it was built it was actually on the shoreline; the arches on its south side housed longboats. The cottage is now the home of the Sydney Harbour National Park Information Centre, which organises tours of the harbour islands (see p107). There's a glassed-off area on the lower level revealing a mass of old drain

work exposed in an archaeological dig, as well as a small museum with a few exhibits.

THE ROCKS DISCOVERY MUSEUM Map p54
☎ 9251 8804; www.rocksdiscoverymuseum .com.au; Kendall Lane, The Rocks; admission free; 🕐 10am-5pm; 🚇 Circular Quay
Housed in a restored 1850s sandstone warehouse, this interesting little museum has a curious collection of knick-knacks and exhibits tracing the inhabitation of the area from Cadigal times to today.

TANK STREAM FOUNTAIN Map p54
Alfred St, Circular Quay; 🚇 Circular Quay
This elaborate, four-part bronze fountain (1981) in Herald Sq near Circular Quay incorporates dozens of sculptures of native Australian animals. The fountain was designed by Stephen Walker and dedicated to 'all the children who have played around the Tank Stream'. Try spotting the echidna.

CAMPBELL'S STOREHOUSES Map p54
7 West Circular Quay, The Rocks; 🚇 Circular Quay
In 1839, Scottish merchant Robert Campbell commenced construction of these storehouses and a private wharf in order to hold supplies of tea, alcohol, sugar and fabric. Construction eventually finished in 1861, and a brick storey was added in 1890. Such storehouses were a common feature of the area into the early 20th century. These 11 surviving storehouses are now given over to restaurants.

OVERSEAS PASSENGER TERMINAL Map p54
West Circular Quay, The Rocks; 🚇 Circular Quay
Passengers from luxury cruise ships such as the QEII disembark here, so what better place to site ultra-fancy drinking and dining establishments? Quay (p140) is among the occupants of the architecturally dynamic modern terminal. For a great harbour view, head up to the observation deck housed in the turret at the north end.

KEN DONE GALLERY Map p54
☎ 9247 2740; www.kendone.com.au; 1 Hickson Rd, The Rocks; admission free; 🕐 10am-5.30pm; 🚇 Circular Quay
The cheerful, almost childlike work of Sydney artist Ken Done is displayed in a gallery in the wonderfully restored

Australian Steam Navigation Building. Expect plenty of vividly coloured, uniquely Australian landscapes and seascapes, plus lots of works that depict the daily minutiae of Done's rather charmed existence.

EAST CIRCULAR QUAY

SYDNEY OPERA HOUSE Map p54
☎ 9250 7111; www.sydneyoperahouse.com; Bennelong Point; ℞ Circular Quay

Gazing upon the Sydney Opera House with virgin eyes is a sure way to send a tingle down your spine. Gloriously white and brilliantly sharp, Australia's most recognisable icon sits dramatically at the tip of Bennelong Point. On a sunny day the Opera House is postcard-perfect, its startling curves and points a pinnacle of architectural genius. These most distinguishing features are seen in many ways – sails, shells and even nuns in a rugby scrum. It's not until you get close that you realise that the seemingly solid expanse of white is actually composed of 1,056,000 self-cleaning cream-coloured Swedish tiles.

The Opera House's construction was itself truly operatic (see p36) – it was even dramatised as The Eighth Wonder, performed here by Opera Australia in 1995. The interiors don't live up to the promise of the dazzling exterior, but if you're curious to see inside there's an informative, hour-long tour (☎ 9250 7250; Guided Tours Office, Lower Concourse; adult/concession $26/18; ☿ 9am-5pm); not all tours can visit all theatres because of rehearsals, but you're more likely to see everything if you go early. A highlight is the Utzon Room, the only part of the house to have an interior designed by the great man himself. Tours run every half hour and you'll save a few bucks if you book online. For a more in-depth nosy around, the two-hour backstage tour (tickets $140; ☿ 7am) includes the stars' dressing rooms.

The Opera House has five regular performance spaces, and hosts concerts, dance, theatre, cabaret and film, as well as opera. Over 2000 events are staged every year (for information on shows, see p169). Kids at the House is the Opera House's pint-size entertainment programme, with music, dance and drama on offer, including the delightful Babies' Proms series.

On Sunday there's a market near the front entrance selling Australian-made arts and crafts.

Disabled access is good for the most part, although some areas of the building require staff assistance. Subtitles are a feature of opera performances and guide dogs are welcome throughout the building and at performances.

ROYAL BOTANIC GARDENS Map p54
☎ 9231 8111; www.rbgsyd.nsw.gov.au; Mrs Macquaries Rd, Sydney; admission free; ☿ 7am-sunset; ℞ Circular Quay

These expansive gardens are the city's favourite picnic spot, jogging route and strolling venue. Bordering Farm Cove, east of the Sydney Opera House, the enchanting gardens were established in 1816 and feature plant life from the South Pacific and around the world. They include the site of the colony's first paltry vegetable patch, but their history goes back much further than that; long before the convicts arrived

FLYING FOXINESS

'Release the bats', vampiric Australian rocker Nick Cave once screamed, and every night at sunset it seems like someone does just that. Although you'll find them throughout the city, it's the great black cloud that passes from the Royal Botanic Gardens (RBG) to Centennial Park that is the most impressive.

There's no need to cower under a crucifix: the grey-headed flying fox (Pteropus ploiocephalus) is a committed vegetarian, preferring to feast on Moreton Bay figs and nectar. These bats are an important part of the region's ecology, spreading seeds and pollinating flowers as they feed. The only damage they are likely to inflict is on the paintwork of your car; as any Sydney motorist will tell you, their droppings are incredibly corrosive.

By day they hang around (literally) in their thousands in the trees behind the RBG café, chittering madly and wrestling for the best roost. Unlike other bats, flying foxes don't live in caves, don't use echolocation and can't see in complete darkness. Also, they don't fly in a jerky manner like their smaller cousins, but rather use their metre-wide wingspan to glide around gracefully, much like birds do.

For more information on these amazing creatures, stop by the RBG visitors centre or check out www.sydneybats .org.au.

this was an initiation ground for the Cadigal people.

The fabulous Sydney Tropical Centre (adult/child $4.40/2.20; ☉ 10am-4pm) is housed in the interconnecting Arc and Pyramid glasshouses. It's a great place to visit on a cool, grey day, with the added advantage of always being warm. The multistorey Arc has a collection of rampant climbers and trailers from the world's rainforests, while the Pyramid houses the Australian collection, including monsoonal, woodland and tropical rainforest plants.

Other attractions in the gardens include the Fernery, Succulent Garden, a sustainable Rose Garden and a rare Wollemi Pine – an ancient tree only discovered in 1994 in the Blue Mountains. As far as wildlife goes, you can't fail to notice the gardens' resident colony of grey-headed flying foxes (see p57), or the large flocks of sulphur-crested cockatoos, whose raucous squawks can be heard for blocks.

Free guided walks (☉ 10.30am) depart from the information booth at the Gardens Shop, and last an hour and a half. You'll need to book ahead for the Aboriginal Heritage Tour (☎ 9231 8134; tours $20; ☉ 2pm Fri), which includes traditional music, dance and bushfood tastings. Self-guided tours can be downloaded from the website.

The park's paths are for the most part wheelchair accessible, although there are some flights of stairs scattered about. Attractions are well signposted throughout, although the estimated walking times are best described as pessimistic. If a sign says something is five minutes away, bank on only about two minutes.

CUSTOMS HOUSE Map p54

☎ 9242 8595; www.sydneycustomshouse.com.au; 31 Alfred St, Circular Quay; admission free; ☉ 8am-7pm Mon-Fri, 10am-4pm Sat & Sun; ⊠ Circular Quay

In June of 2005, 120 years after its construction, Customs House reopened following a major renovation that turned the first three floors into a library (☎ 9242 8555). The grand old building offers attractions for visitors and locals alike. There's a great selection of international newspapers and magazines to read and free internet upstairs (it's not meant to be used for email and the main providers are blocked, but you might get lucky if you use a more obscure mail-server), as well as

temporary exhibitions. In the lobby, look for the swastikas in the tiling (and the plaque explaining their symbolism) and walk over a large scale model of the city sunk beneath a glass floor. On the top floor is the wonderful Café Sydney (p140).

GOVERNMENT HOUSE Map p54

☎ 9931 5222; www.hht.net.au/museums/gh; Macquarie St; admission free; ☉ grounds 10am-4pm, tours 10.30am-3pm Fri-Sun; ⊠ Circular Quay

Government House (1845) is the third of five structures that have served as the official residence of the governor of New South Wales. It dominates the western headland of Farm Cove and plays host to visiting dignitaries, including heads of state and royalty. The governor, who now resides in Admiralty House (p109), still uses it for weekly meetings. It's a marvellous example of the Gothic Revival style. Tours of the house (departing every half-hour) are the only way to see the opulent interior, and can be extremely entertaining and informative. Disabled access is OK, but it's best to call in advance.

JUSTICE & POLICE MUSEUM Map p54

☎ 9252 1144; www.hht.net.au/museums/jp; cnr Albert & Phillip Sts; adult/child/family $8/4/17; ☉ 10am-5pm Sat & Sun; ⊠ Circular Quay

Based in the old Water Police Station (1858), this museum focuses on crime, policing and the Australian legal and penal system. Like the Hyde Park Barracks Museum (p67) it's at once fascinating and depressing. Is it comforting to learn that Sydney's last hanging for carnal knowledge occurred in 1901, or horrifying? Displays include forensic evidence from famous crimes of the past, some nasty-looking weapons, lots of mug shots and at least two stuffed dogs. The museum has wheelchair access to the ground floor only, but Braille and audio guides are available.

MACQUARIE PLACE Map p54

cnr Loftus & Bridge Sts; ⊠ Circular Quay

Under the shady Moreton Bay figs is this historic little area. Look for the cannon and anchor from the First Fleet flagship (HMS Sirius), an ornate drinking fountain (1857), a National Trust–classified gentlemen's convenience (not open), and an obelisk erected in 1818 'to record that all the public roads leading to the interior of the colony are measured from it'. The park is overlooked by the imposing 19th-century Lands Department Building. Nip round to the south façade, which bears statues of Blaxland, Wentworth, Lawson and other notables from the history of Australia's exploration.

SYDNEY CONSERVATORIUM OF MUSIC Map p54

☎ 9351 1222; www.music.usyd.edu.au; Macquarie St; ℞ Circular Quay

'The Con' was built by convict architect Francis Greenway as the stables and servants' quarters of Macquarie's planned new government house. Partly because of the project's extravagance (of which this crenulated castle for horses is evidence), Macquarie was replaced as governor before the house could be completed. In 1915 it was converted into a music conservatorium, which amalgamated with the University of Sydney in 1990. Recent renovations (at a cost of $145 million) have created world-class facilities for study and performance (see p169).

WRITERS WALK Map p54

Circular Quay promenade; ℞ Circular Quay

A series of round metal plaques set into the promenade alongside the wharves hold ruminations from prominent Australian writers (and the odd literary visitor). The likes of Robert Hughes, Germaine Greer, Peter Carey, James Michener and Clive James wax lyrical on subjects ranging from indigenous rights to the paradoxical nature of glass. Genres vary from eloquent poems addressing the human condition to an irreverent ditty about a meat pie by Barry Humphries.

This heady bunch was recently joined by even more illustrious company, namely famous Australian supermodels, several of whom are honoured with plaques in the pavement near the Overseas Terminal.

MINUS 5 Map p54

☎ 9251 0311; www.minus5experience.com; Opera Quays, Circular Quay East; adult/child $30/15; 🕑 noon-10pm Sun-Thu, noon-midnight Fri & Sat; ℞ Circular Quay

On a hot summer's day stepping into this winter wonderland is a surreal experience, particularly if you look out the window at Circular Quay sweltering below. Everything's made of ice, from the furniture to the intricate sculptures. Adults get a complementary vodka cocktail (value $15) served in an ice glass; it's the only option as other alcohol would freeze. Even wearing the big coat and gloves provided, you won't be sorry to be booted out after 30 minutes. Children can only enter before 6pm. It's wheelchair accessible but the lounge itself isn't guide-dog friendly.

A ROCK-QUAY ROAD Walking Tour

1 Observatory Hill Start by taking the lay of the land from this peaceful park, site of the colony's first windmill and, since 1858, Sydney Observatory (p53). When you're ready, follow the path curving down to Argyle Place, a quiet, English-style village green lined with attractive terraced houses.

2 Lord Nelson Brewery Hotel Across the road and slightly west, the Lord Nelson Brewery Hotel (p155) was built in 1836 as a private residence before being converted into a pub in 1841, making it the oldest continually licensed hotel in Sydney. Head back down Argyle Place and turn left into Lower Fort St.

3 Ferry Lane At the corner of Windmill St you'll pass the Hero of Waterloo (see p156), another contender for the 'oldest pub in Sydney' title. Turn left, and cross the road to tiny Ferry Lane. Here you'll find the foundations of Arthur Payne's house; he was the first victim of the 1900 bubonic plague outbreak.

4 Garrison Church Retrace your steps along Lower Fort St to handsome 1843 Garrison Church (p53). Turn left into Argyle St and head through the Argyle Cut, excavated by convict labourers. The work began in 1843 with hand tools, and was completed (with the aid of dynamite) in 1867.

5 Foundation Park Just past the Cut take the stairs to the left and head along Gloucester Walk to the thought-provoking Foundation Park – on the right, in the preserved ruins of an old tenement building. The oversized furniture by artist Peter Cole evokes the cramped conditions experienced by the working-class families that lived here.

6 Suez Canal Continue along the lane, turn right and right again, passing Playfair St's

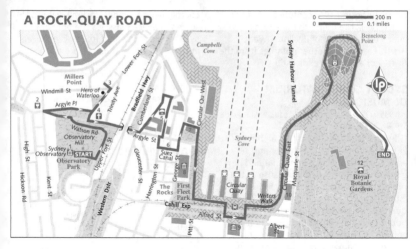

A ROCK-QUAY ROAD

terraced houses. Cross into Harrington and left into Suez Canal. A notorious lurking point for 19th-century push gangs, it tapers as it goes downhill until it's less than a metre wide. Where it intersects Nurses Walk, there's a hoist – once used for hauling goods to the upper floors.

7 Cadman's Cottage Turn left into George St, Sydney's oldest road. Look out for the quirky Harry Potter-ish street numbering. Head down the stairs to the right to Cadman's Cottage (p56); dating from 1816 it's the oldest house in the area.

8 Museum of Contemporary Art Follow Circular Quay to the east past the monolithic Museum of Contemporary Art (p53). Take advantage of the free entry for a quick art fix.

9 Customs House Cut underneath Circular Quay train station to the fabulously renovated Customs House (p58) and re-trace your steps thus far in the scale model of the city set into the floor.

10 Opera Quays Head back to the bustling ferry wharves, and check out the buskers and

WALK FACTS

Start Observatory Hill
End Royal Botanic Gardens
Distance 7km
Duration 2½ hours
Fuel stops Pricey but numerous

Writers Walk plaques (p59) as you follow the quay east then north. Disparagingly referred to as 'the toaster', Opera Quays is a modern set of apartments with a solid strip of bars and restaurants lining East Circular Quay.

11 Sydney Opera House The magnificent white sails of the Sydney Opera House (p57) are directly in front of you. Take some time to wander in and around them. From close up they look strangely smaller than you'd expect and the tile colour is actually far from white.

12 Royal Botanic Gardens After circumnavigating Bennelong Point, follow the water's edge to the gates of the Royal Botanic Gardens (p57) – find a shady spot to rest before heading in search of the bats.

Drinking & Nightlife p156; Eating p140; Shopping p123; Sleeping p189

Before suburban sprawl started in earnest in the mid-19th century, this (along with The Rocks) *was* Sydney. The historic city can be traced in its place names: Bridge St once spanned the Tank Stream, the first water supply, which emptied into Sydney Cove (now Circular Quay); crops were planted in Farm Cove to feed the early convicts and marines, the latter of which were housed at the top of Barrack St; Market St was the site of the bustling produce markets, later moved south to Haymarket.

top picks

CITY CENTRE

- Art Gallery of NSW (p66)
- Queen Victoria Building (p68)
- Hyde Park (p66)
- St Mary's Cathedral (p67)
- State Library of NSW (below)

Today this narrow stretch of land has been transformed into a modern city's towering CBD, the economic engine of Australia. Skyscrapers jostle sandstone colonial buildings and prominent places of worship, making the city's central canyons a great place for architecture buffs to explore. Venerable Macquarie St may be the centre of government, but Martin Place represents Sydney's pulsing commercial heart.

George St cuts through the middle of it all, running 3km north–south from The Rocks to Central Station; underneath, trains race around the City Circle, while the monorail glides by above.

There's plenty to keep shopaholics busy, with an unbroken chain of big-name boutiques and department stores stretching from the Queen Victoria Building (p68) to Pitt St Mall. The city's bars and restaurants cater mainly to the business brigade and, with a few extremely notable exceptions, can be rather dull. A tiny Spanish Quarter takes up a block of Liverpool St between George and Sussex Sts.

At lunchtime, Hyde Park (p66) and The Domain (p66), which form the city's eastern fringe, are full of office workers either seeking solace in the greenery or determined to scratch an hour out of the day to work on staying fit and beautiful.

WYNYARD & AROUND

ST PHILIP'S CHURCH Map pp62–3

☎ 9247 1071; www.stphilips-sydney.org.au; 3 York St, Church Hill; ✆ 9am-5pm Tue-Fri; ⛆ Wynyard

Completed in 1856 by architect Edmund Blacket in the High Victorian Gothic style, St Philip's is the successor of a line descending from Sydney's original Anglican parish church (1793). Today it's a peaceful and unobtrusive structure dwarfed by the area's surrounding skyscrapers. It's usually kept locked, but the parish workers at the neighbouring office are happy to open up the doors to visitors. A handy self-guided tour pamphlet is available.

AUSTRALIA SQUARE Map pp62–3

☎ 8247 5200; www.australiasquare.net; 264 George St; ✆ retail 7am-6pm Mon-Fri; ⛆ Wynyard

Generally acknowledged as Australia's first major office tower, Australia Square (1968) was designed by local phenomenon Harry Seidler. His 50-storey design has a distinctive circular form and an airy open plaza at the base with shops below. A colourful Sol LeWitt mural (2004) in the lobby replaces a rare Le Corbusier tapestry that hung here for decades before being auctioned off by the building's owner. Head up to Orbit (p156) in the 47th-floor revolving restaurant for breathtaking views that will only cost the price of a drink.

MARTIN PLACE & AROUND

STATE LIBRARY OF NSW Map pp62–3

☎ 9273 1414; www.atmitchell.com; Macquarie St; ✆ 9am-9pm Mon-Thu, 9am-6pm Fri, 11am-5pm Sat & Sun; ⛆ Martin Place

This library holds over five million tomes, and has one of the best collections of early works on Australia, including Captain Cook's and Joseph Banks' journals and Captain (later Governor) Bligh's log from the *Bounty*. It's also known for the innovative

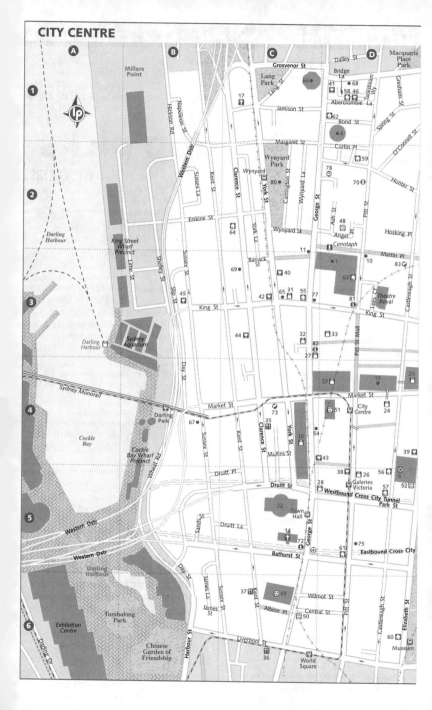

CITY CENTRE

A **B** **C** **D**

Dalley St

Macquarie Place Park

0 Millers Point

Grosvenor St

Bridge La

41 • 68

Lang Park

58 46

Lang St

Abercrombie La

Jamison St

62

17

Bond St

Margaret St

•4

Curtin Pl

59

Wynyard Park

78

70

Hunter St

Wynyard

80

70

Erskine St

48

Hosking Pl

Angel Pl

Wynyard St

Cenotaph

Martin Pl

64

11

•1

10

83

King Street Wharf Precinct

Barrack St

40

63

81

Theatre Royal

King St

69

45

42

65 31 55

77

Darling Harbour

King St

Sydney Aquarium

44

32 33

82

Day St

27

29

19

25

Sydney Monorail

Market St

73

City Centre

24

Darling Park

67

35

54

Cockle Bay

30

39

Mullins St

Cockle Bay Wharf Precinct

43

Druitt Pl

38 26

56

Galeries Victoria

52

Druitt St

28

57

Westbound Cross City Tunnel

Park St

22

Town Hall

14

Druitt La

72

61

75

Darling Harbour

Bathurst St

Eastbound Cross City

Tumbalong Park

37

49

Wilmot St

Exhibition Centre

James La

Albion Pl

Central St

50

60

Museum

Chinese Garden of Friendship

Liverpool St

36

World Square

62

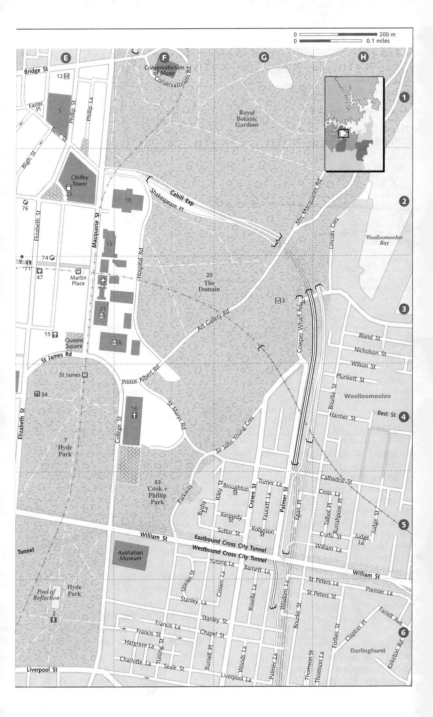

CITY CENTRE

SIGHTS (pp61–70)
1 Martin Place.............................1 D3
Anzac Memorial.........................2 E6
Art Gallery of NSW....................3 G3
Arthouse Hotel...........................(see 38)
Australia Square........................4 D1
Governors Phillip & Macquarie
    Towers..................................5 E1
Great Synagogue........................6 D5
Hyde Park...................................7 E5
Hyde Park Barracks
    Museum.................................8 F3
Marble Bar.................................(see 43)
Martin Place Bank Buildings.......9 E3
Martin Place Bank Buildings.....10 D3
Martin Place Bank Buildings.....11 C2
Museum of Sydney....................12 E1
Parliament House......................13 E2
Queen Victoria Building...........(see 30)
St Andrew's Cathedral...............14 C5
St James' Church.......................15 E3
St Mary's Cathedral...................16 F4
St Philip's Church......................17 C1
State Library of NSW.................18 F2
State Theatre.............................(see 51)
Sydney Hospital........................(see 79)
Sydney Tower............................19 D4
The Domain...............................20 F3
The Mint....................................21 E3
Town Hall..................................22 C5

SHOPPING (pp123–5)
Chifley Plaza.............................23 E2
David Jones...............................24 D4
David Jones...............................25 D4
Dirt Cheap CDs.........................26 D5
Dymocks...................................27 C3
Herringbone..............................(see 1)
Kinokuniya................................28 D5
Myer...29 D4
Queen Victoria Building............30 C4

Red Eye Records.......................31 C3
RM Williams.............................32 C3
Strand Arcade...........................33 D3
Strand Hatters..........................(see 33)

EATING (pp140–1)
Bar Quattro...............................34 E4
Bécasse....................................35 C4
Casa Asturiana..........................36 C6
Est...(see 41)
Tetsuya's...................................37 C6

DRINKING & NIGHTLIFE (pp156–8)
Arthouse Hotel..........................38 D5
Bambini Wine Room..................39 D4
Bavarian Bier Café.....................40 C3
Establishment...........................41 D1
Hemmesphere............................(see 41)
Hotel CBD.................................42 C3
Marble Bar................................43 D4
Orbit...(see 4)
Redoak Boutique Beer Café......44 C3
Slip Inn.....................................45 B3
Statement Lounge.....................(see 51)
Tank..(see 58)
Tank Stream Bar.......................46 D1
Wine Banq................................47 E3

ARTS
Chinese Laundry.......................(see 45)
City Recital Hall........................48 D2
Greater Union George St
    Cinemas...............................49 C6
Metro Theatre...........................50 C6
State Theatre.............................51 D4
Ticketek....................................52 D5

SPORTS & ACTIVITIES
Cook + Phillip Park...................53 F5
Pro Dive....................................54 C4

SLEEPING (pp189–90)
Blacket......................................55 C3
Castlereagh...............................56 D5
Central Park Hotel.....................57 D5
Establishment Hotel..................58 D1
Grand Hotel..............................59 D2
Hyde Park Inn...........................60 D6
Meriton Serviced Apartments
    Pitt St...................................61 D5
Saville 2 Bond St.......................62 D1
Westin Sydney...........................63 D3
Wynyard Hotel..........................64 C2

TRANSPORT
Alitalia......................................65 C3
British Airways...........................66 C1
Japan Airlines............................67 B4
Singapore Airlines.....................68 D1
United Airlines...........................69 C3

INFORMATION
American Express.......................70 D2
City Host Information Kiosk
    (Martin Place).......................71 E3
City Host Information Kiosk
    (Town Hall)............................72 C5
French Consulate.......................73 C4
Japanese Consulate...................74 E3
Map World................................75 D5
New Zealand High
    Commission..........................76 E2
NRMA.......................................77 C3
Poste Restante
    Service..................................78 D2
Sydney Hospital........................79 E3
TransitShop...............................80 C2
Travelex/
    Thomas Cook........................81 D3
Travellers Medical & Vaccination
    Centre...................................82 C3
US Consulate General...............83 D3

temporary exhibitions in its galleries (9am-5pm Mon-Fri, 10am-5pm Sat & Sun).

The main entrance is through elaborately sculpted bronze doors and into the grand atrium of the neoclassical Mitchell wing (1910). Note the map of Tasman's journeys in the mosaic floor. The main reading room is an elegant temple of knowledge clad in milky marble; skylights bring natural light to the rows of long communal tables. Disabled access is excellent.

On the Macquarie St side of the building look for the sculpture of explorer Matthew Flinders, with a statue of his intrepid cat Trim behind him beneath one of the windows.

THE MINT Map pp62–3
 8239 2288; www.hht.net.au/museums/the _mint; 10 Macquarie St; admission free; 9am-5pm Mon-Fri; Martin Place

The main building (1816) in the Mint complex was originally the southern wing of the infamous Rum Hospital, built by two Sydney merchants in return for a monopoly on the rum trade (Sydney's real form of currency in those days). It became a branch of the Royal Mint in 1854, the first to be established outside England. It's now head office for the Historic Houses Trust, with a small historical collection on the premises and a lovely café. You're welcome to peruse those areas not posted off-limits, including the serene rear courtyard and the former coining factory behind it.

PARLIAMENT HOUSE Map pp62–3
 9230 2111; www.parliament.nsw.gov.au; Macquarie St; admission free; 9am-5pm Mon-Fri; Martin Place

Twin of The Mint (left), Parliament House (1816), used by the Legislative Council of the colony from 1829, is still home to the Parliament of New South Wales, making it the world's oldest continually operating parliament building. The front section was originally the northern wing of the Rum Hospital. It blends into a modern addition on the east side.

You'll need to go through a metal detector to gain access. Once inside you're free to check out the changing art exhibitions in the central lobby, and the fascinating historical display in the wood-panelled Jubilee Room. On non-sitting days both assembly chambers are open, but when Parliament's sitting you're restricted to the Public Gallery. Wheelchair access is excellent.

SYDNEY HOSPITAL Map pp62–3
☎ 9382 7111; 8 Macquarie St; ® Martin Place
Originally the Rum Hospital (see opposite) the country's oldest hospital has a grand Victorian sandstone façade and an interesting history. While you can't wander around inside, the central courtyard with its over-the-top enamelled fountain is open to the public. Here you'll find the attractive Gothic Revival Nightingale Wing (1869) – site of the first Nightingale school, and the home of nursing in Australia – and a decent café. In front of the hospital is the large bronze Il Porcellino, a copy of a statue of a boar in Florence, with water dripping from its mouth. Rubbing its polished snout – coupled with a donation that goes to the hospital – is said to bring good luck.

1 MARTIN PLACE Map pp62–3
☎ 9221 5073; 1 Martin Place; ® Martin Place
As iconic as the Opera House in its time, this beautiful colonnaded Victorian building, built in 1874, was formerly the General Post Office and has now been gutted, stabbed with tower blocks and transformed into swanky shops, restaurants, offices and the Westin Sydney (p189) hotel. Inspired

by Italian Renaissance palaces, architect James Barnet caused a minor scandal by basing the faces carved on the sandstone façade on local identities. Queen Victoria dominates the central white-marble statuary, surrounded by allegorical figures. In the basement, hidden under a staircase, is an interesting historical display and a pipe housing what remains of the Tank Stream.

MARTIN PLACE BANK BUILDINGS Map pp62–3
® Martin Place
These cathedrals of commerce were designed to awe in much the same way as their spiritual siblings. The 12-storey Commonwealth Bank building (5 Martin Place) was Australia's first steel-framed 'skyscraper' when it was built in 1916. Its interiors are largely intact and clock-watching tellers can still muse over the inscription – 'The Noiseless Foot Of Time Steals Swiftly By' – on the wall. Another branch (48 Martin Place) has taken over the old State Savings Bank building. This stunning example of inter-war beaux-arts architecture features green-marble Doric columns and a brass-and-marble enclosed teller area. Abutting Martin Place, another grand bank is now the Virgin Megastore (343 George St).

MUSEUM OF SYDNEY Map pp62–3

☎ 9251 5988; www.hht.net.au/museums/mos; cnr Phillip & Bridge Sts; adult/child $10/5; ⏰ 9.30am–5pm; ⓡ Circular Quay

Built on the site of the first government house (the foundations are still visible), the MOS is a top-notch museum that uses installation and multiple-perspective art to explore Sydney's early history. Exhibits encompass the early natural environment, the culture of the indigenous Eora people and convict life. Sydney's early history comes to life in whisper, argument, gossip and artefacts, displayed in clever and engaging ways. Be sure to open some of the many stainless steel and glass drawers (they close themselves).

GOVERNORS PHILLIP & MACQUARIE TOWERS Map pp62–3

Phillip, Young & Bent Sts; ⓡ Circular Quay

With much hullabaloo, plans were drawn up in the 1980s to develop the site of Governor Phillip's first Government House which had been left semi-derelict for 50 years. At the north end of the block the remaining foundations of Government house were converted into First Government House Plaza and the Museum of Sydney (above), with these two towers looming large behind them, clad in steel, granite and glass. Governor Phillip Tower (1993) is Sydney's 6th tallest office block with the third-highest roofline; at 227m it's only 3m from the tallest. Its distinctive metallic-bladed top has earned it the nickname 'the milk crate'.

ST JAMES & AROUND

THE DOMAIN Map pp62–3

Prince Albert Rd; ⓡ St James

The Domain is a large grassy area east of Macquarie St, set aside by Governor Phillip in 1788 for public recreation. Today, it's used by workers for lunchtime sport and as a place to escape the bustle of the city. It's also the Sunday afternoon venue for impassioned soapbox speakers who do their best to entertain, inspire or enrage. Many large-scale public events are held here, including the Tropfest film festival (p17).

Sculptures dot the park, including a Henry Moore reclining figure and Brett Whiteley's Almost Once (1991) – two giant matches, one burnt – rising out of the ground near the Art Gallery of NSW (right).

top picks

PARKS

- Royal Botanic Gardens (p57)
- Chinese Garden of Friendship (p74)
- Observatory Hill (p53)
- Nielsen Park (p116)
- Hyde Park (below)
- Centennial Park (p83)

Heading past the Art Gallery alongside the Royal Botanic Gardens is Mrs Macquaries Point, offering great views over Woolloomooloo, the harbour and the city. Mrs Macquarie's Chair was carved out of the sandstone by convicts in 1816 for the governor's wife's vice-regal bottom.

ART GALLERY OF NSW Map pp62–3

☎ 9225 1744; www.artgallery.nsw.gov.au; Art Gallery Rd, The Domain; admission free; ⏰ 10am–5pm Thu-Tue, 10am-9pm Wed; ⓡ St James

With its elegant classical Greek frontage and modern rear end, the state's main gallery has an outstanding permanent display of Australian art (including a substantial Aboriginal and Torres Strait Islander collection), a well-regarded Asian gallery, a Western collection starting from the 16th century, and some inspired temporary exhibits (prices vary). The frequently controversial, much-debated Archibald Prize exhibition is held here every March, with portraits of the famous and not-so-famous bringing out the art critic in every Sydneysider. There are free guided tours on the hour from 11am to 2pm (Tuesday to Sunday), and wheelchair access is good. Look out for Lin Onus' Fruit Bats (1991), a cheeky bunch of critters painted in Aboriginal cross-hatching hanging from a clothes line.

HYDE PARK Map pp62–3

ⓡ St James & Museum

Hyde Park is the city's lungs. More formal than The Domain (left), it offers a green respite from the surrounding traffic and crowds, and a home to many small creatures. The tree-formed tunnel running down the middle is particularly lovely at night, when it's illuminated by fairy lights. The northern end is crowned by the richly symbolic Art Deco Archibald Memorial Fountain, featuring figures from Greek mythology. At the southern end the shallow Pool of Reflection leads to the exquisite Anzac Memorial (below). Cafés above the train stations at either end offer alfresco dining, and there is a popular life-sized chess set near St James.

ANZAC MEMORIAL Map pp62–3

☎ 9267 7668; Hyde Park; admission free; ⏲ 9am-5pm; ⊠ Museum

This beautiful Art Deco memorial (1934) covered in interesting statues and friezes commemorates the soldiers of the Australia and New Zealand Army Corps (Anzacs) who served in WWI. The centrepiece is *Sacrifice*, a bronze statue of a naked dead soldier draped over a shield, supported by four women (mother, sister, wife and child) standing on a golden sun. In the marble ceiling are 120,000 tiny stars, one for each person from New South Wales who served. An eternal flame burns nearby, and there's a small military museum attached.

ST MARY'S CATHEDRAL Map pp62–3

☎ 9220 0400; www.sydney.catholic.org.au /cathedral; College St; admission free; ⏲ 6.30am-6.30pm Sun-Fri, 7am-7pm Sat; ⊠ St James

Begun in 1868 and consecrated in 1905, St Mary's is the seat of the Catholic Archbishop of Sydney. As you might expect given its importance, the Gothic Revival cathedral is imposingly large (106m long) and has oodles of stained glass (crafted in Birmingham, England); its 75m-high front spires were only completed in 2000. The best time to visit is when the sun streams through the side windows in the early morning and late afternoon. The crypt has an impressive terrazzo mosaic floor depicting *The Creation*, inspired by the *Book of Kells*.

GREAT SYNAGOGUE Map pp62–3

☎ 9267 2477; www.greatsynagogue.org.au; 187A Elizabeth St; adult/child $5/3; ⏲ tours noon Tue & Thu; ⊠ St James

The Great Synagogue (1878) is the spiritual home of Sydney's longest-running Jewish congregation, established in 1831. One of 28 Orthodox synagogues in Sydney, 800 families form its congregation. It's considered the Mother Synagogue of Australia and architecturally the most important in the southern hemisphere. The impressive

ceiling features gold-leaf stars on a night-blue background, supported by ornate white and gold columns forming 12 arches representing the tribes of Israel. An impressive rose window illuminates the eastern wall. It's only open for services and the fascinating tours, which include a presentation on local Jewish history.

ST JAMES' CHURCH Map pp62–3

☎ 8227 1300; www.sjks.org.au; 173 King St; admission free; ⏲ 8am-6pm Mon-Fri, 8am-4.30 Sat, 7am-4pm Sun; ⊠ St James

Another Greenway gem, St James' Church was originally designed to be a courthouse but was consecrated by the Reverend Marsden in 1824 – making it the oldest remaining church in Sydney. Restored in the 1950s, it contains traditional stained glass, but also the striking modern 'creation window' in the Chapel of the Holy Spirit, as well as a choir loft of dark wood and a lovely pipe organ. Free concerts are held at 1.15pm Wednesday from March to December and free tours at 2.30pm weekdays.

HYDE PARK BARRACKS MUSEUM Map pp62–3

☎ 8239 2311; www.hht.net.au/museums/hpbm; Queens Sq, Macquarie St; adult/child $10/5; ⏲ 9.30am-5pm; ⊠ St James

Francis Greenway designed this squarish, decorously Georgian structure (1819) as convict quarters. It later served as an immigration depot, an asylum for women and law courts. Now it's a fascinating if not entirely cheerful museum, focusing on the various phases of the barracks' history and the archaeological efforts that helped uncover it. Read about some of the offences

---

SPIRING TO GREATNESS

Those who say that size doesn't matter should have a word with Sydney's architects. Sydney currently has 10 buildings over 200m tall, but as most men can tell you, how big something is depends on where you measure it from. A large spire can add 80m to a building and an antenna even more.

By any measure, Sydney Tower (p68) at 309m is king of all it surveys. Chifley Tower (1992, p125) is the highest office block, with its spire scraping 244m. However World Tower (2004, 91 Liverpool St), at 230m and 73 floors, has the highest roof.

that got people transported to Australia, or added to their time and punishment once they arrived; many of them were of an astoundingly petty nature. You can wander the courtyard and look at the foyer display for free.

STATE THEATRE Map pp62–3
☎ 9373 6852; www.statetheatre.com.au; 49 Market St; tours $15; ✆ box office 9am-5pm Mon-Fri; ⊠ St James
The splendidly elaborate State (1929) is the city's most ostentatious theatre. It was originally built as a movie palace during Hollywood's heyday and is now a National Trust–classified building, dripping with gilt and velveteen. These days it stages live shows, except during the Sydney Film Festival (p18) in June. If you're lucky, you might make one of the monthly guided tours (☎ 9373 6862).

SYDNEY TOWER Map pp62–3
☎ 9333 9222; www.sydneytoweroztrek.com.au; Podium Level, 100 Market St; adult/child $24/14; ✆ 9am-10.30pm Sun-Fri, 9am-11.30pm Sat; ⊠ St James
This futuristic tower (built 1970–1981) stands 309m high and on clear days the views from the 250m observation floor take in the Blue Mountains, Botany Bay and the length of Sydney Harbour. The admission price entitles you to a goofy virtual-reality ride through Australian 'kulcha'. If you're planning on heading to Sydney Aquarium (p71) or Sydney Wildlife World (p73), check out the discounted combined tickets.

For an added thrill take the 90-minute guided Sky Walk (adult/child $89/73), 10m higher up on the exposed roof. At nearly twice the height of BridgeClimb (p226) there's the added thrill of standing on a glass platform while it extends 2m over the tower's edge.

At the lower four floors is the Centrepoint shopping complex, which opens onto Pitt St Mall.

TOWN HALL & AROUND

QUEEN VICTORIA BUILDING Map pp62–3
QVB; ☎ 9264 9209; www.qvb.com.au; 455 George St; ✆ bldg 24hr, shops 9am-6pm Mon-Wed, Fri & Sat, 9am-9pm Thu, 11am-5pm Sun; ⊠ Town Hall
They don't build 'em like this anymore! The lavish QVB takes up the entire block and houses some 200 shops (p125), cafés and restaurants. Built in 1898 as the city's markets, the colonnaded façade and multiple copper domes are designed to evoke a Byzantine palace. Unbelievably this building was repeatedly due for demolition before it was restored in the mid-1980s.

Inside, look out for the two large suspended clocks, replicas of the crown jewels and the Queen Victoria ballroom. Outside the QVB is an imposing statue of Queen Victoria herself, and nearby is a wishing well featuring a small bronze statue of her beloved pooch, Islay (which, quite disconcertingly, speaks aloud in the deep baritone voice of former radio shock-jock John Laws). Guided tours ($10) leave daily from the concierge desk.

TOWN HALL Map pp62–3
☎ 9265 9189; www.cityofsydney.nsw.gov.au; 483 George St; ✆ 8am-6pm Mon-Fri; ⊠ Town Hall
The High Victorian sandstone wedding-cake exterior of the Town Hall (built 1869-1889) is matched by the elaborate chamber room and wood-lined concert hall inside. The stupendous concert hall (☎ 9265 9007) houses an impressive 8000-pipe organ and is a venue for free, monthly lunchtime concerts. Functions sometimes see Town Hall closed to the casual visitor, but otherwise feel free to poke around the first few halls off the entrance.

ST ANDREW'S CATHEDRAL Map pp62–3
☎ 9265 1661; www.cathedral.sydney.anglican.asn.au; cnr George & Bathurst Sts; admission free; ✆ 10am-4pm Mon, Tue, Fri & Sat, 8am-8pm Wed, 10am-6.30pm Thu, 7.30am-8pm Sun; ⊠ Town Hall
Sporting beautiful stained glass and twin spires inspired by England's York Minster, Anglican St Andrew's is the oldest cathedral in Australia (1868). There are some ugly modifications around the front door but disabled access is good. Organ recitals are held on Friday at 1.10pm and a concert band performs most Wednesdays at 12.30pm. During term time, free 'Young Music' concerts are held at 1pm on Monday and 1.10pm on Thursday.

MARBLE BAR Map pp62–3
☎ 9265 6026; www.marblebarsydney.com.au; Hilton Sydney, 488 George St; ✆ 5pm-1am Mon-Thu, noon-3am Fri & Sat, 6pm-midnight Sun; ⊠ Town Hall

George Adams must have been having a Medici moment when he built this dazzling bar in 1893 at a staggering cost of £32,000. An explosion of opulence coats every inch – from the intricately carved wooden bar to the bronze capitals of the Corinthian columns. When the Adams Hotel was demolished, every slab of marble was carefully dismantled, restored and then reassembled in its present location, under the Hilton Hotel.

ARTHOUSE HOTEL Map pp62–3
☎ 9284 1200; www.thearthousehotel.com.au; 275 Pitt St; ⏰ 11am-midnight Mon & Tue, 11am-1am Wed & Thu, 11am-3am Fri, 5pm-6am Sat; 🚉 Town Hall
Once the School of Arts (1836), this beautifully restored, heritage-listed building houses a creative combination of the artistic and the alcoholic. There are regular exhibitions by emerging Australian artists in the Gallery bar, free life-drawing in the Dome restaurant (Monday from 6.30pm; bring your own media) and Dr Sketchy's Anti-Art School 'where cabaret meets art' in the Attic Bar ($15; Tuesday from 6.30pm). The main bar once housed a chapel (see p157).

A CITY CANYON ADVENTURE
Walking Tour
1 Town Hall Who knows what she'd make of the cheeky city Sydney's become, but Queen Victoria would surely be amused by the High Victorian start to our tour, the elaborate Town Hall (opposite). Cross Druitt St to her imperious statue (and that of her alarming talking dog) and enter her eponymous building.

2 Queen Victoria Building On the site of the city's first markets, the Queen Victoria Building (opposite) blends American and Venetian Romanesque grandeur. Have a good look around as you pass through this shopping mecca, but watch your bank balance. Exit at the far end and turn right into Market St.

3 State Theatre On your right you'll find the extraordinarily extravagant State Theatre (opposite), more like the inside of a cathedral than a thespian venue. Stop to check out the foyer and note the coming shows – something might tempt you to buy tickets to return and see the old girl in action.

4 Hyde Park Continue past giant Sydney Tower (opposite) and into Hyde Park (p66). As you cut across, check out the giant chessboard and the elaborate Archibald Memorial Fountain.

5 St Mary's Cathedral Stop to explore the imposing Gothic Revival sandstone St Mary's Cathedral (p67). Upon leaving head north and, as the road curves around the top of Hyde Park under the watchful eyes of Prince Albert, turn right into Macquarie St.

6 Macquarie Street Governor Lachlan Macquarie commissioned convicted forger Francis Greenway to design this street in the early 19th century. Greenway's Hyde Park Barracks (p67) and St James' Church (p67), guard the south end. Heading north you'll pass on the right, in

WALK FACTS
Start Town Hall
End Martin Place
Distance 6km
Duration 2 hours (not including shop stops)
Fuel stops Plenty

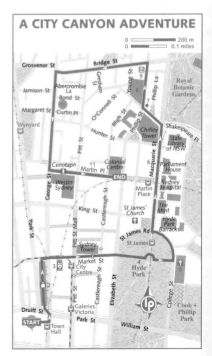

A CITY CANYON ADVENTURE

69

quick succession, The Mint (p64), Sydney Hospital (p65), Parliament House (p64) and the State Library of NSW (p61).

7 Aurora Place Cross the road to the corner of Bent St where much of the block is taken up by Renzo Piano's Aurora Place (2001), one of Sydney's most dynamic (and, at \$500 million, most expensive) commercial towers (now branded ABN Amro). The façade's curves are intended to mirror the Opera House's lines.

8 Governors Phillip & Macquarie Towers
You're now well and truly in the big end of town. Across Phillip St the 227m-high Governor Phillip Tower (1993) is propped up on zinc-plated transfer beams for a monumental 10 storeys before the tower begins. Neighbouring Governor Macquarie Tower (1994) is a comparative pipsqueak (145m).

9 Museum of Sydney From the cutting edge to the historical: head past the surreal façades of Phillip St to the Museum of Sydney (p66). In front of the museum you can see the foundations of the city's earliest significant building, the infamously fetid First Government House.

10 Australia Square Turn left into Bridge St and after five blocks turn left again, back into George St. After two blocks you'll come to Harry Seidler's minimalist/modernist Australia Square (p61). Zip up to the bar in the revolving 47th-floor restaurant for a drink and stunning views – you're nearly finished.

11 Martin Place Continue up George St and left into Martin Place. Near the bottom is the Cenotaph. Flanked by statues of two impossibly handsome servicemen, it commemorates Australia's war dead. Explore the foyers of the majestic buildings (p65) lining this grand pedestrian mall. Note the TV screens on the Colonial Centre windows, to the left past Castlereagh; Channel 7 news is filmed live behind that glass.

DARLING HARBOUR & CHINATOWN

Drinking & Nightlife p158; Eating p141; Shopping p125; Sleeping p190

Hugging the city's western and southern flanks, this once heavily commercial area is now a lively entertainment district.

Darling Harbour, between the city and Pyrmont, was a thriving dockland lined with factories, warehouses and shipyards. After years of decline it was reinvented and opened in 1988 as a bicentennial gift to Sydney – or rather to her tourists. It's now a bizarre futuristic landscape of glass domes and cones which, with the mono-rail whizzing by, looks like a scene from 1960s cartoon *The Jetsons*. Among the masses of restaurants, bars and tourist shops you'll find custom-built attractions to amuse all ages – from pedal boats to the casino.

top picks

DARLING HARBOUR & CHINATOWN

- Sydney Aquarium (left)
- Powerhouse Museum (p74)
- Chinese Garden of Friendship (p74)
- Australian National Maritime Museum (below)
- Sydney Wildlife World (p73)

Bustling Chinatown has been centred on Dixon St Haymarket since the 1920s and now covers much of the city's southern fringe. No longer just Chinese, the area is truly pan-Asian, with plenty of Korean, Singaporean, Vietnamese, Malaysian and Thai businesses adding to the mix.

Apart from the constant hum of activity, the main drawcards here are the food and the shopping. It's the place to come for anything from Chinese medicinal herbs to mobile-phone covers, dirt-cheap clothes and Hello Kitty accessories. On Chinese New Year (p17) it seems that half of Sydney squishes into these tiny lanes to enjoy the dragon dancers and street stalls.

Around Central Station you'll find the mega-hostels, with their attendant bars, internet cafés and the buzz of young travellers. It's not the prettiest part of town, but it's certainly central. The city's busiest intersection, Railway Square has been decorated with colourful towerlike sculptures that resemble DNA strands. To the south, Broadway takes over from George St before becoming the main western route to Parramatta. Sydney's ugliest campus, the University of Technology (UTS), sprawls along its western edge.

DARLING HARBOUR

SYDNEY AQUARIUM Map p72
☎ 8251 7800; www.sydneyaquarium.com.au; Aquarium Pier; adult/child $28/14; ⏰ 9am-10pm; 🚇 Aquarium

Maybe a cute little guy named Nemo has something to do with it, but this place brings in more paid visitors than any other attraction in Australia – even with its hefty admission charges. Along with Nemo and his homies you'll find alien-like phosphorescent jellyfish, colourful corals and some irresistibly cute fairy penguins and platypuses. Underwater tunnels get you up close to seals, immense rays and an intimidating array of sharks. The finale at the Great Barrier Reef 'theatre' is absolutely breathtaking. Needless to say, kids love it. Disabled access is good. Discounted combined tickets are available with Sydney Tower (p68) and/or Sydney Wildlife World (p73).

AUSTRALIAN NATIONAL MARITIME MUSEUM Map p72
☎ 9298 3777; www.anmm.gov.au; 2 Murray St; admission free; ⏰ 9.30am-5pm; MLR Pyrmont Bay

The maritime museum is a fascinating place to learn about Australia's ongoing relationship with the sea. Entry to the permanent indoor collection is free; touring the vessels moored outside varies, with the 'big ticket' (adult/child $25/13) covering the submarine (HMAS *Onslow*), the destroyer (HMAS *Vampire*) and an 1874 square-rigger (*James Craig*). Occasionally a replica of James Cook's *Endeavour* also drops anchor. The huge museum has a curved roof (a little like a low-rent Opera House) and houses numerous displays, including a boat made of beer cans.

Outside, the 100m-long Welcome Wall honours migrants, allowing families to inscribe names and register their history on the database. It's not entirely clear who's doing the welcoming.

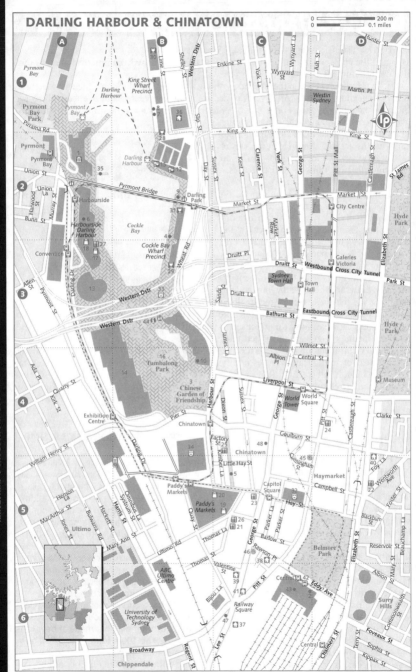

DARLING HARBOUR & CHINATOWN

0 — 200 m
0 — 0.1 miles

DARLING HARBOUR & CHINATOWN

SYDNEY WILDLIFE WORLD Map p72

☎ 9333 9288; www.sydneywildlifeworld.com.au;
Aquarium Pier; adult/child $29/15; ⏰ 9am-10pm;
🚇 Aquarium

Following the same formula as its sister and
neighbour Sydney Aquarium (p71), this large
complex houses an impressive collection
of Australian native reptiles, butterflies,
spiders, snakes and small mammals. The
nocturnal section is particularly good,
bringing the extrovert out in the quolls,
potoroos, echidnas and possums. The kids
may be more interested in holding snakes
and posing with koalas. It's extremely well
done, but it's still not a patch on Taronga
Zoo. You'll save around $10 on a combined
ticket with the Aquarium.

OUTBACK CENTRE Map p72

☎ 9283 7477; www.outbackcentre.com.au;
28 Darling Walk, 1-25 Harbour St; ⏰ 10am-6pm;
🚇 Town Hall

A mixture of the kitsch and the cultural,
this is a combination of souvenir store,
performance space and art gallery. Among
the fluffy koalas and key-rings you'll find
woomeras (spear-throwers), kalis (jumbo-
sized boomerangs), musical clapsticks and
bullroarers (ceremonial musical instruments). The highlight, hidden (strangely
enough) out back, is Australia's Outback Gallery
(p125). A free 'Sounds of the Outback'

didgeridoo performance takes place at
1pm, 3pm and 5pm daily.

TUMBALONG PARK Map p72

⏰ 24hr; 🚇 Town Hall
This friendly grassy area at Darling Harbour's south end has fountains with timed,
acrobatic water jets, a delightful sculpture
of sheep leaping into another dimension
and an amphitheatre that often hosts free
entertainment. Nearby there's an excellent children's playground and a lake with
pricey paddle-boats ($12 for 15 minutes,
maximum three people).

top picks

FOR CHILDREN

- Any of Sydney's beaches and parks
- Taronga Zoo (p106)
- Sydney Aquarium (p71)
- Powerhouse Museum (p74)
- Australian National Maritime Museum (p71)
- Sydney Observatory (p53)
- Sydney Wildlife World (left)
- Australian Museum (p77)
- Royal Botanic Gardens (p57)
- Tumbalong Park (above)

TRANSPORT: DARLING HARBOUR & CHINATOWN

Train The best option; everything's an easy walk from Central or Town Hall Stations.

Bus As well as the routes heading through to The Rocks and Circular Quay (see p53), many leave from Railway Square, including 372 to Coogee via Surry Hills and 378 to Bronte via Oxford St.

MLR Metro Light Rail links Central to Lilyfield via Glebe, with several stops around Haymarket and Pyrmont.

Ferry Services head from Darling Harbour and Pyrmont Bay to Circular Quay.

Monorail The loop links Darling Park, Harbourside, Convention, Paddy's Markets and Chinatown to the city centre.

Parking Try Harbourside car park, under the Novotel (enter from Murray St; one hour $7).

COCKLE BAY WHARF Map p72
☎ 9264 4755; www.cocklebaywharf.com;
⊞ Town Hall

The first vaguely tasteful development in Darling Harbour, Cockle Bay Wharf takes up the city-side frontage as far as Pyrmont Bridge. Its modern architecture is softened by the use of timber and whimsical sculptures. We particularly like the stork fountain and the suspended clear plastic whales. Housing 10 upmarket restaurants and six bars, Cockle Bay helped pull Darling Harbour out of the financial dumps in the 1990s. The eateries are generally good, albeit touristy and pricey. Home (p158) set a new standard for stylish megaclubs, and bucked the colonial trend by spawning an offshoot in London.

KING ST WHARF Map p72
☎ 9299 0622; www.ksw.com.au; Erskine St;
⊞ Wynyard

Cockle Bay Wharf in ultramodern metal drag, this wharf continues the Darling Harbour precinct past the Pyrmont Bridge on the city side. All the luxury apartments in this $800-million development are sold and the office space leased out, but you can still get a taste of the high life at its strip of bars and restaurants.

HARBOURSIDE Map p72
☎ 9281 3999; Darling Dr; ⊙ 10am-9pm;
MLR Convention

The first big Darling Harbour development, Harbourside is like that guy in a trendy nightclub still wearing a pirate shirt and an unreconstructed mullet; its 1980s stylings are no match for the chic constructions loitering on the other side of the harbour. Restaurants line the frontage and a food hall and shops selling cheap clothes and souvenirs fill the interior.

SYDNEY CONVENTION CENTRE & SYDNEY EXHIBITION CENTRE Map p72
☎ 9282 5000; www.scec.com.au; Darling Dr;
MLR Convention

No, you're not in Texas. They like to do things big in Sydney too, like this behemoth on the western edge of Tumbalong Park. It was designed by Australian architect Philip Cox, who also did the aquarium and the maritime museum. The exhibition centre, on the south end of the complex, has steel masts from which its roofs are suspended. The convention centre is the rounder bit located nearer to the harbour. Check the website to find out about opening times and events.

CHINATOWN

CHINESE GARDEN OF FRIENDSHIP Map p72
☎ 9240 8888; www.chinesegarden.com.au;
adult/child/family $6/3/15; ⊙ 9.30am-5.30pm;
⊞ Town Hall

This tranquil, traditional garden – designed by landscape architects from Guangzhou (a sister city to Sydney) – occupies over a hectare of Darling Harbour bordering Chinatown. It was set up by Sydney's Chinese community to commemorate the Australian Bicentenary in 1988. Its ponds, pavilions, waterfalls and lush plant life make a refreshing break from hoofing it about the city's hot pavement, especially if you finish your visit with a pick-me-up in the teahouse (⊙ 10am-4.30pm). Imperial court costumes are available for those who like to play dress up ($5, or $10 including a print).

POWERHOUSE MUSEUM Map p72
☎ 9217 0111; www.powerhousemuseum.com;
500 Harris St, Ultimo; adult/child/under 5 $10/5/free; ⊙ 10am-5pm; MLR Paddy's Markets

Hands down the best museum for kids, the Powerhouse is huge, occupying what was once the power station for Sydney's erstwhile tram system. Grab a map of the museum once you're inside; you'll need it.

The zillion exhibits at the Powerhouse are extremely engaging, covering everything from furniture design to trains, from space shuttles to musical instruments, from robotics to fashion. There's plenty of interaction, including a series of exhibits where you can conduct your own magnetic and electronic experiments. Look out for the Strasburg Clock replica on level 4 and a guitar owned by AC/DC's Angus Young on level 2. Services are available for disabled visitors.

DIXON STREET Map p72
Haymarket; MLR Paddy's Market
The epicentre of Chinatown, bustling Dixon St is a narrow pedestrian mall lined with restaurants, with ornate gates at either end. These *paifang* are topped with fake bamboo tiling and golden Chinese calligraphy (with English translations). Ornamental lions keep evil spirits at bay. This is actually Sydney's third Chinatown. The first formed in The Rocks in the late 19th century, before moving to the Darling Harbour end of Market St. Dixon St's Chinatown dates from the 1920s.

CENTRAL STATION Map p72
Eddy Ave, City; ⒭ Central Station
Sydney's main railway hub was built in 1906 on the site of a cemetery and a convent; the 75m Gothic Revival clock tower was added 15 years later. The main sandstone concourse has an impressive vaulted roof and is the terminus for the intercity and country trains. It also houses the Railway Heritage Centre (☼ 8.30am-5.30pm Mon-Fri, 9am-4pm Sat). Suburban trains chug into the outdoor platforms downstairs on the Surry Hills side. As you're pulling into Central from the south, look out for the ornate, disused Mortuary Station (1869) on your left.

A DARLING CHINATOWN STROLL
Walking Tour
1 Central Station Start upstairs in the main concourse of Central Station (above), taking time to admire the stained glass windows in the

Rail Heritage Centre. Leave by the George St exit, turn left and walk through the small park down to Railway Square. Cross Pitt St and head onto George St.

2 Christ Church St Lawrence At 812 George St step off Sydney's main thoroughfare into the oasis of calm that is this sandstone church (1845). It's a brief respite before the city's main thoroughfare leads you past a sordid collection of sex clubs and adult stores.

3 Sydney City Library Haymarket At the corner of Hay St, this fine Victorian sandstone building (1875) has delicate floral detailing. Inside, look for the photograph of the Chung Shan Society pictured in traditional costumes in Dixon St in 1910.

WALK FACTS
Start Central Station
End Pyrmont Bridge
Distance 4km
Duration 1½ hours
Fuel stops Numerous

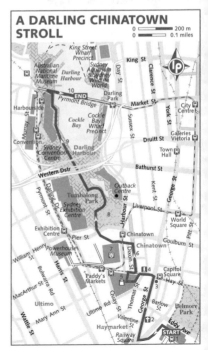

4 Golden Water Mouth Cross George St and head down Hay St. To the right of the road, the Golden Water Mouth drips with gold and water; it's formed from a eucalyptus trunk from Condobolin, the destination of many gold rush–era Chinese. Its feng shui significance is to encourage positive energy and good fortune.

5 Paddy's Markets A little further down Hay St, Paddy's Markets (p126) occupies a large brick building. Although it had its start in the mid-19th century with mainly European traders, the market's tightly packed stalls are more evocative of present-day Vietnam.

6 Dixon Street Double back and enter through the lion-flanked gate to Dixon St (p75), the pedestrian mall at the heart of Chinatown. Look for the fake-bamboo awnings guarded by dragons, dogs and lions to your left, and a lighting fixture reminiscent of an upturned wok while crossing Little Hay St.

7 Sydney Entertainment Centre Exit through the far gate, turn left into Factory St, cross the road and cut across the paved area to the right of the monumentally ugly Entertainment Centre (p169). Veer right in front of the Pump House (1889) and past the garish pink neon that marks the start of Darling Harbour.

8 Chinese Garden Of Friendship As you head towards the water you'll pass the Chinese Garden of Friendship (p74), one of the prettiest spots in the inner city. Consider paying the admission and soaking up the zen atmosphere over a beverage in the tea garden.

9 Darling Harbour You'll pass Tumbalong Park (p73) and the Outback Centre (p73) as you head towards the actual harbour. Follow it around to the left where there's a cool sunken spiral fountain in front of the Convention Centre (p74). The trick is to try to reach the centre while keeping your feet dry.

10 Pyrmont Bridge Continue past the Harbourside (p74) complex to Pyrmont Bridge, a swing bridge dating from 1902. While crossing over you'll get a great view of the city and Darling Harbour, including the Australian National Maritime Museum (p71) and, on the far side, Cockle Bay (p74) and King Street Wharfs (p74), Sydney Aquarium (p71) and Sydney Wildlife World (p73).

Drinking & Nightlife p158; Eating p142; Shopping p126; Sleeping p191

The beginning of Sydney's Eastern Suburbs, the city fringe of Darlinghurst to Potts Point is a sociological stew. Taking in the first part of Oxford St (Sydney's sequinned mile), Darlinghurst is synonymous with the gay community – it's home to most of the city's gay venues and the Mardi Gras parade.

As Darlinghurst borders the city it morphs into East Sydney, with the remains of a tiny Italian enclave centred on Stanley St.

Where busy William St crosses Victoria, the Kings Cross red-light district begins in earnest – fittingly under the scarlet glow of a giant Coca-Cola sign. In the early 19th century this ridge became a popular address for the very rich, escaping the fetid slums of the city. As the slums spread, the wealthy abandoned their mansions to move to the suburbs and Sydney's first blocks of flats started to spring up. By the 1920s a bohemian reputation had stuck, as artists rubbed shoulders with immigrants from Continental Europe. During WWII the area was flooded with refugees and randy Americans on shore leave. Foreign conceptions such as cafés and cabarets sprung up, and eventually strip clubs. By the 1970s and 1980s the Cross was the haunt of crooked cops, ruthless underworld figures and heartbreakingly young junkies and prostitutes.

top picks

DARLINGHURST TO POTTS POINT

- Sydney Jewish Museum (left)
- National Art School (below)
- Elizabeth Bay House (p80)
- Finger Wharf (p80)
- Australian Museum (below)

Now the area's changing again. In recent years the footpaths have been spruced up, obvious drug-dealers moved on and strip-club touts reined in.

Potts Point and Elizabeth Bay are the stylish sisters of tarty Kings Cross. Despite coming from the same gene pool, they've kept themselves nice, and offer fabulous remnants of the Victorian and Art Deco building sprees. Leafy Victoria St has a large concentration of backpacker hostels.

Wedged between the city and the Cross, Woolloomooloo was one of Sydney's most notorious slums and still has pockets best avoided after dark. The wharf and neighbouring streets have been gentrified beyond recognition over the last decade.

DARLINGHURST & EAST SYDNEY

SYDNEY JEWISH MUSEUM Map p78
☎ 9360 7999; www.sydneyjewishmuseum.com.au; 148 Darlinghurst Rd, Darlinghurst; adult/child/family $10/6/22; ☷ 10am-4pm Sun-Thu, 10am-2pm Fri; ☒ 311

This excellent museum has evocative displays on Australian Jewish history from the First Fleet (which included 16 known Jews) to the present day, along with the history of Judaism in general. Video testimony and touch-screen computers are used to good effect. There's a sobering Holocaust section, which includes the moving Children's Memorial. Allow at least two hours to explore this extraordinary place. Free 40-minute tours leave at noon and there's a kosher café on site.

AUSTRALIAN MUSEUM Map p78
☎ 9320 6000; www.amonline.net.au; 6 College St, East Sydney; adult/child $10/5; ☷ 9.30am-5pm; ☖ Museum

This natural-history museum, established only 40 years after the First Fleet dropped anchor, has an excellent Australian wildlife collection (including some cool skeletons) and a gallery tracing Aboriginal history and the Dreamtime. There's a half-hour indigenous performance at noon and 2pm every Sunday, and a whole heap of fun programmes for kids. It's also wheelchair accessible.

NATIONAL ART SCHOOL Map p78
☎ 9337 8744; www.nas.edu.au; Forbes St, Darlinghurst; admission free; ☷ 10am-4pm Mon-Sat; ☒ 311

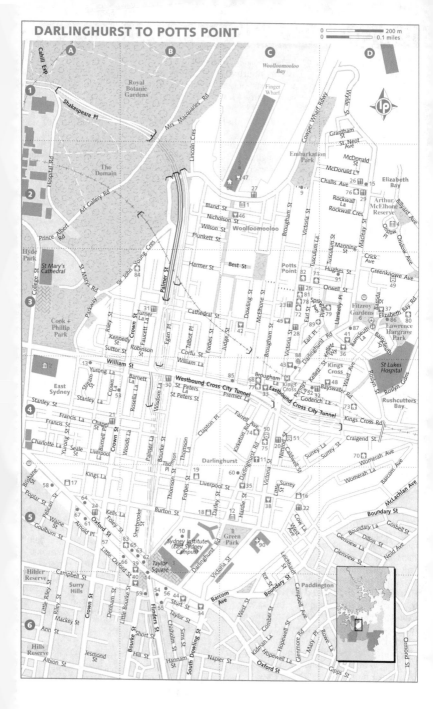

DARLINGHURST TO POTTS POINT

DARLINGHURST TO POTTS POINT

From 1841 to 1912 this bizarre set of sandstone buildings was Darlinghurst Gaol. Writer Henry Lawson was incarcerated here several times for debt (he called the place 'Starvinghurst'). If today's art students ever think they've got it hard, they should spare a thought for the 732 prisoners crammed within these convict-hewn walls, and the 76 hanged here. The circular central building was the chapel; head upstairs for an interesting historical display. A tiny morgue near the Burton St exit has creepy skull and crossbone carvings. There's an excellent gallery on site showcasing students' work.

TAYLOR SQUARE Map p78
cnr Oxford & Bourke Sts, Darlinghurst; 🚌 **380**
You know it's been a rough night if you wake up here. This almost pretty paved area straddling Oxford St is the hub of Darlinghurst's nightlife. The stern Greek Revival

Darlinghurst Courthouse (1842) watches the goings-on, no doubt disapprovingly. Near the courthouse is a heritage-listed Edwardian underground toilet (now closed), while on the Surry Hills side a sporadic fountain shoots enemas at unsuspecting passers-by. Carrying on that theme are metre-high suppositories, which house an outdoor gallery of sorts.

GREEN PARK Map p78
cnr Victoria & Burton Sts, Darlinghurst; 🚌 **311**
Once the residence of Alexander Green, hangman of Darlinghurst Gaol, Green Park is a pleasant place during the day but best avoided after dark. A large illuminated pink triangle backed by black pillars is the Gay & Lesbian Holocaust Memorial. It was founded by the late Dr Kitty Fischer, who as a young Jewish girl in Auschwitz was kept alive by food

Train For Potts Point, Elizabeth Bay and the eastern ridge of Darlinghurst, use Kings Cross Station. For the western end of Darlinghurst and East Sydney use Museum Station. For Woolloomooloo, walk downhill from either St James or Kings Cross.

Bus Route 311 hooks around the entire neighbourhood heading between Circular Quay and Railway Square. Oxford St buses head to Railway Square (378), Circular Quay (373, 380), Watsons Bay via Bondi (380), Bronte (378), Coogee (373) and Newtown via Surry Hills (352). The 389 cuts through the back streets of East Sydney and Darlinghurst from Circular Quay or North Bondi (via Paddington and Woollahra). Routes 324-5 pass through Kings Cross from Circular Quay or Watsons Bay.

Parking Street parking is usually possible, although often metered and limited in duration. Clearways are ruthlessly enforced. Don't leave valuables visible.

smuggled to her by a gay inmate forced to wear the pink triangle. At another corner of the park is a memorial to Victor Chang, the famed heart surgeon who worked at neighbouring St Vincent's Hospital.

ST JOHN'S CHURCH Map p78
☎ 9360 6844; www.stjohnsanglican.org.au; 120 Darlinghurst Rd, Darlinghurst; ☽ 10am-2pm; ⊕ Kings Cross
Grab a pamphlet inside this lovely sandstone church (1858) for an interesting 10-minute, self-guided tour. There's a separate leaflet with information about the historic stained-glass windows. This Anglican congregation runs the Rough Edges Community Centre, working with the area's many homeless.

WOOLLOOMOOLOO

FINGER WHARF Map p78
Cowper Wharf Rdwy; ⊟ 311
A former wool and cargo dock, the Finger Wharf got a huge sprucing up in the late 1990s and has emerged as one of Sydney's most exclusive eating, drinking, sleeping and luxury yacht–mooring addresses. It's still a public wharf so feel free to walk through the centre, past five-star hotel Blue (p193) and its fabulously designery Water Bar (p159). Along the way the wharf's history is etched into glass walls. This bastion of working-class tough has been transformed into a star-spotting paparazzi haunt, so it's fitting that everyman-megastar Russell Crowe has the penthouse at the end.

ARTSPACE Map p78
☎ 9356 0555; www.artspace.org.au; The Gunnery, 51 Cowper Wharf Rdwy; admission free; ☽ 11am-5pm Tue-Sat; ⊟ 311

This cutting-edge 'centre for experimentation' has changing contemporary avant-garde exhibitions that focus on modern Australian life and culture. It's an admirable attempt to liven things up in Sydney's art scene, with sometimes disturbing ideas stretching across the borders that stifle expression. Interdisciplinary works are a speciality; disabled access is excellent.

HARRY'S CAFÉ DE WHEELS Map p78
☎ 9347 3074; Cowper Wharf Rdwy; pies $3-4; ☽ 9am-1am Mon-Wed, 9am-3am Thu, 9am-4am Fri & Sat, 9am-midnight Sun; ⊟ 311
A humble pie cart but a tourist attraction no less, Harry's has been open since 1938 (besides a few years when founder Harry 'Tiger' Edwards was on active service). Photos prove that anyone and everyone comes to Harry's; if you stop to pay homage, you'll be joining the ranks of Pamela Anderson, Frank Sinatra and Colonel Sanders.

KINGS CROSS & POTTS POINT

FITZROY GARDENS Map p78
cnr Macleay St & Darlinghurst Rd, Kings Cross; ⊕ Kings Cross
It's testimony to the 'cleaning up' of the Cross that this once decidedly dodgy park is now a reasonably pleasant place to loiter (probably helped by the Stalinist police station at one end). The dandelion-esque El Alamein Fountain (1961) is one of the area's most notable landmarks, known locally as 'the elephant douche'. On Sundays a small flea market sets up in the plaza.

ELIZABETH BAY HOUSE Map p78
☎ 9356 3022; www.hht.net.au/museums/ebh; 7 Onslow Ave, Elizabeth Bay; adult/child/family $8/4/17; ☽ 10am-4.30pm Tue-Sun; ⊟ 311

Once known as 'the finest house in the colony', Elizabeth Bay House (1839) has been meticulously restored; painted in the original colour scheme and furnished with early-19th-century furniture. The house, with fine harbour views, was designed in English Neoclassical style by architect John Verge for then-colonial secretary of NSW Alexander Macleay (whose memorial tablet is in St James' Church, see p67). The large original grounds of the house served as a sort of botanic garden for Macleay, who collected plants from around the world.

YELLOW HOUSE Map p78
59 Macleay St, Potts Point; 🚌 311
Once a sunflower-yellow symbol of all things bohemian, this former artists' residence housed cultural heroes such as Martin Sharp, Peter Weir, Brett Whiteley and George Gittoes. It fell into disrepair in the '70s but has recently been renovated into a slick commercial gallery (p126) showcasing contemporary Australian and New Zealand art and a café-providore known for its heavenly chocolate cake.

MCELHONE STAIRS Map p78
Victoria St, Potts Point; 🚉 Kings Cross
These wonderful old stone stairs (1870) were built to connect smart Potts Point with the Woolloomooloo slums below. The downhill trip is infinitely easier on the legs and lungs than the 120 steps up from Woolloomooloo.

A RISQUÉ RAMBLE
Walking Tour
1 Taylor Square Start by following the route of the annual Mardi Gras Parade (p17) along Oxford St from Hyde Park; this is the city's main gay strip. Stop at Taylor Square (p79), the heart of the pink 'hood, and note the historic Victorian underground toilets (closed) and the majestic sandstone Darlinghurst Courthouse.

2 National Art School Cut diagonally left across the square and take Forbes St, where you'll pass the old Darlinghurst Police Station. To the right, behind imposing sandstone walls, is the National Art School (p77) – formerly Darlinghurst Gaol. Pass through the gates and search out the chapel, gallery and the creepy morgue.

3 Green Park Leave by the Burton St exit, turn right and head down to the traffic lights. Directly ahead is Green Park (p79), flanked by St Vincent's Hospital and Sacred Heart Hospice. Both the hospital and hospice found themselves at the frontline of the AIDS epidemic when it hit the local community hard in the 1980s.

4 St John's Church Turn into Darlinghurst Rd, passing the Sydney Jewish Museum (p77) on your right (don't stop unless you've got a couple of hours to do it justice). This stretch has some lovely terrace houses and the Darlo Bar (p159), flat-ironed into a corner location. Stop at St John's Church (opposite) and grab a pamphlet for a 10-minute self-guided tour.

5 Victoria Street, Darlinghurst Cut through the church ground and turn left onto the Victoria St restaurant strip. Grab a coffee at Bar Coluzzi (p143) on the right, a local institution since the 1950s. Up ahead you'll see the giant Coca-Cola sign that marks the beginning of Kings Cross.

6 'Top of the Cross' Stop at this busy intersection to take in the view down William St. Behind you, in front of the Elan apartments, is Ken Unsworth's much derided *Stones Against the Sky* sculpture. Locals know it as 'Shits On Sticks', which may be why it's recently been painted from brown to grey.

7 El Alamein Fountain Follow Darlinghurst Rd into the seedy heart of the Cross. Look to the ground for a series of inscriptions offering titbits of local history; just before McDonald's, you'll see one that marks the site of the 1978 Mardi Gras arrests (p183). Continue to Fitzroy Gardens (opposite) and the El Alamein Fountain.

8 Elizabeth Bay Cut past the distinctive round Gazebo tower, turn left into Elizabeth Bay

WALK FACTS
Start Hyde Park
End Woolloomooloo Finger Wharf
Distance 7km
Duration Two hours solid walking
Fuel stops Plenty along Victoria St and Challis Ave; Harry's and the Water bar at the end

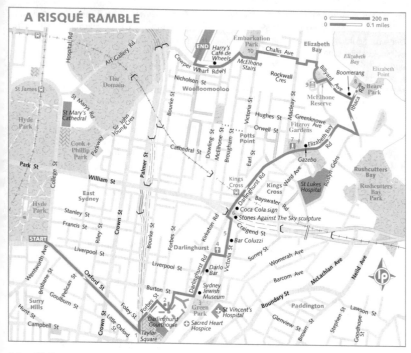

A RISQUÉ RAMBLE

Rd and follow it as it heads downhill and turns sharply right at a roundabout. Turn left when you reach Ithaca Rd and head down to pretty Elizabeth Bay where there's a small park.

9 Elizabeth Bay House Backtrack slightly and turn right into Billyard Ave. As you do you're passing the high walls of Boomerang, one of Australia's most expensive private houses. Take the stairs on the left (by the bus stop) leading up to genteel McElhone Reserve. Across this little park is stately Elizabeth Bay House (p80).

10 Embarkation Park Turn right (downhill) and take the stairs just before 17 Billyard Ave. At the top turn right into Macleay St and then left into highly caffeinated Challis Ave where you'll pass an impressive row of colonnaded mansions. At the bottom is Embarkation Park, offering great views over Woolloomooloo and the city.

top picks

MUSEUMS

- Museum of Contemporary Art (p53)
- Australian National Maritime Museum (p71)
- Sydney Jewish Museum (p77)
- Powerhouse Museum (p74)
- Nicholson Museum (p102)

11 Finger Wharf Head down McElhone Stairs (p81), to the left of the park. As you approach Woolloomooloo Finger Wharf (p80) you'll pass Harry's Café de Wheels (p80), a Sydney institution since 1938. Refuel with a pie or continue into the wharf for a classier finale at the Water Bar (p159).

Drinking & Nightlife p161; Eating p144; Shopping p127; Sleeping p193

The next belt of suburbs to the east is distinctly well-heeled. Pretty Paddington is a residential area of steep leafy streets and tightly packed terrace houses. It was built for aspiring artisans in the later years of the Victorian era, but during the lemming-like rush to the dreary outer suburbs after WWII, the area became an overcrowded slum. A renewed interest in Victorian architecture, combined with a sudden recollection of the pleasures of inner-city life, led to the area's restoration from the 1960s onwards.

Paddington has since turned into a fascinating jumble of beautifully restored terrace homes, elegant boutiques, cosy restaurants with five-star kitchens, sleek art galleries and cool bookshops.

Paddington's main spine is Oxford St, built over an ancient Cadigal walking track. When it passes through the suburb it becomes Sydney's premiere fashion strip. The best time to see Paddington at its liveliest is on Saturday, when the Paddington Markets (p86) and the surrounding boutiques are in full swing.

top picks

PADDINGTON TO DOUBLE BAY

- Australian Centre For Photography (p85)
- Centennial Park (left)
- Victoria Barracks (left)
- Redleaf Pool (p87)
- Rushcutters Bay Park (p87)

In contrast to Paddington, Woollahra was never a slum, and it's this old-money smugness that gives it a genteel, bordering on pompous, ambience. A dash of decent cafés, some great restaurants, upmarket boutiques and a wealth of antique shops (mainly around Queen St) make it a good spot for a combined stroll and shopping spree.

As you head down the hill towards the harbour, Edgecliff is a nondescript transport hub centred on New South Head Rd, sheltering the seriously moneyed mansions of Darling Point. Nicole Kidman has her Sydney home here. Just to the west of the point is peaceful Rushcutters Bay, while to the east Double Bay has a flashy nouveau riche reputation. Colloquially known as 'Double Pay', its pricey boutiques and restaurants aren't as interesting as Paddington's, but it does have some good hotels and the closest beach to the city (which you'd ever contemplate swimming at).

VICTORIA BARRACKS Map pp84–5

☎ 9339 3330; Oxford St, Paddington; admission free; ⏱ museum & tour 10am-1pm Thu, museum only 10am-4pm Sun; 🚌 380
There are free tours of these stately Georgian barracks (built 1841–8) that include a performance by the military band (weather permitting). It's a large complex, brought alive by the old soldiers of the Corps of Guides; expect a good yarn. The museum is jam-packed with military paraphernalia. Disabled access is good.

CENTENNIAL PARK Map pp84–5

☎ 9339 6699; www.cp.nsw.gov.au; Oxford St, Woollahra; ⏱ sunrise-sunset; 🚌 380
Sydney's biggest park, Centennial Park is a leafy 189-hectare expanse popular with horse riders, joggers, cyclists and in-line skaters (for cycle and in-line skate hire see

p217 and p175); it also offers barbecue sites, playgrounds and football fields. Built in 1888 in the grand Victorian tradition, it has wide formal avenues, ponds and numerous statues. The spot where Australia was officially proclaimed a nation (on 1 January 1901) is marked by the Federation Pavilion.

During summer, you can catch the Moonlight Cinema (p170) here, as well as various rock concerts. At the southern edge of the park is Royal Randwick Racecourse (p179), while on its eastern edge it joins Queens Park and continues for another 26 hectares.

MOORE PARK Map pp84–5

☎ 9339 6699; www.cp.nsw.gov.au; Anzac Pde; 🚌 339
Part of the Centennial Parklands – a huge green swathe that cuts from Surry Hills to Bondi – Moore Park covers 115 hectares

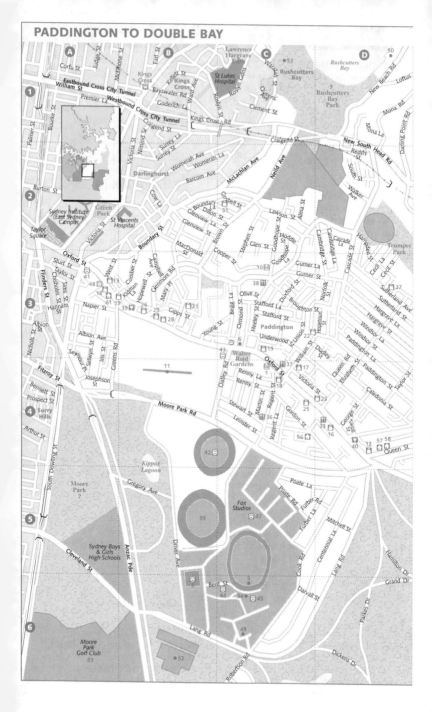

PADDINGTON TO DOUBLE BAY

TRANSPORT: PADDINGTON TO DOUBLE BAY

Bus Routes 378 (to/from Railway Square and Bronte), 380 (between Circular Quay and Watsons Bay via Bondi) and 352 (between Bondi Junction and Newtown via Surry Hills) cover Oxford St. From Oxford St, Woollahra, route 355 connects Bondi Junction to Newtown via Surry Hills, Redfern, Alexandria and Erskineville. Bus 389 connects North Bondi and Circular Quay via Woollahra's Moncur St. Buses 324-5 pass through Edgecliff and Double Bay (to/from Circular Quay and Watsons Bay).

Train Walk downhill from Edgecliff Station to Rushcutters Bay, Double Bay and the bottom of Paddington.

Ferry Services stopping in Double Bay connect Watsons Bay and Circular Quay.

Parking Street parking is usually possible, although often metered and limited in duration.

just south of Paddington, including sports fields, tennis and netball courts, an 18-hole public golf course (p177) and a site for visiting circuses. The broader precinct also includes the homes of the Sydney Swans Aussie rules team, the Sydney City Roosters rugby league team and the Sydney Gay & Lesbian Mardi Gras Party – the historic Sydney Cricket Ground (SCG), Aussie Stadium and the Hordern Pavilion, respectively. Try not to get them confused! Fox Studios and the Entertainment Quarter (p86) add further to the mix.

SCG Tour Experience (☎ 1300 724 737; www.scgt .nsw.gov.au/tours.html; adult/child/family $25/17/65; ◷ tours 10am & 1pm Mon-Fri, 10pm Sat) are behind-the-scenes guided tours of the facilities at Aussie Stadium and the SCG, giving sports fans the chance to run up the players' tunnel from the dressing rooms in their own Grand Final moment.

AUSTRALIAN CENTRE FOR PHOTOGRAPHY Map pp84–5

☎ 9332 1455; www.acp.org.au; 257 Oxford St, Paddington; admission free; ◷ noon-7pm Tue-Fri, 10am-6pm Sat & Sun; 🚌 380

This not-for-profit centre has wonderful regular exhibitions of the work of Sydney's best photographers. You can pick up a copy of the centre's magazine, *Photofile*, while you're there.

SHERMAN CONTEMPORARY ART FOUNDATION Map pp84–5

☎ 9331 1112; www.sherman-scaf.org.au; 16 Goodhope St, Paddington; admission free; ◷ 10am-6pm Tue-Fri, 11am-6pm Sat; 🚌 389

After 21 years as a cutting-edge commercial gallery, at the time of research Sherman Galleries was preparing to celebrate its coming-of-age by re-opening as a not-for-profit gallery. The focus will be on temporary exhibitions of work by influential and innovative artists from Australia and the Asia-Pacific region. Details such as opening hours may change, so it would pay to call ahead.

ENTERTAINMENT QUARTER Map pp84–5

☎ 9383 4333; www.entertainmentquarter.com.au; 122 Lang Rd, Moore Park; ◷ 10am-midnight; 🚌 339

Formerly named after neighbouring Fox Studios (where *Moulin Rouge*, *The Matrix* and two *Star Wars* prequels were made), this very-LA entertainment complex spreads along a palm-lined avenue. It boasts cinemas, shops, restaurants, pubs and performance venues and is home to two popular markets (p124). There's a monster car park and disabled access is very good.

JUNIPER HALL Map pp84–5

www.nsw.nationaltrust.org.au/properties/juniper hall/; 250 Oxford St, Paddington; ◷ 10am-5.30pm Mon-Fri, 10am-4pm Sat; 🚌 380

This magnificently restored Georgian mansion was built by Robert Cooper as a family home in 1824 with profits from his gin business. He named it after a key gin-making ingredient. Paddington's oldest home, it's owned by the National Trust but tenanted as a shop specialising in antiques and decorative arts; there's nothing to stop you having a nosy inside during opening hours.

PADDINGTON MARKET Map pp84–5

☎ 9331 2923; www.paddingtonmarket.com.au; St John's Church, 395 Oxford St, Paddington; ◷ 10am-4pm Sat; 🚌 380

A cultural experience, these quirky, long-running markets turn Saturdays in Paddington into pandemonium. Originating in the heady Whitlam era of the 1970s, Paddington Markets were a beacon for larrikin artists and artisans, Eastern Suburbs punks, skinheads, patchouli-scented hippies and fledgling fashion designers. It's a tad more mainstream now, but still worth checking out for its pricey cutting-edge fashions and vintage clothing, creative crafts, beautiful jewellery, tasty food, palm-reading and holistic treatments. Don't even think about finding a place to park – this is one for public transport.

LINDESAY
☎ 9363 2401; www.nsw.nationaltrust.org
.au/properties/lindesay; 1a Carthona Ave, Darling
Point; admission $6; ⏲ 10am-2pm 1st Thu of the
month; ⚓ Darling Point

It's rarely open but aside from Nicole Kidman inviting you in for tea, this is probably your best chance to look inside an actual Darling Point mansion. Built in 1834, it's still got its Georgian interiors, servants' quarters and long lawn overlooking the harbour.

RUSHCUTTERS BAY PARK Map pp84–5
New South Head Rd, Rushcutters Bay; ⚌ 324-5

This delightful waterfront park is an ideal spot for a quiet walk or jog, surrounded by enormous Moreton Bay figs, luxury yachts and overly pampered pooches. In December this is where you'll find the country's greatest yachties as they prepare for the gruelling Sydney to Hobart race (p19).

REDLEAF POOL Map pp84–5
536 New South Head Rd, Double Bay; ⚌ 324-5

Not really a pool at all, Redleaf is the closest swimmable beach to the city – and as such attracts an urbane collection of inner-eastern locals. A boardwalk runs around the top of a shark-net, giving it an enclosed pool-like feel. This and two floating pontoons are highly sought-after posing platforms for those who confuse beaches with catwalks. The western end is popular with families, who enjoy the sense of security

the shark-net brings, while the eastern is nearly exclusively colonised by gay men.

QUEEN STREET Map pp84–5
Woollahra; ⚌ 389

Despite its status as the premier antique shopping strip in Australia (its first antique shop opened in 1957), elegant tree-lined Queen St retains a village atmosphere, with attractive boutiques that make for great window-shopping. It was once the site of a famous annual street fair until the delicate residents had it shut down in the early 1980s, unhappy with the noise. Paul Keating, former prime minister, owns a grand home here.

FOLLOW THE FASHION TRAIL
Walking Tour

1 Victoria Barracks This place (p83) is still an active Army base, so you'll have to catch a view of the impressive Georgian sandstone structure from the guarded gate. Cross Oxford St, turn left and head down to Glenmore Rd where temptation comes by way of a cluster of boutiques.

WALK FACTS

Start **Victoria Barracks**
End **Centennial Park**
Distance **4km**
Duration **Two hours (not including Centennial Park or extended shopping frenzies)**
Fuel stops **Continuously available**

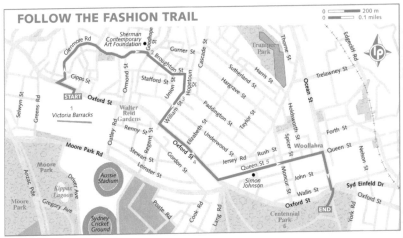

FOLLOW THE FASHION TRAIL

2 Five Ways Turn right into Glenmore Rd and follow it as it curves around for several blocks to Five Ways, a roundabout at the confluence of five roads. While Oxford St is the main strip, this charming collection of cafés and shops is the residential heart of Paddington – surrounded by million-dollar-plus terrace houses.

3 William Street boutiques At Five Ways stop for a quick look around the Sherman Contemporary Art Foundation gallery (p86) at the beginning of Goodhope St, before heading uphill along Broughton St, turning right into Hopetoun St and following this to William St. This quiet side street has sprouted a strip of relaxed boutiques.

4 Oxford Street, Paddington Turn left into Oxford St, Sydney's main fashionista thoroughfare. Both local and international designers are represented, selling swanky threads for women and men. Cafés, pubs and homeware stores join the race to prise your credit card out of your wallet.

5 Queen Street, Woollahra At the end of the strip turn left into Queen St, the beginning of upmarket Woollahra. There are a few leading boutiques at the beginning, but gradually they give way to antique stores and providores. Simon Johnson (p129) at number 55 usually has tastings, so drop in for a free nibble.

6 Centennial Park Turn right into Ocean St and follow this back up to Oxford St. Cross the road and enter Centennial Park (p83). There's a lot of park to explore – if you're not too laden down with shopping bags. Lighten the load by getting stuck into the yummies you couldn't resist buying at Simon Johnson.

SURRY HILLS TO ALEXANDRIA

Drinking & Nightlife p161; Eating p145; Shopping p129; Sleeping p194

Collectively known as South Sydney, this area has long had a reputation as a tough, tightly-knit working class community. While its city-fringe terraces are fast becoming flash, there's still a lively mix of racial and sexual minorities, and the inner city's biggest Aboriginal population.

Squeezed between the east side of Central Station and South Dowling St, Surry Hills is the most obvious recipient of relentless gentrification. Once the hub of the rag trade and print media, it's now increasingly known as Sydney's pre-eminent dining precinct. Gay men are now the most easily identifiable grouping in the suburb.

Not as sleazy as Darlinghurst, Surry Hills' leafy backstreets make a great base for exploring the city – although sleeping options are limited. Crown St, heading south from Oxford St, is the main drag and, along with quiet Bourke St, it has most of the restaurants, funky boutiques and trendy bars. At its south edge, Cleveland St has cheaper dining options including a cluster of vegetarian Indian eateries.

Heading further south, Redfern and Waterloo have held on to their traditional character more tightly but have a grittier reputation as a result.

Tensions boiled over into a night of rioting in 2004 when a 17-year-old Aboriginal boy died while being pursued by police. The Block, an area of Aboriginal housing near Redfern station, is a virtual no-go zone where it's not unusual to see fires lit on the street and dealers openly pushing heroin. No matter how genuinely interested you are in seeing 'the real Sydney' you're not going to win any friends poking around here with your camera.

Bizarrely, the last few years have seen Danks St in Waterloo transform into an art and gourmet food enclave – well worth checking out.

Further south still, Alexandria is a mostly industrial area and a great spot to find bargain-basement factory shops.

BRETT WHITELEY STUDIO Map pp90–1

☎ 9225 1881; www.brettwhiteley.org; 2 Raper St, Surry Hills; adult/concession $7/5; ☺ 10am-4pm Sat & Sun; 🚌 301-303

Down a small lane hides the former studio of this renowned modern Australian artist. You can identify it by the two oversized matches (one burnt, one intact) at the door – a miniature version of his famous sculpture in The Domain (p66). The studio houses a selection of Whiteley's work and has been preserved to show how the artist operated before his untimely death in 1992.

OBJECT GALLERY Map pp90–1

☎ 9361 4555; www.object.com.au; 417 Bourke St, Surry Hills; admission free; ☺ 11am-6pm Tue-Sun; 🚌 380

Also known as the Australian Centre for Craft and Design, Object Gallery focuses on contemporary Australian design in a variety of materials, encompassing everything from furniture to fashion to kitchen utensils. It occupies the delicious chapel of the former St Margaret's Hospital, an intriguing design in itself – round with panels of coloured glass.

TRANSPORT: SURRY HILLS TO ALEXANDRIA

Train Walk uphill from Central for the western edge of Surry Hills, or use Museum for the blocks around Oxford St. Most lines stop at Redfern Station. For Alexandria use Green Square.

Bus To/from Circular Quay, routes 301-3 take Crown St and carry on to Waterloo, routes 309-10 skirt the western edge of Surry Hills before heading through Redfern and Alexandria, and route 339 to Clovelly passes through Surry Hills. Route 372 heads along Cleveland St to/from Railway Square and Coogee. Route 355 and 352 connect Bondi Junction to Newtown via Surry Hills and Redfern (the former through Alexandria and Erskineville, the latter through Oxford St).

Parking Street parking is usually possible, although often metered and limited in duration. Don't leave valuables visible.

SURRY HILLS TO ALEXANDRIA

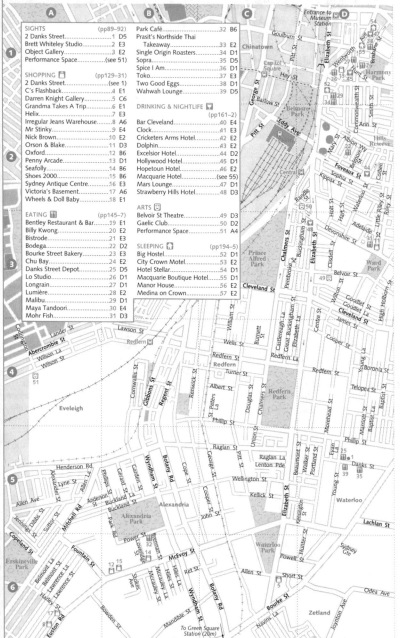

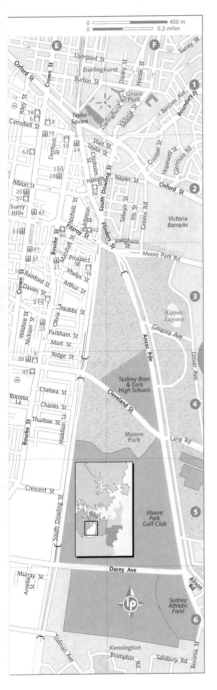

DANKS STREET Map pp90–1

☎ 9361 4555; www.2danksstreet.com.au;
2 Danks St, Waterloo; admission free;
⏰ 11am-6pm Tue-Sat; 🚌 301-303

If the wonderful Danks Street Depot café (p130) isn't enough to tempt you off the beaten track to Waterloo, the nine commercial galleries that inhabit this warehouse conversion should push you over the edge. They encompass a broad range of contemporary art, including Aboriginal and Pacific art, photography, sculpture, painting and jewellery.

PERFORMANCE SPACE Map pp90–1

☎ 9698 7235; www.performancespace.com.au;
245 Wilson St, Redfern; admission free; ⏰ noon-8pm Wed-Sat; 🚆 Redfern

This avant-garde arts project has recently relocated to Carriageworks – a fascinating group of huge Victorian-era factories that were part of the Eveleigh Railyards – where as well as performances (see p171) they have a shed devoted to installation and multi-media art.

A SURRY HILLS STROLL
Walking Tour

1 Taylor Square Start at the Surry Hills end of Taylor Square, near the Taylor Square Hotel. Before you head up Bourke St note the attractive Art Deco Belgenny apartment building (corner Bourke and Campbell Sts) and the antique red post box.

2 Greek Orthodox Church of St Sophia

In the first block of Bourke St there are rare reminders of the neighbourhood's once visible Greek community. At 407, Christopher's Cake Shop has been selling Greek sweets since 1955. A few doors down, St Sophia's church is normally closed unless services are being held.

3 St Margaret's A short stroll further along Bourke is the site of the old St Margaret's Hospital, housing the Object Gallery (p89). Its pricey apartments and restaurants stand in stark contrast to the sandstone Wesleyan Chapel (1847) across the road. Behind its façade the Edward Eager Lodge serves the neighbourhood's many homeless.

A SURRY HILLS STROLL

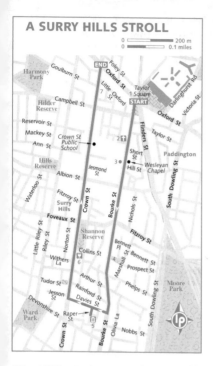

WALK FACTS

Start Taylor Square
End Oxford St
Distance 2km
Duration One hour
Fuel stops The Crown Hotel and many other restaurants, bars and cafés

a straight ex-plumber and a staunch supporter of gay rights.

5 Brett Whiteley's Studio Note the row of particularly grand four-storey terraces starting at No 520. Turn right into Davies St into a tight web of laneways. Raper St is on the left and the large matchsticks on the wall will help you spot Brett Whiteley's Studio (p89).

6 Clock Backtrack then continue left along Davies St until you come out on Crown St, Surry Hills' main strip and a glutton's paradise. Turn right and note for future reference the location of some of the city's best restaurants. If you're getting thirsty, call into the Clock (p162).

7 Secondhand clothing boutiques Continue along Crown St past more terraces and pubs (turn it into a pub crawl if you must). Look out for the stately Crown Street Public School (1849) on your right, with a statue of a WWI digger out the front. When you start to hit the secondhand clothing boutiques you'll know you're nearing Oxford St.

4 Fred Miller Park Continuing along Bourke you'll pass some interesting houses, including a sandstone Georgian block with a deep veranda and some large Victorian terraces, gentrified and otherwise. Just after No 454 a small park commemorates a very-Surry Hills character. Fred Miller was a Labor politician,

BONDI TO COOGEE

Drinking & Nightlife p163; Eating p147; Shopping p131; Sleeping p195

Glorious stretches of golden sand framed by sheer cliffs, the Eastern Beaches are a big part of Sydney's appeal. Most famous of all is the broad sweep of Bondi Beach, only 7km from the CBD yet a world away; the stunning scenery and constant procession of beautiful bods is enough to take anyone's mind off work. This is where Sydney comes to see and be seen – preferably wearing as little as possible. It's not an affirming place for those with body image issues.

Bondi Junction is an innocuous transport hub at the end of Oxford St. Bondi Rd begins here, passing through Bondi proper before swooping down to Campbell Pde, the beachfront road where most of the hotels and pubs are located.

Bondi wasn't always known for million-dollar apartments and flashiness. Traditionally the neighbourhood of choice for New Zealand migrants (including a strong Maori community), until recently it was the frequent butt of sneering 'Kiwi dole-bludger' comments. More noticeable due to their distinctive garb is a large Hassidic Jewish community concentrated around several synagogues in the steep back streets.

top picks

BONDI TO COOGEE

- Bondi Beach (left)
- Clovelly Beach (p97)
- Waverley Cemetery (p96)
- Coogee Ocean Pools (p96)
- Bronte Beach (p96)

South of Bondi, Tamarama (aka 'Glamarama') is a lovely cove with notorious rips. Below Tamarama you'll find family-friendly Bronte and its pretty bowl-shaped park with picnic tables and coin-operated barbecues. While brunching on the popular café strip during the winter months you may catch sight of the watery snorts of migrating whales.

Further south is the shallow, protected lagoon of Clovelly. Swimming is excellent, and the water is home to an abundance of marine life that attracts both snorkellers and divers.

Four kilometres south of Bondi, Coogee is nearly a carbon copy of its famous sister but without the airs and graces. While it takes longer to get here on public transport, budget accommodation options here are generally of a better standard than at Bondi.

Inland, Randwick is home to a famous racecourse and the University of New South Wales.

BONDI

BONDI BEACH Map pp94–5

Campbell Pde, Bondi; 🚌 380

Sydney's (indeed, Australia's) most famous beach, Bondi lures people from around the world with its promise of sun, sand, surf and exposed skin, and all just 8km from the CBD. The average water temperature is a pleasant 21°C. If you don't like it rough, there are saltwater swimming pools at either end – great for the kids.

The two surf clubs – Bondi and North Bondi – patrol the beach between sets of flags. These are positioned to avoid the worst rips and holes; don't be an idiot – swim between them. Try not to be one of the thousands of tourists and locals who have to be rescued every year. Surfers ride breaks at either end of the beach and it's a good place for learners (see p178). Near the

south end of the beach is a popular skate ramp. If posing in your budgie smugglers (Speedos) isn't having enough impact, there's an outdoor work-out area near the North Bondi Surf Club. Coincidentally this is the part of the beach where the gay guys tend to hang out.

Bondi Pavilion (below) has changing rooms and lockers, along with a gelato shop. Ice-cream vendors also strut the sand in summer. At the north end there's a lovely grassy spot with coin-operated barbecues. Alcohol is forbidden on the beach.

BONDI PAVILION Map pp94–5

☎ 8362 3400; www.waverley.nsw.gov.au/info /pavilion/; Queen Elizabeth Dr, Bondi; 🚌 380

'The Pav', just off the esplanade, is a 1929 Mediterranean Georgian Revival-style edifice. It has changing rooms, lockers and

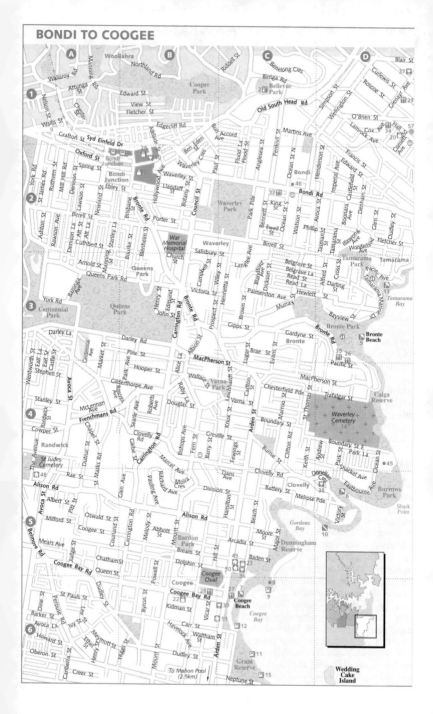

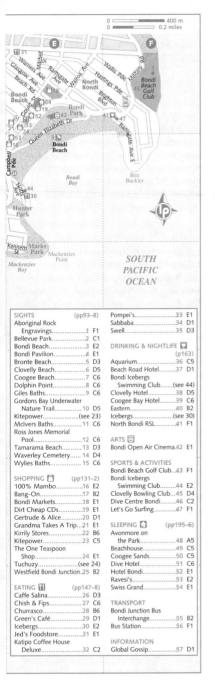

SOUTH
PACIFIC
OCEAN

TRANSPORT: BONDI TO COOGEE

Train Take the train to Bondi Junction for Bondi (then bus 380, 381 or 382), Tamarama (then bus 361), Bronte (then bus 360, 361 or 378), Clovelly (then bus 360) or Coogee (then bus 313, 314 or 353).

Bus For Bondi take bus 380 from Watsons Bay or Circular Quay via Oxford St, or 389 from Circular Quay via Woollahra. For Bronte take bus 378 from Railway Square via Oxford St. For Clovelly take bus 339 from The Rocks via Surry Hills. For Coogee take bus 373 from Circular Quay via Oxford St or bus 372 from Railway Square via Surry Hills. For Bondi Junction take any of the Oxford St routes or 352/355 from Newtown via Redfern and Surry Hills.

Parking Difficult on sunny weekends – be prepared to park and walk. Bronte has only limited-duration meters near the beach.

showers, as well as a theatre and gallery hosting cultural and community events, holiday entertainment for kids and a plethora of classes.

ABORIGINAL ROCK ENGRAVINGS Map pp94–5
Bondi Golf Course, Military Rd, North Bondi; 380
On the golf course a short walk north (and uphill) from Bondi Beach, you'll find some interesting Aboriginal rock engravings. Look for the fenced areas about 20m southeast of the enormous chimney. The original carvings had to be regrooved by Waverley Council in the 1960s in order to preserve them. Some of the figures are a little hard to distinguish, though you should be able to make out the marine life and the figure of a man. There's also a great lookout at the end of Ramsgate Ave with stunning views back over Bondi Beach.

BELLEVUE PARK Map pp94–5
Bellevue Park Rd, Bellevue Hill; 326-7
This quiet suburban park has brilliant views over Bondi and all the heads – North, South and Middle. When the early Irish convicts named it Vinegar Hill, after a battle in the 1798 Irish Rebellion, Governor Macquarie stepped in and officially named

top picks

BEACHES

- Bondi Beach (p93)
- Whale Beach (p112)
- Dee Why (p112)
- Cronulla (p120)
- Balmoral (p111)

it Bellevue Hill, after the beautiful views. The surrounding neighbourhood is home to a large Jewish community and some of Sydney's richest and most famous, including the Packer media clan and actress Toni Collette.

BRONTE

BRONTE BEACH Map pp94–5
Bronte Rd, Bronte; 🚌 339
A superb family-orientated beach hemmed in by sandstone cliffs and a grassy park, Bronte claims to have the oldest surf life-saving club in the world (dating back to 1903). Locals pronounce it 'Bronty', not like the name of the famous authoring sisters. In fact, it's named after Lord Nelson who was the Duke of Bronte, a place in Sicily.

A toy train chugs around during the warmer months offering children's rides. There's a kiosk and changing room attached to the surf club and plenty of outdoor seating near the coin-operated barbecues. Parking is a nightmare.

WAVERLEY CEMETERY Map pp94–5
☎ 9665 4938; www.waverley.nsw.gov.au /cemetery; St Thomas Street, Bronte; 🕐 7am-sunset; 🚌 378
Many Sydneysiders would die for these views, and that's the only way they're going to get them. Perched on the cliffs between Bronte and Coogee the white marble gravestones are dazzling in the sunlight. Eighty-thousand people have been interred here since 1877, including writer and poet Henry Lawson. It's a fascinating place to potter about and a good spot for whale-watching in the winter months.

TAMARAMA BEACH Map pp94–5
Pacific Ave; 🚌 361
When it got its nickname Glamarama in the 1980s, this was probably Sydney's gayest beach. Perhaps it's a sign of increasing acceptance that the gay guys have migrated en masse to North Bondi, leaving the huge waves to the surfers. Surrounded by high cliffs it's a lovely spot with only 80m of water line but a deep tongue of sand and parkland. It's considered the single most dangerous patrolled beach in New South Wales due to its ever-present rips; it's often closed to swimmers. From 1887 to 1911 a rollercoaster looped over the water in Sydney's first coastal amusement park.

COOGEE

COOGEE BEACH Map pp94–5
Arden St, Coogee; 🚌 372-3
Bondi without the glitz and the posers, Coogee has a lovely sweep of golden sand, historic ocean baths (right) and plenty of green space for barbecues and Frisbee-throwing. Locals clip both syllables and pronounce the double 'o' like in the word 'took'. It's believed to have its origins in an Aboriginal word meaning 'smelly place' – probably a reference to the seaweed that gets washed up after storms; nowadays it's cleared before it ever lives up to the name. Between the wars Coogee had an English-style pier, with a 1400-seat theatre and 600-seat ballroom – until the surf took it.

DOLPHIN POINT Map pp94–5
Cnr Beach & Baden Sts, Coogee; 🚌 372-3
This grassy park at Coogee Beach's northern end offers great ocean views, and has a delightful ocean pool. A sobering shrine commemorates the locals killed in the Bali bombings of 12 October 2002. This neighbourhood was hit hard by the tragedy, with 20 locals killed out of a total of 89 Australians. Formerly known as Dunningham Park, its name was changed to honour the six members of the Coogee Dolphins A-grade rugby league team who were killed in the blast.

COOGEE OCEAN POOLS Map pp94–5
Coogee; 🚌 372-3
If you've got kids, shark-paranoia, or surf just isn't your thing, Sydney's blessed with

beautiful man-made ocean pools up and down the coast. Coogee's got the best of the bunch. The Ross Jones Memorial Pool, at the beach's southern end, has sand-castle-like concrete turrets. Perched against the cliffs to the south is McIvers Baths. Well screened from passers-by, this spot has been popular for women's bathing since before 1876. Its strictly women-only policy has made it popular with an unlikely mixture of nuns, Muslim women and topless lesbians. Further south still, Wylies Baths (adult/child $3/50¢) is for serious lap swimmers.

Closer to Maroubra is the Mahon Pool (Marine Pde, Maroubra; ☎ 399), an idyllic rock pool where the surf crashes over the edges at high tide.

CLOVELLY BEACH Map pp94–5
Clovelly Rd; ☎ 339
It might seem a little odd, but this ocean channel with concrete edging is a great place to swim, sunbathe and snorkel. It's safe for the kids, and the water is exceptionally clear. A handy sign identifies the kind of marine life you might encounter in the waters, including a metre-long blue grouper. On the other side of the car park is the entrance to the Gordons Bay Underwater Nature Trail, 500m of chain to guide divers through the reefs, sand-flats and kelp forests.

A COASTAL CRUISE
Walking Tour
1 Dolphin Point Wander past the friendly bustle of Coogee Beach. On calmer days you can snorkel in the rock pool at the northern end of the sand. A short walk north from the beach takes you to Dolphin Point (p96) where there's a sobering memorial to the victims of the 2002 Bali bombings.

WALK FACTS
Start Coogee Beach
End North Bondi
Distance 5km
Duration Two to 2½ hours
Fuel stops Many along the way

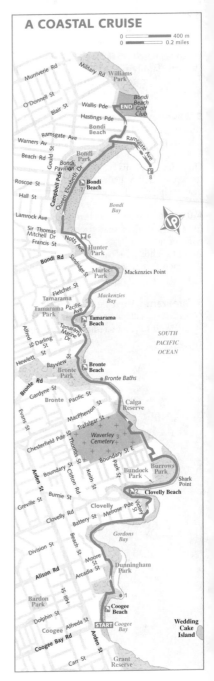

A COASTAL CRUISE

2 Clovelly Pass the native fauna and fishing boats of Gordon's Bay (one of Sydney's most popular dive spots), and continue on to sheltered Clovelly Beach (p97), a favourite with family picnickers. Here you will find a well protected, narrow rock pool for swimming.

3 Waverley Cemetery Further along, the stunning cliff-edge Waverley Cemetery (p96) is the final resting place for some famous Australians, most notably the poet Henry Lawson. On a clear day, this is a prime vantage point for keen whale-watchers. A series of pretty beaches lies ahead.

4 Bronte Descend the cliff-top path, pass (or take a dip) in the Bronte Baths and you will reach Bronte Beach (p96) where you are spoilt for choice for cafés. Cross the beautiful beach and pick up the path on the other side.

5 Tamarama A couple of hundred metres north is the small but prettily formed Tamarama Beach (p96). It has an incredibly deep stretch of sand, quite out of proportion to its width. Pick up the cliff-top path on the opposite side.

6 Icebergs As you wend your way around the coastal curves you will soon see the glorious sweep of Bondi Beach. Pass or go into the lavish Icebergs (p163) complex, depending on your thirst and the size of your wallet. You would need to have booked ahead to have any chance of a meal.

7 Bondi Beach You're now deep in Bondi territory. Head down the stairs, kick off the shoes and cut across the golden sand. Check out the graffiti wall to your left and the iconic Bondi Pavilion (p93). Note a car-sized rock near the very northern tip of the beach – this 235-tonne monster was spat out of the sea during a storm in 1912.

8 Ben Buckler Lookout Right at the end of the beach, head down Ramsgate Ave to the Ben Buckler Lookout and admire the view as well as the ground you have just covered. One worthwhile detour is to head up Military Rd to Bondi Beach Golf Club (p177), which has some interesting Aboriginal rock engravings (p95).

Arguably the city's coolest suburb, Newtown is a melting pot of stoned students, social and sexual subcultures, and spiffed-up home renovators. King St is lined with funky clothes shops, musty bookshops, cheap cafés and an inordinate number of Thai restaurants. While it's definitely moving up the social scale, Newtown comes with a healthy dose of eccentricity and political activism (a McDonald's branch that opened in the 1990s didn't last long).

Erskineville is similar but more upmarket, with an appealing village feel centred on its small hub of pubs and cafés.

On the other side of the university Glebe is home to students, New-Agers, lesbians, a sizable Aboriginal community and more than its fair share of the city's judges. The main thoroughfare, Glebe Point Rd, runs the length of the suburb from Broadway and offers affordable eateries, interesting shops and several good places to stay.

top picks

INNER WEST

- Nicholson Museum (p102)
- Camperdown Cemetery (left)
- Anzac Bridge (p103)
- University of Sydney (below)
- Sydney Park (left)

The area has been inhabited since the First Fleet's chaplain was granted the first church land (or glebe), covering an area of 160 hectares. Mansions started to spring up in 1826, but after 1855 the church leased the remaining land for down-market housing, which deteriorated into slums. In the mid-1970s Gough Whitlam's federal government bought the estate and rejuvenated the area for low-income families, many of whom have lived here for generations.

Once a tough, working-class neighbourhood, Balmain now rivals Paddington in Victorian-era trendiness – with the added advantage of being surrounded by water and only a short ferry ride from the city. Darling St runs the length of the peninsula and makes for a decent pub-crawl. Neighbouring Rozelle is more low-rent, but has some historic English-feeling pubs hidden in its back streets.

Norton St, the main drag of the predominantly Italian suburb of Leichhardt (affectionately known as Dykeheart to its lesbian residents), is known for its Italian restaurants and piazza.

NEWTOWN

CAMPERDOWN CEMETERY Map pp100–1

☎ 9557 2043; 189 Church St, Newtown; ☽ sunrise-sunset; ⊠ Newtown
Take a self-guided tour beyond the monstrous fig tree (which dates from 1848) into this woodsy, spider-web-filled and eerily unkempt cemetery. Many famous Aussies were buried here between 1849 and 1942, including Eliza Donnithorne, the inspiration for Miss Havisham in Dickens' *Great Expectations*. It's a great place to spot some big (up to 10cm) but harmless St Andrew's Cross Spiders.

SYDNEY PARK

Sydney Park Rd; ⊠ St Peters
Popular with dog-walkers and kite-flyers, Sydney Park is a great place to watch the sunrise and sunset. From the barren,

windswept hill the city rises like a volcanic island from a sea of suburbia, while to the south there's a view over the airport to Botany Bay. This 40-hectare site, opposite St Peters Station, has modern sculpture and sculptural-looking chimneys from its days as a brickworks; much of the pit has been converted to wetlands.

GLEBE

UNIVERSITY OF SYDNEY Map pp100–1

☎ 9351 2222; www.usyd.edu.au; Parramatta Rd; ⊠ 422-3
Australia's oldest tertiary institution (1850), the University of Sydney has over 45,000 students and even boasts its own postcode. You don't need to be an academic to grab a free campus map and wander around at your leisure. The Gothic Revival design of the Quadrangle tips its mortar board towards

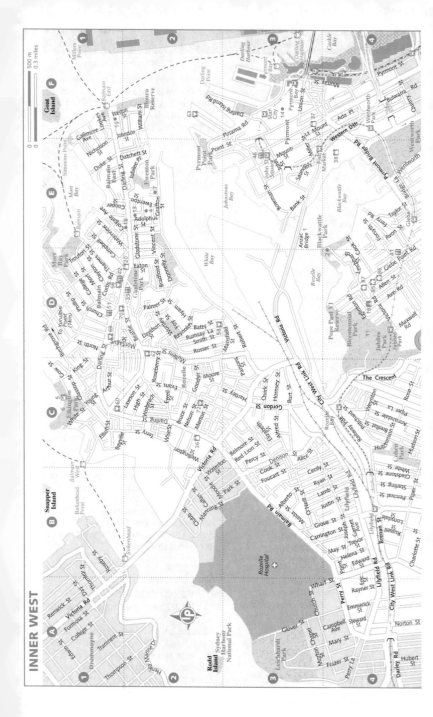

INNER WEST

the stately colleges of Oxford. It boasts two grand halls that wouldn't be out of place in Harry Potter's beloved Hogwarts, as well as the wonderful Nicholson Museum (below) and the small University Art Gallery. Nearby, the Macleay Museum has a musty dead smell associated with either old dons or its historic collection of taxidermied Australian fauna. If you want to be sure of seeing inside the usually locked Great Hall, enquire about guided tours ($11).

NICHOLSON MUSEUM Map pp100–1

☎ 9351 2812; www.usyd.edu.au/museums /about/nicholson.shtml; Bldg A14, Main Quadrangle, University of Sydney; admission free; ☑ 10am-4.30pm Mon-Fri, noon-4pm Sun; 🚊 422-3
Located near the University of Sydney's quad, this museum is a must-see for ancient history buffs. It houses an impressive display of Greek, Roman, Cypriot, Egyptian, and Near Eastern antiquities, including the mummified remains of a cat. It was

founded in 1860 by Sir Charles Nicholson, who was an important figure in the founding of both the University of Sydney and the Australian Museum.

VICTORIA PARK Map pp100–1
cnr Broadway & City Rd; 🚊 422-3
The green gateway to the Inner West and the University of Sydney, Victoria Park is a pleasant 9-hectare grassy space set around pond-like Lake Northam and Victoria Park Pool (p176). Every February 75,000 people descend on the park for the Sydney Gay & Lesbian Mardi Gras Fair Day – a fun family day that includes dog shows, live performances and the Miss Fair Day drag competition.

SZE YUP TEMPLE Map pp100–1
☎ 9660 6465; Edward St; MLR Jubilee Park
This humble temple was opened in 1898 by immigrants from the Sze Yup area of China. At Chinese New Year it's a hive of

activity, with people of various ethnicities coming to make offerings of incense and fruit. It's dedicated to 3rd-century folk hero Kwung Ti whose embroidered image in green robes, flanked by two guards, takes centre place on the altar. Known for his loyalty, physical prowess and masculinity, supplicants look to him as a wise judge, guide and protector. Respectful visitors are welcome to this sacred site. Remove your shoes before entering.

JUBILEE & BICENTENNIAL PARKS Map pp100–1
Glebe Point Rd; MLR Jubilee Park
At the northern tip of Glebe Point Rd these two large grassy parks merge together, offering good views across the bay to Rozelle. Looking towards the city you get a rare combined view of the Anzac and Harbour Bridges. Fig and palm trees dot the landscape and mums and dads stroll along with their kiddies. A new pathway leads along the shoreline to Blackwattle Bay, passing the Victorian Italianate Bellevue Cottage (1896) and a new park set around the temple-like ruins of an industrial incinerator.

PYRMONT
SYDNEY FISH MARKET Map pp100–1
☎ 9004 1100; www.sydneyfishmarket.com.au; Bank St, Pyrmont; ⊗ 7am-4pm; MLR Fish Market
With over 15 million kilograms of seafood sold and shifted out of here annually, this large fish market is the best place to get on first-name terms with a bewildering array of scaly critters. You can witness fish auctions happening in the early mornings, eat sushi or fish and chips all day, attend cooking classes (see left), and buy the freshest seafood in town.

STAR CITY Map pp100–1
☎ 9777 9000; www.starcity.com.au; 80 Pyrmont St, Pyrmont; ⊗ 24hr; MLR Star City
This large casino complex includes a major theatre, retail stores, restaurants, bars and a luxury hotel. It's located on the waterfront in Pyrmont, on the northwestern headland of Darling Harbour. The décor is best described as 'Disney-meets-Outback', complete with a lagoon bar (think indoor waterfall), fake palm trees and flashy lights all over the place.

ANZAC BRIDGE Map pp100–1
Western Distributor
Completed in 1996, Sydney's other eye-catching bridge spans Johnstons Bay, connecting Pyrmont and Rozelle. At 345m in length it's the longest cable bridge in Australia, offering great views as you stroll into the city from the west. The two main towers are shaped like the eye of a needle, with the road as the thread. The Anzac theme is reinforced by an Australian flag atop the eastern tower, a New Zealand flag on the western, and a bronze statue of a soldier.

BALMAIN & LEICHHARDT
ELKINGTON PARK Map pp100–1
cnr Glassop & White Sts; ⚓ Balmain West
This small, peaceful and hilly park on a waterfront escarpment was named in 1883 after a local politician. On its grounds is the oldest swimming club in Australia (1888),

which owns the murky saltwater Dawn Fraser Baths (☎ 9555 1903; adult/child $3.40/$2.30; ☿ 7.15am-6.30pm Oct-Apr), named after Australia's greatest-ever swimmer and local-girl-turned-world-champion.

YURULBIN POINT
Louisa Rd; ⚓ Birchgrove
At the northern tip of the Balmain peninsula, this narrow point stretches to within 300m of the North Shore. Once called Long Nose Point, it was changed back to its original name (meaning 'swift running water') in 1994. It was originally inhabited by the Wangal clan, of which Bennelong is thought to have been a member (see p23). There are great views up the harbour towards the bridge, making this a popular firework-watching spot. Louisa Rd is one of Sydney's most expensive streets; Birchgrove House (c1810) at number 16 was the first residence in the area.

BALMAIN HISTORIC BUILDINGS Map pp100–1
⚓ Balmain East
Balmain's pretty streets are home to dozens of significant buildings, most of which are privately owned. The most notable is Hampton Villa (12b Grafton St), a marine villa in the Georgian style (1847). From 1888 to 1892 it was the home of 'The Father of Federation', NSW Premier Sir Henry Parkes. At least one cabinet meeting was held here during the constitutional debates. Nearby is Clontarf (4 Wallace St), an impressively restored house (1844) saved by local protests, and St Mary's Hall (7 Adolphus St), built around 1851. At 179 Darling St is Sydney's oldest surviving lockup, the Watch House (1854), and at No 12 is Waterman's Cottage (1841)

ITALIAN FORUM Map pp100–1
☎ 9518 3396; www.theitalianforum.com; 23 Norton St, Leichhardt; 🚌 436-8
This re-creation of an Italian piazza has had its fair share of criticism and compliments, and yes, it is a bit cheesy (think Disney does Italy), but the Italian Forum is a good place to partake in fairly authentic Italian grub. Order a gelato or a macchiato, check everyone out and remember to say 'ciao' whenever possible. The Forum is home to shops, family-friendly restaurants and a library.

A WILD WESTERN WANDER
Walking Tour
1 Erskineville Village As you come out of the train station turn left and walk through Erskineville village. On your left you'll pass the lovely tiled pub, Rose of Australia (p164), and on your right the defunct South Sydney City Council Chambers (it was merged with the City of Sydney in 2004) and the Art Deco Erskineville Hotel.

2 Imperial Hotel If you experience déjà vu as you reach the Imperial Hotel (p184) at the corner of Union St, it may be that you recognise this as the spot the bus set off from in classic Aussie flick *The Adventures of Priscilla, Queen of the Desert*. The Sydney drag scenes were filmed inside.

WALK FACTS
Start **Erskineville Station**
End **Glebe Point Rd**
Distance **4km**
Duration **Two hours plus bookshop browsing time**
Fuel Stops **Hard to avoid**

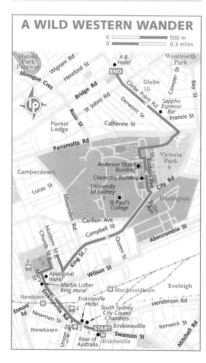

A WILD WESTERN WANDER

3 Union Street An unassuming house on this quiet suburban street was the setting for the 'Battle of Union St' in June 1931, one of several eviction battles during the Great Depression. Hundreds of people jeered on the street as police brutally evicted the occupants, including members of the Unemployed Workers Movement, who had barricaded themselves inside.

4 Green Bans Park Another Socialist landmark is a small park a block further along Erskineville Rd, just before the railway bridge, which owes its existence to the Green Bans. Ceramic tiles tell the story of the 1992 union construction ban that led to this land being retained as a park for the local community.

5 Camperdown Memorial Rest Park Cross the bridge and head to King St, Newtown. Across the road is a large mural honouring Martin Luther King. Cross King St and cut down Mary St, noting the Aboriginal mural on the wall. Directly ahead is the Camperdown Memorial Rest Park, Newtown's green meeting place.

6 Camperdown Cemetery Turn right then left into Church St. You'll find the evocatively ramshackle Camperdown Cemetery (p99) on your left. Grab a self-guided tour pamphlet from the box near the gate and explore.

7 King Street, Newtown Leaving the cemetery go straight ahead then turn right into Hordern St – noting the mix of grungy and gentrified villas – before turning left into King St. As you pass the boutiques, bookshops and bars, notice the lovely old buildings forming Newtown's largely intact old streetscape.

8 University of Sydney By the time you pass Carillon Ave, you're in Sydney Uni (p99) territory. You can catch glimpses of grand St Paul's College behind the wrought iron fence. Enter the campus by the drive opposite Butlin Ave and follow Eastern Ave past the Norman-looking Madsen Building, the ugly Chemistry block and the gorgeous Gothic Revival Anderson Stuart Building.

9 Victoria Park Ahead is the main university building, housing the Quadrangle, Nicholson Museum (p102), MacLaurin Hall and the Great Hall. Wander around and explore whatever's open. Leave by the main entrance and take the grand path through Victoria Park (p102), veering to the left at the bottom of the stairs, keeping the pond on your right.

10 Glebe Cross busy Parramatta Rd and head down Glebe Point Rd. It's a little like Newtown's begun again, with an eclectic collection of cafés, health stores and some excellent bookshops. Finish with a coffee at the Sappho Espresso Bar (p149) or, if you're after something harder, continue down to the A.B. Hotel (p165).

Drinking & Nightlife p166; Eating p150; Sleeping p197

The amorphous sprawling suburbs north of the harbour are lumped together under the umbrella of the North Shore.

The Harbour Bridge reaches to Milsons Point which, along with McMahons Point to the west and Kirribilli to the east, is a pleasant harbourside suburb with stunning city views. To the north the towers of North Sydney are a continuation of the CBD, but without the pizzazz. It's the preserve of advertising and recruitment agencies, and a handful of pubs. There's not a lot to do here, but the proximity to the city makes it worth considering as a place to stay.

Military Rd is the main artery heading east towards Manly. It passes through the largely residential areas of Neutral Bay, Cremorne and Mosman (one of Sydney's wealthiest suburbs), all of which have pretty bays, strips of bushland and multi-million-dollar houses.

It's due to its military use that the scrub-covered coast leading to Middle Head has been left much as the First Fleet would have found it. While the navy still controls some land, most has been turned over to Sydney Harbour National Park (below).

The beachside suburb of Balmoral faces Manly across Middle Harbour. It has a fine beach and some good restaurants.

top picks

NORTH SHORE

- Taronga Zoo (left)
- Fort Denison (opposite)
- Balmoral (p111)
- Whale Beach (p112)
- Manly Scenic Walkway (p110)

Sydney's other iconic beach, Manly straddles a narrow peninsula that ends at the cliffs of North Head (p109). Proving that even Sydney's first governor wasn't beyond checking out the locals' bods, His Excellency named it after the 'manly' physique of the indigenous people he met here.

This popular beachside village boasts a lively holiday-resort atmosphere along with a keen sense of local identity. Most of The Corso (the cheeky pedestrian mall that links the harbour with the ocean) is lined with touristy shops, mediocre eateries and boozy bars – its brashness a refreshing change from the prim surrounding suburbs.

Spread out over 25km and reaching to Sydney's northern limits, the Northern Beaches are some of the city's finest.

LOWER NORTH SHORE

TARONGA ZOO Map p108

☎ 9969 2777; www.zoo.nsw.gov.au; Bradleys Head Rd, Mosman; adult/child $32/18; ☼ 9am-5pm; 🚢 Taronga Zoo

Not even the governor general has views as good as Taronga's residents. A definite Sydney highlight, this exceptional zoo boasts a spectacular location, which over 3000 furry, scaly and feathered critters (including a substantial number of Australian natives) call home. The animals are well looked after, and there are more natural open enclosures than cages. A zoo fave is the nocturnal platypus habitat, in which day and night have been switched to give you an opportunity to see the little guys partying. The koala and giraffe displays offer great photo ops ($3), and the seal and bird shows are also popular (so find a seat in advance).

Ferries leave regularly, taking only 12 minutes from Circular Quay. From the wharf there's a cable car and bus that will whisk you to the main entrance, allowing you to traverse the zoo downhill back to the ferry. A ZooPass (adult/child $39/21), sold at Circular Quay and elsewhere, includes return ferry rides and zoo admission. Parking ($10) is available for 500 cars. Disabled access is good, even if arriving by ferry, and wheelchairs are available.

SYDNEY HARBOUR NATIONAL PARK Map pp50–1

www.nationalparks.nsw.gov.au/parks.nsf

One of the qualities that make Sydney such a wonderful city is its close proximity to beautiful bushland and stunning seascapes. The Sydney Harbour National Park protects the large swathe of bushland around the harbour and includes several small islands (below). It offers great walking tracks, scenic lookouts, Aboriginal carvings, beaches and a handful of historic sites. While the park incorporates South Head (p116) and Nielsen Park (p116) on the south side, the largest part of it is on the North Shore – including Bradleys Head, Middle Head, Dobroyd Head and North Head (p109). Free brochures, including self-tours, are available from the park office in Cadman's Cottage (p56), which itself is part of the park.

LUNA PARK Map p108

☎ 9922 6644; www.lunaparksydney.com; admission free; 1 Olympic Dr, Milsons Point; ⏰ 10am-6pm Sun, 11am-6pm Mon & Thu, 11am-11pm Fri, 10am-6pm Sun; ﹦ Milsons Point

A colourful landmark, this old-fashioned amusement park opened in 1935 but served a long spell locked up before its toothy gates reopened in 2004. You can pay as you go, or buy a height-based unlimited ride pass (over 130cm/106-129cm/85-105cm $42/32/20). Kids under 85cm can ride the Ferris wheel and carousel for free. If you're creeped out by clowns and ventriloquist dolls, avoid looking too hard at the painted signs. Even John Wayne Gacy would find the disastrous dentistry and spiky metal eyelashes of the clown entrance a bit sinister. During school and public holidays Luna Park opens daily, with extended hours.

MARY MACKILLOP PLACE Map p108

☎ 8912 4878; www.marymackillopplace.org.au; 7 Mount St, North Sydney; adult/concession/family $7.50/5/15; ⏰ 10am-4pm; ﹦ North Sydney

This museum tells the life story of Australia's first hope for a saint, a dedicated and

TRANSPORT: NORTH SHORE

Ferry The nicest way to travel between Circular Quay and McMahons Point, Milsons Point, Kirribilli, North Sydney, Neutral Bay, Cremorne, Mosman, Taronga Zoo and Manly.

Train Milsons Point and North Sydney are stops on the North Shore and Northern lines. The Northern Line will take you all the way to the outskirts of Ku-ring-gai Chase National Park.

Bus From Wynyard Park in the city, buses pass through North Sydney, Cremorne and Mosman en route to Taronga Zoo (247), Balmoral (246), Obelisk Bay (244), The Spit (248-9, 172-3), Manly (169), Dee Why (178) and the tip of the Northern Beaches (L88, L90). Routes 272-3 head to Chatswood via North Sydney. Bus 257 connects Balmoral with Chatswood. Bus 135 runs from outside Manly Wharf to North Head and the Quarantine Station. Buses 136 and 139 head from Manly Wharf to Freshwater and Curl Curl.

Parking There's metered street parking all over the North Shore.

outspoken educator and pioneer who prevailed over conservative Catholic hierarchical ideals despite being excommunicated for six months. The building was blessed by Pope John Paul II on the day of MacKillop's beatification (19 January 1995). You'll find her tomb inside the chapel.

NUTCOTE Map p108

☎ 9953 4453; www.maygibbs.com.au; 5 Wallaringa Ave, Neutral Bay; adult/child $8/3; ⏰ 11am-3pm Wed-Sun; ﹦ Neutral Bay

HARBOUR ISLANDS

Previously known as Pinchgut, Fort Denison (Map pp50–1) is a small, fortified island off Mrs Macquaries Point. It was originally used for punishment of troublesome convicts until it was fortified in the mid-19th century during the Crimean War amid fears of a Russian invasion. It now has a café, which may be one of the best places to have coffee in all of Sydney in terms of views and location. Take your pick of either the daily heritage tour (adult/child $22/18; ⏰ 11.45am-3pm) or the brunch tour (adult/child $47/43; ⏰ 9am-1pm Sat & Sun).

The largest island in the bay, Goat Island (Map pp50–1), near Balmain, has been a shipyard, quarantine station and gunpowder depot in its previous lives. The island is currently closed to visitors, although regular tours should resume towards the end of 2008.

Clark Island off Darling Point, Rodd Island at Iron Cove near Birkenhead Point and Shark Island off Rose Bay make great picnic getaways, but to visit you'll need a permit from Cadman's Cottage (landing fees are $5 per person). These three islands are open from 9am to sunset daily; all have drinking water and toilets available. There's a ferry service from Circular Quay to Shark Island (adult/child $16/14, four daily) but you'll need to hire a water taxi (see p217) or have access to a boat to reach the others.

For more information and tour bookings contact the Sydney Harbour National Park office at Cadmans Cottage (p56).

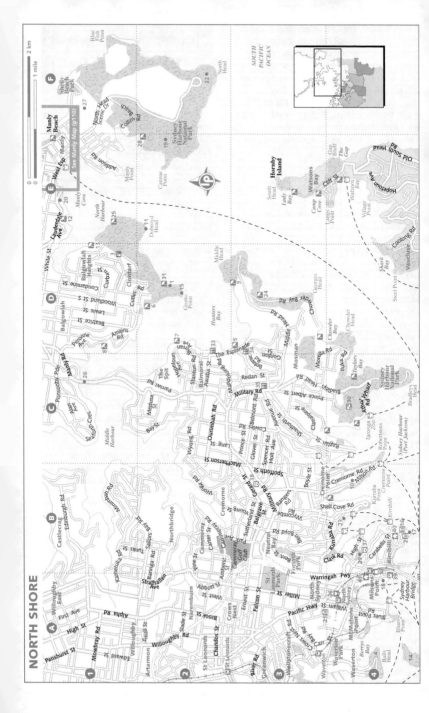

NORTH SHORE

108

NORTH SHORE

Nutcote (1925) is the former home of well-known and much-loved Australian children's author May Gibbs (author of *Snugglepot and Cuddlepie*). It's now a museum, restored to its 1930s style, and has exhibits on her life and work. Volunteer guides can show you around and there are beautiful gardens, a tearoom and a gift shop. It's a five-minute walk from the wharf.

BALLS HEAD RESERVE Map p108
Balls Head Rd; 🚆 Waverton
Balls Head Reserve not only has great views of the harbour and skyline, but also wonderful water-line and inland paths, ancient Aboriginal rock paintings and carvings (although they're not easily discernible) and barbecue facilities. It gives a great idea of how pre-European Sydney was. From Waverton train station turn left and follow Bay Rd, which becomes Balls Head Rd (just before the harbour, turn right). It's a 10-minute walk.

CREMORNE POINT Map p108
🚢 Cremorne Point
Cremorne Point is an excellent spot for a swim or a picnic on the grass reserve, with great views of the harbour. It's especially popular on Christmas Day, and on New Year's Eve as a vantage point for the annual fireworks.

KIRRIBILLI POINT Map p108
🚢 Kirribilli
The Sydney residences of the governor general and the prime minister are on Kirribilli Point, east of the Harbour Bridge. John Howard bucked tradition by making his home the Gothic Revival–style Kirribilli House (1854), as opposed to The Lodge in Canberra. The governor general's digs are in Admiralty House (1846), the one nearer the bridge (and the one everyone dreams of living in, if it came without the job). Both houses are better spotted from the water than by peering through the heavily-guarded gates.

To the north of Kirribilli Point is the Sydney Flying Squadron (p179) headquarters for the Royal Yacht Squadron. Yachting has been popular on the harbour since the 1830s.

MANLY

NORTH HEAD Map p108
North Head Scenic Dr; 🚢 Manly then 🚌 135
Spectacular North Head, about 3km south of Manly, offers grand views of the ocean, harbour and city skyline. The area is believed to have been used as a ceremonial site by the native Camaraigal people. The peninsula boasts dramatic cliffs, lookouts and the Manly Quarantine Station (opposite); it's

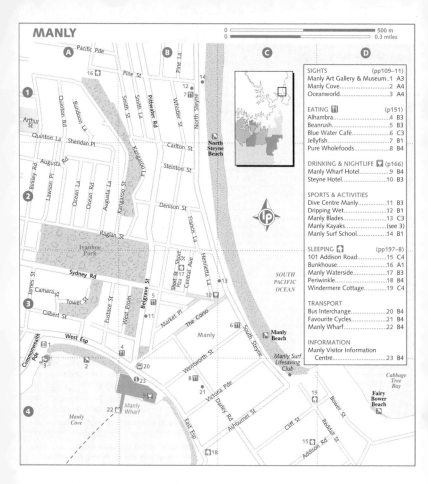

0 — 500 m
0 — 0.3 miles

SIGHTS   (pp109–11)
Manly Art Gallery & Museum..1 A3
Manly Cove......................2 A4
Oceanworld......................3 A4

EATING 🍴   (p151)
Alhambra........................4 B3
Beanrush........................5 B3
Blue Water Café..............6 C3
Jellyfish........................7 B1
Pure Wholefoods............8 B4

DRINKING & NIGHTLIFE 🍷 (p166)
Manly Wharf Hotel..........9 B4
Steyne Hotel.................10 B3

SPORTS & ACTIVITIES
Dive Centre Manly..........11 B3
Dripping Wet................12 B1
Manly Blades................13 C3
Manly Kayaks..............(see 3)
Manly Surf School.........14 B1

SLEEPING 🛏   (pp197–8)
101 Addison Road..........15 C4
Bunkhouse...................16 A1
Manly Waterside............17 B3
Periwinkle...................18 B4
Windermere Cottage......19 C4

TRANSPORT
Bus Interchange............20 B4
Favourite Cycles...........21 B4
Manly Wharf................22 B4

INFORMATION
Manly Visitor Information
Centre.......................23 B4

great to explore by bike. Most of the head-land is in the Sydney Harbour National Park (p106); contact the National Parks and Wildlife Service office (NPWS; ☎ 9977 6522) near the Quarantine Station for information. Parking in the area costs $3.

MANLY SCENIC WALKWAY Map p108
🚌 168 to The Spit, 🚢 Manly

This classic, well-marked, four-hour walk wanders through pricey residential areas and beautifully preserved, undulating native bushland with breathtaking harbour views. Starting from the Spit Bridge it winds its way along the edge of secluded bays before reaching Clontarf Beach (opposite) and its grassy picnic grounds. It's then sign-posted to isolated Castle Rock Beach, within

the wonderfully native Sydney Harbour National Park (p106). A little later it turns towards Grotto Point, which has great views beside a whitewashed old lighthouse. Nearby there are ancient Aboriginal rock carvings, just to the right of the main track.

Further down the track, a 200m detour inland leads to the Arabanoo Lookout for lovely vistas over Manly and North Head. Views are just as good from Dobroyd Head, off a short path to the right, not far from Reef Beach (opposite). There is an inland detour you can take if access to the picnic areas and beach of Forty Baskets Reserve is cut off at high tide. Beyond the reserve the path follows the road (not the stairs) to the top, and then goes on to Fairlight Beach, which has water fountains and a lovely saltwater pool. The walkway finishes in Manly Cove near Oceanworld (below).

Take comfortable shoes, water and snacks – supplies along the way are limited.

MANLY QUARANTINE STATION Map p108

☎ 9977 5145; www.q-station.com.au; North Head Scenic Dr; 🚢 Manly then 🚌 135

A favourite haunt of ghost-hunters, this station was used as a quarantine area from 1828 to 1972 in an attempt to limit the spread of cholera, smallpox and bubonic plague. It was then used until 1984 to house illegal immigrants. At present access is limited to guided tours, but this is about to change. There are controversial plans afoot to turn the station into a major full-time tourist attraction, with its own ferry stop. Phone ahead or check the website before attempting a visit.

OCEANWORLD Map p110

☎ 8251 7877; www.oceanworld.com.au; West Esplanade; adult/child $18/10; 🕙 10am-5.30pm; 🚢 Manly

Manly's shabby aquarium isn't a patch on its big sister in Darling Harbour (p71), but if you're staying locally and you're stuck with grumpy kids on a wet day, it starts to justify the admission charge. There are plenty of aquariums and an underwater tunnel for viewing the sharks and stingrays. Snakes and reptiles also make an appearance. There's reasonable access for wheelchairs and prams. After 3.30pm the admission price drops 15%.

MANLY ART GALLERY & MUSEUM Map p110

☎ 9949 1776; West Esplanade; adult/child $3.60/free, free Wed; 🕙 10am-5pm Tue-Sun; 🚢 Manly

Next to Oceanworld on the Manly Cove foreshore, this tiny gallery has a small local history section with old photos and newspapers, an exhibition space and a ceramics collection.

ST PATRICK'S COLLEGE Map p108

Darley Rd; 🚢 Manly

The college is the large building (1889) on the hill, southeast of Manly's town centre. It was a seminary for years and the first

top picks

SYDNEY HARBOUR BEACHES – NORTHSIDE

Obelisk (Map p108) Isolated gay and nudist beach surrounded by bushland in the Middle Head section of Sydney Harbour National Park (p106). It loses the sun quickly in the afternoon.

Cobblers Beach (Map p108) Also nudist and secluded, on the other side of Middle Head.

Balmoral (Map p108) A large, sweeping beach near Mosman with several fancy eateries, grassy parkland for picnics and a small island (connected by a footbridge) to explore. Popular on weekends.

Chinaman's Beach (Map p108) Gorgeous, peaceful and serene, despite its proximity to busy Balmoral. Good for picturesque swimming.

Clontarf Beach (Map p108) Another popular and sheltered beach for families, with large grassy areas for picnics. It faces towards the Spit Bridge.

Washaway Beach (Map p108) Rugged and beautiful, this is a secluded spot near Grotto Point on the Manly Scenic Walkway (opposite).

Reef Beach (Map p108) Also on the stunning Manly Scenic Walkway, this beach is not nudist, despite what you may have heard.

Forty Baskets Beach (Map p108) Past Reef Beach, just outside of Sydney Harbour National Park. It has a picnic area, which is cut off at high tide.

Manly Cove (Map p110) A decent sheltered beach with shark nets, next to Manly Wharf. For party action or surf simply cross the peninsula.

Store Beach (Map pp50–1) A hidden gem on Little Manly Cove only reachable by kayak or boat. A fairy penguin breeding ground, access is prohibited from dusk when the penguins return from feeding.

Catholic training college to be built in Australia; you can read about it in author Thomas Keneally's early works. It's now a tourism and hotel management school, and the recipient of a Unesco award for cultural heritage conservation.

UPPER NORTH SHORE

KU-RING-GAI CHASE NATIONAL PARK Map p113

☎ 9472 8949; www.nationalparks.nsw.gov.au /parks.nsf; per car $11, boat landing fee adult/child $3/2; ☯ sunrise-sunset; 🚉 Berowra, Mt Kuring-Gai or Turramurra then 🚌 577, 🚌 594 express from Town Hall, ⛴ from Palm Beach

This 14,978-hectare national park is 24km north of the city centre and borders the southern edge of Broken Bay and the western shore of Pittwater. It has that classic Sydney mixture of sandstone, bushland and water vistas, plus walking tracks, horse-riding trails, picnic areas, Aboriginal rock engravings and spectacular views of Broken Bay. The park has over 100km of shoreline and several through-roads (enter from Bobbin Head Rd, North Turramurra; Ku-ring-gai Chase Rd off Pacific Hwy, Mt Colah; or McCarrs Creek Rd, Terrey Hills). Camping (adult/child per night $10/5) is allowed only at the Basin (call ☎ 9974 1011 to book).

There's an information centre in the historic Bobbin Inn at Bobbin Head on Cowan Creek, which also has a marina, picnic areas, a café (serving hot meals, coffee and snacks) and a boardwalk leading through mangroves.

Elevated parts of the park offer superb views across inlets such as Cowan Creek and Pittwater, and from West Head, in particular, there's a fantastic view across Pittwater to Barrenjoey Head and Lion Island. You may also be lucky enough to see lyrebirds in this area during their May to July mating season.

West Head Rd offers access to some of the best places within the park to see Aboriginal engravings and handprints, listed here in order from east to west. Nearly at West Head itself is the Resolute picnic area, from which you can amble 100m to Red Hands Cave for a look at some very faint ochre handprints. About another 500m along Resolute Track (after a short steep section) is an engraving site. You can turn around or continue to one more site and make a 3.5km loop that takes in Resolute Beach.

Back on West Head Rd, just less than 2km west of the picnic area, is the Echidna

---

NORTHERN BEACHES

It requires an effort to reach them, but many rate the Northern Beaches as Sydney's finest. For surf freaks and *Home and Away* devotees they're a must-see. No trains run here and bus services seem to take forever. Consider hiring a car to beach-hop at your leisure. Heading north from Manly, these are the best of them:

Freshwater (Map p113; ⛴ Manly, then 🚌 139) This is a nice sheltered beach with an ocean pool, popular with local teenagers. Good for beginner surfers.

Curl Curl (Map p113; ⛴ Manly, then 🚌 136) A well-balanced mix of family groups and experienced surfers, with a lush lagoon nearby. Bring food and water.

Dee Why (Map p113; 🚌 178) Big and popular with local families, and with one of the best point breaks in Sydney (suitable for experienced surfers who can handle heavy take-offs). Near plenty of services.

Collaroy (Map p113; 🚌 L88, L90) A long beach that's a good spot to unwind, with a relaxed family atmosphere. Good for learning to surf.

Narrabeen (Map p113; 🚌 L88, L90) This is surfing turf, so get experienced before trying the consistent breaks here. Not the best for swimming, but there's a pool and lagoon.

Bilgola (Map p113; 🚌 L88, L90) With its saltwater pool, this beach seems like a bit of a secret gem. Good swimming, and some services available.

Avalon (Map p113; 🚌 L88) This medium-sized beach has challenging surf and tangerine sand. Great services like cafés, shops and picnic tables.

Whale Beach (Map p113; 🚌 L88 to Avalon, then 🚌 193) Heavenly, remote and clean, this gorgeous beach is ideally sized and not touristy. Good for surfers and families; no services.

Palm Beach (Map p113; 🚌 L90) The tip of Sydney and supremely blissful. Kids should stick to beach pools; cafés provide nourishment. Site of cheesy TV series *Home and Away* and the Barrenjoey lighthouse (opposite).

Track, whose boardwalk provides good disabled access to engravings very near the road. Less than a kilometre up the road from Echidna is the Basin Track, which makes an easy stroll to a good set of engravings.

Please note that it's unwise to swim in Broken Bay because of sharks, but if you're dying for a dip in waters that seem free of the usual hordes of tourists, there are safer netted swimming areas at Illawong Bay and the Basin.

BARRENJOEY LIGHTHOUSE Map p113
Palm Beach; 🚌 L90
Located at the tip of the northern beaches peninsula (and in an annexe of Ku-ring-gai Chase National Park) is this historic lighthouse (1881). You'll need to don sturdy shoes for the steep 40-minute hike (no toilets!), but superb views across Pittwater await. On Sundays short tours (adult/child $3/2) start every half hour from 11am to 3pm; no need to book ahead.

LANE COVE NATIONAL PARK
☎ 9412 1811; www.nationalparks.nsw.gov .au/parks.nsf; Lady Game Dr, Chatswood; per car $7; ⏰ 9am-6pm (till 7pm in summer); 🚌 292
This 601-hectare park lies about 10km northwest of Sydney's centre and is a good option for bushwalks. It's home to dozens of critters including some endangered species of owl and toad. The best time to visit is in spring, when the water dragons are getting horny and the native orchids and lilies are in flower. The Lane Cove River is great for rowing boats and kayaks, but swimming is inadvisable. You can cycle and camp, and wheelchair access is available in parts.

ROSE SEIDLER HOUSE
☎ 9989 8020; www.hht.nsw.gov.au/museums /rose_seidler_house; 71 Clissold Rd, Wahroonga; adult/child $8/4; ⏰ 10am-5pm Sun; 🚆 Turramurra then 🚌 575
World-famous architect Harry Seidler designed this modest house (built 1948–50) for his mother and father, Rose and Max. It's a Modernist construction and its interior reflects the style of the time, with plenty of open spaces, a muted colour scheme and

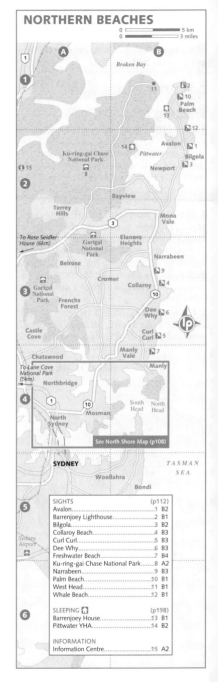

NORTHERN BEACHES

0 ——————— 5 km
0 ——————— 3 miles

the hippest furnishings of the era. Every year the Historic Houses Trust holds a Fifties Fair (usually in August) on the grounds of the house. Only serious architecture fans or true retro buffs need visit.

A NORTH SHORE HIKE
Walking Tour

1 Cremorne Point Take a ferry from the city to Cremorne Point (p109), which is surrounded by the jungle-like strip of native shrubs and trees that make up Cremorne Reserve. Make your way to the tip of the reserve, Robertson's Point, for some truly magnificent views.

2 Mosman Rowing Club Heading north, you'll pass some well-tended plots of palms, ferns, philodendrons and other tropical flora in Lex and Ruby's garden, which has been lovingly tended for decades. Keep wandering along the path to Mosman Rowing Club (☎ 9953 7713); if you catch it open you can stop for a meal .

3 Mosman Bay After a refreshing break, amble around exclusive Mosman Bay (which used to be an old whaling cove). Note the

historic stone building called the Barn, an early colonial structure that's now a scout hall. Just beyond is the Wharf Store; go up the stairs to Mosman St, following it up to McLeod St.

4 Little Sirius Cove Cross Musgrave St and take the stairs down to the other side, then cross Raglan St where you'll find more stairs that head down to the shore. Wind around Little Sirius Cove and take the stone steps onto a shoreline path, which leads to the border of Taronga Zoo.

5 Taronga Zoo To visit a secluded little strip of sand, take the stairs down to Whiting Beach (look for the 'No Dogs' sign). After heading further along this lush, shaded path you'll

WALK FACTS

Start **Cremorne Point**
End **Balmoral Beach**
Distance **5½km**
Duration **Three to 3½ hours**
Fuel stop **Mosman Rowing Club, Chowder Bay Naval Base**

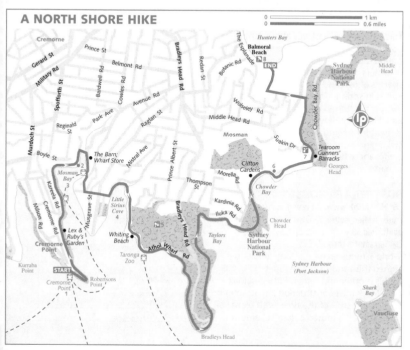

A NORTH SHORE HIKE

finally reach the Taronga Zoo (p106) entrance and ferry wharf, where there's a stand selling drinks and snacks.

6 Chowder Bay Naval Base Keep following the path through Bradleys Head and Clifton Gardens, where you'll link up with a recently opened track with spectacular views of the headlands. You will soon reach Chowder Bay Naval Base, now open to pedestrians. For refreshments there's a kiosk and the Tearoom Gunners' Barracks.

7 Lookout Wander to the lookout to the right, which has a glorious cityscape panorama and views over the gun stations that guarded the entrance to Sydney Harbour. Continue down the path as it cuts through bush and scrubland, passing an artists' colony on the left-hand side.

8 Balmoral Beach Follow the path and take in the magnificent gnarled red gum trees on the right-hand side. The path will lead you down some steps to the delightfully low-key Balmoral Beach (p111). If you are on a dawn stroll you'll probably catch t'ai chi and aerobics classes in action. Stop here to pick up some well deserved refreshment.

OTHER NEIGHBOURHOODS

Give up the idea that every Sydneysider has a harbour or beach view from their front veranda, or even that central Sydney is at the centre of the city. The geographical midpoint is Parramatta, 24km west along the Parramatta River. From this point Sydney's suburbs sprawl for at least 25km in every direction; this is where the majority live – and it's not all pretty.

The prosperous eastern harbour suburbs are close to the city and quickly reached by bus or ferry. The further-flung sights to the west and south are well connected by public transport and within the normal daily commute of many thousands of Sydneysiders.

EAST

VAUCLUSE HOUSE Map pp50–1

☎ 9388 7922; www.hht.nsw.gov.au; Wentworth Rd, Vaucluse; adult/child/family $8/4/17; ☼ 10am-4.30pm Tue-Sun; ☒ 325

Vaucluse was a desirable address even in the colony's early days, so it's interesting to note that one of its finest mansions was built by William Wentworth, a prominent explorer, patriot and barrister who, as a result of his free thinking and vocal advocacy of self-government, suffered a sort of social ostracism.

Built in fine grounds (1828–62), sumptuous Vaucluse House is an imposing example of a Gothic Revival marine villa and is one of Australia's finest mansions. The interior is laden with beautiful period pieces from Europe, including Bohemian glass, Meissen china and a Venetian dining setting. Life may well have been privileged for the Wentworths, but it also had its share of sorrow, which you'll discover as you tour the house and read the fascinating signs that accompany the rooms (disabled access on ground floor only). The lush 10-hectare grounds are a delight and well worth a picnic.

NIELSEN PARK Map pp50–1

Vaucluse Rd, Vaucluse; ☼ 5am-10pm; ☒ 325

Nielsen Park is a beautiful bush area and part of Sydney Harbour National Park (p106).

top picks

OTHER NEIGHBOURHOODS

- South Head (right)
- Vaucluse House (above)
- Nielsen Park (above)
- Sydney Olympic Park (opposite)
- Cronulla (p120)

Attractions include a decent netted beach, some gentle walking tracks and Greycliffe House (1851), a beautiful rustic Gothic sandstone pile (not open to visitors). The best time to come is on a weekday, when it's not too busy and the other layabouts are just mums, kids, oldies and people throwing sickies from work.

SOUTH HEAD Map pp50–1

Old South Head Rd; ⚓ Watsons Bay, ☒ 324-5, 380

The narrow peninsula heading to the harbour's southern head is one of Sydney's most sublime spots. Best approached from Bondi, the view as Old South Head Rd leaves the sheer ocean cliffs to descend to Watsons Bay is breathtaking; all at once Sydney Harbour as far as the Bridge is laid out before you.

Nestled on the harbour side, Watsons Bay was once a small fishing village, a fact that is still evident in some of the tiny heritage cottages that pepper the suburb's narrow streets (and now cost a fortune). While you're here, tradition demands that you sit on the sunny terrace of the beer garden at Doyles Palace Hotel (p166). At sunset the sun falls behind the disembodied Harbour Bridge that juts out above Bradley's Head.

On the ocean side of the peninsula, opposite Watsons Bay, is The Gap, a dramatic cliff-top lookout with the surf crashing far below. It has a macabre reputation as a suicide spot.

Past Watsons Bay is small family-friendly swimming beach Camp Cove (opposite). At its north end the South Head Heritage Trail begins, leading into yet another section of Sydney Harbour National Park (p106). It passes old battlements and a path heading down to little nudist/gay beach Lady Bay (opposite) before continuing to the candy-striped Hornby Lighthouse and Lightkeepers' Cottages (1858) on the tip of the head itself.

MACQUARIE LIGHTHOUSE Map pp50–1

Old South Head Rd; 📟 380
When the original Francis Greenway-designed lighthouse (1818) fell into disrepair, the current lighthouse (1883) was built in front of it as an exact replica and the original dismantled. It's a pleasant spot to visit, with large surrounding grassy lawns and heavenly ocean views, best enjoyed while ambling along the Coastal Cliff Walk. Before the lighthouse was built a series of fires were lit along Sydney's headland to alert ships to the treacherous cliffs below.

WEST

SYDNEY OLYMPIC PARK Map pp50–1

www.sydneyolympicpark.com.au; Homebush Bay; admission free; 🚉 Olympic Park, 🚢 Sydney Olympic Park
More than just a nostalgic reminder of the glorious, glitzy, over-the-top 2000 Olympic Games, Sydney's Olympic Park is a sprawling sustainable world unto itself, 14km west of the city centre. In the years since the Olympics the surrounding land has been transformed into nature reserves, 35km of cycleways and whole new residential suburbs.

The best way to explore this 23-hectare site is to hire a bike (per 1/2/4/8hr $12/17/22/32) from the Visitor Centre (☎ 9714 7888; 1 Showground Rd; 🕙 9am-5pm), where you can also pick up maps and information on tours and events. Get a heads-up on the park's layout from the Observation Centre (adult/child $4/2.75; 🕙 10am-4pm) on the 17th-floor of the Novotel.

The main Olympic venues are near the train station, including the Aquatic Centre (p175). Also here is the Sydney Showground – the home of the annual Royal Easter Show (p17) and Big Day Out (p16) music festival – and a massive new Skate Park. Newington Armoury, at the complex's north edge, hosts the weekend-long Great Escape (p17) music festival.

Telstra Stadium (formerly Stadium Australia, see p118) is an imposing oval bedpan with a colourful sculpture of native feathers spiralling over its main entrance. It's used for large sporting events including the Rugby League Grand Final (p18) and State of Origin (p17) matches, and rugby union internationals.

On the approach to the stadium is Games Memories, an outdoor multimedia museum of sorts, constructed of 480 poles. Interspersed between the names of 74,000

top picks

SYDNEY HARBOUR BEACHES – SOUTHSIDE

Redleaf Pool A small city beach with floating pontoons and a boardwalk (see p87).

Shark Beach (Map pp50–1) Despite its name, this easily accessible beach is netted and safe. It's in Nielsen Park (opposite) and popular for family picnics; there are services and lush walks nearby.

Parsley Bay (Map pp50–1) A real gem, with a large calm lagoon to swim in, grassy areas for picnics and a cute suspension bridge to cross.

Camp Cove (Map pp50–1) An attractive family-friendly beach with a kiosk and historic past. Close to South Head (opposite).

Lady Bay (Map pp50–1) Nudist and gay beach, with boulders and sand on which to sun, and great views of the harbour. On the popular path to South Head (opposite), but reasonably private.

volunteers are poles decorated with bits of track surfaces, rowing oars, javelins and movement-activated TV screens. Look for Ian Thorpe's pole, a mirrored one celebrating Kylie Minogue's closing ceremony performance, and one dedicated to 'Fatso the big-arsed wombat', the mascot of an irreverent nightly TV roundup screened during the games. A circular theatre fast-forwards the entire games experience with 12 screens simultaneously broadcasting highlights. Nearby, the silver flying saucer that burst into Olympic flame has been converted into a striking fountain.

A new addition is the architecturally stunning Brickpit Ring Walk (🕙 sunrise-sunset), a brightly coloured circular walkway supported 18m above an abandoned brickworks on what looks like metal chopsticks. Between 1911 and 1988 three-billion bricks were made here, but it's now been reclaimed by several native species including the endangered green and golden bell frog. Built into the loop are multimedia exhibits about the brick-workers and their amphibious replacements.

Native critters also have possession of various woodland and wetland reserves around Homebush Bay, Haslams Creek and the Parramatta River. The site has the

WHOSE STADIUM?

There are Olympic stadiums all over the world – from Montreal to Munich – but not in Sydney, home of the 2000 Olympic Games. Perhaps you may vaguely remember Sydney's stadium being referred to as Stadium Australia – a patriotic name for a grandiose venue. But you won't find a Stadium Australia these days either. There is an Aussie Stadium, but that's in Moore Park, not Olympic Park. Confused?

Sydneysiders seem unperturbed that their iconic Olympic stadium and Sydney Football Stadium have been rechristened in corporate branding deals as Telstra Stadium and Aussie Stadium (after sponsor Aussie Home Loans) respectively. Of course, this does nothing to dispel the rest of the country's impression that Sydneysiders would sell their grandmothers for a harbour view. One can't imagine the same indignity happening at the beloved MCG (Melbourne Cricket Ground).

prettiest sewage works you're ever likely to see or smell. Each year 850 milllion litres of water are captured in the park's water features, reducing its demand on the city's water supply by half. Banks of solar panels generate much of the site's electricity.

A variety of tours of the area are available; contact the visitors centre or check the website for more details.

PARRAMATTA

🚇 Parramatta or 🚢 Parramatta

Sydney's reserves of glamour are running dry by the time you head this far west, but for those on longer stays in Sydney – particularly those with a historical bent – a river journey to Parramatta is an interesting diversion and a chance to see more of the 'real Sydney'.

The second European settlement in Australia, Rose Hill was founded by First Fleet convict labour when Sydney Cove proved to be a poor area for farming. While this name survives in an inner Parramatta suburb, the town became known by what is actually a mishearing of the name of the local Aboriginal people, the Burramattagal. It roughly translates to 'eel creek' – the slippery critters giving their name to the area's rugby league team. Consumed by Sydney's westward sprawl, Parramatta is a thriving commercial centre, with some historic gems nestled among the mostly dreary modern developments.

If arriving by RiverCat, follow the river west to the knowledgeable Parramatta Heritage & Visitors Centre (☎ 8839 3311; 346A Church St; 🕐 9am-5pm) and grab a History & Heritage brochure outlining walking routes that take in the major sights. The centre is a museum in its own right, with temporary exhibits by local artists, as well as a fine permanent exhibition on Parramatta's history and culture.

Bicentennial Sq (on Church St, south of Macquarie St) is the civic centre, containing St John's Cathedral (with towers dating to 1819) and the Parramatta Town Hall (1883). St John's Cemetery (O'Connell St), three blocks south-west of the cathedral, contains the graves of many of the first settlers.

OLD GOVERNMENT HOUSE

☎ 9635 8149; www.friendsofogh.com; adult/concession/family $8/5/18; 🕐 10am-4pm Mon-Fri, 10.30am-4pm Sat & Sun; 🚇 Parramatta

The country residence of the early governors, this elegant Georgian Palladian building is situated in Parramatta Park, site of the first farm. The earliest part dates from 1799, making it the oldest remaining public building in Australia. Entry is by way of an interesting hour-long tour around rooms furnished with original colonial furniture and painstaking reproductions. An extra $2 will get you a joint ticket giving access to Experiment Farm (opposite). Phone for details about monthly ghost nights.

ELIZABETH FARM

☎ 9635 9488; www.hht.net.au/museums/ef; 70 Alice St, Rosehill; adult/child/family $8/4/17; 🕐 10am-5pm; 🚢 Parramatta or 🚇 Rosehill

Built as the home of John and Elizabeth Macarthur, this lovely homestead is the oldest surviving building in Australia (1793). Macarthur may be heralded as the founder of Australia's wool industry, but he wasn't a nice man. An officer turned ruthless capitalist, his misuse of power made him immensely wealthy and a thorn in the side of successive governors. His house is much more pleasant. Unlike Old Government House (above) all of the furniture is reproduction; you're allowed to swan around, touch things and sit in the chairs as if you own the colony – just like Macarthur did.

EXPERIMENT FARM COTTAGE

☎ 9635 5655; www.nsw.nationaltrust.org
.au/properties/efc; 9 Ruse St, Harris Park; adult/
concession/family $6/4/14; ⏱ 10.30am-3.30pm
Tue-Fri, 11am-3.30pm Sat & Sun; 🚊 Parramatta or
🚆 Harris Park

A block east of Elizabeth Farm is this colonial
bungalow (1835), built on the site of the
first land grant issued to a convict. Only a
year after arriving, Governor Phillip granted
12 hectares of land to James Ruse in an
experiment in self-sufficiency (much to the
consternation of some of the military). Down
the hill, Hambledon Cottage (☎ 9635 6924; 63 Hassell
St; adult/child $4/2; ⏱ 11am-4pm Wed-Sun) is older
still (1824) and surrounded by nearly 200-
year-old camphor laurels and English oaks.

SOUTH

BOTANY BAY NATIONAL PARK

www.nationalparks.nsw.gov.au/parks.nsf; per car
$7; 🚆 Cronulla then 🚌 987 to Kurnell, 🚌 393-4
to La Perouse

This 456-hectare national park straddles the
entrance of Botany Bay, 15km south of Sydney Harbour. If all had gone according to
plan, this would have been the site of Sydney. It was here that Captain Cook landed
in 1770. The bay was named in honour of
the many botanical specimens his natural-
ist Joseph Banks found here. Banks was the
one who suggested it as a good place to
plant the new penal colony. When the First
Fleet arrived in the height of summer 18
years later, they weren't inclined to agree;
the scorched vegetation and limited water
supplies a far cry from the paradise Banks
had visited in winter.

Cook's landing place is marked on the
Monument Track, a 1.5km walk at Kurnell on
the southern side of the bay. The nearby
Discovery Centre (☎ 9668 9111; ⏱ 11am-3pm Mon-
Fri, 10am-4.30pm Sat & Sun) has material relating
to Cook's life and expeditions, an exhibition
about the first contact between Cook's
crew and the local people, and information
on the surrounding wetlands.

La Perouse is on the northern side of the
bay at the spot where the First Fleet laid
anchor, followed by French explorer
Jean-François de Galaup, Comte de La
Pérouse just six days later. His arrival was
utterly coincidental, and gave the Brits
quite a scare. However the La Pérouse
expedition was purely scientific; he and
his men camped at Botany Bay for a few
weeks, then sailed off into the Pacific and
vanished. Many years later the wrecks of
their ships were discovered on a reef near
the Solomon Islands.

SHE'LL BE WHITE, MATE

One of the great contradictions of Australian life is the easy-going 'she'll be right, mate' self-image that stands in sharp
contrast to a nasty racism boiling away under the surface in some sections of society. Two recent race riots in Sydney
make it hard to deny. The White Australia policy may have been officially shelved by government in 1973 but perhaps
some attitudes linger on.

In 2004 Redfern erupted in a night of rioting following the death of an Aboriginal teenager in a police pursuit. The
following year it was images of white youths bashing people of different ethnicities while brandishing slogans such as
'Aussie Pride' and 'Wog Free Zone' that made headlines around the world.

The catalyst for the Cronulla riots of December 2005 was an assault of local surf life-savers by four young men, who some
in the media were quick to point out were Lebanese Australians. Whipped up by talkback radio shock jocks and an SMS
message issuing the call to 'come to Cronulla this weekend to take revenge' a crowd of 5000 white youth gathered in what
started as a party atmosphere, but degenerated into drunken racially motivated mob attacks on any passer-by who looked
vaguely Middle Eastern. Retaliatory attacks from both sides of the racial divide continued over the next few days.

It would be wrong to stereotype Sydneysiders as racist. After all, 250,000 people took to the streets in 2000 in support of Aboriginal reconciliation. But this is a nation where some politicians and sections of the media pander to racism
with relative impunity. Visitors are often shocked to hear casual references to 'Abos', 'Lebs' and 'Wogs' (a catch-all that
covers anyone of Mediterranean extraction) in otherwise polite conversation.

After the Australian Communications and Media Authority ruled that shock jock Alan Jones broadcast comments in
the lead up to the riot likely to encourage violence and vilify people of Middle Eastern background, Prime Minister John
Howard leapt to his defence, saying that Jones 'is a person who articulates what a lot of people think'. Jones is popular
with the lower-middle-class 'Aussie battlers' that are a key part of Howard's constituency.

Back in Cronulla, most locals were horrified by what had happened. One positive outcome has been the formation
of On The Same Wave, a successful collaboration between the local council, Surf Life Saving and the Department of Immigration and Citizenship aimed at increasing participation of people from ethnic minorities in surf life-saving.

The La Perouse area has strong links with the Aboriginal community. Laperouse Museum & Visitor Centre (☎ 9311 3379; adult/child $5.50/3.30; ✆ 10am-4pm Wed-Sun) has an interesting Aboriginal gallery, as well as relics of the La Pérouse expedition and antique maps. There's a monument commemorating the explorer, built in 1828 by French sailors searching for him.

The French connection continues in the name of Sans Souci, one of the sprawling suburbs that line Botany Bay – although in the local accent it's made to rhyme with 'man-floozy'.

CRONULLA
🚇 Cronulla

In the last edition of this book this surf town south of Botany Bay was described as having 'an atmosphere that couldn't be more relaxed without reaching the comatose level'. Then came the Cronulla riots (see p119). Things have calmed down again and visitors should have no qualms enjoying what this top beach has to offer: great surf, endless sand dunes and a pleasant beachfront promenade with dozens of eateries and bars nearby.

BLUELIST[1] (blu‿list) *v.*
to recommend a travel experience.
What's your recommendation? www.lonelyplanet.com/bluelist

SHOPPING

top picks

SHOPPING

Brash, hedonistic Sydney has elevated shopping to a universal panacea. Feeling good? Let's go shopping. Feeling bad? Let's go shopping. The credit card bills getting you down? Let's go shopping.

Many locals see shopping as a recreational activity and in some cases as a competitive sport. We know people in well-paid jobs who scour the markets and op-shops for 'rich bitch cast-offs' to sell on eBay to supplement their income so they can shop even more.

Shopping in Sydney can be fun, frantic and frivolous, and service is generally reasonable, although travellers from the US may find it a bit laid-back at times. Sycophancy isn't the Australian way, but generally neither is snobbiness. You shouldn't face condescension if you rock into a boutique in your thongs and a singlet, but neither will you be treated like a princess just because you've splashed $5000 on daddy's credit card.

SHOPPING AREAS

The city centre offers the broadest shopping potential, with its numerous department stores, shopping centres, malls and arcades. Paddington is the place to go for art and smart fashion, while new and secondhand boutiques around Newtown and Surry Hills cater to a hipper, more alternative crowd. Double Bay, Mosman and Balmain are a bit more 'mother of the bride'. If you're chasing bargains, head to Chinatown or the Alexandria factory outlets.

Newtown and Glebe have many of the best book and record stores. For surf gear, head to Bondi or Manly. Woollahra, Newtown (around St Peters station) and Surry Hills are good for antiques. Souvenirs – from exquisite opals to tacky T-shirts – are easily found around The Rocks, Circular Quay and Darling Harbour.

OPENING HOURS

Most stores are open from 9.30am to 6pm Monday to Wednesday, Friday and Saturday, and until 9pm Thursday. Sunday trading is common but expect shorter hours, such as noon to 4pm or 5pm.

BARGAINING

Bargaining is generally frowned upon, though you could try your luck at some of the grungier markets around the city, or if you're buying in bulk. Sales are usually held in early January and July.

DUTY FREE

Apart from the 10% goods and services tax (GST) the only other sales duties remaining are on naughty things such as alcohol and tobacco, which are best bought at the airport. The GST tourist refund scheme (see p227) has basically replaced traditional duty free shopping.

WARRANTIES & GUARANTEES

Under local law, all purchases (including secondhand) have an implied warranty that the goods are of merchantable quality (unless the customer is informed otherwise), are fit for the purpose supplied, and match the sample or description provided. If this is not the case you are legally entitled to a refund; which is all very well if you're still in the country.

Many suppliers (particularly of electrical goods) will offer written warranties (guarantees) for fixed terms. Check that they are worldwide and include service in your country of residence.

REFUNDS & EXCHANGES

Many stores have formal refund and exchange policies – you're best to check them before you purchase. If no policy exists you shouldn't presume that a refund will be allowed, except in the situation described above under warranties. That said, if you're not happy with a purchase some stores will consider exchanges, particularly if you have a receipt and haven't disturbed the packaging.

SHIPPING GOODS

There are several options if you find that a shopping frenzy has overfilled your bags. Firstly, check with your airline regarding excess baggage or unaccompanied baggage rates. It may be cheaper to post a parcel back. Enquire at any post office or check the handy country-based pull-down list on Australia Post's website (www.auspost.com.au). If you're buying big items, such as art or cases of wine, some vendors will arrange a shipping service for a fee. There are stacks of shipping companies operating out of Sydney listed in the telephone directory (www.yellowpages.com.au).

WHAT TO BUY

Opals and Aboriginal art are two of the most popular souvenirs particular to Australia. Along with iconic Akubra hats, Drizabone coats, Blundstone boots, boomerangs and didgeridoos they say more about the outback than urban Sydney, but you won't have any problems finding them here.

Sydney has a thriving fashion scene, and a slinky summer dress or pair of Speedos won't take up much luggage space. Enquire at a CD or book store about what's hot from local bands and authors, or grab a Sydney-based movie on DVD. Hunter Valley wine makes a great gift – check your country's duty free allowance before buying a case.

If you're after a more substantial purchase, check out the many galleries featuring local artists – indigenous or otherwise.

THE ROCKS & CIRCULAR QUAY

Not a place that locals would ever choose for a shopping spree, this neighbourhood caters mainly to wealthy-tourist tastes. It's not a bad spot for opal hunting, duty-free shopping and tacky souvenirs; explore around George St and the Quay itself.

As well as the stores following there's a Herringbone (p129) branch at 7 Macquarie Pl.

PUPPET SHOP AT THE ROCKS
Map p54   Children's
☎ 9247 9137; 77 George St, The Rocks; ☾ 10am-5pm; ☒ Circular Quay
Both fascinating and a little creepy, all manner of stringed things and bizarre, jointed toys dangle from the ceiling of this wonderful underground treasure chest. Kids love this shop, as do grown-ups who haven't watched too many horror movies about killer mannequins.

AUSTRALIAN WINE CENTRE
Map p54   Food & Drink
☎ 9247 2755; Goldfields House, 1 Alfred St, Circular Quay; ☾ 9.30am-6.30pm Mon-Sat, 11am-5pm Sun; ☒ Circular Quay

If you don't make it to the Hunter Valley, this place offers a cellar-door experience in the heart of the city – with wines available for tasting. You'll find wines from every Australian and New Zealand wine-growing region, which the centre will package and deliver to your door.

DONE ART & DESIGN
Map p54   Souvenirs
☎ 9251 6099; 125 George St, The Rocks; ☾ 10am-6pm; ☒ Circular Quay
Ken Done's bright, cartoonish Matisse-on-Prozac images adorn T-shirts, shorts, towels, bathing suits, robes, dresses and any other kind of resort item you can think of. For more, check out his nearby gallery (p56) or the outlet store in Market City (p126).

CITY CENTRE

Sydneysiders head city-ward if they've got something special to buy or when serious retail therapy is required. The central city's diverse range of mainly upmarket stores – centred on Pitt St Mall, Market St and George St – offers plenty of choice for gifts and treats.

There are also branches of Dirt Cheap CDs (p132) and Herringbone (p129) in the centre.

DYMOCKS Map pp62–3   Books
☎ 9235 0155; 424 George St; ☾ 8.30am-6.30pm Mon-Wed & Fri, 8.30am-9pm Thu, 9am-6pm Sat, 10am-5.30pm Sun; ☒ St James
This huge bookstore has more than 250,000 titles spread over three floors; look for the Lonely Planet aisle! Great for almost any book you might be after, plus there's a café. There are several other branches around the city.

KINOKUNIYA Map pp62–3   Books
☎ 9262 7996; level 2, 500 George St; ☾ 10am-7pm Mon-Wed, Fri & Sat, 10am-9pm Thu, 10am-6pm Sun; ☒ Town Hall
Located in the Galeries Victoria, this large Japanese bookstore has great art, design, travel and children's sections, as well as plenty of magazines, stationery and Japanese language titles.

RM WILLIAMS
Map pp62–3   Clothing & Accessories
☎ 9262 2228; 389 George St; ☾ 8.30am-6pm Mon-Wed & Fri, 8.30am-9pm Thu, 9am-5pm Sat, 11am-5pm Sun; ☒ St James
This long-established manufacturer and distributor of Aussie outdoor gear – such as

TO MARKET, TO MARKET

Sydney's markets offer a fun way to shop, and the wide range of goods available will suit a variety of tastes and budgets. While some are quite touristy, others have a distinct local vibe – running the gamut from groovy to snooty.

Balmain Markets (Map pp100–1; ☎ 0418 765 736; St Andrew's Church, 223 Darling St, Balmain; ⏰ 8.30am-4pm Sat; 🚌 433 & 434) This small local market offers high-quality creative crafts such as handmade candles, soaps, funky jewellery, exotic textiles, artwork and used clothing and books. The feel is friendly, social and low-key, and there are some great Asian food stalls to try.

Bondi Markets (Map pp94–5; ☎ 9315 8988; Bondi Beach Public School, cnr Campbell Pde & Warners Ave, Bondi; ⏰ 10am-5pm Sun; 🚌 380) Sitting across from the beach at the northern end of Campbell Pde, this small market is good for hip clothing, exotic imports, jewellery, fashion accessories, knick-knacks and skimpily-dressed-people watching.

Entertainment Quarter (Map pp84–5; ☎ 9383 4333; www.entertainmentquarter.com.au; 122 Lang Rd, Moore Park; 🚌 339) The Farmers' Market (⏰ 10am-3.30pm Wed & Sat) has loads of fine regional produce including delicious cheese and yoghurt, while the craft-based Merchandise Market (⏰ 10am-5pm Sun) covers similar bases to The Rocks Market (see below).

Glebe Markets (Map pp100–1; ☎ 4237 7499; Glebe Public School, cnr Glebe Point Rd & Derby Pl, Glebe; ⏰ 10am-4pm Sat; 🚌 431-4) This large and slightly grungy market hawks a wide assortment of books, records, vintage clothes, glassware, leather goods, herbal teas, hippie crafts, oddities and curios. It takes over the neighbourhood on Saturdays, so crowds will be heavy everywhere.

Kirribilli Markets (Map p108; ☎ 9922 4428; Bradfield Park, Milsons Point; ⏰ 7am-3pm 4th Sat every month; 🚆 Milsons Point) A wonderful monthly market offering everything from vintage clothes to real (and faux) antiques to kids' gear to all kinds of jewellery. Plenty of exotic foods too, and a great lively atmosphere.

Paddington Markets (Map pp84–5; ☎ 9331 2923; www.paddingtonmarkets.com.au; St John's Church, 395 Oxford St, Paddington; ⏰ 10am-4pm Sat; 🚌 380) Very popular, upmarket and pricey, with vintage clothing, creative crafts, beautiful jewellery, tasty food and holistic treatments. Some fledgling designers get their start here.

Paddy's Markets (Map p72; ☎ 1300 361 589; www.paddysmarkets.com.au; 9-13 Hay St, Haymarket; ⏰ 9am-5pm Thu-Sun; 🚆 Central) This Sydney institution is a great place to find cheap souvenirs, clothing, wigs, electronics, sheepskin rugs, cosmetics, mobile phone covers and plenty of knick-knacks. In the basement there's a good selection of fresh fruit, vegetables and seafood.

The Rocks Market (Map p54; ☎ 9240 8717; www.therocksmarket.com; George St, The Rocks; ⏰ 10am-5pm Sat & Sun; 🚆 Circular Quay) At the top end of George St, this market is definitely on the touristy side but still fun for a browse. Crafts made of metal, ceramic, stone, leather and glass abound, along with souvenirs. It's close to many pubs and cafés, so your non-shopping partner can sit, drink and wait it out.

Rozelle Markets (Map pp100–1; ☎ 9818 5373; www.rozellemarkets.com.au; cnr Darling & National Sts, Rozelle; ⏰ 9am-4pm Sat & Sun; 🚌 432-4) This is one of Sydney's best markets for bargain hunters, and you're unlikely to run into fellow tourists. Hippie jewellery, recycled clothes, plants, books, knick-knacks, live folk music, palm readings, exotic food stalls and some basic junk can be sifted through. It's lots of fun.

Surry Hills Markets (Map pp90–1; ☎ 9310 2888; Shannon Reserve, Crown St, Surry Hills; ⏰ 9am-4pm first Sat every month; 🚆 Central) There's a lively community feeling with mainly locals renting stalls to sell/recycle their old stuff – clothes, CDs, books and bric-a-brac. Some good bargains to be had.

drought-breakers (oilskin riding coats) and moleskin trousers – attracts every urban cowboy and cowgirl within the city limits. One of the best sellers is the classic elastic-sided boot, which is nothing less than an Aussie icon.

STRAND HATTERS

Map pp62–3   Clothing & Accessories
☎ 9231 6884; Strand Arcade, 412 George St; ⏰ 9am-6pm Mon-Wed & Fri, 9am-8pm Thu, 9.30am-4pm Sat, 11am-4pm Sun; 🚆 St James

Wearing a hat to protect oneself from the sun is a good idea in this country – wearing the iconic rabbit-felt Akubra (around $155) will ensure you'll look like you came straight from the outback.

DAVID JONES
Map pp62–3   Department Store
☎ 9266 5544; cnr Elizabeth & Market Sts; ⏰ 9.30am-6pm Mon-Wed & Fri, 9.30am-9pm Thu, 9am-6pm Sat, 10am-6pm Sun; 🚆 St James
Bright and sparkling, this is considered the city's premier department store, straddling

two diagonally-opposite buildings. The one on the corner of Castlereagh and Market Sts has menswear, homewares and electrical goods, along with a luxury food hall. The Elizabeth St store sells women's and children's goods. David Jones also takes up a sizeable chunk of Westfield Bondi Junction (p132).

MYER Map pp62–3   Department Store
☎ 9238 9000; 436 George St, City; ⏱ 9am-6pm Mon-Wed & Sat, 9am-9pm Thu, 9am-7pm Thu, 10am-6pm Sun; ⏴ St James

At seven storeys, Myer (ex-Grace Bros) is one of Sydney's largest stores and a prime venue for after-Christmas sales. It's marginally less swanky than David Jones, but you'll still find plenty of high-quality goods, along with slick cafés when you tire of lugging those bags. More branches in the suburbs, including Westfield Bondi Junction (p132).

RED EYE RECORDS Map pp62–3   Music
☎ 9299 4233; 66 King St; ⏱ 9am-6pm Mon-Wed & Fri, 9am-9pm Thu, 9am-5pm Sat, 11am-5pm Sun; ⏴ Wynyard

A great store for music junkies, the large and unusual stock covers Japanese, European and US imports along with Australian artists and plenty of independent releases. A secondhand section upstairs includes collectable CDs, DVDs, vinyl, books and posters. Knowledgeable staff will take orders for the hard-to-find.

CHIFLEY PLAZA Map pp62–3   Shopping Centre
☎ 9221 6111; 2 Chifley Sq; ⏱ 9.30am-6pm Mon-Fri, 9.30am-4pm Sat; ⏴ Martin Place

For many Sydneysiders, luxury shopping starts and ends at the base of Sydney's tallest office block, where overseas name brands compete with Leona Edmiston (p127), Herringbone (p129), Oxford (p131) and RM Williams (p123).

QUEEN VICTORIA BUILDING
Map pp62–3   Shopping Centre
QVB; ☎ 9264 9209; www.qvb.com.au; 455 George St; ⏱ 9am-6pm Mon-Wed & Fri & Sat, 9am-9pm Thu, 11am-5pm Sun; ⏴ Town Hall

The magnificent QVB (also p68) takes up a whole block and boasts nearly 200 shops on five levels. It's the city's most beautiful shopping centre, with tenants including Herringbone (p129), Oxford (p131) and Victoria's Basement (p131).

STRAND ARCADE Map pp62–3   Shopping Centre
☎ 9232 4199; enter Pitt St Mall or 412 George St; ⏱ 9.30am-5.30pm Mon-Wed & Fri, 9.30am-8pm Thu, 9am-4pm Sat, 11am-4pm Sun; ⏴ St James

With its stained-glass windows, iron-lacework balconies and three floors of boutique shops this quirky shopping centre makes for a truly atmospheric splurge. Shops here include Lisa Ho, Leona Edmiston (p127), Third Millennium, Hussy and Dinosaur Designs (p128), among others. Built in 1892, this is the city's only Victorian arcade to survive in its original form.

DARLING HARBOUR & CHINATOWN

Shopping is one of Chinatown's big drawcards, with plenty of bargains to be had of the 'Made in China/Taiwan/Korea' type. The insane buzz of the markets is half the fun. Darling Harbour's a bit like The Rocks – a good place for traditional touristy stuff like opals and souvenirs, otherwise forget it.

AUSTRALIA'S OUTBACK GALLERY
Map p72   Art, Souvenirs
☎ 9283 7477; www.outbackgallery.com.au; 28 Darling Walk, 1-25 Harbour St, Darling Harbour; ⏱ 10am-6pm; ⏴ Town Hall

Part of the Outback Centre (p73), this excellent gallery features a mix of collectable and emerging Aboriginal artists, meaning you might find a small canvas for $135 or a large piece by a well-known artist for up to $13,000. For a cheaper memento you can always grab a fluffy koala next door.

GAVALA ABORIGINAL ART CENTRE
Map p72   Art, Souvenirs
☎ 9212 7232; Harbourside, Darling Harbour; ⏱ 10am-9pm; MLR Convention

Proudly proclaiming itself as Sydney's only Aboriginal-owned retail centre and gallery, this is a great place to source everything from a T-shirt to a bark painting, a boomerang or an Aboriginal flag.

BLACK RIDGE JEWELLERS
Map p72   Jewellery
☎ 9281 5140; Harbourside, Darling Harbour; ⏱ 10am-9pm; MLR Convention

Australia produces 95% of the world's opals and NSW 99% of black opals, so in many ways these radiant sparklers are the perfect

Sydney souvenir – even if they are a bit nana-ish. All of Sydney's tourist traps have opal shops. We like this one for its delightfully tacky mineshaft entrance.

MARKET CITY Map p72 Shopping Centre
☎ 9212 1388; 9-13 Hay St, Haymarket; ✆ stores 10am-7pm Fri-Wed, 10am-8pm Thu, centre 10am-late; ☒ Central
This mammoth shopping centre includes Paddy's Markets (p124), a big food court, heaps of fashion outlet stores, Chinese cinemas and video-game parlours. Shops include Done Art & Design (p123), Bracewell (p130) and Oxford (p131).

DARLINGHURST TO POTTS POINT

The most established shopping strip in this part of town is probably the row of adult shops lining Kings Cross. There are a few gay-oriented businesses in Oxford St, Darlinghurst (see also p183), some of which have crossover appeal for the inner-city club crowd. A smattering of secondhand stores and established art galleries dot the back streets.

MARTIN BROWNE FINE ART
Map p78 Art
☎ 9331 7997; www.martinbrownefineart.com; 59 Macleay St, Potts Point; ✆ 11am-6pm Tue-Sun; ☒ 311
The clientele may be more bourgeois than bohemian, but it's nice that there's still art in the famous Yellow House (p81). Focussing on the contemporary, Browne represents several prominent Australian and international artists.

ROBIN GIBSON GALLERY Map p78 Art
☎ 9331 6692; www.robingibson.net; 278 Liverpool St, Darlinghurst; ✆ 10am-6pm Tue-Sat; ☒ 311
Housed in a beautiful three-storey terrace, this gallery represents a coterie of Australian artists, but also stages the occasional exhibition by superstars like Hockney and Picasso.

BLUE SPINACH
Map p78 Clothing & Accessories
☎ 9331 3904; 348 Liverpool St, Darlinghurst; ✆ 10am-6pm Mon-Wed & Fri & Sat, 10am-7pm Thu; ☒ Kings Cross
Consignment clothing at its most high-end, with penny-pinching label-lovers – both men and women – flocking to this shockingly blue corner shop to source secondhand designer duds (think YSL, Gucci and Collette Dinnigan) at (relatively) bargain prices.

HOUSE OF PRISCILLA
Map p78 Clothing & Accessories
☎ 9286 3023; level 1, 47 Oxford St, Darlinghurst; ✆ 10am-6pm Mon-Wed & Fri & Sat, 10am-7pm Thu; ☒ Museum
Not only is Priscilla the queen of the desert, she also has her own boutique – not bad for a cinematic bus. Run by some of the city's leading drag artistes, Priscilla is the place for feathered angel wings and boas, naughty nurse outfits, wigs, thigh-high boots and sequinned frocks to fit front-row forwards. Very camp women also welcome.

KOOKABURRA KIOSK
Map p78 Clothing & Accessories
☎ 9380 5509; 112A Burton St, Darlinghurst; ✆ 11am-6pm; ☒ 311
This small, long-running secondhand clothing store has some fab finds from the fashion archives. It concentrates on unique vintage pieces and manages to avoid that fabric-explosion atmosphere that plagues so many similar shops. Sort through the sale racks out the front for bargains.

SAX FETISH
Map p78 Clothing & Accessories
☎ 9331 6105; 110A Oxford St, Darlinghurst; ✆ noon-6pm Sun-Mon, 11am-7pm Tue-Wed & Fri, 11am-8pm Thu, 11am-6pm Sat; ☒ Museum
Sax addicts come from all over the world for the high-quality leather- and rubber-wear at the black heart of this shop. Both men and women are catered for, and the 'accessories' range goes a little further than your standard shoes and handbags. Cufflinks and ties have quite a different meaning here.

top picks

SOUVENIRS & GIFTS

- Gavala Aboriginal Art Centre (p125)
- Paddy's Market (p124)
- Outback Centre (p73)
- Strand Hatters (p124)
- Australian Wine Centre (p123)

CENTRAL STATION Map p78 — Music
☎ 9361 5222; 46a Oxford St, Darlinghurst; ☺ 10am-6pm Mon & Sat, 10am-7pm Tue-Wed & Fri, 10am-9pm Thu, noon-5pm Sun; ⓜ Museum
You'll hear this store before you see it – the pumping beats lead down a long corridor to this temple to dance music. You can buy everything from slamming compilation CDs to technical DJ gear, and there's a self-contained hip-hop store onsite. Ask at the counter about upcoming events and party tickets.

PADDINGTON TO DOUBLE BAY

As well as encompassing two of Sydney's premier shopping strips in Oxford St, Paddington (fashion, homewares) and Queen St, Woollahra (antiques, fashion), this neighbourhood is known for its numerous commercial galleries and Double Bay's overpriced boutiques.

You can also find branches of Berkelouw Books (p134), Gertrude & Alice (p131), Oxford (p131) and Bracewell (p130).

PADDINGTON
HOGARTH GALLERIES ABORIGINAL ART CENTRE
Map pp84–5 — Art
☎ 9360 6839; www.aboriginalartcentres.com; 7 Walker Lane, Paddington; ☺ 10am-5pm Tue-Sat; ⓜ 380
This hard-to-find gallery has been exhibiting Aboriginal work from all over Australia since 1972. A wide range of art (bark and canvas paintings, weavings, carvings) is on display, including works by young artists Lisa Michl, Rosella Namok and Fiona Omeenyo. From Oxford St take Shadforth Rd, turn right onto Walker Lane and right again to enter from the side lane.

ROSLYN OXLEY9 GALLERY
Map pp84–5 — Art
☎ 9331 1919; www.roslynoxley9.com.au; 8 Soudan Lane, Paddington; ☺ 10am-6pm Tue-Fri, 11am-6pm Sat; ⓜ 389
For 25 years this high-powered commercial gallery has showcased innovative contemporary work, representing artists such as Tracey Moffatt, Fiona Hall, Bronwyn Oliver and Bill Henson. It's great for a nosy even if you're not crazy-wealthy.

top picks
ART
- Martin Browne Fine Art (opposite)
- Roslyn Oxley9 Gallery (left)
- Stills Gallery (below)
- Hogarth Galleries Aboriginal Art Centre (left)
- 2 Danks St (p130)

STILLS GALLERY Map pp84–5 — Art
☎ 9331 7775; www.stillsgallery.com.au; 36 Gosbell St, Paddington; ☺ 11am-6pm Tue- Sat; ⓜ 389
This large gallery is a brilliant place for a gander at cutting-edge photography. It represents a swag of internationally recognised photographers, including William Yang, Anne Noble and Sandy Edwards.

ARIEL Map pp84–5 — Books
☎ 9332 4581; 42 Oxford St, Paddington; ☺ 9am-midnight; ⓜ 380
Ariel focuses on art and design books, with plenty of temptation for those planning on weighing down the coffee table with the biggest and best. Fiction and travel are well represented and there's plenty for kids too.

COLLETTE DINNIGAN
Map pp84–5 — Clothing & Accessories
☎ 9360 6691; www.collettedinnigan.com; 33 William St, Paddington; ☺ 10am-6pm Mon-Sat, noon-5pm Sun; ⓜ 380
Dinnigan is one of Australia's most successful international designers, and this sugar-coated boudoir of a shop shows why. Her wonderfully slinky designs include beautiful, intricately hand-beaded evening dresses, all made in Sydney. And it's not just for size-6-wearing models, either – real women can enjoy her creations as well.

LEONA EDMISTON
Map pp84–5 — Clothing & Accessories
☎ 9331 7033; www.leonaedmiston.com; 88 William St, Paddington; ☺ 10am-6pm Mon-Wed & Fri, 10am-8pm Thu, 10am-5.30pm Sat, noon-5pm Sun; ⓜ 380
Leona Edmiston knows what women fancy in a frock, whether of the little and black variety, whimsically floral or all-out sexy. A line of accessories includes heels and handbags, with exotic Asian fabrics thrown in for

CLOTHING SIZES

Women's clothing

Aus/UK	8	10	12	14	16	18
Europe	36	38	40	42	44	46
Japan	5	7	9	11	13	15
USA	6	8	10	12	14	16

Women's shoes

Aus/USA	5	6	7	8	9	10
Europe	35	36	37	38	39	40
France only	35	36	38	39	40	42
Japan	22	23	24	25	26	27
UK	3½	4½	5½	6½	7½	8½

Men's clothing

Aus	92	96	100	104	108	112
Europe	46	48	50	52	54	56
Japan	S		M	M		L
UK/USA	35	36	37	38	39	40

Men's shirts (collar sizes)

Aus/Japan	38	39	40	41	42	43
Europe	38	39	40	41	42	43
UK/USA	15	15½	16	16½	17	17½

Men's shoes

Aus/UK	7	8	9	10	11	12
Europe	41	42	43	44½	46	47
Japan	26	27	27½	28	29	30
USA	7½	8½	9½	10½	11½	12½

Measurements approximate only, try before you buy

good measure. Also at Chifley Plaza (p125) and Westfield Bondi Junction (p132).

MORRISSEY Map pp84–5 Clothing & Accessories

☎ 9380 7422; 372 Oxford St, Paddington; 10am-6pm Mon-Wed & Fri, 10am-8pm Thu, 10am-5.30pm Sat, noon-5pm Sun; bus 380

One of Sydney's most recognised fashion identities, Peter Morrissey brings classic style and simplicity with a touch of sexy sparkle to his men's and women's ranges. Also at Westfield Bondi Junction (p132).

QUICK BROWN FOX

Map pp84–5 Clothing & Accessories

☎ 9331 3211; 100 Oxford St, Paddington; 10am-6pm Mon-Wed & Fri & Sat, 10am-8pm Thu, noon-5pm Sun; bus 380

No lazy dogs here, that's for sure, but plenty of fast-looking, tanned vixens snapping up a range of funky vintage fashions that veer between Hello-Kitty-cuteness and indecent-exposure-sexiness. Catchy patterns and fabrics and very hip boots and bags. There's also a branch at 312 King St, Newtown.

SASS & BIDE Map pp84–5 Clothing & Accessories

☎ 9360 3900; www.sassandbide.com; 132 Oxford St, Paddington; 10am-6pm Mon-Wed & Fri & Sat, 10am-8pm Thu, 11am-5pm Sun; bus 380

Brisbane's Heidi Middleton and Sarah-Jane Clarke got their start with a stall on London's Portobello Rd before heading to Sydney in 1999 and starting the label that has made them international fashion stars. Come here for sassy super-low-cut women's jeans, body-hugging jackets and minidresses.

SCANLAN & THEODORE

Map pp84–5 Clothing & Accessories

☎ 9380 9388; 122 Oxford St, Paddington; 10am-6pm Mon-Wed & Fri, 10am-8pm Thu, 10am-5.30pm Sat, noon-5pm Sun; bus 380

Scanlan & Theodore excel at beautifully made and finely silhouetted women's outfits for the evening or the office. Plenty of sophisticated patterns and colours complement fabrics you just can't help but fondle.

CAMBODIA HOUSE

Map pp84–5 Clothing & Accessories, Homewares

☎ 9332 1101; 445 Oxford St, Paddington; 9.30am-5.30pm Mon-Fri, 9.30am-5pm Sat, 11am-5pm Sun; bus 380

Consumerism with a conscience, this not-for-profit store has a cool collection of Khmer arts and crafts, including hand-loomed silks made into handbags, scarves and bedding. You'll also find nifty lanterns, candles, tableware and carved statues.

DINOSAUR DESIGNS

Map pp84–5 Jewellery, Homewares

☎ 9361 3776; 339 Oxford St, Paddington; 10am-6pm Mon-Sat, noon-5pm Sun; bus 380

If the Flintstones opened a store, this is what it would look like. Oversized, colourful and chunky resin jewellery competes with vibrantly coloured home accessories (such as salad bowls and vases) that prove your urban coolness. Also in Strand Arcade (p125).

WOOLLAHRA

AKIRA ISOGAWA

Map pp84–5 Clothing & Accessories

☎ 9361 5221; 12A Queen St, Woollahra; 10.30am-6pm Mon-Wed & Fri, 10.30am-7pm Thu, 10am-6pm Sat, 11am-4pm Sun; bus 380

One of Sydney's most famous designers, Akira Isogawa creates fastidiously crafted dresses (some utilising his own dyeing techniques) which are masterpieces of feminine geometry worthy of a modern art collection. If you can afford his pieces, you'll be sure to attract some attention.

HERRINGBONE
Map pp84–5   Clothing & Accessories
☎ 9327 6470; 102 Queen St, Woollahra; ⏰ 10am-6pm Mon-Wed & Fri, 10am-7.30pm Thu, 9am-6pm Sat, 11am-5pm Sun; 🚌 389
Combining Australian design with Italian woven fabrics, Herringbone produces something surprisingly English-looking – beautiful men's and women's shirts with crisp collars and bright colours. City branches are at 7 Macquarie Pl, QVB (p125), Chifley Plaza (p125) and 1 Martin Place (p65).

ORSON & BLAKE
Map pp84–5   Clothing & Accessories, Homewares
☎ 9326 1155; 85 Queen St, Woollahra; ⏰ 9.30am-5.30pm Mon-Wed & Fri & Sat, 9.30am-6pm Thu, noon-5pm Sun
Sydney's most stylish spot to source homewares, with something for the bath (glorious lotions, soaps, towels), bedroom (sheets, robes, pillows) and backyard (statues, urns, pots). Also stuffed bunnies, scented candles and exotic furniture, along with a whole women's fashion collection upstairs. The branch at 483 Riley St, Surry Hills offers a café, more furniture, men's threads and crazy books.

SIMON JOHNSON Map pp84–5   Food & Drink
☎ 9328 6888; 55 Queen St, Woollahra; ⏰ 10am-6.30pm Mon-Fri, 9am-5.30pm Sat, 10am-4.30pm Sun; 🚌 389
Stock up your high-class picnic hamper at this gourmet wonderland. You'll find the

tastiest olives, creamiest Belgian chocolates and crispiest English biscuits, along with a great selection of imported olive oil and vinegar. The refrigerated case holds imported *prosciutto,* salami, and cheeses. The Pyrmont store (181 Harris St) hosts cooking seminars (p139).

SURRY HILLS TO ALEXANDRIA

Just as this area's restaurants have taken off, so too have its boutiques. The bottom end of Crown St has some great vintage stores, while local designers have a low-key presence throughout Surry Hills. Alexandria's factory shops attract busloads of Gold Coast shoppers every weekend.

Orson & Blake (left) also has a branch here.

SURRY HILLS
SYDNEY ANTIQUE CENTRE
Map pp90–1   Antiques
☎ 9361 3244; 531 South Dowling St; ⏰ 10am-6pm; 🚌 301-3
The Paddy's Market of antiques, this large red-and-black building houses dozens of individual stallholders selling everything from jewellery to furniture, ancient artefacts to vintage posters and homewares.

C'S FLASHBACK
Map pp90–1   Clothing & Accessories
☎ 9331 7833; 316 Crown St; ⏰ 10am-6pm Mon-Wed & Fri & Sat, 10am-9pm Thu, 11am-5.30pm Sun; 🚌 380
Looking for a mad secondhand sequinned or beaded number for a party? How about a groovy cowboy shirt? We're not sure exactly what C was on, but her flashback is pretty damn camp. This secondhand store sells both men's and women's threads. There's another branch at 180 King St, Newtown.

GRANDMA TAKES A TRIP
Map pp90–1   Clothing & Accessories
☎ 9356 3322; 263 Crown St; ⏰ 10am-6pm Mon-Wed & Fri & Sat, 10am-8pm Thu, noon-5pm Sun; 🚌 380
We don't know where Granny's gone, but she sure left a crazy wardrobe behind her. So did Grandpa by the looks of things. This upmarket secondhand boutique has an attention-grabbing collection of freaky threads. Also at 79 Gould St, Bondi Beach.

top picks

WOMEN'S FASHION
- Sass & Bide (opposite)
- Leona Edmiston (p127)
- Scanlan & Theodore (opposite)
- Wheels & Doll Baby (p130)
- One Teaspoon (p131)

HELIX Map pp90–1 Clothing & Accessories
☎ 9319 1599; 595 Bourke St; ◷ 11am-6pm
Mon-Wed & Fri, 11am-8pm Thu, 10am-6pm Sat;
🚌 301-3

A magical Pandora's Box of vintage beads and unique local women's fashion awaits in this backstreet boutique. Everything's produced locally in Surry Hills and you needn't worry about some scrag showing up in the same frock; only a handful of each design is produced. Lead designer Lisa Stack handmakes her own silk screens.

MR STINKY Map pp90–1 Clothing & Accessories
☎ 9310 7005; 482 Cleveland St; ◷ noon-6pm
Mon-Wed & Fri, noon-7pm Thu, 11am-5pm Sat;
🚌 301-3

The Stinkmeister deals in groovy vintage gear for cool dudes and saucy babes. The range is wide, the prices reasonable, and the staff friendly and helpful – with no discernable odour.

NICK BROWN
Map pp90–1 Clothing & Accessories
☎ 9360 7334; 397 Bourke St; ◷ 11am-6pm Mon-Wed & Fri, 11am-8pm Thu, 10am-6pm Sat; 🚌 380

If women have little black dresses as their essential fashion item, the men's equivalent should be the crisp cotton shirt. A new Nick Brown short-sleeve may well be the perfect accompaniment to a Sydney summer. He even does made-to-measure to perfectly showcase that worked-out torso.

PENNY ARCADE
Map pp90–1 Clothing & Accessories, Furniture
☎ 9281 8830; 15 Foster St; ◷ 10am-5.30pm Mon-Fri, 10am-3pm Sat; 🚉 Central

This unusual concept store from well-known Sydney designer Michael Bracewell brings together his own label and vintage women's clothes he's sourced from Paris and London.

It then adds to the mix a funky collection of retro furniture, particularly sought-after Danish and Australian pieces. You'll find straight-up Bracewell stores at Westfield Bondi Junction (p132) and 274 Oxford St, Paddington, and a factory outlet in Market City (p126).

WHEELS & DOLL BABY
Map pp90–1 Clothing & Accessories
☎ 9361 3286; 259 Crown St, Surry Hills; ◷ 10am-6pm Mon-Wed & Fri & Sat, 10am-8pm Thu, noon-5pm Sun; 🚌 380

This boutique is rock chick, posh punk or Parisian scruff (your choice), and a great place to snag an upmarket girly-girl costume. Join Deborah Harry and own a piece of this action, whether it be a polka-dot skirt, floral spaghetti-strap dress, Victorian corset or baby-doll T-shirt. Male rockers will have to settle for T-shirts.

WATERLOO

2 DANKS STREET Map pp90–1 Art, Jewellery
☎ 9361 4555; 2 Danks St; ◷ 11am-6pm Tue-Sat; 🚌 301-303

If you're after a more significant purchase as a memento of your Sydney visit, this large space houses nine separate contemporary art galleries and an antiques store. The jewellery may be slightly easier to pack than a 3m steel sculpture or a large Aboriginal painting.

DARREN KNIGHT GALLERY
Map pp90–1 Art, Jewellery
☎ 9699 5353; www.darrenknightgallery.com; 840 Elizabeth St; ◷ 11am-6pm Tue-Sat; 🚉 Green Square

This little off-the-beaten-track gallery showcases established and up-and-coming artists from Australia and New Zealand – including Ricky Swallow, whose work hangs in New York's MOMA and the National Gallery of Australia.

ALEXANDRIA
IRREGULAR JEANS WAREHOUSE
Map pp90–1 Clothing & Accessories
☎ 9550 3588; 33-49 Euston Rd; ◷ 9.30am-5.30pm Mon-Sat, 10am-5pm Sun; 🚌 370

Just as it sounds, this large factory outlet has trestle tables and racks laden down with denim and more, from brands big and small. You'll also find shirts, skirts, jackets and accessories.

top picks

VINTAGE CLOTHING

- C's Flashback (p129)
- Grandma Takes a Trip (p129)
- Mr Stinky (above)
- Penny Arcade (above)
- Frolic (p133)

OXFORD Map pp90–1 Clothing & Accessories

☎ 9318 1718; 141-143 McEvoy St; ⏱ 9am-5.30pm
Mon-Fri, 9am-5pm Sat, 10am-5pm Sun; 🚌 355

Another bargain store from a big local brand, Oxford is best known for reasonably priced but stylish menswear, although it has now launched a women's range. Think business to smart casual, including well-tailored shirts, suits and ties. For its latest range head to 246 Oxford St, Paddington or the city stores in QVB (p125) and Chifley Plaza (p125).

SEAFOLLY Map pp90–1 Clothing & Accessories

☎ 9690 1955; 111-117 McEvoy St; ⏱ 9am-5pm
Mon-Sat, 11am-4pm Sun; 🚌 355

Here's where the famous Aussie women's swimwear label sells its seconds, samples and discontinued lines. As well as battling over bikinis there are sarong, boardshort and tracksuit bargains to be had.

SHOES 2000

Map pp90–1 Clothing & Accessories, Homewares, Perfume

☎ 9698 1092; 135-139 McEvoy St; ⏱ 9am-5.30pm
Mon-Fri, 9am-5pm Sat, 10am-5pm Sun; 🚌 355

The biggest of the lot, Shoes 2000 off-loads a large range of men's and women's branded footwear, including iconic Aussie boot brands Blundstone, Redback and Mack – along with some big name imports. This giant warehouse incorporates three other factory outlets: Perfumes On The Move, POTM Clothing and Linen One.

VICTORIA'S BASEMENT

Map pp90–1 Homewares

☎ 9557 1954; cnr Euston Rd & Harley St; ⏱ 10am-5pm; 🚌 370

This large warehouse is packed to the rafters with high-quality kitchen and tableware at bargain-basement prices. It's the best place to come for wedding or house-warming gifts. Despite banning shopping tour buses it's always frantic on the weekends. You'll find its full-price outlet in the QVB (p125).

BONDI TO COOGEE

You'll still find surf shops galore, but as Bondi Beach has gentrified it has attracted its own set of big-name local designers, mainly based around Gould St. Up in Bondi Junction, serious shoppers from all over the city flock to the giant mall.

There are branches of Grandma Takes a Trip (p129) and Kirrily Stores (p134) here, too.

GERTRUDE & ALICE Map pp94–5 Books

☎ 9130 5155; 46A Hall St, Bondi; ⏱ 9am-11pm; 🚌 389

This secondhand bookstore offers good-quality beach-reading tomes and a wonderfully casual atmosphere. The café makes hanging out easy and there are regular poetry and acoustic music sets upstairs. There's another branch at 78 Oxford St, Paddington.

KITE POWER Map pp94–5 Children's

☎ 9315 7894; 126 Beach St, Coogee; ⏱ 9.30am-5.30pm; 🚌 372-3

Whether you're a kid or just a kid at heart, if you're looking for beach entertainment this is the place to come. This small shop is chock-full of beach balls, Frisbees, boomerangs, smashball racquets, hula hoops, juggling paraphernalia, games and, of course, lots of kites. Test your purchases in the nearby grassy reserve.

100% MAMBO

Map pp94–5 Clothing & Accessories

☎ 9365 2255; 80 Campbell Pde, Bondi;
⏱ 9.30am-6.30pm Fri-Wed, 9.30am-7pm Thu;
🚌 380

Bold, off-the-wall, comic-bookish graphics adorn street-, skate- and surfwear for men and women at this popular store. Mambo artist and musician Reg Mombasa is a local legend – he even designed the shirts for the Australian Olympic team in 2000. Expect a wide range of goodies (including watches, backpacks and coffee-table books). Also at 80 the Corso, Manly.

BANG-ON Map pp94–5 Clothing & Accessories

☎ 9386 1231; Westfield Bondi Junction; ⏱ 10am-6pm Mon-Wed & Fri, 10am-9pm Thu, 10am-7pm Sat & Sun; 🚇 Bondi Junction

Our favourite custom T-shirt place, Bang-On has an extensive range of supercool decals to print on non-sweatshop American Apparel tees. You'll find everything from obscure 1970s album covers to your favourite socialist icons and David Hasselhoff prints.

ONE TEASPOON SHOP

Map pp94–5 Clothing & Accessories

☎ 9365 1290; www.oneteaspoon.com.au; 86 Gould St, Bondi; ⏱ 10am-6pm Fri-Wed, 10am-7pm Thu; 🚌 380

Rising star Sydney designer Jamie Blakey has her young women's streetwear range in

David Jones and Harrods, but this concept store gives her space all of her own to show off her cleavage-revealing dresses, as well as bikinis, belts and shoes.

TUCHUZY
Map pp94–5   Clothing & Accessories
☎ 9365 5371; 90 Gould St, Bondi; ⏰ 9am-6pm Mon-Wed & Fri & Sat, 9am-7pm Thu, 10am-6pm Sun; 🚌 380
Tuchuzy stocks an edgy collection of local and imported labels for budding male or female rock stars, including Sass & Bide (p128), Karen Walker, Rock Stars & Angels and American Apparel. They have flashy accessories and contemporary vintage selections as well. If you've been wondering where you'll find your baby's first Che Guevara T-shirt, look no further.

DIRT CHEAP CDS
Map pp94–5   Music
☎ 9365 5222; 180 Campbell Pde, Bondi; ⏰ 10am-7pm Sun-Thu, 10am-10pm Fri & Sat; 🚌 389
Missing that hard-to-find fifth Flaming Lips CD, or has your LP of Rolling Stones' *Goat's Head Soup* finally given up the ghost? This is the place for brand new back-catalogue CDs, most priced around $10. There's also a branch at 238 Pitt St in the city.

WESTFIELD BONDI JUNCTION
Map pp94–5   Shopping Centre
☎ 9947 8000; 500 Oxford St, Bondi Junction; ⏰ 10am-6pm Mon-Wed & Fri, 10am-9pm Thu, 10am-7pm Sat & Sun; 🚉 Bondi Junction
Vast. That's the only word to describe Australia's flashest shopping mall. Expect to get lost; the space-time continuum does funny things as you wander around the 438 stores spread over six levels in two interlinking buildings straddling Oxford St. It's even worse in the maze-like underground car park.

Its leading-edge store design showcases some of Australia's biggest names in fashion including Morrissey (p128), Bracewell (p130), Leona Edmiston (p127) alongside the big international brands (Hugo Boss, Armani, Versace). Australia's two big department stores – Myer (p125) and David Jones (p124) – do battle, as do the two main supermarkets (Coles and Woolworths). There's plenty of opportunity for daddy daycare in the form of TV screens, plush couches, cinemas and bars. The food court puts all others to shame.

INNER WEST
Newtown and Glebe are the places to look for anything punky, alternative, Socialist, greenie, intellectual or in shades of black. King St has an interesting collection of boutiques, second-hand stores and (along with Glebe Point Rd) the city's best bookstores. There are now enough homeware shops to strike the fear of gentrification into the hearts of long-term residents.

There are also branches of Simon Johnson (p129), Quick Brown Fox (p128) and C's Flashback (p129) to be found here.

NEWTOWN & ERSKINEVILLE
NEWTOWN OLD WARES
Map pp100–1   Antiques
☎ 9519 6705; 439 King St, Newtown; ⏰ 11am-5pm Tue, 10am-5pm Wed-Sat, 11am-4pm Sun; 🚉 Newtown
Yearning for a vintage Cilla Black poster? This funky antique store is home to much that's cool and kitsch from 'deco to disco'. There are old transistor radios, TV sets and telephones as well as groovy furniture, lamps and knick-knacks. It's a great shop to potter about in.

BETTER READ THAN DEAD
Map pp100–1   Books
☎ 9557 8700; 265 King St, Newtown; ⏰ 9.30am-9pm Mon-Thu, 9.30am-10pm Fri & Sat; 🚉 Newtown
This is our favourite Sydney bookshop, and not just because of the clever name and great selection of Lonely Planet titles. Nobody seems to mind if you waste hours perusing the beautifully presented aisles, stacked with high-, medium- and deliciously low-brow reading materials.

GOULD'S BOOK ARCADE
Map pp100–1   Books
☎ 9519 8947; 32 King St, Newtown; ⏰ 9am-midnight; 🚌 422-3
Possibly the scariest secondhand bookstore in the world, the floor-to-ceiling racks and stacks seem in perpetual danger of burying you under a ton of Stalinist analysis. While all manner of musty out-of-print books are stocked, owner Bob's leftie leanings are reflected in one very large wall. You'll find a whole fixture devoted to Trotsky, another to Marxist philosophy and three to the British labour movement.

top picks

BOOKSHOPS

- **Better Read Than Dead** (opposite)
- **Berkelouw Books** (p134)
- **Gleebooks** (right)
- **Ariel** (p127)
- **Gertrude & Alice** (p131)

FASTER PUSSYCAT

Map pp100–1   Clothing & Accessories
☎ 9519 1744; 431A King St, Newtown; 🕒 11am-6pm Mon-Wed & Fri & Sat, 11am-7pm Thu, noon-5.30pm Sun; 🚇 Newtown

Inspired by 'trash pop culture, hot rods and rock and roll' this cool cat coughs up clothing for all genders and ages (including baby punkwear) in several shades of New-town black.

FROLIC   Map pp100–1   Clothing & Accessories
☎ 9519 9895; 461 King St, Newtown; 🕒 11am-6pm Tue-Fri, 10.30am-6pm Sat, 11am-5pm Sun; 🚇 Newtown

You'll find funky tees, sunnies, hats and vintage frocks in this store specialising in 1950s to 1980s secondhand men's and women's clothes, as well as stocking several local brands. Masquerade as a local with a Newtown Jets T-shirt.

HOLY MOLEY

Map pp100–1   Clothing & Accessories
☎ 9550 4033; 325 King St, Newtown; 🕒 11am-6pm Mon-Wed & Fri & Sat, 11am-7pm Thu, noon-5pm Sun; 🚇 Newtown

You won't miss this one; its very-Newtown murals (Robert DeNiro in *Taxi Driver*, a skeleton with a mohawk) are the first thing you see as you step out of the station. Inside it's all spunky-punky T-shirts, baby-doll dresses and sexy lingerie.

PRETTY IN PINK

Map pp100–1   Clothing & Accessories
☎ 9516 2331; 533 King St, Newtown; 🕒 10.30am-4pm Tue, 10.30am-5.30pm Wed & Fri & Sat, 10.30am-6.30pm Thu, 11am-5pm Sun; 🚇 St Peters

Sydney designer Jessica McKenzie delivers women's clothes with retro flair and a flirty fun spin in her signature store. You'll find heavily patterned baby-doll skirts along with dresses, lingerie and accessories. Everything is made locally.

BEEHIVE GALLERY

Map pp100–1   Clothing & Accessories, Homewares, Jewellery
☎ 9550 2515; 441 King St, Newtown; 🕒 11am-5pm Tue-Wed & Fri & Sun, 11am-7pm Thu, 11am-6pm Sat; 🚇 Newtown

As long as it's homemade it has a home in this store, focussing on quality art and crafts. There are some interesting small photos of Sydney scenes printed on canvas squares that might make a good souvenir.

ENLIGHTENED ELEPHANT

Map pp100–1   Gifts, Jewellery
☎ 9517 9957; 43 Erskineville Rd, Erskineville; 🕒 10am-5pm Wed-Sun; 🚇 Erskineville

This shop stocks fascinating things with a feel-good factor – or as they put it 'gifts that give twice' – made by HIV-positive mothers from Cape Town. There are intricately beaded toys, jewellery, bags made from recycled car tires, coasters and beaded Fosters cans. All are sourced from not-for-profit community-based groups who channel money directly to the artisans.

EGG RECORDS   Map pp100–1   Music
☎ 9550 6056; 3 Wilson St, Newtown; 🕒 10am-6.30pm Mon-Wed & Fri & Sat, 10am-8pm Thu, 11am-5pm Sun; 🚇 Newtown

There's something of the *High Fidelity* too-cool-for-school vibe to this secondhand and new CD and record store, but it's an excellent place to, say, complete your collection of 1980s David Bowie 12" singles.

GLEBE

GLEEBOOKS   Map pp100–1   Books
☎ 9660 2333; 49 Glebe Point Rd, Glebe; 🕒 9am-9pm Mon-Sun; 🚌 431-4

One of Sydney's best and most loved, you'll find everything from quality fiction to academic tomes at the main store. Children's books, antiquarian and used books are further down the road (191 Glebe Point Rd).

BROADWAY SHOPPING CENTRE

Map pp100–1   Shopping Centre
☎ 9213 3333; cnr Broadway & Bay St, Glebe; 🕒 10am-7pm Mon-Wed & Fri, 10am-9pm Thu, 9am-6pm Sat, 10am-6pm Sun; 🚌 422-3

Located in the grand old Grace Bros building, this large complex offers dozens of shops, a food court, a Hoyts cinema complex and two late-night supermarkets. Parking is free for the first three hours – great for a cheeky stop for brunch in Glebe or to visit the University of Sydney (p99).

BALMAIN & LEICHHARDT
BERKELOUW BOOKS

Map pp100–1   Books
☎ 9560 3200; 70 Norton St, Leichhardt; ☺ 9am-10pm Sun-Mon, 9am-11pm Tue-Sat; 🚌 435-8
Six generations of Berkelouws have specialised in secondhand books and printed rarities since setting up shop in Holland in 1812, but its modern stores are just as good for finding new releases and sipping coffee. There's another branch at 19 Oxford St, Paddington.

KIRRILY STORES

Map pp100–1   Clothing & Accessories
☎ 0424 930 206; 317 Darling St, Balmain; ☺ 9am-8pm; 🚢 Balmain
A slice of Newtown in Balmain (and also at 175 Coogee Bay Rd, Coogee), Kirrily has casual cool women's wear that won't break the bank; a welcome change from the upmarket couturiers of the area.

BLUELIST[1] (blu,list) *v.*
to recommend a travel experience.
What's your recommendation? www.lonelyplanet.com/bluelist

EATING

top picks

- **Pier** (Seafood, p151)
- **Guillaume At Bennelong** (Mod Oz, p140)
- **Spice I Am** (Thai, p145)
- **Chu Bay** (Vietnamese, p145)
- **Billy Kwong** (Chinese, p145)
- **Toko** (Japanese, p146)
- **Zaaffran** (Indian, p141)
- **Fifi's** (Lebanese, p148)
- **Lo Studio** (Italian, p145)
- **Bathers' Pavilion** (French, p150)

EATING

Not content with proving itself world class in the swimming pool, on the cricket pitch and on the big screen, Australia has finally taken the competition to the kitchen. Good old-fashioned Aussie parochialism has turned chefs into celebrities to rival *Home and Away* starlets. Take Tetsuya (Wakuda) and Bill (Granger); their eponymous restaurants have granted them a first-name recognition amongst Sydney sophisticates equal to Kylie, the great one-named diva herself.

The simple fact is that Sydney's cuisine now rivals that of any world city. While Melbourne has made much of its Mediterranean melting pot, Sydney more than any other Australian city has woken up and found itself on the Pacific Rim. It's in its food that White Australia is finally being laid to rest. Nowadays Cheryl and Darryl from Rooty Hill are just as likely to head out for Thai, Vietnamese or Lebanese as they are for fish and chips or a roast.

The country is blessed with excellent produce from its farms and its fisheries. A simple rule of thumb in Sydney: when in doubt, order the prawns – they're generally large and luscious. The tropical north provides pineapples, mangoes and even winter strawberries, while the cooler southern climate lends itself to fine wines and cheeses. These come together in a fresh, flavoursome, multicultural mix on dining tables throughout the harbour rim.

Sydney is also blessed with enlightened licensing laws that allow you to bring your own (BYO) wine and sometimes beer to those restaurants that offer the choice. You'll usually be charged corkage (even if your bottle's got a screw cap) at either a per-person or per-bottle rate, but it's generally cheaper than choosing off the wine list – and at least you know what you're getting.

While Sydney's top restaurants are properly pricey, eating out needn't be expensive. There are plenty of ethnic eateries where you can grab a cheap and tasty pizza or a bowl of noodles. Judicious ordering can even land you a reasonably priced meal at some of Sydney's celebrity kitchens – try brunch at bills (p142) or share vegetarian dishes at Billy Kwong (p145).

Any taste can be catered to. You can greet the day with a heart-starting espresso and some ricotta hot cakes in Potts Point; chow down the freshest catch of the day at a waterfront restaurant in Darling Harbour; stave off afternoon hunger pangs with tapas in Glebe; gobble a pie with sauce at an evening footy game at Aussie Stadium; rise above it all with a glittering harbour view and the snazziest top-end cuisine on the North Shore; or spend the wee hours in a post-midnight supper at one of Chinatown's great-value eating dens.

MOD OZ

At one point those making a case for a distinctly Australian cuisine would have pointed to pavlova, lamingtons and Anzac biscuits (risking pistols at dawn from the New Zealand Countrywomens' Institute) or 'bush tucker'. While eating the Coat of Arms (kangaroo and emu, with a crocodile starter) is a distinctly Australian experience and worth trying (kangaroo is quite tasty and has a gamey quality, reminiscent of venison), it doesn't a cuisine make.

At which point the country's most innovative chefs reverted to convict stereotypes; eyeing the surroundings carefully, they determined what to steal from their neighbours and wove it all into something better than the sum of its parts – something just right for the location and climate.

This mix of European traditions with exotic flavours is what is casually termed 'Mod Oz' (Modern Australian) cuisine – an amalgamation of Mediterranean, Asian, Middle Eastern and Californian cooking practices that emphasise lightness, experimentation and healthy eating. It's a hybrid style, shaped by migrant influences, climatic conditions and local ingredients. It is essentially a culinary adventure built around local, seasonal produce that plays freely with imported ingredients, along with their accompanying

top picks

MOD OZ

- Guillaume At Bennelong (p140)
- Ripples (p150)
- Bentley Restaurant & Bar (p145)
- Café Sydney (p140)
- Quay (p140)

cooking techniques and traditions. In Sydney this magpie style has filtered down from sophisticated restaurants to modest corner bistros and pub grub.

HISTORY & CULTURE

While the original convicts and marines came close to starvation in the early years of the settlement, the local Aboriginal tribes had millennia of experience in deriving sustenance from the land. You can see examples of the edible plants harvested by the Cadigal, Darug and D'harawal people in the *Cadi Jam Ora* (First Encounters) beds of the Royal Botanic Gardens (p57). The existence of huge middens in the city centre show that shellfish were a staple, and fish, birds, snakes and kangaroo provided further sources of protein.

The settlers aspired to the bland food of England – roast meat, pies and boiled vegetables. In lean times, the city's poor would fall back on rabbit. Eventually 'meat and three veg' dinners followed by tinned fruit and cream became the standard Australian home-cooked meal, with 'throwing some prawns on the bar-be(-cue)' for the more adventurous.

Waves of immigrants brought their cuisine with them, starting with the Chinese in the 1850s. Mediterranean migrants (particularly Italians and, to a lesser extent, Greeks and southern Slavs) started to have an impact on local fare from the early 20th century, especially in the area around Kings Cross. They also started a love affair with coffee that has spread to every corner of the city.

In the latter half of the century, wars in Vietnam and Lebanon brought new waves of refugees and new ways of cooking – although it's only recently that these cuisines have crossed into the mainstream. In the 1980s and '90s the number of young Thai students burgeoned, firmly establishing one of Sydney's most popular ethnic cuisines.

It's no exaggeration to say that in Sydney today you could experience a different culture's cuisine every night for a month without doubling up. You'll find everything from Maltese to Nepalese within a few kilometres of the city centre.

HOW SYDNEY PEOPLE EAT

Breakfast is a social event for many Sydneysiders. Many now prefer to conduct business over a café latte and a bowl of porridge instead of an upmarket power lunch or fine

top picks

ETHNIC EATING AREAS

- Thai King St, Newtown
- Vietnamese Chinatown; King St, Newtown; Cabramatta
- Chinese Chinatown; Chatswood
- Indian Cleveland St, Surry Hills
- Balkan Oxford St, Darlinghurst
- Italian Leichhardt; Haberfield; Stanley St, East Sydney
- Spanish Liverpool St, City

dinner, and friends often choose to start the day with scrambled eggs, gossip and giggling. The prime neighbourhoods for this are Potts Point, Surry Hills and Bronte, but it would be surprising not to find a respectable breakfast café in any part of Greater Sydney.

Breakfast time can start around 6am and extend to a late-morning brunch, although many cafés serve all-day breakfasts, especially on weekends. The all-day option is perfect for hardened party animals and is therefore more common in the inner east and west. If you're an early riser, a well-positioned breakfast table can prove an entertaining platform for watching the detritus of the night before, spilling out of Darlinghurst and Kings Cross clubs. Yum cha in Chinatown is a popular weekend brunch option.

It's in the coffee stakes that Sydney (and indeed most Australasian cities) wipes the floor with London and Los Angeles. You won't have to settle for wussy drip filters here – it's espresso all the way. The big international chains have sprouted up, but are generally considered by the city's hipsters to be the last refuge of the boring and unimaginative. Chose a local café and order a flat white (espresso with warm milk), café latte (similar but milkier, often served in a glass), cappuccino (espresso topped with frothed milk and chocolate or cinnamon), long or short black (espresso without milk and with varying amounts of water), *macchiato* (a short black with a tiny splash of milk) or *ristretto* (harder to find, but basically a very concentrated espresso currently fashionable due to Ian Thorpe). Most cafés now offer soy or 'skinny' milk.

For most working Sydneysiders, lunch means a quick sandwich or salad gobbled at their desk or in a nearby park. Others head to shopping centre food halls (generally serving a selection of ethnically diverse bain-marie fare) – though there are many restaurants that provide an upmarket option. Chinatown sees large lunchtime crowds jamming its good-value eateries – it's a great place to go for a casual and delicious meal.

Dinner is more important on the social scale, but unless it's a special event, casual is usually the go. Jeans, tidy T-shirts and trainers are generally fine in all but the most exclusive joints. At Asian, Lebanese and Indian restaurants, sharing dishes is the norm – hogging your own is regarded as bad form, unless you're the only vegetarian.

At a European-style restaurant many Sydneysiders would stop at two courses, only going 'all the way' for a special occasion at a special place (or when work's paying). When it comes to the pointy end of the night there's usually a discussion as to whether to split the bill or pay for your own. Splitting is more common, but if you've knocked back the lobster and a bottle of Dom Perignon, you should insist on paying extra.

VEGETARIANS & VEGANS

Sydney is not a difficult city for herbivores. Vegetarians should have no trouble finding satisfying choices on most menus – unless you wander into a steak house by mistake. Some of Sydney's leading restaurants offer separate vegetarian menus, which at Tetsuya's (p141) and the Bathers' Pavilion (p150) stretch to multiple course degustation.

At Asian eateries it pays to inquire as to whether the vegetable dishes are cooked with oyster or fish sauce. Usually they'll be happy to make soy-based substitutions. Many of the more established restaurants such as Thai Potong (p148) specifically mark strictly vegetarian options on the menu. Southeast Asian vegetarian dishes are usually a good option for vegans also, but once again it pays to check.

The more socially progressive suburbs, such as Newtown and Glebe, have the widest range of veggie options. Also worth noting is the cluster of mainly vegetarian South Indian restaurants on Cleveland St, Surry Hills, between Crown and Bourke Sts.

HOOKING A BETTER CATCH

No wonder Sydney's restaurants feature seafood so prominently – the island nation's fishing zone is the third-largest in the world, comprising 133 different fisheries. These generate over two billion dollars annually, making it Australia's fourth-biggest income-earning industry. But what toll does the removal of 287,000 tonnes of fish and associated by-catch (dolphins, seals and other species snagged unintentionally) have on the oceans? Is this sustainable?

Anissa Lawrence is the CEO of Ocean Watch Australia, a body set up by the fishing industry to work towards sustainability. Some of its innovations to improve fishing methods are deceptively simple, such as hanging streamers from hook and line fisheries to deter sea birds from getting snagged. Others are more high-tech; Ocean Watch is working on a trawl net design to allow undersized fish to escape the haul. The body also works with coastal councils to install recycling bins for the disposal of leftover fishing line – reducing the likelihood of marine creatures becoming tangled.

So what can we do to make a difference? Australians consume an average of 16kg of seafood per person each year. However 75% of that is imported (such as canned fish), often from less well-regulated countries, while 75% of Australia's higher quality catch is exported. The remaining 25% is what's served up to you in restaurants.

Lawrence wants to see a grassroots momentum build from people asking at their supermarkets 'Is this fish sustainable?' She also suggests seeking out the Marine Stewardship Council logo – you'll currently find it on West Australian rock lobsters, John West salmon (but not its tuna), New Zealand Hoki, and Sealord and Bird's Eye products.

She agrees that line-caught fishing is generally better than trawling and suggests avoiding ordering shark and orange roughy – both are long lived, slow growing species that produce relatively few offspring.

The independent Australian Marine Conservation Society (☎ 07-3393 5811; www.amcs.org.au) goes further still with its handy pocket-sized Australia's Sustainable Seafood Guide. It splits commercial species into three categories – say no, think twice and better choice – depending on how they've been caught and reared. The society doesn't approve of sea-cage aquaculture.

Given that neither you nor your waiter are likely to know exactly how the fish made their way onto the menu, we've used their guide to put together the following rough suggestions on the very worst and best things to order:

Worst: Atlantic salmon, blue warhou, broadbill swordfish, commercial scallop, eastern gemfish (hake), ocean trout, orange roughy, oreos, rays, redfish (nannygai), shark (flake), silver trevally, snapper, southern bluefish tuna

Best: abalone, Australian salmon, blue swimmer crab, bream, calamari, crayfish, cuttlefish, flathead, leatherjacket, marron, mullet, mussels, octopus, oysters, squid, trevally (but not silver), western rock lobster, whiting, yabbies

Catering specifically to vegans are the Iku Wholefoods chain (www.iku.com.au), which has cafés throughout Sydney, and Pure Wholefoods (p151).

COOKING COURSES

If food's your thing and you want to leave Sydney with more than some happily gained inches around your belt, several seminars enable you to expand your culinary repertoire while indulging in food and wine tastings or even full meals.

One of the city's leading providores Simon Johnson (p129) hosts the excellent 'Talk Eat Drink' series, featuring a two-hour class from a leading chef ($90). They are usually held on Saturday mornings from 10.30am at the Pyrmont store (see www.simonjohnson.com.au).

The Sydney Fish Market (p103) attracts 14,000 people per year to its regular 'Sydney Seafood School' sittings. Courses start from $75 and run from 11am to 3pm on weekends and from 6.30pm to 8.30pm about three nights per week (see www.sydneyfishmarket.com.au). They, too, feature celebrity chefs and culminate in a food and wine tasting.

For a more Ocker experience, try the Bar-Be School (☎ 9460 2700; www.bar-beschool.com.au). It offers a series of three sessions for a hefty $250 (or single sessions for $99), where you'll learn to barbecue meat, seafood or vegetable skewers. The 2½-hour classes are held from 11.30am or 3pm on Saturdays at either the Union Hotel, North Sydney or the Fairland Pavilion, Centennial Park – culminating in a full meal and wine tasting.

PRACTICALITIES

Opening Hours

Cafés and restaurants generally open seven days a week. If they do close, it's usually on a Sunday night or Monday. Cafés often serve food throughout the day from around 7am until 5pm, unless they offer a dinner menu. Restaurant serving hours are more rigid; noon to 3pm is a usual lunch sitting and 6pm to 9pm is typical for dinner. Only hours that differ substantially from these are mentioned in the reviews.

How Much?

Eating in Sydney can be as thrifty as a $4 foccacia or a $7 Chinese noodle soup. At midrange restaurants you can expect to pay

PRICE GUIDE	
$$$	mains over $25
$$	mains $12-25
$	mains under $12

between $12 and $25 for a main course. At the city's top restaurants you can easily be looking at $30 to $50 for a main course, and over $100 for a degustation menu.

Booking Tables

Most restaurants take reservations for both lunch and dinner. For the best restaurants it's safest to book at least a week ahead, although you can sometimes sneak in with less notice, particularly for a mid-week lunch. For some, such as Tetsuya's, months are required.

Luckily for tourists some of Sydney's top tables don't take bookings at all; if you're prepared to wait a couple of hours you'll snaffle a table. These restaurants often have a bar or arrangement with a nearby pub – put your name on the list and have a liquid appetiser.

Tipping

Waiting staff at cafés and restaurants are paid a living wage, so tipping is not compulsory. If the service is up to snuff, it's common to tip around 10%, particularly at better restaurants. If anything gets your goat, you don't have to tip at all. At cafés where you order and pay at the counter, tipping is not expected but there's often a jar where customers can throw their change.

Self-Catering

Sydney's two big supermarkets are Coles and Woolworths, with branches everywhere. Some are open 24 hours or until midnight. Every suburb worth its weight will have a decent delicatessen.

THE ROCKS & CIRCULAR QUAY

If you feel like a splurge, this is the place to come. The charismatic back lanes of The Rocks are dotted with little eateries, from 24-hour pancake joints to white-linen palaces. Following the horseshoe around from the Harbour Bridge to the Opera House you'll find dozens of upmarket restaurants, all with glorious water views. It should come as no surprise that this most touristy of precincts is also the priciest. If at all possible, budget for at least one night where you can throw on your glad rags and let Sydney's showiness seduce you.

THE ROCKS

QUAY Map p54 Mod Oz $$$
☎ 9251 5600; upper level, Overseas Passenger Terminal; mains $48-65; ☽ lunch Tue-Fri, dinner daily; ⚇ Circular Quay

Quay is shamelessly guilty of breaking the rule that good views make for bad food. Peter Gilmore may be one of Sydney's younger celebrity chefs, but Quay's exquisite cuisine proves he's at the top of his game (doubters should try the crispy-skin Murray cod with shitake). And the view? Like dining in a postcard. Bookings are recommended.

HARBOUR VIEW HOTEL
Map p54 Mod Oz $$$
☎ 9252 4111; 18 Lower Fort St; mains $22-29; ☽ lunch Mon-Fri, dinner Mon-Sat; ⚇ Circular Quay

Request a table with a view in the intimate upstairs dining room of this lovingly restored 1920s pub, nearly directly underneath the Harbour Bridge. An old-fashioned ambience (crisp white linen and antique crockery mounted on the walls) matches hearty but interesting meals, accompanied by complementary damper and consommé.

GUMNUT TEAGARDEN
Map p54 Café $$
☎ 9247 9591; 28 Harrington St; mains $8-17; ☽ 8am-5pm Sat-Tue, 8am-10pm Wed-Fri; ⚇ Circular Quay

Housed in the leafy backyard of a wonderfully preserved Rocks cottage (1829), the Gumnut serves good, old-fashioned nosh such as sandwiches, pies and ploughmen's platters. The antique theme carries through to tables fashioned from Singer sewing machine bases. Expect quality coffee and cakes Granny would be proud of. Chill out to live jazz on Friday nights and Sunday afternoons.

EAST CIRCULAR QUAY

ARIA Map p54 Mod Oz $$$
☎ 9252 2555; 1 Macquarie St; mains $44-54; ☽ lunch Mon-Fri, dinner daily; ⚇ Circular Quay

Carrying on the operatic theme of its famous neighbour, Aria offers a winning combination of artful dishes (the roasted duck breast with rhubarb *tarte tatin*, parsnip puree and black pepper sauce is music for the mouth), superb harbour views, an award-winning wine list and flawless service. Reservations essential.

GUILLAUME AT BENNELONG
Map p54 Mod Oz $$$
☎ 9241 1999; Sydney Opera House; mains $38-50; ☽ lunch Thu & Fri, dinner Mon-Sat; ⚇ Circular Quay

Located under the smallest of the Opera House's iconic sails, a meal at Guillaume won't fail to be a treasured Sydney memory. Award-winning chef Guillaume Brahimi's masterful style is evident in every divine dish. Just thinking about the rib-eye of Wagyu beef cooked on the bone ($180 for two) is enough to induce palpitations (on two counts). Book well ahead.

CAFÉ SYDNEY Map p54 Mod Oz $$$
☎ 9251 8683; Customs House, 31 Alfred St; mains $28-39; ☽ noon-11pm Mon-Fri, 5-11pm Sat, noon-5pm Sun; ⚇ Circular Quay

At Café Sydney you never know if your meal will come out of a saucepan, wok, tandoori oven or wood-fired grill, but you can always be sure that the views will come straight from heaven. Easing into the roasted barramundi with yabbies ($39) on a lazy Sunday afternoon while live jazz plays is one of the more sublime Sydney experiences.

TRAMEZZINI ESPRESSO
Map p54 Café $
☎ 9232 0422; 50 Bridge St; mains $4-7; ☽ 6.30am-5pm Mon-Fri; ⚇ Circular Quay

There aren't a lot of good places in the city for a reasonably priced healthy bite, so this Italian café in the foyer of the AMP building is worth remembering. Unsurprisingly the clientele is extremely suity, but don't let that and all the ostentatious marble get in the way of a delicious egg and parmesan breakfast roll.

CITY CENTRE

The biggest names have tended to gravitate to the big end of town, where the big bucks are. Without harbour views, the city's central restaurants tend to be discreet upmarket spots, perfect for secret handshakes over million-dollar deals. Some have beaten geography by perching themselves up towers, while others stake out a sunny spot in the parks.

Expect a reverse gradation of prices, starting at the water and lightening considerably as you head inland. For a cheap lunch, make like an office worker – grab something at one of the numerous food halls and sandwich bars and head for Hyde Park. There's a tiny Spanish Quarter taking up a stretch of Liverpool St west of George St.

TETSUYA'S Map pp62–3 French-Japanese $$$

☎ 9267 2900; www.tetsuyas.com; 529 Kent St; degustation $185; ⏲ 6-11pm Tue-Fri, noon-11pm Sat; ⓡ Town Hall

Tetsuya's has been ranked within the top five best restaurants in the *world* – come here with a palate that seeks a culinary journey rather than a simple stuffed belly. The degustation menu offers 10 courses of amazingly creative morsels of art (portions are small) and tastes that are pure, refined and exhilarating. It pays to book months in advance.

EST Map pp62–3 Mod Oz $$$

☎ 9240 3010; Level 1, Establishment Hotel, 252 George St; mains $48; ⏲ lunch Mon-Fri, dinner Mon-Sat; ⓡ Wynyard

Legendary Sydney chef Peter Doyle and sommelier Franck Moreau keep the business crowds powering through deal-sealing corporate lunches at this slick eatery. Portions are small but high quality and the dining room more suited to groups than to intimate meals, but this classy place still exemplifies Sydney dining at its best. Thick wallet and fancy threads a must.

BÉCASSE Map pp62–3 French $$$

☎ 9283 3440; 204 Clarence St; mains $38-48; ⏲ lunch Mon-Fri, dinner Mon-Sat; ⓡ Town Hall

As you enter through the heavy black velvet drapes you'll know you're somewhere special. The bling of crystal chandeliers brings Sydney sparkle into an elegant but austere dining room, currently ranked Sydney's best. Try the degustation menu ($120): 10 courses of gustatory heaven, superbly created by chef Justin North and complemented by unsullied service. Book ahead and dress up.

CASA ASTURIANA Map pp62–3 Spanish $$

☎ 9264 1010; 77 Liverpool St; tapas $9-15, mains $23-29; ⏲ noon-10pm; ⓡ Town Hall

Tapas is flavour of the month in Sydney, but this atmospheric little eatery in Sydney's tiny Spanish Quarter predates the current trend. Try the delicious seafood, meat and vegetarian titbits and order a fine

Spanish wine, sangria or Asturian cider to wash it all down. If you're in the mood for a *cazuela* (baked fish fillet), paella or even weekend flamenco, you're in luck.

BAR QUATTRO Map pp62–3 Italian $$

☎ 9267 0299; St James Station, Hyde Park; mains $12-25; ⏲ 7am-5pm Mon-Fri, 8am-5pm Sat & Sun; ⓡ St James

As you sit admiring Hyde Park, you wouldn't think that less than a decade ago this pleasant sandstone café was one of Sydney's most notorious public toilets. The goings on are much more genteel these days – generally involving chatting, drinking coffee and choosing items off a traditional Italian menu. It's a lovely spot and the seafood pasta is delicious.

DARLING HARBOUR & CHINATOWN

'See water, seafood' is the simple equation offered in Darling Harbour, and you'll find uninterrupted rows of restaurants lining the Harbourside (p74), Cockle Bay (p74) and King St Wharf (p74) developments. Most are pricey tourist-driven affairs that are generally good without being outstanding.

Chinatown is one of the city's best bets for a cheap, satisfying meal – especially after midnight. While Chinese rightly dominates, it also has excellent Vietnamese, Malaysian and Korean restaurants.

ZAAFFRAN Map p72 Indian $$$

☎ 9211 8900; Level 2, 345 Harbourside, Darling Harbour; mains $17-38; ⏲ lunch & dinner; MLR Convention

Indian food doesn't come fancier than this, with Chef Vikrant Kapoor (of Singapore's Raffles fame) whipping up an unfaultable assortment of both traditional dishes and his own creations. Case in point is the tempting dessert menu featuring Indian twists on European favourites. The Darling Harbour views spice things up even further.

EMPEROR'S GARDEN BBQ & NOODLES Map p72 Chinese $$

☎ 9281 9899; 213 Thomas St, Haymarket; dishes $8-26; ⏲ 9.30am-11pm; ⓡ Central

With barbecued ducks dangling in the window and bright lighting and basic furnishings inside, this is the real Chinatown deal. Try the gow gee and the delicious softshell crab, or if you're more adventurous there's always the pig's blood jelly congee. Servings are large, so expect to share the pricier dishes.

MARIGOLD RESTAURANT
Map p72   Chinese $$
☎ 9281 3388; Level 5, 683 George St, Haymarket; yum cha (4-5 serves) $15-25, banquet $30-60; ⏰ 10am-3pm & 5.30-midnight; 🚉 Central
This vast yum cha palace is a constant whirl of trolley dollies in silk dresses and waiters in bowties bustling around the 800 seats. It's hard to resist gorging as the Cantonese delights are presented for inspection – dim sum, dumplings, steamed pork buns, chickens' feet and all the other usual suspects. On weekends expect to queue.

SUPER BOWL Map p72   Chinese $$
☎ 9281 2462; 41 Dixon St, Haymarket; dishes $7-24; ⏰ 8am-2am; 🚉 Central
Take it as an extremely good sign that this is the place on Dixon St always crammed with Chinese diners. From the street-side tables you're well positioned to soak up the Chinatown vibe and slurp up a bowl of noodles. It's a good place for a post-midnight snack.

XIC LO Map p72   Vietnamese $
☎ 9280 1678; 215A Thomas St, Haymarket; mains $8-14; ⏰ 11am-10.30pm; 🚉 Central
Serving up authentic favourites such as pho bo (beef rice-noodle soup) and rice paper rolls, this slick diner is a worthy crowd-pleaser. The food is excellent – fresh, tangy and as well-balanced as Vietnamese cuisine is supposed to be.

JAIPUR SWEETS Map p72   Indian $
☎ 9280 1111; 188 Elizabeth St, Sydney; mains $6-14; ⏰ 10.30am-10.30pm; 🚉 Museum
While Jaipur has plenty of Indian desserts on offer, it dishes up excellent meals as well. Vegetarian options dominate, with plenty of thali and curry to choose from. You can't get better value than the $6 'dhal of the day' – served with two roti, a small salad and spicy lime chutney.

SEA BAY RESTAURANT
Map p72   Chinese $
☎ 9267 4855; 372 Pitt St, Sydney; dishes $10-13; ⏰ 11am-10pm Mon-Sat; 🚉 Museum
Sea Bay has slipped the touristy tethers of Chinatown and drifted a few blocks north,

but the aesthetic is the same. Expect brightly lit, basic surroundings and simple, satisfying food. The shredded potato with chilli is a winner, as are the pancakes and dumplings.

DARLINGHURST TO POTTS POINT

With the exception of the row of upmarket restaurants lining Woolloomooloo Finger Wharf (p80), this neighbourhood doesn't offer the razzle-dazzle of the harbour. What it has instead is a buzzy set of small spunky bistros and cafés with charisma. Charming Stanley St still has long-standing Italian survivors, now sharing space with sushi bars. Victoria St offers an eclectic mix of ethnic cuisines as it passes through Darlinghurst and Potts Point. Tiny Challis Ave houses the city's coolest micro-cafés.

DARLINGHURST & EAST SYDNEY

BILLS Map p78   Mod Oz $$$
☎ 9360 9631; 433 Liverpool St, Darlinghurst; breakfast $5-18, mains $19-30; ⏰ 7.30am-10pm Mon-Sat, 8.30am-3pm Sun; 🚉 Kings Cross
Although it's now cloned throughout the Eastern Suburbs, the original bills still has the best vibe. The tucked-away location and large communal table lend a casualness not normally associated with celebrity chef establishments. Bill Granger is Mr Scrambled Egg, so dropping in for brunch is an affordable way of sampling the best bits of one of Sydney's iconic culinary talents.

BAR REGGIO Map p78   Italian $$
☎ 9332 1129; 135 Crown St, East Sydney; mains $12-24; ⏰ 10am-10.30pm Mon-Thu, 10am-11pm Fri & Sat; 🚉 Museum
While most of East Sydney's celebrated Italian restaurants have closed or gone up-market, Bar Reggio has kept its old-school atmosphere. Try for a seat in the courtyard lined with travel brochure murals and dig in to a traditional pizza, pasta or grill. For a cheap, satisfying lunch try a half ($4) or full ($6 to $7) foccacia.

DON DON Map p78   Japanese $
☎ 9331 3544; 80 Oxford St, Darlinghurst; mains $9-14; ⏰ 11.30am-10.30pm Tue-Sat; 🚉 Museum
We've worked our way backwards and forwards through the handy photo menu

for years and have only had consistently delicious dishes at this tiny Oxford St eatery. Expect everything from chicken *katsu-don* to sashimi, with most meals served with rice, miso and Japanese pickles on the side. It's a popular spot, so be prepared to wait.

TEN BUCK ALLEY Map p78 Café $
☎ 9356 3000; 1/185 Bourke St, Darlinghurst; mains $5-14; ⏰ 7am-4pm Mon-Fri; ⑧ Kings Cross
The name pays homage to the back laneway, once a notorious hangout for transsexual prostitutes. The cheeky chappies at this tiny café continue the alley's bang-for-your-buck tradition, only with delicious food and even better coffee.

BAR COLUZZI Map p78 Café $
☎ 9380 5420; 322 Victoria St, Darlinghurst; counter food $5-10; ⏰ 5am-7pm; ⑧ Kings Cross
One of Sydney's legendary cafés, Coluzzi's been here since 1957 and still attracts an odd-ball mix of older Italian gentlemen, judges, shady Kings Cross 'characters', Darlinghurst gay guys, bohemians and suits. Chose from the tasty selection of bagels, foccacia and pastries available at the counter and grab a table on the street.

WOOLLOOMOOLOO

TOBY'S ESTATE Map p78 Café $
☎ 9358 1196; 129 Cathedral St, Woolloomooloo; counter food $4-9; ⏰ 7am-6pm Mon-Fri, 8am-4pm Sat, 9am-4pm Sun; ⑧ St James, ⑧ 311
While coffee is undoubtedly the main attraction at this tucked away roasters, it's a great place to drop in for a fresh baguette, toasted sandwich, nori roll or cake. As for the brown gold – it's strong, perfectly brewed and usually fair trade.

HARRY'S CAFÉ DE WHEELS
Map p78 Café $
☎ 9347 3074; Cowper Wharf Rdwy, Woolloomooloo; pies $3-4; ⏰ 9am-1am Mon-Wed, 9am-3am Thu, 9am-4am Fri & Sat, 9am-midnight Sun; ⑧ 311
Ok, so it's just a pie cart – but it has been here since 1938 and at 3am after a night on the turps you'll rate it higher than Tetsuya's. Try a Tiger – a pie with mushy peas, potato and gravy on top. Just watch out for the scavenging seagulls (during the day) and rats the size of cats (at night).

KINGS CROSS & POTTS POINT

FRATELLI PARADISO Map p78 Italian $$$
☎ 9357 1744; 12 Challis Ave, Potts Point; mains $20-33; ⏰ 7.30am-10pm Mon-Fri, 7am-6pm Sat & Sun; ⑧ 311
An ever-changing and always interesting menu keeps the locals returning to this small, stylish eatery. Portions aren't large, allowing plenty of room for multiple courses. If you're not a regular the service can be cool, but the food is well worth the wait and the people-watching often excellent.

JIMMY LIK'S Map p78 Southeast Asian $$$
☎ 8354 1400; 188 Victoria St, Potts Point; mains $16-32; ⏰ 6-11pm; ⑧ Kings Cross
This chic eatery offers a menu inspired by Southeast Asian street food, served on a long communal table. The flavours are bold, balanced and invariably delicious. There's usually a wait for restaurant seating – an opportunity to enjoy the bar snacks and adventurous cocktails.

DOV @ DELECTICA Map p78 Café $$
☎ 9368 0600; 130 Victoria St, Potts Point; mains $17-24; ⏰ 7.30am-3pm Sun-Tue, 7.30am-10pm Wed-Sat; ⑧ Kings Cross
Opening onto the nicest part of leafy Victoria St, Dov has a vibe that will tempt you to linger all morning over your newspaper and coffee. The menu varies throughout the day, starting with reasonably priced brekkie ($5 to $14) and lunch (check out the savoury tart of the day) before culminating in substantial evening meals from the ever-changing blackboard menu.

LA BUVETTE Map p78 Café $$
☎ 9358 5113; 35 Challis Ave, Potts Point; mains $11-17; ⏰ 6am-9pm Sun-Thu, 6am-5.30pm Fri & Sat; ⑧ 311
Like its sister Spring next door, La Buvette is absolutely teeny. That doesn't stop it being crammed with the beautiful, the famous and the guppies (gay urban professionals in the latest designer sunglasses). The menu features salads, sandwiches and crepes, but our favourite is the baked eggs with chorizo. Excellent coffee.

SPRING ESPRESSO Map p78 Café $$
☎ 9331 0190; 35 Challis Ave, Potts Point; mains $12-16; ⏰ 6am-5pm; ⑧ 311
It's hard to differentiate this place from La Buvette (same size, clientele, standard –

similar menu) and even more difficult before the first coffee of the day, so just grab whichever has the first table available. Spring's salmon breakfast hits the spot every time.

DOLCETTA Map p78 Italian $$
☎ 9326 9899; 165 Victoria St, Potts Point; mains $10-16; ☺ 6am-10pm Mon-Fri, 6am-3pm Sat & Sun; ⓡ Kings Cross

Perhaps it's because it doubles as a *providore* that this friendly little neighbourhood eatery can offer beautiful meals at such reasonable prices. Where else in Sydney can you find fresh, zingy blue swimmer crab pasta with garlic and lemon zest for $12.50? Try the truffled scrambled eggs for breakfast.

ULIVETO Map p78 Café $$
☎ 9357 7331; 33 Bayswater Rd, Kings Cross; mains $10-15; ☺ 7am-6pm Mon-Fri, 7am-5pm Sat & Sun; ⓡ Kings Cross

Great coffee and muffins are the staples of this chilled-out café, set in a tree-lined plaza. The people-watching's not bad either.

PADDINGTON TO DOUBLE BAY

In this conservative stretch restaurants offer good eating that shies away from the aggressively modern tendencies of its neighbours. Here's where you'll find an appreciation of the just-so steak with the perfect wine, and subdued, well-mannered service to match.

PADDINGTON

VAMPS Map pp84–5 French $$$
☎ 9331 1032; 227 Glenmore Rd, Paddington; mains $12-28; ☺ 6.30-10.30pm Tue-Fri, 9am-2.30pm & 6.30-10.30pm Sat, 9am-2pm Sun; ☒ 389

This romantic little old-style French restaurant serves classics such as duck *à l'orange* and *crêpe suzette* in the evenings. However, it's the weekend Breakfast Club that keeps us coming back. After a hard night out grab a seat in the pretty courtyard, order lots of coffee and a hearty breakfast ($4 to $13) and vamp it up with the waiters.

SLOANES Map pp84–5 Café $$
☎ 9331 6717; 312 Oxford St, Paddington; mains $10-15; ☺ 6.15am-5.30pm Mon-Sat, 7am-5.30pm Sun; ☒ 380

Don't be put off by the tiny interior, head down the back where there's a sweet courtyard surrounded by mature trees. The breakfast and coffee are great, and the lunch blackboard is always crammed with fancy pies, salads, wraps and soups. This is the place where former jailbird Paris Hilton famously, like, totally wandered off without paying her bill. Like, shut up!

RELISH ON REGENT Map pp84–5 Deli $
☎ 9380 8699; 55 Regent St, Paddington; sandwiches $7-9; ☺ 7.30am-7.30pm Mon-Fri, 8am-2pm Sat & Sun; ☒ 380

This little deli in the backstreets of Paddington has a large communal table and sunny window seats. Chose from the enticing salads, filo pastries and frittatas at the counter or direct the construction of your own sandwich from the fresh ingredients. This is a great place to assemble a picnic on the way to Centennial Park or the beaches.

CHOCOLATE BY THE BALD MAN MAX BRENNER Map pp84–5 Café $
☎ 9357 5055; 437 Oxford St, Paddington; sweets $3.50-5; ☺ 9am-11pm Mon-Thu, 9am-midnight Fri & Sat, 10am-10.30pm Sun; ☒ 380

The crazy bald guy has taken a leaf from Willy Wonka's book. Shiny copper pipes lead to big vats of liquid heaven, while shelves bulge with all sorts of tempting treats to takeaway. Try the warm chocolate fondue for two, served with fruit, banana bread and marshmallows ($16), or just sneak in for a coffee and brownie.

WOOLLAHRA

BISTRO MONCUR Map pp84–5 French $$$
☎ 9363 2519; Woollahra Hotel, 116 Queen St, Woollahra; mains $28-40; ☺ lunch Tue-Sun, dinner daily; ☒ 389

With a striking monochromatic mural running the length of one wall and highly regarded chef Damien Pignolet creating marvels in the kitchen, Bistro Moncur has long been a favourite. The menu changes seasonally, but signature dishes such as the French onion soufflé gratin and grilled sirloin *Café de Paris* delight diners all year round. The service is impeccable.

JONES THE GROCER Map pp84–5 Deli $$
☎ 9362 1222; 68 Moncur St, Woollahra; mains $10-14; ☺ 7.30am-5.30pm Mon-Sat, 9am-5pm Sun; ☒ 389

Jones has a reputation as one of Sydney's finest providores – stocking wonderful cheese, chutneys and *charcuterie*. Grab a seat at the communal table for a tasty deli-fresh roll or pasta.

SURRY HILLS TO ALEXANDRIA

Surry Hills' transformation into Sydney's cuisine mecca has been shockingly sudden – roughly coinciding with the 1999 opening of the Eastern Distributor, which made peaceful tree-lined backstreets out of Crown and Bourke Sts (once the main link between the airport and the bridge). In the 2007 *Sydney Morning Herald Good Food Guide*, Surry Hills restaurants nabbed half of the main awards. Even more surprising is the birth of Danks St in rough-edged Waterloo as a new gourmet strip. For a delicious cheap vegetarian meal, try the row of Indian eateries on Cleveland St, between Crown and Bourke.

SURRY HILLS

BILLY KWONG Map pp90–1   Chinese $$$
☎ 9332 3300; 355 Crown St, Surry Hills; mains $20-42; 🕑 dinner; 🚍 301-3
There's something wonderfully egalitarian about top restaurants where queuing's required – perfect for travellers who don't have the luxury of booking weeks ahead. Chef Kylie Kwong serves up a tempting seasonal menu made from the best organic, sustainable, fair-trade ingredients available.

LONGRAIN Map pp90–1   Thai $$$
☎ 9280 2888; 85 Commonwealth St, Surry Hills; mains $28-39; 🕑 lunch Mon-Fri, dinner Mon-Sat; 🚍 Central
Set in a large warehouse conversion with long communal tables, Longrain pushes the boundaries of modern Thai cuisine. Try the caramelised pork hock with chilli vinegar and the eggnet – a large ball of prawns, sprouts and coriander yumminess encased in an egg lattice.

BENTLEY RESTAURANT & BAR
Map pp90–1   Mod Oz $$$
☎ 9332 2344; 320 Crown St, Surry Hills; mains $29-34; 🕑 noon-1am Tue-Sat; 🚍 Museum
The reincarnation of this old corner pub as an upmarket restaurant hasn't thrown the bar out with the bathwater. The mains are an artful take on English pub fare (roast chicken

and duck, slow cooked pork loin, pan-roasted jewfish), while imaginative tapas ($4 to $12) takes the place of bar snacks. Add to the mix faultless service and an extensive wine list.

LO STUDIO Map pp90–1   Italian $$$
☎ 9212 4118; 55 Brisbane St, Surry Hills; mains $24-34; 🕑 lunch Mon-Fri, dinner Mon-Sat; 🚍 Central
The sexy Deco curves of the Paramount Pictures office add glamour to this newcomer to the Surry Hills scene. The modern Italian menu covers a wide base of meat, seafood and vegetarian dishes and is unafraid to be adventurous.

BISTRODE Map pp90–1   French $$$
☎ 9380 7333; 478 Bourke St, Surry Hills; mains $27-33; 🕑 lunch Fri, dinner Tue-Sat; 🚍 301-3
A celebration of all things meaty and fishy, the Bistrode menu will be challenging for some. The lily sure isn't gilded in the descriptions – it's more likely dipped in offal or served in the warm pig's head salad with pickled egg dressing. The food is exceptional – hearty yet intricate with plenty of unusual twists.

SPICE I AM Map pp90–1   Thai $$
☎ 9280 0928; 90 Wentworth Ave, Surry Hills; mains $8-26; 🕑 lunch & dinner Tue-Sun; 🚍 Central
In Sydney parlance this is definitely 'a thing right now'. Once the preserve of local Thais wanting an authentic taste of home, it now has queues out the door. No wonder, as everything we've tried from the over-70 reasonably priced dishes on the menu is wonderful – fragrant and spicy. Expect to be hurried out as soon as you're finished.

BODEGA Map pp90–1   Spanish $$
☎ 9212 7766; 216 Commonwealth St, Surry Hills; tapas $6-26; 🕑 lunch Thu & Fri, dinner Mon-Sat; 🚍 Central
The coolest progeny of the current tapas frenzy, Bodega has a casual vibe, impossibly handsome staff and a very funky matador mural. The dishes vary widely in size and price, with a substantial serve of ocean trout at the upper end. Wash them down with a tipple from the wide range of Hispanic wine, sherry, port and beer.

CHU BAY Map pp90–1   Vietnamese $$
☎ 9331 3386; 312A Bourke St, Surry Hills; mains $12-25; 🕑 dinner; 🚍 380
It's a little sad to be blowing the cover of this local hideaway, but this wonderful

family-run eatery is one of our very favourites. This is an authentically Vietnamese establishment – the pink walls and moving waterfall 'paintings' prove it. The food is always fresh and flavoursome and the service welcoming.

PRASIT'S NORTHSIDE THAI TAKEAWAY Map pp90–1   Thai $$
☎ 9332 1792; 395 Crown St, Surry Hills; mains $12-20; ⏲ lunch & dinner; 🚌 301-3
There are only a handful of tables upstairs at this popular plum-painted eatery, so put your name on the list and grab a drink nearby. The menu covers a wide range of Thai specialities; look for the sublime Moreton Bay Bug in curry sauce in the specials.

MOHR FISH Map pp90–1   Seafood $$
☎ 9318 1326; 202 Devonshire St, Surry Hills; mains $10-20; ⏲ 10.30am-9.30pm; 🚊 Central
Don't expect to find yourself in a fancy eatery when you come to Mohr Fish – this small but popular place takes up a space that's about the size of your living room. It has a very casual atmosphere and only a short, simple menu of excellent seafood – think fancy fish and chips.

TOKO Map pp90–1   Japanese $$
☎ 9357 6100; 490 Crown St, Surry Hills; dishes $7-18; ⏲ lunch Thu-Sat, dinner Mon-Sat; 🚌 301-3
A new concept for Sydney, Toko dishes up delicious modern Japanese tapas – such as a superb soft shell crab ($16) and eggplant with miso ($9). Expect to spend upwards of $30 a meal, more if you're a sashimi junkie (about $6 for two pieces). Check out the brilliant lighting feature made of chopsticks in the so-cool-it-hurts cocktail bar.

LUMIÈRE Map pp90–1   Café $$
☎ 9331 6184; 425 Bourke St, Surry Hills; mains $9-15; ⏲ 7.30am-4.30pm Mon-Fri, 8am-4.30pm Sat & Sun; 🚌 380
It's a sheer delight to sit in the bakery section of this café and watch all manner of gorgeous things being readied for the ovens. For brunch you can't go past the ricotta hot cakes with sour cherries, honeycomb and mascarpone.

TWO GOOD EGGS Map pp90–1   Café $$
☎ 9283 9694; 2/148 Goulburn St, Surry Hills; mains $9-15; ⏲ 7am-4pm Mon-Fri, 8am-3pm Sat; 🚊 Central
We love the egg-shaped lighting fixtures and industrial feel of this corner café on the

lower slopes of Surry Hills. It's a great spot for a weekday breakfast, killer coffee and, yes, eggs dominate.

MAYA TANDOORI Map pp90–1   Indian $
☎ 8394 9799; 472 Cleveland St, Surry Hills; mains $8-11; ⏲ 10am-10.30pm; 🚌 372
On a strip of mainly vegetarian Indian restaurants, Maya Tandoori is proof that the prettiest is not always the best. Don't be put off by the bright lights, nasty furniture and general lack of ambience. The food's authentic, spice-tastic and one hell of a bargain ($13 for four curries, raita, pickles, rice, two roti and dessert).

MALIBU Map pp90–1   Café $
☎ 9280 2233; 62 Foster St, Surry Hills; mains $4-10; ⏲ 8am-2.30pm Mon-Fri; 🚊 Central
It's not often that a simple sandwich shop gets foodies excited, but this tiny hole-in-the-wall is an exception. The sandwiches are absolutely massive and the ingredients fresh and first-rate.

SINGLE ORIGIN ROASTERS
Map pp90–1   Café $
☎ 9211 0665; 60-64 Reservoir St, Surry Hills; mains $4-9; ⏲ 7am-3pm Mon-Fri; 🚊 Central
It's hard to imagine a more passionate bunch of caffeine junkies than this crew – they practically bounce off the walls in their enthusiasm, happy to chat about the fair trade or environmental credentials of their various beans. The food's simple but delicious, including a great bircher muesli.

BOURKE STREET BAKERY
Map pp90–1   Café $
☎ 9669 1011; 633 Bourke St, Surry Hills; mains $3-7; ⏲ 7am-4pm Mon-Fri, 8am-4pm Sat; 🚌 301-303
Foodies go nuts about this little place, and quite right, too. The fresh baking is impeccable, particularly the sourdough bread. Grab a seat and a coffee and pick from the alluring array of pizza slices, pies, tarts and pastries.

WATERLOO & ALEXANDRIA
DANKS STREET DEPOT
Map pp90–1   Café $$$
☎ 9698 2201; 1/2 Danks St, Waterloo; breakfast $5-18, dinner $25-28; ⏲ 7.30am-4pm Mon, 7.30am-11pm Tue-Fri, 8am-11pm Sat, 9am-4pm Sun; 🚌 301-303

Upon its opening this industrial-chic café quickly become a brunch-time gourmet favourite, with the creamed eggs with roasted mushrooms and truffle oil ($17.50) assuming near legendary status.

WAHWAH LOUNGE Map pp90–1   Café $$
☎ 9699 3456; 2/1 Danks St, Waterloo; mains $11-21; ☽ 7am-4pm Mon-Sat, 8am-3pm Sun; ☒ 301-303

With its über-modern interior, friendly staff and great name, this is a dependable spot for a first-rate cooked breakfast or lunch, a healthy sandwich or a daytime wine tipple.

PARK CAFÉ Map pp90–1   Café $$
☎ 9690 0393; 11 Power Ave, Alexandria; mains $11-20; ☽ 7am-3pm; ☒ 309-310

Tucked away in a surprisingly leafy pocket of Alexandria with the factory outlets only a block away, Park Café is a great spot to refuel during a shopping frenzy or to celebrate your bargains with a glass of wine on the sunny terrace. The food's fresh and fabulous with a distinctly Mediterranean feel and the coffee's excellent.

SOPRA Map pp90–1   Italian $$
☎ 1300 552 119; 7 Danks St, Waterloo; mains $15-18; ☽ 10am-3pm Tue-Fri, 8am-3pm Sat; ☒ 301-303

Gastronomes in the know pour into this place, tucked away above one of the city's best gourmet providores. The menu's very seasonal, using the best of the fresh and imported produce on offer downstairs. On Fridays the huge *fritto misto di pesce* (seafood) platter is a highlight.

BONDI TO COOGEE

Sydney's eastern beaches restaurants are an eclectic mix. Bondi offers everything from chin-up, tits-out glamour to funky surfie cafés. Bronte Rd is unbeatable for brunch – particularly when you can spot migrating whales over your cappuccino. For the Ritz of food halls, check out Westfield Bondi Junction (p132) – or stock up with stuff for cooking on the coast's well-maintained coin-operated beachside barbecues. If that sounds like too much hassle, you can always snaffle fish and chips on the sand.

BONDI

ICEBERGS Map pp94–5   Italian $$$
☎ 9365 9000; 1 Notts Ave, Bondi; mains $38-46; ☽ lunch & dinner Tue-Sun; ☒ 380

Maurice Terzini's sleek celebrity magnet absolutely sizzles at its supreme cliff-top locale. His food is to Italian what Mod Oz is to meat and two veg; the upmarket menu is laced with unusual delights. Reservations definitely required.

POMPEI'S
Map pp94–5   Italian $$
☎ 9365 1233; 126 Roscoe St, Bondi; mains $17-20; ☽ 3-11pm Tue-Thu, 11am-11pm Fri-Sun; ☒ 380

While the pizza here is good, it's the northern Italian dishes whipped up by expat George Pompei that are really special. Try the delicious handmade ravioli stuffed with spinach, ricotta and nutmeg, but be sure to leave room for the flavoursome sorbets and gelati.

SABBABA Map pp94–5   Israeli $
☎ 9365 7500; 82 Hall St, Bondi; mains $7-16; ☽ 11am-10pm; ☒ 389

Despite being situated in a block catering mainly to Bondi's Hassidic Jewish community, this Israeli falafel shop attracts more punters in board shorts than black coats (it's not strictly kosher). The vegetarian falafels in pita bread ($7) are a tasty bargain, or if that sounds too healthy, try a meat grill ($16).

GREEN'S CAFÉ
Map pp94–5   Café $$
☎ 9130 6181; 140 Glenayr Ave, Bondi; mains $10-15; ☽ 8am-4pm Wed-Sun; ☒ 389

This institution-green neighbourhood café has a 1950s nana-chic aesthetic and is prone to doing oddball things like hosting tea towel and apron exhibitions. Devonshire teas are served, but the menu is contemporary café fare, with excellent all-day breakfasts (try the delicious parmesan scrambled eggs).

KATIPO COFFEE HOUSE DELUXE
Map pp94–5   Café $
☎ 9387 7399; 101 Bondi Rd, Bondi; mains $5-15; ☽ 6am-9.30pm Mon & Tue, 6am-10pm Wed-Sat, 8am-10pm Sun; ☒ 380

Named after New Zealand's only poisonous spider this unassuming café offers a little extra bite in everything it does. Even the tap water is subtly flavoured with fresh fruit and delivered with a smile. For breakfast try the Nouveau Hippy Vego Feast – a banquet of eggs, herb-roasted tomato, garlic mushrooms, kumera and wilted greens.

JED'S FOODSTORE Map pp94–5 Café $
☎ 9365 0022; 60 Warners Ave, Bondi; mains $5-14; ⏰ 6.30am-3.30pm Mon-Fri, 6.30am-4.40pm Sat & Sun; 🚌 389

With a skateboard and a single trainer hanging from the roof, this sunny corner café is the epitome of slacker cool. Breakfast treats include a delicious quesadilla and the popular breakfast bowl (mountains of berries, muesli and yoghurt). Toasted sambos (sandwiches to the uninitiated) go by the names of Rock Hudson and Errol Flynn (a hammier version).

BRONTE
SWELL Map pp94–5 Mod Oz $$$
☎ 9386 5001; 465 Bronte Rd, Bronte; mains $28-32; ⏰ 7am-10pm; 🚌 378

Swell is an apt name for the swankiest place on the Bronte strip. Expect a skillful blend of European and Asian flavours, with simpler meals available at lunch (from $16) and a popular breakfast menu (from $7).

CAFFE SALINA Map pp94–5 Café $$
☎ 9369 4012; 479 Bronte Rd, Bronte; mains $17-22; ⏰ 7am-5pm Sun-Tue, 7am-9pm Wed-Sat; 🚌 378

Friendly Salina's is on to a winner with its long brunches and hangover specials (bacon, egg, steak, roast tomatoes, chips and a glass of iced Berocca). Who doesn't want hearty food, great coffee and soothing seaside when you're feeling poorly? Delicious, healthy picnic baskets to enjoy across the road at Bronte Beach can be ordered.

COOGEE
CHURRASCO Map pp94–5 Brazilian $$$
☎ 9665 6535; 240 Coogee Bay Rd, Coogee; skewers $30; ⏰ dinner; 🚌 372-374

At this swanky Brazilian barbecue, illuminated by a strange mix of trendy hanging globes and chandeliers, black-clad waiting staff proffer wave upon wave of South American–spiced chorizo, chicken and tender steak skewers. Share a salad ($11) to avoid meat overload. The vegetarian version (at the same price, which hardly seems fair) swaps in vegetables and haloumi.

CHISH N FIPS Map pp94–5 Seafood $
☎ 9664 7100; Coogee Beach; mains $6-12; ⏰ 5.30am-9pm weather dependent; 🚌 372-374

Oh the sheer Ockerness of it all – quality fish and chips on a golden-sand beach! This well-placed snack bar also has great fish burgers and, for those seeking a healthier alternative, plentiful salads.

INNER WEST
The tastes differ across these inner-city suburbs. Newtown's King St is undoubtedly one of the city's best eat streets. It has a staggering number of Thai restaurants, the Vietnamese have colonised the blocks south of Missenden Rd, and you'll also find African, Macedonian, Lebanese and Mexican scattered around. Glebe has a good selection of reasonably priced cafés, while things are a little more upmarket on Balmain's Darling St. Italian is the tradition in Leichhardt and Haberfield – the restaurants lining the piazza in Norton St's Italian Forum (p104) are great fun for families.

NEWTOWN & ERSKINEVILLE
THAI POTHONG Map pp100–1 Thai $$
☎ 9550 6277; 294 King St, Newtown; mains $14-28; ⏰ lunch Tue-Sun, dinner daily; 🚉 Newtown

The ever popular Thai Pothong is gradually taking over King St. It's now at least four times bigger than its original size, yet the food is just as impressive and the service as attentive. All of the prawn dishes are sublime.

FIFI'S Map pp100–1 Lebanese $$
☎ 9550 4665; 158 Enmore Rd, Enmore; mains $12-25; ⏰ dinner Tue-Sun; 🚉 Newtown

Chef Fifi Fudda brought the secret of her deliciously smoky baba ganouge dip with her from Beirut. Her restaurant gives Lebanese cuisine the respect it deserves, with white linen and classy décor. Opt for either a three-course omnivore or vegetarian banquet ($30) or supersize to five courses ($39).

VARGA BAR ESPRESSO Map pp100–1 Café $
☎ 9517 1932; 10 Wilson St, Newtown; mains $8-14; ⏰ 7am-6pm Mon-Fri, 8am-5.30pm Sat & Sun; 🚉 Newtown

This cute little dark pink café with an electric blue coffee machine is a great place to sit and watch Newtown's black parade. It's a mission to choose from the tantalising brunch options but the breakfast burrito usually wins out.

CAFÉ SOFIA Map pp100–1   Café $

☎ 9519 1565; 7 Swanson St, Erskineville; mains $5-14; ⏰ 6.30am-5pm Mon & Tue, 6.30am-9pm Wed-Fri, 7am-9pm Sat, 8am-4pm Sun; 🚉 Erskineville

In the heart of Erskineville village, Café Sofia's sunny back courtyard is a popular spot to enjoy an all-day breakfast and great coffee. The salmon muffin with poached eggs and salad is a steal at $5.50, and the friand and cake selection is always fresh and luscious. Greek mezze is served after 6pm.

KILIMANJARO Map pp100–1   African $

☎ 9557 4565; 280 King St, Newtown; mains $10-13; ⏰ noon-10pm Sun-Thu, noon-11pm Fri & Sat; 🚉 Newtown

With a giant map of Africa on the side of the building, bright yellow walls and staff in colourful robes, you won't mistake Kilimanjaro. The owners are Senegalese but the menu is sourced from all over the continent, including a delicious North African tagine. Try the *sossou-gorgiguan* ('homosexual' in Wolof, apparently) – tuna steamed with spices. How very Newtown.

GUZMAN Y GOMEZ TAQUERIA

Map pp100–1   Mexican $

☎ 9517 1533; 175 King St, Newtown; mains $8-10; ⏰ noon-10pm Tue-Sat, noon-9pm Sun; 🚉 Newtown

Delivering a healthy and delicious alternative to fast food, this clean and modern diner uses fresh local produce to prepare authentic Mexican tacos, burritos and quesadillas. Everything's marinated and grilled daily, with only the *baja*-style fish cooked in oil.

GLEBE & PYRMONT

ALMUSTAFA Map pp100–1   Lebanese $$

☎ 9660 9006; 23 Glebe Point Rd, Glebe; mains $10-28; ⏰ 5.30-10.30pm Sun-Thu, 5.30-11.30pm Fri & Sat; 🚌 431-434

With belly dancers on the weekends and water pipes for afters, Almustafa is a fun place to eat – which wouldn't matter if the food wasn't first rate. Try not to fill up on the more-ish *hummus* and *baba ghanooj* dips; save room for stuffed vine leaves, sizzling lamb *kofta,* chicken *shwarma* and the other greatest hits of Lebanese cuisine.

FIDEL'S BAR Map pp100–1   Mexican $$

☎ 9692 0973; 4/45 Harris St, Pyrmont; mains $10-22; ⏰ 5-10pm Tue-Thu & Sun, 5-11pm Fri & Sat; MLR John St Sq

Housed under an inconspicuous apartment block, there's nothing unassuming about Fidel's. Photos of Mexican revolutionary Pancho Villa adorn the walls, fiesta fajitas come sizzling out on hot plates and the enigmatic owners ensure the tequila flows freely.

DIGI.KAF Map pp100–1   Café $$

☎ 9660 3509; 174 St Johns Rd, Glebe; mains $6-19; ⏰ 7am-5pm Mon-Fri, 8am-5pm Sat, 9am-4pm Sun; 🚌 432-434

It's great to find an internet café that hasn't neglected the café bit. This one promises 'coffee, cake and cyberspace' and delivers much more than that, including a cracking brunch. There's a tiny side lane for alfresco dining and nary a gaming nerd to be seen.

FAIR TRADE COFFEE COMPANY

Map pp100–1   Café $

☎ 9660 0621; 33 Glebe Point Rd, Glebe; mains $5-15; ⏰ 6.30am-9.30pm Mon-Fri, 8.30am-10pm Sat & Sun; 🚌 431-434

Unashamedly hippie and slightly grungy, this is great spot for guilt-free coffee and a community atmosphere. The food raids a number of cuisines, from a Mediterranean platter to Colombian *arepas* and Moroccan meatballs. Serves are tasty and substantial.

YUGA Map pp100–1   Café $

☎ 9692 8604; 172 St Johns Rd, Glebe; mains $7-12; ⏰ 8am-5pm Mon-Fri, 9am-4pm Sat & Sun; 🚌 432-434

This is an odd combination – not just florist and café, but stylish and reasonably priced, fancy and friendly. Set in a beautiful old house with tables on the terrace, Yuga offers healthy Western-style breakfasts morphing into Japanese-flavoured lunches.

BAKERY CAFÉ Map pp100–1   Café $

365 Glebe Point Rd, Glebe; mains $4-10; ⏰ 8am-7pm Mon-Fri, 8am-5pm Sat & Sun; 🚌 431

It doesn't look like much, but this little bakery serves satisfying breakfasts, fresh baguettes and filling pasta meals. It's well positioned for the backpackers down the road and a friendly change from other too-cool cafés on the strip.

SAPPHO ESPRESSO BAR Map pp100–1 Café $

☎ 9552 4498; 51 Glebe Point Rd, Glebe; mains $4-9; ⏰ 8am-6.30pm Mon-Sat, 9am-6.30pm Sun; 🚌 431-434

Hidden away in the back of a sprawling bookshop, Sappho is a wonderfully

bohemian garden café where the walls
are scrawled with generations of graffiti.
The coffee's excellent, the staff adorable
and the food a healthy selection of salads,
panini and light breakfast options.

BALMAIN

BLUE GINGER Map pp100–1   Southeast Asian $$
☎ 9818 4662; 241 Darling St, Balmain; mains $13-
25; ⏰ 6-10.30pm; ⛴ Balmain
If you own the cookbook, you'll definitely
want to try chef Les Huynh's fresh and
fragrant dishes first hand. Not restricted to
his Vietnamese roots, Huynh borrows from
Thai, Malay and Chinese cuisine to bring
the best of the region to his long communal table.

PINTO THAI Map pp100–1   Thai $$
☎ 9555 9236; 315 Darling St, Balmain; mains $13-
24; ⏰ noon-11pm; ⛴ Balmain
Avoid the fast and furious takeaway downstairs and try to hook a table in the little
upstairs dining room – there are surprising
harbour bridge views. Most of the usual
Thai faves (curries and stir-fries) are under
$20 but you'll shell out a little more for
crab (blue swimmer or soft shell with a
lychee salad).

ALL ABOUT... RAMONA'S
Map pp100–1   Café $
☎ 9555 1140; 260 Darling St, Balmain; mains
$10-14; ⏰ 7am-5pm Mon-Sat, 8am-5pm Sun;
⛴ Balmain
It's all about the vibe in this funky café,
featuring cool art on the walls and a fish
tank fashioned from a 1950s TV set. It's a
great place to kick back with a free newspaper, a coffee and a slice of exquisite
cheesecake. Sam I Am fans should try
the green eggs and ham (scrambled with
pesto).

LEICHHARDT

CAFÉ JOLLY Map pp100–1   Italian $$
☎ 9560 2434; 158 Norton St, Leichhardt; mains
$13-19; ⏰ 11am-10pm Mon-Fri, 9am-10pm Sat &
Sun; 🚌 440
Jolly by name and nature you won't find
any surly *prima donnas* here. The food is
classic Italian – pasta, risotto and grills.
The substantial weekend fry-up breakfasts
are Jolly Special, once again by name and
nature.

LA DISFIDA Map pp50–1   Italian $$
☎ 9798 8299; 109 Ramsay Rd, Haberfield; mains
$14-18; ⏰ 6-9.30pm Wed-Sun; 🚌 437-438
Just up the road in Haberfield, this humble
local pizzeria of 13 years' standing serves
decent pasta as well, but don't even think
about it. Head straight for a delicious
traditional thin-crust pizza, hot out of the
wood-fired oven. It's been rated the best in
Sydney, so don't be surprised if you have to
wait for a table.

LA CREMERIA DE LUCA Map pp100–1   Gelato $
☎ 9564 1127; 106 Norton St, Leichhardt; 3 scoops
$6; ⏰ 6-11pm Mon, 4-11pm Tue, 3-11pm Wed-Fri,
noon-midnight Sat, noon-8pm Sun; 🚌 435-438
A main contender for Sydney's best ice
cream, the artisans at De Luca whip up all
the favourite flavours as well as the more
exotic; try the sublime rose petal or chocolate and chilli. They even turn out a beer-
flavoured *gelato* for St Paddy's Day.

NORTH SHORE

The best restaurants north of the bridge dip
their feet in the water, some affording fantastic
views of the city. Manly's beach-town vibe
has resulted in dozens of average restaurants
lining the streets, with a couple of starlets in
their midst. Local surfie hippies have ensured a
sprinkling of organic and vegetarian options.

LOWER NORTH SHORE

BATHERS' PAVILION Map p108   French $$$
☎ 9969 5050; The Esplanade, Balmoral Beach; 3
courses/degustation $115/150; ⏰ lunch & dinner;
🚌 257
Perhaps it's the beachside setting that
lends an appealing casualness to this finest
of dining experiences. The menu is highly
seasonal, focussing on produce from small
local providers, with plenty of seafood.
There's a full alternative menu for vegetarians, including a complete eight-course
degustation. A two-course option is available for weekday lunches ($75).

RIPPLES Map p108   Mod Oz $$$
☎ 9929 7722; Olympic Dr, Milsons Point; mains
$22-29; ⏰ 7am-11pm
Flanked by the Harbour Bridge and the
manic grin of Luna Park, the food does well
to compete with the view and come out a
winner. Expect lots of seafood with subtle
Asian and European flavours on the

ever-changing menu, along with fish and chips ($22) cooked to crispy perfection.

BOTTOM OF THE HARBOUR
Map p108   Seafood $$
☎ 9969 7911; 21 The Esplanade, Balmoral Beach; fish & chips $9-22; ⏱ 7am-9pm; 🚌 257
Fish and chips and Balmoral Beach go hand in hand so ignore the stylish dining room and grab some takeaway. Yep, it's pricey but this upmarket chippie uses only free-range, organic and sustainable products – meaning that your tuna will have been line-caught, not trawled.

SOURCE Map p108   Café $
☎ 9969 1368; 6/914 Military Rd, Mosman; sandwiches $7.50-8.50; ⏱ 6.30am-4.30pm Mon-Fri, 7am-4pm Sat, 7am-1pm Sun; 🚌 257
If you're hankering for a coffee en route to Balmoral or the zoo, grab a seat at the communal table at this new, modern café. These guys are more than passionate about the stuff. Prepare to be tempted by the selection of fresh sandwiches and cakes.

MANLY
BLUE WATER CAFÉ Map p110   Café $$
☎ 9976 2051; 28 South Steyne, Manly; mains $16-29; ⏱ 7.30am-10pm; 🚊 Manly
The huge portions are a major drawcard at this bustling beach café adorned with surfboards. Choose between pasta, burgers, wraps, *pide* and grills, mostly under $20 but up to $29 for a juicy sirloin.

ALHAMBRA Map p110   Spanish $$
☎ 9976 2975; 54 West Esplanade, Manly; mains $20-26; ⏱ lunch & dinner Mon-Sat, noon-10.30pm Sun; 🚊 Manly
Equal parts Spanish and Moorish, at Alhambra tapas compete with tagine for your attention. In the later part of the week, live guitar and flamenco dancers add to the atmosphere. In winter it's closed from Monday to Tuesday evening.

JELLYFISH Map p110   Café $$
☎ 9977 4555; 95 North Steyne, Manly; mains $9-26; ⏱ 7am-9pm; 🚊 Manly
There are much better places for coffee, but this similarly surfboard-strewn café is a

good choice for a light lunch or heftier dinner. Keep an eye on the surf as you munch on salt and pepper squid or a tasty smoked salmon and avocado wrap ($11).

PURE WHOLEFOODS Map p110   Café $
☎ 8966 9377; 10 Darley Rd, Manly; mains $6-15; ⏱ 7.30am-6pm Mon-Sat, 8am-5pm Sun; 🚊 Manly
Where Manly's hippie surfers come to refuel, this wholefood mini-market has a great little street café where you can chose from all manner of organic vegetarian goodies, including flavour-filled flans, salads, nori rolls, cakes and cookies. Those on more restrictive diets (including vegan, sugar-free, gluten-free and dairy-free) are also catered for.

BEANRUSH Map p110   Café $
☎ 9977 2236; 7 Whistler St, Manly; mains $7-10; ⏱ 6am-5pm Mon-Fri, 7am-3pm Sat; 🚊 Manly
A small blue box with a little outdoor space, this café serves great coffee made from wonderfully exotic, organic beans; the snacks are mighty fine, too. Worth a visit if your engine needs revving.

OTHER NEIGHBOURHOODS
Sydney's gastronomic delights aren't limited to the inner-city neighbourhoods. If you're driving up the Northern Beaches there are excellent restaurants to explore. Down south, Cronulla's beachfront is lined with upmarket eateries. Way out west, economically deprived Cabramatta is a magnet for fans of authentic Vietnamese food. Parramatta has some good options, mainly on the riverside.

PIER Map pp50–1   Seafood $$$
☎ 9327 6561; 594 New South Head Rd, Rose Bay; mains $44-49; ⏱ lunch & dinner; 🚊 Rose Bay
Jutting out over pretty Rose Bay, Pier has a well-deserved reputation for delicately cooked, incredibly fresh seafood that is unsurpassed in Sydney and quite possibly the whole country. A recently added tasting room offers bite-sized versions of the grown-up portions next door; it's still not exactly a cheap option ($18 to $ 34) and don't expect to walk away replete.

DRINKING & NIGHTLIFE

top picks

- Lord Nelson Brewery Hotel (p155)
- Arthouse Hotel (p157)
- Green Park Hotel (p159)
- Gazebo Wine Garden (p160)
- Doyles Palace Hotel (p166)
- Orbit (p156)
- Bank Hotel (p164)
- Beauchamp Hotel (p159)
- Home (p158)
- Colombian (p183)

DRINKING & NIGHTLIFE

In a city where alcohol was once the main currency (see p23), it's little wonder that drinking is a big part of the social fabric – whether it's knocking back some tinnies on the beach or meeting mates at the pub.

These days Sydney offers plenty of choice in drinking establishments, from the flashy to the trashy. If the mood to tie one on hits, you should find no difficulty finding a place that suits. Sydneysiders are generally gregarious and welcoming of visitors, and the easiest place to meet them is at the pub.

Many areas have kept their historic corner pubs – an appealing facet of British life that the colonists were loathe to leave behind. Given the Australian weather the addition of beer gardens was an obvious improvement on the formula. Over the last few years those pubs lacking them have scrambled to graft on rooftop terraces to cater to smokers; smoking is now banned from all substantially enclosed licensed premises. It's a cruel irony that the most pleasant open-air areas are now often the stinkiest.

While it might not seem the case, NSW licensing laws are quite restrictive. Setting up a new venue requires buying an existing premises or paying through the nose to transfer a license. The result is that the licenses tend to go to where the money is – huge booze barns with racks of poker machines. Unlike Melbourne, small wine bars and cocktail bars are uncommon – unless attached to a kitchen or part of a larger complex.

Poker machines ('pokies' in the local lingo) are the scourge of Sydney's bars – changing many a lovely local into a circus of flashing lights, beeps, whistles and hypnotised gamblers. It's a brave licensee who forgoes this cash cow in favour of a more pleasant drinking environment (in NSW they suck up more than $4 billion annually), but bigger complexes have the luxury of hiding them in a separate annexe.

LIVE MUSIC & DJS

From the 1950s jazz music made inroads into Sydney venues, and in the 1970s and '80s Aussie pub rock became a force to be reckoned with – spawning the likes of INXS, Midnight Oil, Men At Work and Cold Chisel. Although Sydney fell into a house-induced trance in the '90s, live music has started to make a comeback. You can catch a band any night of the week in dozens of inner-city pubs and clubs. Pick up the free street mags (*Drum Media, Revolver*) and check Friday's Metro section of the *Sydney Morning Herald* for what's on.

Sydney's obsession with dance music was born out of the gay scene's legendary bacchanalias – Mardi Gras, Sleaze Ball and numerous other megaparties (see p182). The crossover into mainstream youth culture in the 1990s coincided with the worldwide explosion of dance music and a flood of ecstasy tablets. Now it's so ubiquitous that it is unusual to step into any venue without a four-to-the-floor doof-doof soundtrack.

Apart from some truly world-class nightclubs, plenty of upmarket bars have DJs and dance floors. Sydney's not quite like New York or London where you can party large any night of the week, but if your booty needs shaking there are plenty of options from Wednesday through Sunday. Look for flyers, a free copy of *3D World* magazine, or call into Central Station (p127) for information and tickets for coming events.

Sydney's nightlife has had a druggy reputation for years, but that didn't prepare it for the horrible toll that an influx of crystal-methamphetamine has had on the scene (aka crystal meth, ice, P, Tina); the inane grins of e-heads have all too often given way to the psychotic grimaces of crystal addicts. Without wanting to sound like a nana, this incredibly addictive and destructive substance is best avoided.

OTHER ENTERTAINMENT

Poker competitions are the current hip addition to many pubs' midweek entertainment line-up. Other old favourites include trivia and karaoke, and you'll occasionally find comedy or poetry nights as well. Life drawing is a current fad; although we suspect the venues that offer it just like to have naked people hanging around. Most places have Sky TV for screening sports.

WHEN TO GO

Pubs generally open midmorning (later on weekends) until around midnight. In livelier areas they'll crack on until the wee small hours, and some stay open continuously. Places get busier as you head towards the weekend. The post-beach Sunday sundowner is extremely popular, and Sunday nights attract plenty of hospitality workers and hairdressers.

Clubs don't normally open their doors until 10pm, but don't expect them to get pumping until after midnight. Most close around 5am.

WHAT TO WEAR

Yes, Sydney can be flashy, but it's also very casual. Men will nearly always get away with tidy jeans, T-shirts and trainers. Thongs (flip-flops, jandals), singlets (vests) and shorts are usually fine in pubs in the daytime, but can be more problematic at night. At ritzier bars and clubs it's safest to dress up. If you're a guy, getting your tits out on the dance floor is de rigueur if any two of the following three is true: a) it's a gay bar; b) it's incredibly hot; and c) you're incredibly hot.

Women can generally wear whatever the hell they like, and many take this as an excuse to wear as little as possible. Dress up for cocktail bars and nightclubs. Some gay bars have a no-open-toed-shoes policy, ostensibly for safety (avoiding broken glass) but generally aimed at keeping straight women out.

WHAT TO DRINK

Beer is the staple; Tooheys New, Victoria Bitter and Carlton Cold are the most popular on tap. Order by the schooner (425ml), middy (285ml), or, if you're sharing, a jug. The cheapest places to drink are the Returned Services League (RSL) clubs. In a tourist-friendly irony, locals are prevented from entering unless they're members, but visitors who live more than 5km away are welcome. You'll need to bring proof.

Australian wine is very good and most house wine available at pubs is quite drinkable. Many places now offer extensive wine lists. Cocktails (often with an Asian or Latin twist) are all the rage in the more upmarket venues, usually costing upwards of $15.

THE ROCKS & CIRCULAR QUAY

The Rocks has had a boozed-up reputation since convict times, and several of its pubs date to that era. On George St you'll discover a tiny pub every few doors, many with live musicians performing throughout the week. While The Rocks is quite tourist-orientated, it's still an interesting stretch to explore. Cross Sydney Cove for a completely different experience; East Circular Quay is lined with modern bars serving pricey drinks to view-hungry tourists at tables spilling out onto the promenade.

BLU HORIZON BAR

Map p54   Bar

☎ 9250 6000; 176 Cumberland St, The Rocks; ⏰ 5pm-1am Mon-Thu, noon-2am Fri, 5pm-2am Sat, 5pm-midnight Sun; 🚇 Circular Quay
You'll need to dress up to get in here (trainers are strictly forbidden, no matter how cool or clean), but the views and slick décor justify the effort. Perched on the top of the Shangri La hotel tower, it's worth heading up here for one over-priced drink and a walk on the glitzy side of Sydney life.

LENIN Map p54   Bar

☎ 9251 0311; Opera Quays, East Circular Quay; ⏰ 11am-11pm Sun-Thu, 11am-1am Fri & Sat; 🚇 Circular Quay
The Soviet décor is so inspiring it's tempting to sit inside and miss the view. Vodka lovers can choose between 12 Russian varieties, 23 Polish, nine Swedish, seven French and 23 from other unlikely places, including Ireland, New Zealand and the Ukraine. Upstairs is icy Minus 5 (p59) and swanky cocktail lounge Bubbles.

LORD NELSON BREWERY HOTEL

Map p54   Bar

☎ 9251 4044; www.lordnelson.com.au; 19 Kent St, Millers Point; ⏰ 11am-11pm Mon-Sat, noon-10pm Sun; 🚌 431-4
There are pubs in older buildings, but the Lord Nelson Brewery Hotel is Sydney's oldest continually licensed pub. Since 1841 it's been pouring pints and by now it's pretty good at it. Try one of the natural ales brewed in the stainless steel vats at the back.

HARBOUR VIEW HOTEL
Map p54   Bar, Live Music
☎ 9252 4111; 18 Lower Fort St, The Rocks;
⊙ 11am-midnight Mon-Sat, 11am-10pm Sun;
🚊 Circular Quay
Built in the 1920s, the Harbour View was the
main boozer for the Harbour Bridge builders and now it's fulfilling that role for the
BridgeClimbers (p226). Head to the lovely 2nd-
floor balcony and wave to the hardy souls
as they traverse the nearby girders. On the
weekends bands play in the main bar.

HERO OF WATERLOO
Map p54   Bar, Live Music
☎ 9252 4553; 81 Lower Fort St, The Rocks;
⊙ 9am-midnight Mon-Sat, noon-10pm Sun;
🚌 431-4
Enter into the roughly hewn stone interior,
meet some of the boisterous locals and
enjoy the nightly music (piano, folk, jazz
or Irish tunes) of this historic, old-time bar.
Downstairs is an original dungeon, where
drinkers would sleep off a heavy night
before being shanghaied to the high seas.

BASEMENT Map p54   Live Music
☎ 9251 2797; www.thebasement.com.au;
29 Reiby Pl, Circular Quay; admission $15-50;
⊙ noon-1.30am Mon-Thu, noon-2.30am Fri,
7.30pm-3am Sat, 7pm-1am Sun; 🚊 Circular Quay
This subterranean jazz bar offers dinner-and-
show tickets or standing-room tickets to
live jazz, blues, cabaret and the occasional
rock and pop gig. It's an intimate setting
that sometimes attracts huge names. Prince
played an impromptu set here in 2003.

CITY CENTRE
The centre of town has a diverse selection of
bars, none of which you would describe as
cosy locals. Some are worth seeking out for
their views, boutique beverages, sumptuous
décor or historical interest. Most are what
Sydney wags might call 'drycleaners' – good
places to pick up suits. Many of them close on
Sunday when the suits are shed in favour of
Speedos and cocktails in the inner suburbs.

WYNYARD & AROUND
BAVARIAN BIER CAFÉ Map pp62–3   Bar
☎ 8297 4111; www.bavarianbiercafe.com.au; 24
York St; ⊙ 10am-11pm Mon-Fri, 11.30am-11.30pm
Sat; 🚊 Wynyard

top picks

LIVE JAZZ

- Basement (left)
- Wine Banq (opposite)
- El Rocco Jazz Cellar (p160)
- Strawberry Hills Hotel (p162)
- Unity Hall Hotel (p165)

The handle glasses hanging over the central bar twinkle like a chandelier whether
you're wearing beer goggles or not. This
super-slick spot has Löwenbräu and Fran-
ziskaner on tap and an extensive beer
menu, along with wine and food.

ESTABLISHMENT Map pp62–3   Bar
☎ 9240 3000; 252 George St; ⊙ 11am-2am
Mon-Fri, 6pm-3am Sat; 🚊 Wynyard
Flashier than greased lightning is this
upmarket yuppie bar that brings together
white Corinthian columns, a 42m marble
bar, leather sofas and cashed-up crowds
convinced it's still the '80s. The garden out
the back is a fine place to enjoy tapas and
smooth music.

ORBIT Map pp62–3   Bar
☎ 9247 9777; Level 47, Australia Sq, 264 George
St; ⊙ 5pm-midnight; 🚊 Wynyard
For the price of a trip up Sydney Tower (p68)
you can get four happy-hour cocktails
(5pm to 9pm Monday to Wednesday) at this
47th-floor lounge bar at the top of Australia
Square (p61). Sink into an Eero Saarinen tulip
chair under the glow of an Alex Noble lamp
and watch Sydney spin around far below.
No thongs, shorts or singlets allowed.

REDOAK BOUTIQUE BEER CAFÉ
Map pp62–3   Bar
☎ 9262 3303; www.redoak.com.au; 101 Clarence
St; ⊙ 11am-midnight Mon-Sat; 🚊 Wynyard
Even beer-haters will find something drinkable here, whether it's a honey ale or Belgian chocolate stout. Redoak has been the
most awarded brewery in the Australian
International Beer Awards for three years
running. Try a beer and food tasting – four
beers individually matched with finger food
(choose from meat, vegetarian, seafood,
cheese or dessert) for $20.

TANK STREAM BAR

Map pp62–3   Bar

☎ 9240 3109; 1 Tank Stream Way; ☽ 4pm-midnight Mon-Thu, noon-midnight Fri; ☷ Wynyard
Hidden down a dark alley in the bowels of the swanky Establishment Hotel is this upmarket and atmospheric bar, populated mainly by suits getting over their working days. Flashes of steel and high stools add elegance to the original warehouse features.

HOTEL CBD Map pp62–3   Bar, DJ

☎ 8297 7000; 75 York St; ☽ 11.30am-2am Mon-Fri, 5pm-3am Sat; ☷ Wynyard
This lovely old corner pub is a multilevel escape for those who've had a tough day making money in the CBD. The ground-floor bar gets crowded after work but there are quieter options upstairs and a celebrated bistro.

HEMMESPHERE

Map pp62–3   Bar, DJ, Live Music

☎ 9240 3040; Level 4, 252 George St; ☽ 5.30pm-1am Tue & Wed, 5.30pm-1.30am Thu, 3pm-2am Fri, 6pm-2am Sat; ☷ Wynyard
Like a giant living room that serves cocktails, this exclusive lounge is a quiet, low-slung alternative to the frenetic energy of the other drinking dens in the Establishment complex. DJs lay down soulful funk and lounge, and on Friday nights there's live music. Reservations are advised.

SLIP INN Map pp62–3   Bar, Cub

☎ 9240 3000; 111 Sussex St; ☽ noon-1am Mon-Thu, noon-4am Fri, 6pm-4am Sat; ☷ Wynyard
This historic complex offers plenty of choice if you're looking for bars, pool tables, a beer garden or dance floor. Friday night is breaks night at the Chinese Laundry nightclub (enter Slip St; before/after 10pm $10/15), while Saturday is Laundry night (before/after 10pm $10/20), featuring a changing roster or local and international DJs.

TANK Map pp62–3   Club

☎ 9240 3094; 3 Bridge Lane; admission $15-20; ☽ 10pm-6am Fri & Sat; ☷ Wynyard
Basement spaces never looked so good. Dress up as fine as you're able, pretend you're a movie star and crash the VIP room; you might just run into someone famous. The punters here are young and thin, and gyrate to the funky house music whipped up by some of Sydney's best spinners.

ST JAMES & AROUND

BAMBINI WINE ROOM Map pp62–3   Bar

☎ 9283 7098; 185-187 Elizabeth St; ☽ noon-10pm Mon, noon-11pm Tue-Fri, 5-11pm Sat; ☷ St James
Don't worry, this bar doesn't sell wine to *bambinis* – it is a very grown-up affair. This tiny darkwood-panelled room with a huge chandelier is the sort of place where you might expect to see Oscar Wilde holding court in a corner. There's an extensive wine list (including the rarely seen sparkling shiraz), superb table service, and free almonds and breadsticks.

WINE BANQ Map pp62–3   Bar, Live Music

☎ 9222 1919; www.winebanq.com.au; 53 Martin Pl; ☽ noon-midnight Mon-Fri, 6pm-1am Sat; ☷ Martin Place
This looks like an architect's dream bunker and a brilliant wine list only adds to the appeal. It's the sexiest spot to hear live jazz (admission $10, check website). Past performers include Wynton Marsalis, Barbara Morrison and Harry Connick Jr, but you'll catch lesser luminaries several nights a week.

TOWN HALL & AROUND

STATEMENT LOUNGE

Map pp62–3   Bar, Cabaret

☎ 9373 6758; 49 Market St; ☽ 5pm-midnight Mon-Fri, 6pm-midnight Sat; ☷ Town Hall
Hidden underneath the State Theatre, this low-lit jazz-era bar blends Deco features with a modern makeover. Slink into this atmospheric locale for a quiet drink (it's rarely busy) or a show tune belted out by a cabaret chanteuse.

ARTHOUSE HOTEL

Map pp62–3   Bar, DJ, Cabaret, Club, Live Music

☎ 9284 1200; www.thearthousehotel.com.au; 275 Pitt St; ☽ 11am-midnight Mon & Tue, 11am-1am Wed & Thu, 11am-3am Fri, 5pm-6am Sat; ☷ Town Hall
The art-meets-alcohol theme carries throughout this sumptuous multistorey heritage site (see p69). Friday nights see live jazz in the Dome Lounge, while on Satur-day the whole downstairs becomes Kink (admission $25), one of Sydney's hottest club nights.

MARBLE BAR Map pp62–3   Bar, Live Music
☎ 9265 6026; www.marblebarsydney.com.au;
Hilton Sydney, 488 George St; ⏱ 5pm-1am Mon-
Thu, noon-3am Fri & Sat, 6pm-midnight Sun;
🚇 Town Hall
There's no place better for putting on the
Ritz (even if this is the Hilton) than Syd-
ney's most sumptuous bar (p68). Live musi-
cians play anything from jazz to funk from
Wednesday to Saturday. It's full of suits on
Friday nights, getting seedier as the night
progresses.

DARLING HARBOUR & CHINATOWN

The bright lights of Darling Harbour house
some glitzy bars that get more clublike as
the night progresses, as well as Sydney's only
real super-club. There's easy fun to be had in
the backpacker bars attached to the hostels
around Central Station. You won't find many
locals (unless they're hoping to indulge their
Swedish backpacker fantasies), but you'll find
plenty of boozed-up Europeans.

HOME
Map p72   Bar, Club, Live Music
☎ 9266 0600; www.homesydney.com; Cockle Bay
Wharf; admission free-$49; ⏱ bar 11am-late daily,
club 9pm-late Thu-Sun; 🚇 Town Hall
This monster-sized pleasuredome took club
design to a new level when it opened 10
years ago; at the time of research it was
about to get a million-dollar overhaul,
including a Roger Sanchez–designed DJ
booth. Apart from special events, admission
is around $20 to $25. Thursday's Rebel Rebel
indie night is free and features live bands.
The legendary Sublime (trance, hard house)
is on Friday, Famous (house) on Saturday
and Home on Sunday has an electro tinge.

CARGO BAR
Map p72   Bar, DJ
☎ 9262 1777; www.cargobar.com.au; 52-60 The
Promenade, King St Wharf; ⏱ 11.30am-midnight
Sun-Thu, 11.30am-4am Fri & Sat; 🚇 Wynyard
By day you can relax on the smooth wood
benches or leather sofas while enjoying
the water views; plant yourself under a
white umbrella among the preeners and
romantics to take in the airy breezes and
sweet cocktails. By night, DJs have this joint
jumping until the wee small hours.

top picks

CLUBS

- Home (left)
- Arq (p184)
- Kink, Arthouse Hotel (p157)
- Yu (p161)
- Lady Lux (p160)

LOFT
Map p72   Bar, DJ, Live Music
☎ 9267 7099; www.theloftsydney.com; 3 Lime St,
King St Wharf; ⏱ 4pm-1am Mon-Wed, 4pm-3am
Thu, noon-3am Fri & Sat, noon-1am Sun;
🚇 Wynyard
From its heavily carved wooden roof panels
to the beaded lighting fixtures and rope
sculpture, The Loft screams out flashy-but-
sophisticated – as do its punters. There's
live 'music for grownups' on Thursday and
Sunday nights, while weekend afternoons
offer traditional high tea or pitchers of
Pimms.

PONTOON
Map p72   Bar, DJ, Live Music
☎ 9267 7099; www.pontoonbar.com; The Promenade, Cockle Bay Wharf; ⏱ 11am-midnight
Mon-Wed & Sun, 11am-3am Thu-Sat;
🚇 Town Hall
One of the most popular drinking dens at
Darling Harbour, offering water breezes,
high-tech atmosphere and cool sounds.
There's dancing on weekends, when DJs lay
down the R&B and hip-hop (Saturday $10,
free before 10pm) and live jazz chills the air
on Sunday afternoons.

DARLINGHURST TO POTTS POINT

Sydney's premier party precinct, this neighbourhood has stacks of decent bars ranging
from snug locals to super-slick posing palaces.
Kings Cross is the destination of choice for
suburban party kids, glamming up for a night
on the tiles. Darlinghurst is still the epicentre
of gay nightlife (see p183), although some hor-
ribly trashy straight clubs have elbowed their
way into the famed Oxford St strip.

DARLINGHURST

BEAUCHAMP HOTEL Map p78 — Bar

☎ 9331 2575; 267 Oxford St; ☺ 10am-2am; 🚌 380

The design police have transformed this cool corner pub into something very groovy indeed. On weekends it gets packed – and incredibly noisy – with a stylish mixed crowd. There's an attractive terrace upstairs but the highlight is the cave-meets-boudoir Velvet cocktail lounge in the basement (Friday and Saturday nights only). Order a Sex-On-The-Beach(um) for a handy clue to the pub's pronunciation.

DARLO BAR Map p78 — Bar

☎ 9331 3672; 306 Liverpool St; ☺ 10am-midnight Mon-Sat, noon-midnight Sun; 🚌 311

A good spot for a quiet one during the week, the Darlo attracts a boisterous crowd on weekends. The service is friendly, the furniture retro, the music groovy and the lighting makes things bright but cosy. Add an interesting neighbourhood and you've got a winner.

GREEN PARK HOTEL Map p78 — Bar

☎ 9380 5311; 360 Victoria St; ☺ 10am-2am Mon-Sat, noon-midnight Sun; 🚌 311

Who's gay and who's straight? Who knows or cares at this place. It's the ultimate 'whatever' inner-city bar, where locals of all persuasions come to drink beer, shoot pool and chill out.

JUDGEMENT BAR Map p78 — Bar

☎ 9360 4831; level 1, 189 Oxford St; ☺ 11.30am-4am Mon-Thu, 24hr Fri-Sun; 🚌 380

Many Sydneysiders only know the grungy Judgement Bar as a blurry memory before being trundled into a taxi at the end of a big night. It's a shame, as it's actually a nice spot to sneak into during the day for a quiet, unpretentious bevvie and filling pub grub. The best that can be said for the main Courthouse Hotel bar downstairs is that it beats drinking on Taylor Sq.

KINSELAS Map p78 — Bar, DJ

☎ 9331 3100; 383 Bourke St; ☺ 9am-6am; 🚌 380

In what used to be a funeral parlour, this Taylor Sq institution has come back from the dead more times than we can recall. The downstairs is all Deco stylings (spot the chapel), while Middle Bar upstairs is chic, modern and popular with cocktail-swilling bright young things. It has the best balcony in town and a bitchin' lesbian night (Bitch) every Friday.

RUBY RABBIT Map p78 — Bar, DJ

☎ 9332 3197; 231 Oxford St; admission free-$15; ☺ 9pm-6am Tue-Sat; 🚌 380

If you can make it past the door Nazis, Ruby Rabbit offers a sumptuous, stylish trio of long thin bars that might have been designed by Liberace. There's no room for pretension when the décor's this camp. Entry to Versailles-inspired De Nom on the top floor is only by reservation, membership or referral.

WOOLLOOMOOLOO

OLD FITZROY HOTEL

Map p78 — Bar

☎ 9356 3848; www.oldfitzroy.com.au; 129 Dowling St; ☺ 11am-midnight Mon-Fri, noon-midnight Sat, 3-10pm Sun; 🚇 Kings Cross

A slice of London's Islington in the back streets of Woolloomooloo, this is a proper theatre pub (see p172) but also a decent old-fashioned boozer in its own right. The little balcony is unbeatable on a hot steamy night and there are airy street-side tables. Wednesday night trivia ($3 per person) is a hoot.

WATER BAR Map p78 — Bar

☎ 9331 9000; Finger Wharf, 6 Cowper Wharf Rdwy; ☺ 4-11pm Sun & Mon, 4pm-midnight Tue-Sat; 🚌 311

Like stepping into the pages of Wallpaper* magazine, this stylish bar sits in the cavernous heart of the Woolloomooloo Finger Wharf (p80). The drink menu is long (18 different tequilas!), the ceilings are high and the sofas are so comfy you may well find yourself horizontal in record time.

TILBURY Map p78 — Bar, DJ

☎ 9368 1955; 18 Nicholson St; ☺ 9am-midnight; 🚌 311

By all means prop up the bar nearest the restaurant or nab a table out the front, but to get the best of this place head up and out – to the 1st-floor bar and its spacious terrace. The Tilbury consistently has friendly staff, schmick décor, chilled beats and a good wine list, but it really comes into its own on a Sunday afternoon when a more bohemian, mixed crowd descends.

KINGS CROSS

FAVELA Map p78 — Bar, Club

☎ 9380 7950; www.favela.com.au; 1 Kellett Way; club admission $10-20 Thu-Sun; ⏰ 6pm-midnight Tue & Wed, 6pm-3am Thu-Sun; ⓡ Kings Cross

This place may actually be too flashy even for Sydney. A nondescript entrance leads into a designer's dream bar populated by dressed-up 20-somethings. If you want to splash your roubles, $600 will get you and your four most impressionable friends a Gold Room table (gold-tiled ceiling and walls) and two bottles of Moët. In the up-stairs club, the ceiling's 8000 golden light-globes groove in time to the house beat.

GAZEBO WINE GARDEN

Map p78 — Bar, DJ

☎ 9357 5333; www.gazebowinegarden.com.au; 2 Elizabeth Bay Rd; ⏰ 3pm-midnight Mon-Fri, noon-midnight Sat & Sun; ⓡ Kings Cross

A hip wine bar in skanky old Fitzroy Gardens? Who would have believed it 10 years ago? This place is awesome – super-groovy décor, interesting mixed clientele and a high-tech storage system that shoots gas into open bottles, meaning 55 sometimes obscure wines are available by the glass to join the 300 by the bottle.

PEPPERMINT LOUNGE

Map p78 — Bar, DJ

☎ 9356 6634; www.peppermintlounge.com.au; 231 Victoria St; ⏰ 6pm-3am Wed-Sat; ⓡ Kings Cross

Remember when getting into a nightclub meant guys needed a nice collared shirt and leather shoes? Nothing's changed here, and the spiffy young crowd love it. Curl into the padded booths seemingly carved out of the wall by a melon-baller and order a cocktail while listening to deep house with an electro and hip-hop flavour.

top picks

SUNDAY SUNDOWNER

- Tilbury (p159)
- Gazebo Wine Garden (above)
- Clovelly Hotel (p163)
- Doyles Palace Hotel (p166)
- Welcome Hotel (p165)

WORLD BAR Map p78 — Bar, DJ, Live Music

☎ 9357 7700; 24 Bayswater Rd; ⏰ 1pm-1am Mon, 1pm-4am Tue & Thu, 1pm-3am Wed, 1pm-6am Fri, 1pm-7am Sat, 1pm-3am Sun; ⓡ Kings Cross

Three floors of cool spaces attract the backpacking crowd (especially on Tuesday's Krapp Karaoke night) to this former bordello, and cheap drinks keep them rockin'. There's an airy tropical terrace out the front, different genre DJs nightly (electro, indie, hip-hop, boogie house) and live indie bands on Friday.

BAR ME & EL ROCCO JAZZ CELLAR

Map p78 — Bar, Live Music

☎ 9368 0894; 154 Brougham St; admission free-$35; ⏰ 5pm-1am Mon-Fri, 6pm-1am Sat & Sun; ⓡ Kings Cross

Sydney's first jazz club, between 1955 and 1969 this was the city's premier bohemian haunt, hosting performances by Frank Sinatra and Sarah Vaughan. Those heady days are long gone but live jazz is back on the agenda in the legendary rock-hewn basement. There's a free open mic night on Monday.

LADY LUX Map p78 — Club

☎ 9361 5000; www.myspace.com/ladyluxnight club; 2 Roslyn St; admission $10; ⏰ 10pm-5am Fri-Sun; ⓡ Kings Cross

There's a sophisticated cosiness to this small-ish club with its funky floral metallic wallpa-per and cushioned couches. Friday nights are for underground house 'from deep to minimal tech', with loads of international DJs. Sundays are huge, attracting a very young, dressed-to-the-nines crowd sticking it out until the first train back to the suburbs.

POTTS POINT

JIMMY LIK'S Map p78 — Bar

☎ 8354 1400; 188 Victoria St; ⏰ 5pm-midnight; ⓡ Kings Cross

Long benches and a longer cocktail list (try the Japanese pear with lemon juice, sake and vodka) fit the highfalutin' atmosphere of this slim joint, next to the excellent restaurant (above).

SOHO BAR & LOUNGE Map p78 — Bar, DJ

☎ 9358 6511; www.sohobar.com.au; 171 Victoria St; ⏰ 10am-4am Mon-Thu, 10am-6am Fri, 9am-6am Sat & Sun; ⓡ Kings Cross

The beautiful Art Deco Piccadilly Hotel is a dark, relaxed establishment whose smooth

top picks

COCKTAILS

- Jimmy Lik's (opposite)
- Longrain (p145)
- Toko (p146)
- Bank Hotel (p164)
- Velvet, Beauchamp Hotel (p159)

leather lounges have felt the weight of Keanu Reeves', Nicole Kidman's and Ewan McGregor's celebrity booties. It's rumoured to be where Kylie met Michael Hutchence. Soho is actually the upstairs cocktail bar (evening's only), but the ground-floor Piccadilly Room is just as elegant.

YU Map p78   Club
☎ 9358 6511; www.yu.com.au; 171 Victoria St; admission $10-20; ☽ 10pm-6am Thu-Sun; ⧓ Kings Cross
Yu wants you to get down to the best of house, funk and electro, played by some of Sydney's most venerable DJs and overseas guests. This slick-looking club is attached to the fancy Soho bar.

PADDINGTON TO DOUBLE BAY

Some cool Darlinghurst-style local bars spill over into Paddington, but generally this area is a little more hoity-toity and a lot less interesting. The pretension disappears completely after big matches when the sports fans spill out of Aussie Stadium and the Sydney Cricket Ground and into the neighbouring pubs. The Entertainment Quarter (p86) is worth checking out for its handful of decent venues.

LIGHT BRIGADE HOTEL Map pp84–5   Bar
☎ 9331 2930; www.lightbrigade.com.au; 2A Oxford St, Woollahra; ☽ 10am-1am Mon-Sat, 10am-10pm Sun; ⧓ 380
Charge into this glorious Art Deco pub for a relaxed ground-floor bar with a decent menu, pool table and snazzy sofa lounges. Happy hours run daily from 3pm to 6pm, and it's usually packed until closing on the weekends. Upstairs there's a chic cocktail lounge (Thursday to Saturday only).

FRINGE BAR Map pp84–5   Bar, Comedy
☎ 9360 3554; 106 Oxford St, Paddington; ☽ noon-1am Mon-Wed, noon-3am Thu-Sat, noon-midnight Sun; ⧓ 380
Sumptuous fringed red-velvet curtains cover exposed brick in this cool bar hung with chandeliers and gilt mirrors. There's a busy weeknight schedule; comedy Monday, trivia Tuesday, fashion Wednesday and, the backpacker's friend, $10 all-you-can-eat pizza Thursday.

GOLDEN SHEAF HOTEL
Map pp84–5   Bar, DJ, Live Music
☎ 9327 5877; www.goldensheaf.com.au; 429 New South Head Rd, Double Bay; ☽ 10am-1am Mon-Thu, 10am-2am Fri & Sat, 10am-midnight Sun; ⧓ 323-6
This handsome old pub complex rambles through a shady beer garden, large sports bar with pool tables, TAB, bistro, pokie palace, cocktail bar, dance floor and live music space. The music policy covers rock, soul, hip-hop, samba, house and funked-up folk – both live and DJ-delivered (see website for details). Something for everyone.

WOOLLAHRA HOTEL
Map pp84–5   Bar, Live Music
☎ 9327 9777; www.woollahrahotel.com.au; 116 Queen St, Woollahra; ☽ noon-midnight Mon-Sat, noon-10pm Sun; ⧓ 389
It's a bit snooty and suity most of the time, but it's worth checking out the free live Latin, jazz and Brazilian funk on Sunday (6.30pm to 9.30pm) and Thursday (7.45pm to 10.45pm).

SYDNEY COMEDY STORE
Map pp84–5   Comedy
☎ 9357 1419; www.comedystore.com.au; Entertainment Quarter; tickets $15-30; ☽ shows 8.30pm Tue-Sat; ⧓ 339
In its purpose-built home in the Fox Studios, this comedy venue has stand-up and open-mic nights. Acts have included the crème of local and international talent.

SURRY HILLS TO ALEXANDRIA

There are two types of Surry Hills cool. There are the chic newly renovated designer bars that go hand in hand with the new restaurants. Then there are the long-standing, grungy, back-street pubs, many hosting live music. Cocktail connoisseurs should investigate the sleek bars attached to the Longrain (p145), Toko (p146) and Lo Studio (p145) restaurants, as well as those listed below.

BAR CLEVELAND Map pp90–1 Bar
☎ 9698 1908; www.barcleveland.com.au; 433 Cleveland St, Surry Hills; ☽ 10am-2am Mon-Thu, 10am-4am Fri & Sat, 10am-midnight Sun; ☒ 372
Very much a relaxed local pub despite its sexy Deco curves, this is great spot to watch the footy, shoot pool or relax with mates. The clientele ranges from the bohemian to the blokey, but it's still gay-friendly. Cocktail cravers should try the $6 Wednesday night specials (6pm to 8pm).

CLOCK Map pp90–1 Bar
☎ 9331 5333; www.clockhotel.com.au; 470 Crown St, Surry Hills; ☽ 11.30am-midnight; ☒ 301-3
Slip a coin into the jukebox, play some pool, dissolve into a booth or check the time back home (there are 11 clocks with international times). The outside tables are nice and airy, as is the wraparound balcony upstairs where you can order happy-hour cocktails (6pm to 7pm) and tapas.

CRICKETERS ARMS HOTEL
Map pp90–1 Bar
☎ 9331 3301; 106 Fitzroy St, Surry Hills; ☽ noon-midnight Mon-Sat, noon-10pm Sun; ☒ 301-303
The zenith of Surry Hills grunge, a cosy vibe fills this friendly pub with friendly locals who gather around the wraparound bar or, in winter, open fireplaces. There are tapas available, a small beer garden with wooden benches, and an intimate upstairs area.

DOLPHIN Map pp90–1 Bar
☎ 9331 4800; www.dolphinhotel.com.au; 412 Crown St, Surry Hills; ☽ 10am-midnight Mon-Sat, 10am-10pm Sun; ☒ 301-3
Slick as all get-out is this large refurbished pub. The Dolphin's a smart beast that's been spruced up and given a smoking terrace. The pretty things head upstairs to the is-that-actually-someone's-lounge-room addition, while non-boofhead sports fans gravitate to the big screens downstairs. There's a decent bistro attached.

MARS LOUNGE Map pp90–1 Bar, DJ
☎ 9267 6440; www.marslounge.com.au; 16 Wentworth Ave, Surry Hills; ☽ 5pm-midnight Wed, 5pm-3am Fri, 7pm-3am Sat, 7pm-1am Sun; ☒ Museum

Someone call David Bowie and tell him that there is life on Mars – and it's young, hip, holding a cocktail and swaying to some smooth house in this red-tinged upmarket warehouse conversion.

HOLLYWOOD HOTEL
Map pp90–1 Bar, DJ, Live Music
☎ 9281 2765; 2 Foster St, Surry Hills; ☽ 11am-midnight Mon-Wed, 11am-3am Thu & Fri, 6pm-3am Sat; ☒ Museum
This Art Deco pub looks nondescript from the outside but its dark intimate inside reveals a somewhat bohemian gay-friendly crowd and great place to kick-start a weekend. There's live jazz on Tuesday nights and a loungy DJ set on Thursday.

MACQUARIE HOTEL
Map pp90–1 Bar, DJ, Live Music
☎ 8262 8844; www.macquariehotel.com; 44 Wentworth Ave, Surry Hills; ☽ 10am-midnight; ☒ Museum
The Mac's a good down-home pub with stuff on every night, whether that be a pool or poker comp, wine tasting or live music. It also brews its own beer.

EXCELSIOR HOTEL Map pp90–1 Bar, Live Music
☎ 9211 4945; 64 Foveaux St, Surry Hills; admission free-$12; ☽ 11am-midnight Mon-Wed, 11am-3am Thu-Sat, noon-10pm Sun; ☒ Central
This casual, grungy joint is good for an outdoor schooner on a sunny afternoon, but it's at night when it really rocks out. A hub of local alternative music, it attracts an eclectic crowd to its nightly live gigs.

HOPETOUN HOTEL Map pp90–1 Bar, Live Music
☎ 9361 5257; 416 Bourke St, Surry Hills; admission free-$12; ☽ 3pm-midnight; ☒ Central
This great little venue offers live music every night, running the gamut from folk to rap. You'll occasionally catch internationally well-known indie acts playing here.

STRAWBERRY HILLS HOTEL
Map pp90–1 Bar, Live Music
☎ 9698 2997; 453 Elizabeth St, Surry Hills; admission free; ☽ 24hr; ☒ Central
This basic pub features the live jazz of the Eclipse Alley 5 (4pm to 7pm Saturday) and Bill Dudley's New Orleanians (5pm to 8pm Sunday). Plus there's happy hour from 2.30pm to 6pm, so throw down some $3 schooners before the show.

BONDI TO COOGEE

If you're in the mood to seriously knock some back, you'll find plenty of company in the backpacker haunts along the coast. In the egalitarian Eastern Beaches some of the cheapest boozers have the best views. However, it's not all raucous pub-rock venues – you'll find slick credit card–maxing cocktail joints as well.

BONDI

ICEBERGS Map pp94–5   Bar

☎ 9365 9000; 1 Notts Ave, Bondi; ⏰ noon-midnight Tue-Sat, noon-10pm Sun; 🚌 380

You can't get more modern and trendy than this classy spot, attached to the famous Icebergs (p147) restaurant. The hanging chairs, colourful sofas and elegant cocktails are just fine, but the view's the absolute killer. Make sure your bank account's up to the strain.

EASTERN Map pp94–5   Bar, DJ

☎ 9387 7828; www.theeastern.com.au; 500 Oxford St, Bondi Junction; ⏰ 10am-3am Mon-Sat, 10am-midnight Sun; 🚆 Bondi Junction

This delicious Deco pub was saved from the wrecking ball and fully renovated when Westfield Bondi Junction (p132) was built all around it. It now has elegant but relaxed bars, a snazzy rooftop terrace, a decent restaurant and a popular electro-pop club-night on Wednesday.

BEACH ROAD HOTEL

Map pp94–5   Bar, DJ, Live Music

☎ 9130 7247; 71 Beach Rd, North Bondi; ⏰ 10am-12.30pm Mon-Tue, 10am-1.30am Wed-Sat, 10am-10.30pm Sun; 🚌 389

Behold the sight of the beautiful, bronzed and boozed-up at play. This huge multi-level fortress of rough-edged fun hosts live music and some good local DJs. Wednesday and Sunday the place gets crowded, as do the banks of pool tables. There's a decent beer garden.

BONDI ICEBERGS SWIMMING CLUB

Map pp94–5   Bar, Live Music

☎ 9130 3120; 1 Notts Ave, Bondi; ⏰ 10am-11pm Sun-Thu, 10am-midnight Fri & Sat; 🚌 380

Located just below Icebergs bar, this is a more affordable and laid-back place with practically the same views. Bring ID: if you're not a member, you need to prove

you live at least 5km away. There's live music Friday nights and Sunday afternoons.

NORTH BONDI RSL

Map pp94–5   Bar, Live Music

☎ 9130 8770; 120 Ramsgate Ave, North Bondi; admission free; ⏰ noon-10pm Mon, noon-11pm Tue-Fri, 10am-midnight Sat, 10am-11pm Sun; 🚌 380-389

This place isn't fancy, but with priceless views and cheap drinks, who cares? Bring ID, as you need to prove that you live at least 5km away to justify your lack of a membership. There are live bands most weekends and poker comps on Monday and Thursday.

COOGEE

AQUARIUM Map pp94–5   Bar, DJ

☎ 9664 2900; www.beachpalacehotel.com.au; 169 Dolphin St, Coogee; ⏰ 11.30am-midnight summer, 4pm-midnight winter; 🚌 372-3

Taking up the top floor of the historic Beach Palace (1887), a massive booze barn at the north end of the beach, Aquarium is the place to be on a Sunday afternoon – or if you're a backpacker or under 26, any old time. The views from the large terrace are magnificent; best enjoyed over a chilled glass.

CLOVELLY HOTEL Map pp94–5   Bar, DJ, Live Music

☎ 9665 1214; www.clovellyhotel.com.au; 381 Clovelly Rd, Clovelly; ⏰ 11am-10.30pm Sun-Thu, 11am-midnight Fri & Sat; 🚌 339

An old-style local pub with a nice shady terrace and water views, it's the perfect post-beach Sunday afternoon spot to crack a coldie to the accompaniment of acoustic musos. DJs crank it up on Saturday nights.

COOGEE BAY HOTEL

Map pp94–5   Bar, DJ, Live Music

☎ 9665 0000; www.coogeebayhotel.com.au; cnr Coogee Bay Rd & Arden St, Coogee; ⏰ 9am-3am Mon-Thu, 9am-5am Fri & Sat, 9am-midnight Sun; 🚌 372-4

Heaven for Brit backpackers and those wanting to score them, the Coogee Bay is a big rowdy boozer with a massive beer garden, resident DJs and a popular sports bar. It's also a well-known live music venue that attracts some big names from time to time.

INNER WEST

Devotees of the comfortable, atmospheric local pub will find much cause for celebration throughout the Inner West. Historic Balmain and Rozelle are the best pub crawl locations in Sydney, with a chain of interesting hotels within easy walking distance of each other. The Inner West's large student population supports a wealth of live music, with some big-name venues located in Annandale and Newtown. Sydney's second gay hub, Newtown supports a couple of venues for gay men and several weekly events catering to lesbians.

NEWTOWN & ERSKINEVILLE

BANK HOTEL Map pp100–1   Bar
☎ 8568 1900; www.bankhotel.com.au; 324 King St, Newtown; ☷ 10am-midnight Sun-Tue, 10am-2am Wed & Thu, 10am-4am Fri & Sat; ⊠ Newtown
After a $5 million refit, the Bank is brighter and shinier than ever, with a new rooftop terrace and cocktail bar, back-end beer garden and beautiful bogs. It still attracts a queer mix of lesbians, students, sport fans, gay men and just about everyone else – although they're all a little snazzier dressed than before. There's a long-running lesbian night on Wednesday.

MARLBOROUGH HOTEL Map pp100–1 Bar, DJ
☎ 9519 1222; 145 King St, Newtown; ☷ 10am-3am Mon-Sat, 10am-midnight Sun; ☐ 422-3
A straighter version of the Bank, this place has a rough-edged front sports bar, a shady beer garden and an attractive large cocktail floor with a cool wraparound terrace.

ZANZIBAR Map pp100–1   Bar, DJ
☎ 9519 1511; 323 King St, Newtown; ☷ 10am-4am Mon-Thu, 10am-6am Fri, 10am-5am Sat, 10am-midnight Sun; ⊠ Newtown

Eastern opulence continues all the way to the roof in Newtown's late night option. Catch the sublime sunset views from the rooftop, settle into a cushioned couch or shoot some pool in the downstairs bar.

ROSE OF AUSTRALIA
Map pp100–1   Bar, Live Music
☎ 9565 1441; 1 Swanson St, Erskineville; ☷ 10am-11pm Mon, 10am-midnight Tue-Sat, 10am-10pm Sun; ⊠ Erskineville
Renovations to this gorgeous old corner pub haven't dinted the tiled front bar's charm one iota (see below). Locals of all persuasions hang out here, catching the afternoon sun at the streetside tables, a footy game on the big screens, a meal upstairs, or the live performers on Wednesday and Friday nights.

SANDRINGHAM HOTEL
Map pp100–1   Live Music
☎ 9557 1254; 387 King St, Newtown; admission free-$10; ☷ 9.30am-midnight Mon-Wed, 9.30am-2am Thu & Fri, 10am-2am Sat, 10am-10pm Sun; ⊠ Newtown
Minimal (or no) cash will score you a live music fix at this intimate venue where God comes for a tipple, according to local legends The Whitlams. There's a beer garden, free internet and happy hours (4pm to 7pm).

VANGUARD Map pp100–1   Live Music
☎ 9557 7992; www.thevanguard.com.au; 42 Kings St, Newtown; tickets $10-25; ☷ 7pm-midnight Tue-Sun; ☐ 422-3
This atmospheric, intimate restaurant and live venue has performers six nights a week, including some well-known names. Although it's primarily a jazz, blues and roots club, you can hear anything from a Led Zep covers band to the latest pop starlet. Dinner and show deals are available ($75 to $99 for two). Check the website for line-ups.

A NIGHT ON THE TILES

Sydney's old tiled pubs may look quaint now, but you wouldn't have thought so if you ventured into one at 5.45pm on a weeknight 60 years ago. In NSW, 1916 to 1955 was the era of the infamous six o'clock swill. In an effort to reduce drunkenness and get husbands back to their families in time for dinner, all pubs were forced to close at 6pm. The effect of this wasn't the increase in public decorum that the temperance movement had hoped for. Instead, workers would rush to the bars as soon as they knocked off and imbibe as much as humanly possibly in the hour before closing.

Pubs built during this time tended to have large central bars to allow easy service to the maximum number of punters and extensive tiling so that the whole rancid mess of slopped beer, vomit and urine could be hosed out afterwards. Erskineville's Rose Of Australia (above) is a good example. The central tiled bar looks a little like a urinal, with a drain around it, and one wall has 'There It Is' printed in the tiles with a large hand pointing to the gents. It seems that in this ballistic binge no-one wanted to lose their place at the bar, not even for a toilet stop.

GLEBE & PYRMONT

FLYING FISH Map pp100–1   Bar
☎ 9518 6677; Jones Bay Wharf, 21 Pirrama Rd, Pyrmont; ☻ noon-midnight Sun & Tue-Fri, 6pm-midnight Mon & Sat; MLR Star City

One for the romantics, let the city lights sparkling over the harbour work their magic at the quiet end of this wharf, aided by an indulgent cocktail ($18). If you're not the mushy type, check this bar out for the coolest toilets in town – the clear glass stalls frost over only when you lock the door.

A.B. HOTEL Map pp100–1   Bar, Cabaret
☎ 9660 1417; 225 Glebe Point Rd, Glebe; ☻ 10am-midnight Mon-Sat, 10am-10pm Sun; 🚍 431-4

Another old favourite to have a $5-million facelift, the former Ancient Briton is looking mighty fine – particularly the Pacific Penthouse with live fish swimming around inside the bar. Large portraits of Lenin adorn the wall and on Thursday nights you can catch a fabulous Bette Midler lookalike performing cabaret. That's Glebe for you.

FRIEND IN HAND HOTEL
Map pp100–1   Bar, Comedy, Poetry
☎ 9660 2326; 58 Cowper St, Glebe; ☻ 8am-midnight Mon & Tue, 6am-midnight Wed-Fri, 5am-midnight Sat, 10am-10pm Sun; 🚍 431-4

This early opening down-home pub offers life drawing ($10) on Monday, poetry slams on the first Tuesday of the month, crab races every Wednesday and comedy gigs every Thursday. Or just grab an eyeful of the bric-a-brac around you, and say hi to the cockatoo. The punters are a mix of grizzly old timers and raucous young 'uns.

ROZELLE

BALD ROCK HOTEL Map pp100–1 Bar, Live Music
☎ 9818 4792; 17 Mansfield St, Rozelle; ☻ 11am-11pm Mon, 11am-midnight Tue-Sat, noon-10pm Sun; 🚍 432-4

This tucked-away workingman's pub (1876) has skungy carpet but lots of charm. There's free pool on Wednesday, Trivia on Thursday, live rock and blues on Saturday and live jazz on Sunday.

WELCOME HOTEL Map pp100–1   Bar
☎ 9810 1323; 91 Evans St, Rozelle; ☻ 11am-midnight Mon-Sat, noon-10pm Sun; 🚇 Balmain; 🚍 432-4

Extending a warm welcome since 1877, this cosy local pub hasn't lost any of its atmos-phere. Come to watch the rugger, have a slap-up meal, while away a Sunday arvo in the beer garden, or commune with the ghost of Winston, a foxhound that supposedly haunts the place.

BALMAIN

EXCHANGE HOTEL Map pp100–1   Bar
☎ 9810 1171; cnr Beattie & Mullens Sts, Balmain; ☻ 11am-midnight Mon-Sat, noon-10pm Sun; 🚇 Balmain; 🚍 432-4

The beautiful Exchange (1885) in Balmain's back streets has been lushly renovated and now houses an upmarket restaurant. Stake a place on the terrace for a $5 cocktail late on a Sunday afternoon.

MONKEY BAR Map pp100–1   Bar
☎ 9810 1749; 255 Darling Rd, Balmain; ☻ noon-midnight Mon-Thu, noon-2am Fri & Sat, 11am-10pm Sun; 🚇 Balmain

Flirty monkeys should add this upmarket meat market to their Friday night pub crawl.

TOWN HALL HOTEL Map pp100–1   Bar, DJ
☎ 9818 8950; 366 Darling St, Balmain; ☻ noon-midnight Mon-Thu, noon-1am Fri, 10am-midnight Sat & Sun; 🚍 433-4

The upstairs of this smart old bar has lots of little nooks and crannies and a wrap-around balcony that's great for brunch or a late afternoon tipple. Friday and Saturday nights see DJs (with the odd live accom-panist) pulling in the single-seeking-other punters downstairs.

UNITY HALL HOTEL
Map pp100–1   Bar, DJ, Live Music
☎ 9810 1331; 292 Darling St, Balmain; ☻ 9am-midnight Mon-Thu, 9am-3am Wed-Fri, 10am-3am Sat, 11am-10pm Sun; 🚇 Balmain

Its late hours make this ungentrified pub (1875) Balmain's traditional last port of call. It has its own house band that plays trad jazz on Sunday afternoons and Friday even-ings. There's more live music on Thursday (acoustic) and Saturday (various), while booty-shakers are looked after by a DJ play-ing upstairs every Saturday night.

CAT & FIDDLE Map pp100–1   Bar, Live Music
☎ 9810 7931; www.thecatandfiddle.net; 456 Darling St, Balmain; admission free-$10; ☻ 10am-midnight Mon-Sat, noon-9pm Sun; 🚍 432-4

Around 30 live bands (mainly rock, blues and folk) perform here every week, from

top picks

LIVE ROCK

- Excelsior Hotel (p162)
- Annandale Hotel (below)
- Sandringham Hotel (p164)
- Hopetoun Hotel (p162)
- Cat & Fiddle (p165)

Wednesday through Sunday. Prop yourself up on the tall stools and enjoy the sounds, or escape for a bite to eat at the bistro in the main bar.

ANNANDALE

ANNANDALE HOTEL
Map pp100–1   Bar, Live Music
☎ 9550 1078; www.annandalehotel.com; 17 Parramatta Rd, Annandale; ☽ 11am-midnight Mon-Sat, 4-10pm Sun; 🚌 436-8
The Yeah Yeah Yeahs and the Dandy Warhols are some of the bigger names to have fired up the stage at this alternative venue that hosts live music from Tuesday to Sunday (tickets $11 to $30). Cult movies screen on Monday nights.

EMPIRE HOTEL Map pp100–1   Bar, Live Music
☎ 9557 1701; www.empirelive.com.au; 103 Parramatta Rd, Annandale; Fri & Sat admission free-$15; ☽ 10am-midnight Mon & Tue, 10am-3am Wed-Sat, 10am-10pm Sun; 🚌 438
Blues (along with ska, pop and rockabilly) buffs should investigate the Empire for live acts, aided by a very good sound system.

NORTH SHORE

You'll find bars scattered throughout the North Shore, but not many are worth travelling for. North Sydney has a Friday night after-work swill, but on most nights people are keen to leave this dull commercial centre and escape to their home suburbs. Manly has its own lively party circuit centred on the Corso.

GREENWOOD HOTEL Map p108   Bar, DJ
☎ 9964 9477; www.greenwoodhotel.com; upstairs Greenwood Plaza, 36 Blue St, North Sydney; ☽ 11.30am-midnight Mon-Wed, 11.30am-3am

Thu, 11.30am-12.30am Fri, noon-10.30pm Sun; ☽ Newtown
It's all about the sandstone; the conversion of this impressive building (1878) from a school to one of the Shore's pumping-est pubs has left it largely unadorned apart from a giant mirror ball. School is not a distant memory for many of the punters, apart from the Friday night after-work brigade. Booty-shake to hip-hop and R&B on Thursday nights, or grab a ticket ($15) to the Sounds-On-Sunday day party for uplifting house in the substantial courtyard.

MANLY WHARF HOTEL
Map p110   Bar, DJ, Live Music
☎ 9977 1266; www.manlywharfhotel.com.au; East Esplanade, Manly; ☽ 11.30am-midnight Mon-Fri, 11am-midnight Sat, 11am-10pm Sun; ☽ Manly
Taking the phrase 'open plan' to the nth degree, this breezy place is designed to resemble a 1950s waterside weekender – feature walls, bamboo, lots of stone. This is justifiably Manly's most popular bar and it gets seriously packed on the weekends. A chilled bottle of wine at the Jetty Bar on a summer's day is magical.

STEYNE HOTEL Map p110   Bar, DJ, Live Music
☎ 9977 4977; www.steynehotel.com.au; 75 The Corso, Manly; ☽ 10am-midnight Sun-Wed, 10am-3am Thu-Sat; ☽ Manly
Boasting nine bars on two levels, this place has a spot for everyone – from sport bogans to club kids. The internal courtyard isn't flash, but the upstairs veranda more than makes up for it with wicked views over the beach. Live bands and DJs play every day.

OTHER NEIGHBOURHOODS

DOYLES PALACE HOTEL
Map pp50–1   Bar, Live Music
☎ 9337 5444; 1 Military Rd, Watsons Bay; ☽ 10am-11pm; ☽ Watsons Bay
One of the great pleasures in life is languishing in the rowdy beer garden of the Doyles Palace Hotel with mates over a jug of sangria after a day at the beach. Stay to watch the sun go down over the city and grab some seafood if you're hungry – fish and chips or a fiddly platter complete with crabs and cray.

BLUELIST[1] (blu͵list) *v.*
to recommend a travel experience.
What's your recommendation? www.lonelyplanet.com/bluelist

THE ARTS

top picks

- Sydney Theatre Company (p172)
- Opera Australia (p172)
- Bangarra Dance Theatre (p171)
- Moonlight Cinema (p170)
- Australian Chamber Orchestra (p171)

THE ARTS

It's too easy to categorise Sydney as shallow and silly, when it actually has a thriving and sophisticated arts scene. It's not a complete accident that its main icon is an opera house, after all.

Probably the most exciting genre to explore during your stay is the theatre, which has given birth to many major international stars. One of these is Oscar-winner Cate Blanchett, whose early career included stints with the Griffin (p172) and Sydney (p172) theatre companies. She's now returned to pay her dues, taking on a three-year contract (started in 2008) as co-artistic director of Sydney Theatre Company, along with her husband, playwright Andrew Upton. Sydney's very excited by the prospect.

On the live music front, all the big names head through Sydney and you might just find your trip coincides with one of your favourites. Check the main ticketing websites when you're planning your trip (below).

Without having the extensive repertoires of European cities, there's always plenty of classical music on offer to give you an excuse to check out the interiors of that famous set of sails by the harbour.

One of the best sources of 'what's on' information is Friday's Metro section in the *Sydney Morning Herald*. It lists events for the week ahead and includes gallery listings, film reviews, and music and theatre interviews.

TICKETS & RESERVATIONS

MOSHTIX
☎ 9209 4614; www.moshtix.com.au
A local outfit handling tickets for lots of smaller and independent concerts, theatre and other performances.

TICKETEK Map pp62–3
☎ 9266 4800; www.ticketek.com.au; 195 Elizabeth St, City; ⏱ 9am-5pm Mon-Wed, 9am-7pm Thu & Fri, 9am-4pm Sat; ⓡ St James
The main booking agency for theatre, concerts and sport. Book by phone, internet or outlets around town.

TICKETMASTER
☎ 13 61 00; www.ticketmaster.com.au
The other biggie for music, sports, arts and theatre ticketing; there's an outlet at the Sydney Entertainment Centre (opposite).

PERFORMANCE VENUES

ACER ARENA Map pp50–1
☎ 8765 4321; www.acerarena.com.au; Olympic Blvd, Sydney Olympic Park; tickets $29-150; ⓡ Olympic Park
This is Australia's largest indoor entertainment and sporting venue (21,000 seats). Everything from concerts to Disney On Ice to off-road-vehicle shows are hosted here. Disabled access is excellent.

CAPITOL THEATRE Map p72
☎ 9320 5000; www.capitoltheatre.com.au; 13 Campbell St, Haymarket; tickets $65-215; ⓡ Central
Lavishly restored, this large theatre is home to big-name concerts and long-running musicals.

CITY RECITAL HALL Map pp62–3
☎ 8256 2222; www.cityrecitalhall.com; 2 Angel Pl, City; tickets $45-103; ⓡ Martin Place
This is a world-class, 1200-seat venue with wonderful acoustics for live music performances. Its architecture is based on the 19th-century European blueprint, and it's an excellent place to hear the Australian Brandenburg Orchestra (p171), Australian Chamber Orchestra (p171) and Australian String Quartet, among others.

ENMORE THEATRE Map pp100–1
☎ 9550 3666; www.enmoretheatre.com.au; 130 Enmore Rd, Newtown; tickets $20-150; ⓡ Newtown
The lovely old Enmore plays host to major Australian and overseas acts (Jet, Alice Cooper, Oasis), plus comedy and jazz. The Rolling Stones played an intimate concert here in early 2003.

GAELIC CLUB Map pp90–1
☎ 9211 1687; www.thegaelicclub.com; 64 Devonshire St, Surry Hills; tickets $10-35; ⓡ Central
Whether it's the latest darlings of the British music press or a particularly successful

local band, concerts at the Gaelic are a cosy affair bridging the gap between the pub scene and the larger theatres.

HORDERN PAVILION Map pp84–5
☎ 9921 5333; www.hordernpavilion.com.au; 1 Driver Ave, Moore Park; tickets $54-72; 🚌 339
Holding over 4000 people, the historic Hordern (1924) hosts plenty of big-name rock gigs and, along with neighbouring venues, the spectacular Sydney Gay & Lesbian Mardi Gras Party. If these walls could talk…

LYRIC THEATRE Map pp100–1
☎ 9657 8500; www.starcity.com.au; Star City, 80 Pyrmont Rd, Pyrmont; tickets $50-103; MLR Star City
The large Lyric in the casino stages flashy musical extravaganzas (*Priscilla, Miss Saigon*) and has good acoustics.

METRO THEATRE Map pp62–3
☎ 9287 2000; www.metrotheatre.com.au; 624 George St, City; tickets $13-60; 🚆 Town Hall
Easily the best place to see local and alternative international acts (plus the odd DJ) in well-ventilated comfort. Other offerings include comedy, cabaret, music and theatre.

NATIONAL INSTITUTE OF DRAMATIC ART
☎ 9697 7600; www.nida.edu.au; 215 Anzac Pde, Kensington; tickets $25-35; 🚌 393-394
Former stomping ground of Mel Gibson, Cate Blanchett and Geoffrey Rush, NIDA is a good place to see future stars. Student and graduate plays are presented throughout the year at its attractive 725-seat theatre or intimate 120-seat studio.

NEW THEATRE Map pp100–1
☎ 9519 3403; www.newtheatre.org.au; 542 King St, Newtown; tickets $10-27; 🚆 St Peters
Australia's oldest continuously performing theatre (happy 75th!), the eclectic New Theatre produces cutting-edge drama in addition to traditional pieces.

STATE THEATRE Map pp62–3
☎ 9373 6852; www.statetheatre.com.au; 49 Market St, City; tickets $17-210; 🚆 St James
The beautiful, 2000-seat State Theatre is a lavish, gilt-laden, chandelier-dangling palace. It hosts the Sydney Film Festival (p18), concerts, comedy and the odd musical. For more details, see p68.

SYDNEY CONSERVATORIUM OF MUSIC Map p54
☎ 9351 1222; www.music.usyd.edu.au; Macquarie St, City; tickets free-$28; 🚆 Circular Quay
This historic music venue (p59) showcases the talents of its students and their teachers. Choral, jazz, operatic and chamber concerts are held from March to September, along with free lunch-time recitals on Wednesdays at 1.10pm.

SYDNEY ENTERTAINMENT CENTRE Map p72
☎ 1300 883 622; www.sydentcent.com.au; 35 Harbour St, Haymarket; tickets $68-165; MLR Paddy's Market
A big concrete box purpose-built for superstar extravaganzas, seating just over 12,000 fans.

SYDNEY OPERA HOUSE Map p54
☎ 9250 7111; www.sydneyoperahouse.com; Bennelong Point; 🚆 Circular Quay
The glamorous heart of performance in Australia, with the Concert Hall and Opera Hall holding about 2600 and 1500 people respectively. Witness theatre, comedy, music, dance and ballet, but it's opera that really shines.

SYDNEY THEATRE Map p54
☎ 9250 1999; www.sydneytheatre.org.au; 22 Hickson Rd, Walsh Bay; tickets $65-75; 🚆 Circular Quay
Opened in 2004, this venue is the most significant theatre built in the city since the Sydney Opera House. The state-of-the-art theatre seats 850 and is managed by Sydney Theatre Company.

WHARF THEATRE Map p54
☎ 9250 1777; www.sydneytheatre.com.au; Pier 4, Hickson Rd, Walsh Bay; tickets $25-125; 🚆 Circular Quay
Sydney Theatre Company's own theatre is also home to the Bangarra Dance Theatre (p171) and the Sydney Dance Company (p171). The Wharf restaurant delivers excellent pre- and post-show fare.

CINEMA

Most suburbs have their own mainstream cinemas (often in shopping centres), while art-house cinemas hover around the inner city. Movie listings can be found in Sydney's daily newspapers.

CHAUVEL CINEMA Map pp84–5

☎ 9361 5398; www.chauvelcinema.net.au; cnr Oxford St & Oatley Rd, Paddington; adult/child $16/9; ☽ 11.30am-midnight; 🚌 380
Occupying the former ballroom of the Paddington Town Hall since 1977, the much-loved Chauvel plays quality art-house releases both new and old (with a liberal does of the quirky and out-there), and hosts various themed festivals.

DENDY NEWTOWN Map pp100–1

☎ 9550 5699; www.dendy.com.au; 261 King St, Newtown; adult/child $14/9.50; ☽ 10am-9.30pm; 🚆 Newtown
Sydney's premier art-house chain, Dendy screens first-run independent films in comfortable theatres. Discount nights are Mondays ($9). There's another lavish Dendy at Opera Quays (☎ 9247 3800; 2 Circular Quay East).

GOVINDAS Map p78

☎ 9380 5155; www.govindas.com.au; 112 Darlinghurst Rd, Darlinghurst; dinner & movie $17, movie only $8; ☽ 5.45-10.30pm; 🚆 Kings Cross
Hare Krishna–run Govindas has an all-you-can-gobble vegetarian smorgasbord that you can combine with mainstream blockbusters, art-house fare and old favourites. There's incense in the air and plenty of cushions on the floor.

GREATER UNION GEORGE ST CINEMAS Map pp62–3

☎ 9273 7431; www.greaterunion.com.au; 505 George St, City; adult/child $16/12; ☽ 10am-11.30pm; 🚆 Town Hall
This monster movie palace has 18 screens, plenty of eateries and some youth-oriented distractions. It's an orgy of popcorn-fuelled mainstream entertainment, and disabled access is good. Discount night ($8.50) is colloquially known as Tight-Arse Tuesday.

OUTDOOR CINEMAS

You can't keep Sydneysiders indoors for long in summer, not even for the flicks. Join the bats in Centennial Park to watch Moonlight Cinema (Map pp84–5; Ticketek ☎ 132 849; www.moonlight.com.au, tickets $15) or risk being distracted by the incredible city views at OpenAir Cinema (Map p54; ☎ 1300 366 649; www .stgeorgeopenair.com.au, tickets $23), where the screen is erected over the water at Mrs Macquaries Point. The roar of the surf adds to the soundtrack at Bondi Openair Cinema (Map pp94–5; Moshtix ☎ 9209 4614; www.bondiopenair.com.au, tickets $13).

HAYDEN ORPHEUM PICTURE PALACE Map p108

☎ 9908 4344; www.orpheum.com.au; 380 Military Rd, Cremorne; adult/concession $16/11; ☽ 10.30am-9.30pm; 🚌 151
Return to cinema's golden age via this fabulous Art Deco gem (1935). It still has its original Wurlitzer organ, which is played at special events and the monthly Wednesday Luncheons (movie, lunch and coffee $13).

HOYTS EQ Map pp84–5

☎ 9332 1633; www.hoyts.com.au; Bent St, Moore Park; adult/child $16/11; ☽ 10.30am-midnight; 🚌 339
The large movie complex in the Entertainment Quarter (p86) has more than a dozen cinemas. These include La Premiere, the cinematic equivalent of a 1st-class cabin, offering snuggle-friendly lounges, glasses of wine, and cheese platters ($35). Art-house films and ethnic film festivals tend to screen in Cinema Paris, just down Bent St.

IMAX CINEMA Map p72

☎ 9281 3300; www.imax.com.au; 31 Wheat Rd, Cockle Bay; adult/child $17/12; ☽ 10am-10pm; 🚆 Town Hall
If you're into being wowed (or made motion-sick) by the world's biggest movie screens, then Imax is for you. Movies shown tend to be either thrill-fests or nature documentaries (some in 3D).

PALACE VERONA Map pp84–5

☎ 9360 6296; www.palacecinemas.com.au; 17 Oxford St, Paddington; adult/concession $16/9; ☽ 10.15am-9.30pm; 🚌 380
This cinema has a café and bar, useful for discussing the artistic merits of the latest nonblockbuster flick you've just seen. Other Palace cinemas include Palace Academy Twin (Map pp84–5; ☎ 9331 3457; 3A Oxford St, Paddington; 🚌 380), home of the Mardi Gras Film Festival, and Palace Norton St (Map pp100–1; ☎ 9564 5620; 99 Norton St, Leichhardt; 🚌 435-8).

CLASSICAL MUSIC

Sydneysiders live with an image of being self-absorbed, sports fanatics, but there is still an active audience for classical music. While Sydney's relative youth means there's no confusion as to whether you're in Old Europe or Sin City, concerts occur year-round. The Sydney Opera House is a good place to start.

Broadcasts (live and prerecorded) of major concerts can be heard on the ABC's radio network (ABC Classic FM 92.9). Check the Guide in the *Sydney Morning Herald* on Monday for details. See also right.

AUSTRALIAN BRANDENBURG ORCHESTRA
ABO; ☎ 9328 7581; www.brandenburg.com.au; tickets $50-103
The ABO is a distinguished part of Australia's artistic landscape, playing baroque and classical music on instruments of those periods. Leading international guest artists appear frequently. Performances are held at City Recital Hall (p168) and various local churches.

AUSTRALIAN CHAMBER ORCHESTRA
ACO; ☎ 8274 3800; www.aco.com.au; tickets $45-80
Since 1975 the ACO has been making chamber music sexy and adventurous, especially under the tutelage of artistic director and lead violinist Richard Tognetti. Concerts are staged throughout the year at both the Sydney Opera House (p169) and the City Recital Hall (p168). Cheaper tickets are often available for the under 30s.

MUSICA VIVA AUSTRALIA
☎ 1800 688 482; www.mva.org.au
Musica Viva is the largest stager of ensemble music in the world, providing some 2,500 concerts around Australia in a number of musical styles (including chamber music, a cappella, experimental and jazz).

SYDNEY PHILHARMONIA CHOIRS
☎ 9251 2024; www.sydneyphilharmonia.com.au
If you want your world rocked by 300 enthusiastic voices, this is your choir. They also have a 100-voice symphonic choir, 32-voice motet choir and a youth-based choir. Internationally renowned, you can generally find them at the Sydney Opera House, City Recital Hall and St Andrew's Cathedral.

SYDNEY SYMPHONY ORCHESTRA
SSO; ☎ 8215 4600; www.sso.com.au
The SSO is blessed with chief conductor and artistic director Gianluigi Gelmetti and plays with famous local and international musicians. Catch them at the Sydney Opera House or City Recital Hall.

DANCE
With its idolisation of the body beautiful, it seems only logical that Sydney has a vital dance culture. Performances range from straight-down-the-line traditional ballet with tutus and packed-lunchbox tights to edgy, liberating 'physical theatre'. Australian dancers have a reputation for fearlessness in performance, resulting in some breathtaking displays of physical skill and bravado (and sometimes a lack of costume).

AUSTRALIAN BALLET
☎ 1300 369 741; www.australianballet.com.au
The Melbourne-based Australian Ballet performs a wide repertoire of classic as well as contemporary works. See them perform at the Sydney Opera House.

BANGARRA DANCE THEATRE Map p54
☎ 9251 5333; www.bangarra.com.au; Pier 4, Hickson Rd, Walsh Bay; tickets $25-125; ⊠ Circular Quay
Widely regarded as one of Australia's finest dance companies, Bangarra regularly performs in Sydney and around Australia. Artistic director and national treasure Stephen Page creates a fusion of contemporary and traditional influences, blending indigenous and Western dance styles.

PERFORMANCE SPACE Map pp90-1
☎ 9698 7235; www.performancespace.com.au; 245 Wilson St, Redfern; tickets $20-30; ⊠ Redfern
This edgy artists' hub stages performances of new dance, acrobatic, multimedia works… basically anything that can be lumped under the broad umbrella of The Arts.

SYDNEY DANCE COMPANY Map p54
☎ 9221 4811; www.sydneydancecompany.com; Pier 4, Hickson Rd, Walsh Bay; ⊠ Circular Quay
Australia's best dance company has a reputation for innovative choreography, spellbinding performances and great production values with the sexiest dancers.

OPERA
Despite its relatively small population, Australia has produced some of the world's most magnificent opera singers, including Dames Nellie Melba and Joan Sutherland. While the Opera House may be the symbol of the city, supporting such a cost-heavy art form, however, is a difficult prospect. While new and more

obscure works are staged, it's the big hits that pull in the punters. The opera season lasts from January to March and then from June to November.

OPERA AUSTRALIA
☎ 9318 8200; www.opera-australia.org.au
Opera Australia is a big player on the Sydney arts scene, based at the Sydney Opera House and at Melbourne's State Theatre.

PINCHGUT OPERA
☎ 9518 1082; www.pinchgutopera.com.au
This relative newcomer stages one intimate, often neglected, chamber opera every December at the City Recital Hall.

THEATRE

There's no distinct theatre district in Sydney, but that doesn't mean theatre-lovers suffer. The city offers a vigorous calendar of productions from Broadway shows to experimental theatre. Tickets prices vary widely.

BELVOIR ST THEATRE Map pp90–1
☎ 9699 3444; www.belvoir.com.au; 25 Belvoir St, Surry Hills; tickets $32-52; ⓡ Central
In a quiet corner of Surry Hills, this intimate venue hosts the often experimental and consistently excellent Company B. Shows sometimes feature big stars, like Geoffrey Rush.

DARLINGHURST THEATRE Map p78
☎ 8356 9987; www.darlinghursttheatre.com; 19 Greenknowe Ave, Elizabeth Bay; tickets adult/concession $30/25; ⓡ Kings Cross
This relative newcomer has been developing a good name for high quality productions in its comfortable little theatre.

ENSEMBLE THEATRE Map p108
☎ 9929 0644; www.ensemble.com.au; 78 McDougall St, Kirribilli; tickets $45-61; ⓐ North Sydney

The long-running Ensemble presents eight or nine mainstream productions per season. Playwrights can be Australian or international, and well-known Australian actors are generally featured. It caters to a mature crowd.

GRIFFIN THEATRE COMPANY Map p78
☎ 9250 7799; www.griffintheatre.com.au; 10 Nimrod St, Kings Cross; tickets adult/concession/under 30 yr $42/32/25; ⓡ Kings Cross
The Stables Theatre is the home of this important little company, dedicated to the development and production of new Australian plays since 1970. Cate Blanchett started her professional career here. On Mondays there are 'pay what you can' 6.30pm sessions.

OLD FITZROY THEATRE Map p78
☎ 9356 3848; www.oldfitzroy.com.au; 129 Dowling St, Woolloomooloo; tickets $10-28; ⓡ Kings Cross
Is it a pub? A theatre? A bistro? Actually it's all three. Grab a bowl of laksa, see the acting stars of tomorrow and wash it all down with a beer. The ticket-laksa-beer deal costs from $16 to $34. Old Fitzroy is grassroots with a good reputation, and has premiered dozens of new Australian plays.

SYDNEY THEATRE COMPANY Map p54
STC; ☎ 9250 1777; www.sydneytheatre.com.au; level 2, Pier 4, Hickson Rd, Walsh Bay; tickets $73; ⓡ Circular Quay
Established in 1978, the STC is Sydney's top company and has been an important step in the careers of many famous Australian actors, including Mel Gibson, Judy Davis, Hugo Weaving, Miranda Otto, Geoffrey Rush, Toni Collette and Cate Blanchett. Expect meticulously crafted works that appeal to mainstream sensibilities while still managing to push a few buttons.

SPORTS & ACTIVITIES

top picks

- Watching a rugby league match (p179)
- Kayaking around the harbour (p176)
- Cycling in Centennial Park (p174)
- Learning to surf (p178)
- Swimming in a pool with a view (p175)

SPORTS & ACTIVITIES

Who wants to be stuck inside on a sunny day? Certainly not most Sydneysiders. Give them any excuse and they'll be stripping off every item of clothing not absolutely essential for public decorum and hitting the beaches, parks and pools. If you're going to spend a considerable chunk of your leisure time with bits of flesh revealed, it follows that you're more likely to make an effort to keep in shape.

You only need head out into the suburbs to see that not all Sydneyites are Bondi lifesaver types. Plenty settle for watching rather than participating in the rough and tumble of sporting life. Conveniently, the most popular spectator sports happen in the winter, not interrupting the beach schedule too much.

HEALTH & FITNESS

With looking good such an obvious concern to many Sydneysiders, the city's devised a myriad of ways to stay built, bronzed and beautiful. Oh, and healthy, too. When in Rome…

CYCLING

Sydney's narrow streets and busy traffic aren't ideal, but a few adventurous eco-warriors get about on their wheeled mounts. Some roads have designated cycle lanes but these often run between parked cars and moving traffic. With less-hectic traffic and long cycle paths, both Manly and Centennial Park are popular pedalling spots.

Bicycles can travel on suburban trains for child rates during peak hours, and for free outside peak times. See p217 for bike hire.

BICYCLE NSW
☎ 9281 4099; www.bicyclensw.org.au
Lots of information for bikers and an excellent range of cycling books on its online store.

ROAD TRANSPORT AUTHORITY
RTA; ☎ 132 213; www.rta.nsw.gov.au
The RTA issues free maps of metropolitan Sydney's cycle path network. You can pick them up at bicycle retailers or download them from the website.

GYMS

Many large hotels have a small gym for guests' use, usually free. Casual sessions at Sydney's top inner-city gyms can be steep, but combined gym/swim deals at the public swimming pools can be cheaper – see Aquatic Centre (opposite),

Bondi Icebergs Swimming Club (opposite), Cook + Phillip Park (p176), North Sydney Olympic Pool (p176) and Victoria Park Pool (p176).

BAYSWATER FITNESS Map p78
☎ 9356 3555; www.bayswaterfitness.com.au; 33 Bayswater Rd, Kings Cross; admission $19; ⏰ 6am-midnight Mon-Thu, 6am-11pm Fri, 7am-10pm Sat, 7am-9pm Sun; ⓡ Kings Cross
As well as friendly staff and good equipment, this place offers lots of classes and a great discount for backpackers ($12 casual, $35 weekly, $99 monthly).

CITY GYM Map p78
☎ 9360 6247; www.citygym.com.au; 107 Crown St, East Sydney; admission $18; ⏰ 24hr; ⓡ Museum
This sweaty gym has been pumping hard bodies for over 30 years. Classes (aerobics, pilates, yoga) are available, along with massage, chiro and spray-tan services. The steam room's only for the gay-curious.

HEALTH & DAY SPAS

GINSENG BATHHOUSE Map p78
☎ 9356 6680; Crest Hotel, 111 Darlinghurst Rd, Kings Cross; adult/child from $28/14; ⏰ 9.30am-9.30pm Mon-Fri, 9am-9.30pm Sat & Sun; ⓡ Kings Cross
Korea comes to Sydney in this marvellous bathhouse, which will eliminate your toxins and have your circulation firing in no time. Separate men's and women's facilities have ginseng spas, hot/cold baths and wet/dry saunas. Pay extra for various massages or be scrubbed to within an inch of your life and emerge on the mean streets of the Cross as smooth as a baby's bottom.

SPA CHAKRA Map p78

☎ 9368 0888; www.spachakra.com; Finger Wharf, Woolloomooloo; treatments from $140; ☿ 9am-9pm Mon-Sat, 10am-6pm Sun; 🚌 311

This day spa offers all the pampering your credit card can handle, using the magical unctions of Guerlain Paris.

INLINE SKATING & SKATEBOARDING

The beach promenades at Bondi and Manly are favoured spots for rollerblading, but Centennial Park is the best for a serious workout. There's a decent skate ramp at the south end of Bondi Beach (p93) and a new skate centre has opened at Sydney Olympic Park (p117). There's always a crowd of teenage skater dudes pulling stunts in front of St Mary's Cathedral.

MANLY BLADES Map p110

☎ 9976 3833; www.manlyblades.com.au; 49 North Steyne, Manly; 🚢 Manly

The Manly twin of Skater HQ (see below) offers the same deal.

SKATER HQ Map pp84–5

☎ 9368 0940; www.skaterhq.com.au; Entertainment Quarter, Moore Park; 🚌 391-2

Well positioned for Centennial Park, this busy place will get you sorted for blades, skateboards, razor scooters and bikes (all $15 per hour), or you can look sweet on a bicycle built for two ($25 per hour).

JOGGING

In the city centre, the Royal Botanic Gardens (p57) and The Domain (p66) are great for joggers. Running across the Harbour Bridge (p52) or Anzac Bridge (p103) makes for a popular and healthy commute to the city. Centennial Park (p83) gives a good escape from traffic fumes.

For a good glute workout, nothing beats a soft-sand shuffle in your swimmers along one of the beaches, offering the added advantage of a cooling dip at the end. Bondi (p93) is popular for bronzed gods and goddesses, particularly in the early morning and late afternoon; you don't have to a supermodel to jog here, but it helps. If it's steep challenges you're after, the Bondi to Coogee walkway is a scenic sweat-fest.

For a serious running club, contact Sydney Striders (www.sydneystriders.org.au). For information on August's 14km City2Surf Run, see p18.

SWIMMING

Sydney offers both sheltered harbour beaches and crazy surf. In areas patrolled by lifeguards, swim between the flags; there are some treacherous rips, even at Sydney's most popular beaches. Many of the surf beaches have seawater pools built into the headlands; most are free.

Despite the clear-looking water, after heavy rains avoid swimming in the ocean for a day and the harbour for three days. The stormwater carries all of the cigarette butts and grime of the streets, as well as sewage overflow, straight into the ocean.

Australians are obsessed by swimming and Sydney boasts over 100 public pools within the city limits. Many outdoor pools close at the end of April for the cooler months and reopen in early October.

See also Coogee Ocean Pools (p96) and Dawn Fraser Baths (p103).

ANDREW 'BOY' CHARLTON POOL
Map pp50–1

☎ 9358 6686; www.abcpool.org; Mrs Macquaries Rd, The Domain; adult/child $5.20/3.60; ☿ 6am-8pm Sep-Apr; 🚌 441

Sydney's best saltwater pool, smack bang next to the harbour and a magnet for water-loving gays, straights, mums and fashionistas. It attracts serious lap swimmers, so keep to your lane if you're a leisurely swimmer. Worth it for its five-star change rooms alone. Wheelchair accessible.

AQUATIC CENTRE Map pp50–1

☎ 9752 3666; www.aquaticcentre.com.au; Olympic Blvd, Sydney Olympic Park; adult/child $6.40/5.10; ☿ 5am-9pm Mon-Fri, 6am-7pm Sat & Sun; 🚉 Olympic Park

Indulge your Ian Thorpe or Misty Hyman fantasies in the actual record-shattering pool used in the 2000 Olympics. There's also a leisure pool with a cool whirlpool in one corner, a state-of-the-art gym ($13 with pool), large outdoor patio area, café and swim shop; childcare and massage services also available. Wheelchair accessible.

BONDI ICEBERGS SWIMMING CLUB
Map pp94–5

☎ 9130 4804; 1 Notts Ave, Bondi; adult/child $4.50/2.50; ☿ 6.30am-6.30pm Fri-Wed; 🚌 380

With supreme views of Bondi Beach, this place is an institution (with membership hard to get). Casual swimming is open to all and available year-round. There's also a gym ($15 including pool entry) on the premises.

COOK + PHILLIP PARK Map pp62–3
☎ 9326 0444; www.cookandphillip.com.au; 4 College St, City; adult/child $6/4.40; ☽ 6am-10pm Mon-Fri, 7am-8pm Sat & Sun; 🚇 St James
This Olympic-sized underground indoor pool also has a hydrotherapy area and gym ($16 with pool use). Also available are massage services, acupuncture, a basketball court, yoga, swimming lessons and a fun wave pool that the kids will love.

NORTH SYDNEY OLYMPIC POOL
Map p108
☎ 9955 2309; Alfred St South, Milsons Point; adult/child $5.10/2.50; ☽ 5.30am-9pm Mon-Fri, 7am-7pm Sat & Sun; 🚇 Milsons Point
Next to Luna Park these beautifully situated pools include an Olympic-sized outdoor one, a 25m indoor one, some kids' splash zones and a gym ($14 with pool access). The views are unbelievable.

VICTORIA PARK POOL Map pp100–1
☎ 9351 2812; cnr Broadway & City Rd; adult/child $4.20/2.10; ☽ 6am-7.15pm Mon-Fri, 7am-5.45pm Sat & Sun; 🚌 422-3
This 50m outdoor pool – heated to a minimum of 25°C year-round – serves as Newtown and Glebe's beach. There's also a gym ($9.50 with pool access), crèche, café and swim shop.

TENNIS
MILLER'S POINT TENNIS COURT
Map p54
☎ 9256 2222; Kent St, The Rocks; per hr $25; ☽ 8am-10.30pm; 🚌 431-4
This synthetic-surface, old-school court has a charming, secret-location feeling. Call ahead or reserve through the concierge at the Observatory Hotel (p188).

RUSHCUTTERS BAY PARK TENNIS
Map pp84–5
☎ 9357 1675; Waratah St, Rushcutters Bay; per hr $20-24; ☽ 7am-11pm; 🚇 Kings Cross
The courts here are open to the public, with the cheapest rates available before 4pm weekdays. It's a relaxed place for a game, and racket hire ($3) is available.

YOGA
You'll find yoga classes offered at many gyms, pools and community centres.

ASHTANGA YOGA SPACE Map pp84–5
☎ 9360 7602; www.ashtangayogaspace.com.au; Verona Cinema Bldg, 17 Oxford St, Paddington; per class $17; 🚌 380
Ashtanga Yoga Space adheres to Ashtanga and offers wonderful Mysore-style classes that'll make your muscles sing. Find nirvana at its spacious, wood-floored studio in the lane between the Verona Cinema and Berkelouw's, and follow the smell of incense up the stairs.

SYDNEY YOGA SPACE Map p78
☎ 9360 0577; www.sydneyyogaspace.com; Level 3, 63 William St, East Sydney; per class $10-20; 🚇 Museum
Iyengar Yoga classes (emphasising standing asanas, precision and alignment) are offered at this large studio at three different skill levels.

ACTIVITIES
If you're bored with wandering around sights, Sydney offers plenty of outdoorsy opportunities to do something active. Don't forget the sun block.

CANOEING & KAYAKING
MANLY KAYAKS Map p110
☎ 0411 247 917; West Esplanade; 1hr hire/lesson $15/45; ☽ 9am-5pm Mon-Wed & Fri, 6.30am-5pm Thu, 7am-5pm Sat, 8am-5pm Sun; 🚢 Manly
As long as you can swim you can hire a kayak from this stand near Oceanworld. You'll be provided with a lifejacket and instruction on how to paddle, including recommendations on secluded beaches to visit. Hours dependent on weather.

NATURAL WANDERS
☎ 9899 1001; www.kayaksydney.com.au; per half-day tour $90
Natural Wanders has exhilarating kayak tours of the harbour that pass under the bridge and stop in secluded islands and bays.

NEW SOUTH WALES CANOEING
☎ 8116 9730; www.nswcanoe.org.au
This association has information on canoe courses and hire around Sydney.

SYDNEY HARBOUR KAYAKS

☎ 9960 4389; www.sydneyharbourkayaks.com.au
Based near the Spit Bridge, Mosman, rentals (per hour $15) are offered, along with half-day eco-tours ($99).

DIVING

The best shore dives in Sydney are the Gordons Bay Underwater Nature Trail, north of Coogee; Shark Point, Clovelly; and Ship Rock, Cronulla. Popular boat dive sites are Wedding Cake Island, off Coogee; around the Sydney Heads; and off the Royal National Park. In Manly, you can make beach dives from Shelly Beach.

DIVE CENTRE BONDI Map pp94–5

☎ 9369 3855; www.divebondi.com.au; 192 Bondi Rd, Bondi; 🚌 380
This Professional Association of Diving Instructors (PADI) five-star centre offers double boat dives ($170) or shore dives ($120), including gear, as well as various courses.

DIVE CENTRE MANLY Map p110

☎ 9977 4355; www.divesydney.com; 10 Belgrave St, Manly; 🚢 Manly
One of the largest dive shops in Sydney, offering shore and boat dives. An open-water PADI course costs $395.

PRO DIVE Map pp62–3

☎ 9264 6177; www.prodivesydney.com; 478 George St, City; 🚉 Town Hall
Another PADI five-star centre, offering everything from introductory dives ($135) to three-day open-water courses ($395). It's conveniently located in the city, but operates out of Manly.

GOLF

BONDI BEACH GOLF CLUB Map pp94–5

☎ 9130 1981; www.bondigolf.com.au; 5 Military Rd, North Bondi; 9 holes/18 holes/unlimited/club hire $15/20/45/19; 🚌 380
It's not much of a course (nine holes, par 28) but the views are breathtaking and hazards come in the form of Aboriginal rock engravings (p95) and the Pacific Ocean. Try not to hit any passing surfers or whales.

MOORE PARK GOLF CLUB Map pp84–5

☎ 9663 1064; www.mooreparkgolf.com.au; cnr Anzac Pde & Cleveland St, Moore Park; 18 holes $45 Mon-Fri, $50 Sat & Sun; 🚌 391-2
Moore Park is the most central of Sydney's public golf courses, with 18 holes and par 70.

HORSE RIDING

CENTENNIAL PARKLANDS EQUESTRIAN CENTRE Map pp84–5

☎ 9332 2809; cnr Cook & Lang Rds, Moore Park; per hr $50; 🚌 391-2
Those looking for some horseplay will enjoy the large indoor arena and 3.6km of track at this world-class centre, near the Entertainment Quarter in Moore Park.

KITEBOARDING

KITEPOWER Map pp94–5

☎ 9315 7894; 126 Beach St, Coogee; 🚌 372-3
Sydney Harbour's too busy and the ocean too rough, but Botany Bay is a great spot for indulging in this exhilarating combination of kite flying and surfing. Brush up your kite-flying skills before booking one of these courses (half-/full day $210/350).

LAWN BOWLS

Generally the pastime of old-age pensioners, lawn bowls has experienced something of a revival in recent years. Young folks are playing thanks to the sports' qualities of affordability, accessibility to all fitness levels, and the tradition of drinking and smoking while balls are rolling. A certain retro-kitsch vibe doesn't hurt.

CLOVELLY BOWLING CLUB Map pp94–5

☎ 9665 1507; www.clovellybowlingclub.com.au; cnr Ocean & Boundary Sts, Clovelly; 🕑 3.30-6.30pm Mon, noon-6.30pm Tue-Thu, noon-7.30pm Fri, 11am-6.30pm Sat, 9am-6.30pm Sun; 🚌 360
This club offers glorious ocean views and something of a hipster scene on weekends. Being right on the Bondi to Coogee walk (p97) means folks pop in for a refreshing drink, but if you want to bowl it'll cost you $10 (be sure to book). There's free coaching for beginners.

SAILING

With such a glamorous harbour, an introductory sailing lesson can be a fun way of getting out on the harbour (though it's not for the budget-conscious). More experienced sailors can skipper their own boat.

EASTSAIL Map pp84–5

☎ 9327 1166; www.eastsail.com.au; d'Albora Marina, New Beach Rd, Rushcutters Bay; 🚉 Edgecliff
Nobody ever said that yachting was a cheap sport. These guys offer an 18-hour

SPORTS & ACTIVITIES ACTIVITIES

course for $475, or you can arrange a charter (four hours $575 $995, skippers available for $55 per hour).

SYDNEY BY SAIL Map p72
☎ 9280 1110; www.sydneybysail.com; Festival Pontoon, Darling Harbour; 🚢 Pyrmont Bay
Departing daily from outside the Australian National Maritime Museum, Sydney by Sail offers plenty of cruises (three hours $130) and courses, including a weekend introductory sail course ($425).

SURFING
South of the Heads, the best spots are Bondi (p93), Tamarama (p96), Coogee (p96) and Maroubra. Cronulla (p120), south of Botany Bay, is also a serious surfing spot. To the north, the best beaches are Manly, Curl Curl, Dee Why, North Narrabeen, Mona Vale, Newport Reef, North Avalon and Palm Beach (see p112). For current wave activity check www.coastalwatch.com.

DRIPPING WET Map p110
☎ 9977 3549; 95 North Steyne, Manly; 🕑 9am-5.30pm Mon-Fri, 8am-6pm Sat & Sun; 🚢 Manly
This surf shop also hires surfboards (one hour/two hours/four hours/day/week, $15/25/35/50/150), bodyboards (one hour/two hours/four hours/day/week, $5/8/15/20/60) and wetsuits (same as bodyboards).

LET'S GO SURFING Map pp94–5
☎ 9365 1800; www.letsgosurfing.com.au; 128 Ramsgate Ave East, Bondi; 🚌 380
You can hire gear (board and suit one hour/two hours/four hours/day/week $25/30/50/150) or learn to surf with this outfit. It caters to practically everyone, with classes for grommets aged seven to 16 (two hours $79), adults' classes (two hours $69 to $79), women-only classes (same price) and private tuition (one hour $120). Bondi's a great beach for learners, but Maroubra's quieter and the classes cheaper (two hours $49).

MANLY SURF SCHOOL Map p110
☎ 9977 6977; www.manlysurfschool.com; North Steyne Surf Club, Manly; adult/child $55/45; 🚢 Manly
Offering surf lessons year-round at Manly and Palm Beach; boards and wetsuits provided. Also surfing safaris up the Northern Beaches – which include a lesson, lunch and gear ($110).

WAVES SURF SCHOOL
☎ 1800 851 101; www.wavessurfschool.com.au; surf trips from $75
This popular surf school offers one- to five-day surf camps to Royal National Park, Seal Rocks and Byron Bay.

SPECTATOR SPORT
With so much national pride hung around sporting success, supporting their teams is like a religion to many Australians. Sport dominates the telly most weekends, but nothing beats catching a game live. Sydney's big passion is rugby league, creating the most intense atmosphere for spectators. Otherwise, a big test between Australia and New Zealand in any code (but particularly rugby union) will get the blood pumping.

AUSTRALIAN RULES FOOTBALL
Sydney's never been much of an Aussie Rules city – until now. The Sydney Swans (www .sydneyswans.com.au) brought home the pennant for the first time in 2005, and their fan base is devoted and expanding. Catch the Swannies in their skimpy shorts and vests from March to September at the SCG (below; tickets from $36) or Telstra Stadium (p117; tickets from $20). Book through Ticketek (p168).

CRICKET
SYDNEY CRICKET GROUND Map pp84–5
SCG; ☎ 9360 6601; www.sydneycricketground .com.au; Driver Ave, Moore Park; 🚌 339
The SCG is the venue for sparsely attended Pura Cup (interstate) matches, well-attended five-day tests and sell-out one-day internationals. The cricket season lasts from October to March. Daily admission for a test match costs upwards of $47. Book through Ticketek (p168).

NETBALL
Despite taking it in turns with New Zealand as world champions, and being Australia's top women's game and one of the most played sports in the country, netball doesn't get either the coverage or the money that the football boys rake in. During its winter season, you can catch the Sydney Swifts or a test international at Acer Arena (p168) for as little as $16. Book through Ticketek (p168).

RACING

HAROLD PARK PACEWAY Map pp100-1
☎ 9660 3688; www.haroldpark.com.au; Ross St,
Glebe; adult/child $8/free; MLR Jubilee Park
Close to the city, the Harold Park trots are
easy to get to and a lot of fun, especially on
a Friday night.

ROSEHILL GARDENS Map pp50-1
☎ 9930 4000; www.theraces.com.au; James Ruse
Dr, Rosehill; admission $7-12; ℝ Rosehill
Located near Parramatta, this is one of Sydney's most famous racecourses. Its premier
event is the Golden Slipper (see p17).

ROYAL RANDWICK RACECOURSE
Map pp50-1
☎ 9663 8400; www.ajc.org.au; Alison Rd, Randwick; admission from $11; ⬛ 372-4
Royal Randwick attracts some glamorous
types, plus the usual array of 'colourful' racing identities. Races are usually on Monday,
Wednesday and Saturday, with gates generally opening at 11am, and the last race at
around 5pm. The big event on the calendar
is the Easter Carnival (see p17).

WENTWORTH PARK Map pp100-1
☎ 9552 1799; www.wentworthparksport.com.au;
Wentworth Park Rd, Glebe; admission $5.50;
☾ 6-10.30pm Mon & Sat; MLR Wentworth Park
Wentworth Park is Australia's premier grey-
hound-racing complex, with skinny, fast dogs
salivating madly after tin hares every Saturday and Monday evening. Races have been
held at these grounds since 1932 and the
grounds hold a café, some bars and a bistro.
There's a lovely old-fashioned feel about the
place, like something from another era.

RUGBY LEAGUE
Sydney is one of rugby league's world capitals,
and this is the city's big game. The National
Rugby League's (NRL) Telstra Premiership
(www.nrl.com) runs from March to October,
culminating in the sell-out Grand Final at Telstra Stadium (see p18). You can catch games
every weekend during the season, played at the
home grounds of Sydney's various tribes. The
easiest to access is Aussie Stadium, home of the
Sydney City Roosters (tickets from $22).

The other big rugby league series is the annual State of Origin (p17) comp, when Queensland battles New South Wales. Sydney games

are at Telstra Stadium (tickets from $42). Book
through Ticketek (p168).

RUGBY UNION
Rugby union, which has a more upper-class
reputation despite its biff content, has a less
fanatical following, but Australia's team, the
Wallabies, is one of the world's best. The
Waratahs are NSW's team, calling Aussie
Stadium home. The annual Tri Nations series
(Australia, New Zealand and South Africa)
usually has a game in Sydney. The Australia
vs New Zealand Bledisloe Cup matches in
particular are huge on atmosphere and well
worth attending. Visit www.rugby.com.au to
find out when matches are being played, and
where.

SOCCER
Soccer comes in a poor fourth among the
football codes, although Australia's qualification for the World Cup in 2006 has increased
its popularity. Visit Football Federation Australia's website (www.footballaustralia.com
.au) for information on catching a game.

SURF LIFESAVING CARNIVALS
Surf lifesaving originated in Sydney, and the
volunteer lifesaver is one of the country's
icons. Despite the macho image, many life-
savers are women and in 2007 a contingent
of lifesavers marched for the first time in the
Sydney Gay & Lesbian Mardi Gras Parade.
You can see these dedicated athletes in action
each summer at surf carnivals held all along
the coast. Check at a local surf lifesaving club
for dates or contact Surf Life Saving NSW (☎ 9984
7188; www.surflifesaving.com.au).

YACHTING
The yachting season runs from September to
April, with lots of races on the harbour. South
Head (p116) offers a good vantage point. The
Sydney to Hobart Yacht Race (p19) departs on
Boxing Day.

SYDNEY FLYING SQUADRON Map p108
☎ 9955 8350; www.sydneyflyingsquadron.com.au;
76 McDougall St, Milsons Point; ⬛ North Sydney
Ferries depart from this club to watch skiff
racing from 2pm to 4.30pm on Saturdays
during the yachting season (adult/child
$15/5.50).

GAY & LESBIAN SYDNEY

top picks

- **Sydney Gay & Lesbian Mardi Gras Festival** (p182)
- **Drinking at the Colombian** (p183)
- **Beaching and cruising at Lady Bay** (p117)
- **Drag queens at the Imperial** (p184)
- **Drag kings at the Sly Fox** (p185)

Sydney is indisputably one of the world's great gay cities. Gays and lesbians have migrated here from all over Australia, New Zealand, the region and the world, adding to a community that is visible, vibrant and an integral part of the city's social fabric. It's hard to imagine another metropolis putting a gaggle of drag queens into the closing ceremony of its Olympic Games. Yet that moment was so typically Sydney – cheeky, flirtatious, glitzy, light-hearted and self-deprecating.

Darlinghurst is the city's main gay ghetto, with most of the bars, clubs and gay-targeted businesses based around Oxford St. Newtown's King St comes a close second. Most of the inner suburbs have a sizable queer element, particularly Surry Hills, Potts Point, Kings Cross, Paddington, Redfern, Erskineville, Enmore, Glebe, Leichhardt and the Eastern Beaches.

These days few city dwellers would bat an eyelid at same-sex couples holding hands on the street. The battle for acceptance has been long and protracted. As recently as the early 1990s, several murders were linked to hate crimes and a stroll up Oxford St could result in a chorus of abuse from car windows. Sydney is now relatively safe but it still pays to keep your wits about you, particularly at night.

NSW's gays and lesbians enjoy legal protection from discrimination and vilification, and an equal age of consent (16 years). Marriage/civil unions and adoption rights are the next big hurdles. Other challenges include the ongoing impact of HIV/AIDS (there are over 300 new infections in Sydney annually) and the growing scourge of crystal-meth addiction.

PARTY TIME

There's no doubt about it, Sydney gives good party. By good, read big, lavish and flashy. Some party animals treat it like a professional sport, spending months preparing for the big fixtures, which can resemble endurance events.

Sydney's famous gay and lesbian Mardi Gras is now the biggest annual tourist-attracting date on the Australian calendar. While the straights focus on the parade, the gay and lesbian community throws itself wholeheartedly into the entire festival, including the blitzkrieg of partying that surrounds it. There's no better time for the gay traveller to visit Sydney than this month-long lead-up to the parade and party, held on the first Saturday in March. Along with film festivals, theatre, art exhibitions, talks, gay zoo tours and cruisy harbour cruises, the big events are the launch, fair day and the pool party (for information on all things Mardi Gras related, visit www.mardigras.org.au).

On the big night itself, the parade kicks off around sunset proceeded by the throbbing engines of hundreds of dykes on bikes. Heading up Oxford St from Hyde Park it veers right into Flinders St, hooking into Moore Park Rd and culminating outside the party site in Driver Ave. The whole thing takes about 90 minutes and attracts up to half a million spectators.

It's best to watch from an apartment lining the street (better make friends with those locals quickly), but if you're forced to stand on the street, the gayest section is between Crown St and the first part of Flinders St. If you're running late, the crowd thins out considerably near the end – although by this stage the participants' enthusiasm is on the wane. Another fun option is to volunteer as a marshall – you'll need to attend a few meetings and arrive hideously early on the day, but you'll get the best view and a discounted party ticket for your trouble.

The party (tickets $130 from Ticketek, p168) is an extravaganza in every sense of the word – attended by over 16,000 revellers it stretches over several large lavishly decorated halls featuring the best DJs and lighting designers the world has to offer. Performers have included Kylie Minogue (twice), Boy George and Chaka Khan.

Mardi Gras also runs the annual Sleaze Ball (p18) in late September/early October. Inquisition (www.sydneyleatherpride.org; tickets $95), Sydney Leather Pride's big night, is held in May. Toybox (www.toyboxparty.com.au) is a hugely popular daytime party held several times a year in Luna Park. While Mardi Gras is the city's main Gay Pride festival, the Stonewall Hotel (p184) organises a minifestival around the traditional Stonewall commemorations in late June.

SHOPPING

Oxford St has most of the stores targeting gays and lesbians. At opposite ends of the spectrum, House of Priscilla (p126) and Sax Fetish (p126) offer plenty of opportunity to play dress-up.

TOOLSHED Map p78   Adult
☎ 9332 2792; www.toolshed.com.au; 81 Oxford St, Darlinghurst; ☽ 10am-1am Mon-Thu & Sun, 10am-3am Fri & Sat
Two-foot dildos, life-size dolls, codpieces, S&M paraphernalia and tons of porn – or just call in to buy tickets to upcoming parties. It has another store nearby at 191 Oxford St. Shop online if you're shy.

BOOKSHOP DARLINGHURST
Map p78   Books
☎ 9331 1103; 207 Oxford St, Darlinghurst; ☽ 10am-10pm Mon-Wed, 10am-11pm Thu, 10am-midnight Fri & Sat, 11am-11pm Sun; ◉ 380
This excellent bookshop specialises in gay and lesbian literature, with everything from queer crime and lesbian fiction, to glossy coffee-table books and porn. A fun browse, to say the least.

DRINKING & NIGHTLIFE

Sydney's gay scene is notoriously fickle. What's popular one week may be completely dead as soon as the next new venue opens, so it pays to pick up the excellent free street press (Sydney Star Observer, SX, LOTL) to find out what's 'so hot right now' – or better still, ask a local.

Most of the venues listed below attract a predominately gay male clientele. Despite Sydney's size, there are no permanent lesbian bars, but rather a series of lesbian nights, including the weekly Wednesday night sessions at the Bank Hotel (p164) and the Sly Fox, Friday nights at Middle Bar (p159) and the monthly Moist nights at Arq (p184)

Most inner-city bars are gay friendly. On Sunday afternoons, every gay man who thinks they're too cool (or butch, or old) for the scene seems to descend on the Green Park Hotel (p159). The Bank (p164), The Tilbury (p159) and Kinselas (p159) attract a similarly mixed crowd. Home (p158) started as a mainly gay club, and it still runs the hugely popular homosexual parties on the Sundays of long weekends.

DARLINGHURST

COLOMBIAN Map p78   Bar, DJ
☎ 9360 2151; 117 Oxford St; ☽ 10am-4am; ◉ Museum
Insanely popular, this swanky drinking spot offers an intoxicating mix of cute guys, thumping music and heady drinks. The décor is to die for and the window seats makes it oh so easy to cruise the street.

MANACLE Map p78   Bar, DJ
☎ 9357 4166; 1 Patterson Lane; ☽ 8pm-1am Thu & Fri, 7am-1am Sat & Sun, 7am-4pm Mon; ◉ Museum
A fittingly dodgy entrance down a set of stairs in a back lane leads to the pits of hell – or at least to Sydney's main leather bar. Actually, it's more about the cult of masculinity; there's no strict dress code, but women and drags shouldn't bother trying. Dudes that just can't stop can descend into the gloom on the weekend and pretend the sun never came up.

OXFORD HOTEL Map p78   Bar, DJ
☎ 9331 3467; 134 Oxford St; ☽ 24hrs; ◉ Museum
Another year; another owner; another refit; another panic that this treasured venue may

---

PARADES & POLITICS

On 24 June 1978 a Sydney icon was violently born. There had been other gay rights marches (in 1973 activists were arrested in Martin Place), but this one was different. Two thousand people followed a truck down Oxford St in a carnival-type atmosphere, encouraging punters out of the bars to join them.

After harassing the participants for much of the route, the police corralled the remaining marchers in Darlinghurst Rd, Kings Cross, beating and arresting 53 of them. Worse still, the names of the all of the arrestees were published in the Sydney Morning Herald and many of them lost their jobs.

The following year 3000 people joined the march, dubbed the 'Gay Mardi Gras', and in 1981 the decision was made to move the event to summer. The current parade still has a serious political edge; more than just a protest, many consider that the parade itself has helped to transform Australian society into a more accepting place for lesbians and gay men.

top picks

GAY BEACHES

- North Bondi (p93)
- Lady Bay, aka Lady Jane (p117)
- Obelisk (p111)
- Redleaf Pool (p87)

(shudder) go straight. So far, so gay. The new incarnation still attracts a cross-section of gay blokedom to its spacious street-level main bar with outdoor seating and a video juke-box, and a mini danceclub in the basement.

MIDNIGHT SHIFT Map p78   Bar, Club, Drag
☎ 9360 4319; www.themidnightshift.com; 85 Oxford St; ☾ noon-4am Mon-Wed, noon-6am Thu & Fri, 2pm-6am Sat & Sun; 🚇 Museum
The grand dame of the Oxford St scene, the Shift boasts two quite distinct venues. Downstairs is a video bar attracting an unpretentious mix of blokes, twinks and bears, and a music policy that ranges from Top 40 to camp classics. Upstairs is a seri-ous tits-to-the-wind club (open from 10pm; Fridays $5 before midnight, $15 after; Saturdays $10 before midnight, $25 after), with grinding beats (and teeth) and lavish drag productions.

STONEWALL HOTEL Map p78   Bar, DJ, Drag
☎ 9360 1963; www.stonewallhotel.com; 175 Oxford St; ☾ 11am-6am; 🚇 Museum
Spreading over a gorgeous three-storey heritage building opening boldly on to the street, Stonewall has a fun vibe and attracts a younger crowd. Hosted by the wonderfully glamorous Ricca Paris, there are drag shows every night of the week, as well as movie nights, karaoke and the ever-popular male-box night (wear a numbered sticker and send each other messages). A few years ago, the ceiling collapsed on the dance floor, causing one DJ to proclaim 'I finally brought the house down!'

ARQ Map p78   Club, Drag
☎ 9380 8700; www.arqsydney.com.au; 16 Flinders St; admission free-$20; ☾ 9pm-7am Thu, 9pm-9am Fri-Sun; 🚌 380
Sydney's gay superclub is a beautiful venue split over two levels. Downstairs

is cool and loungy, with amoeba-shaped sofas and pool tables. Upstairs you'll find the cutting-edge light and sound system being worked by the city's top DJs. Look out for the notorious foam parties (Fomo), hilarious drag king fuelled women's nights (Moist), retro nights (Retrosexual), amateur drag comps (Fabulon) and the ever-popular weekly Saturgays.

PALMS ON OXFORD Map p78   Club, Drag
☎ 9357 4166; 124 Oxford St, Darlinghurst; ☾ 8pm-1am Thu & Sun, 8pm-3am Fri & Sat; 🚇 Museum
No-one admits to coming here, but the occasional queues prove them liars. In this underground dance bar the heyday of Stock Aitken Waterman never ended. It may be uncool, but if you're not screaming when Kylie's played you'll be the only one.

PHOENIX Map p78   Club, Live Music
☎ 9331 2956; 34 Oxford St, Darlinghurst; admis-sion $10; ☾ 10pm-6am Thu-Sun; 🚇 Museum
The epitome of down and dirty; if you don't come out drenched in sweat you're not doing it right. This tiny underground club attracts a queer mix of bohemians, party dykes and shirts-off butch dudes. Thursdays are straighter and veer towards indie, with live performances.

BODYLINE Map p78   Sauna
☎ 9360 1006; 10 Taylor St, Darlinghurst; admission $23; ☾ noon-7am Mon-Thu, 24hr noon Fri-7am Mon; 🚇 Museum
This three-level gay mens' sauna offers plenty of heat and steam, particularly on big party weekends.

INNER WEST

IMPERIAL HOTEL Map pp100–1   Bar, DJ, Drag
☎ 9519 9899; 35 Erskineville Rd, Erskineville; ☾ 3-11.30pm Mon, 3pm-midnight Tue & Wed, 3pm-4am Thu, 3pm-6am Fri & Sat, 1pm-midnight Sun; 🚉 Erskineville
Like a comfortable old sequinned pump, the Imperial's always there in the back of the closet to slip on when you want a really trashy night. Famous as the setting of *Priscilla, Queen of the Desert*, drag is still very much on the menu – from the hysteri-cal Bingay (gay bingo) on Tuesdays, to the multi-act extravaganzas in the cabaret room from Thursday to Saturday. At the time of

research the fabulously skanky cellar dance bar was getting a sluice out and refit.

NEWTOWN HOTEL Map pp100–1   Bar, DJ, Drag
☎ 9517 1728; 174 King St, Newtown; ☼ 11am-midnight Mon-Fri, 10am-midnight Sat, 10am-10pm Sun; ⓡ Newtown

In Sydney's other gay enclave, the comfortable Newtown does a roaring trade with a mixed gay crowd looking to shoot pool, play pinball and watch lavish drag shows on the tiny stage (Friday through Sunday).

SLY FOX Map pp100–1   Bar, DJ, Drag-King
☎ 9557 1016; 199 Enmore Rd, Enmore; ☼ 11am-midnight Mon-Fri, 10am-midnight Sat, 10am-10pm Sun; ⓡ Newtown

This fairly blue-collar bar hosts Sydney's biggest weekly lesbian night on Wednesdays, where drag kings pack their crotches and take to the stage, proving that gay men don't have a monopoly on gender illusion in this town.

SLEEPING

It would be very surprising (not to mention illegal) for gay couples to strike problems finding rooms in any Sydney establishment. Accommodation fills up fast and prices shoot up throughout the city at Mardi Gras time, but particularly in Darlinghurst, Surry Hills and Paddington. Both the Wattle (p191) and the Manor House (p194) are on the actual parade route, while other handy gay-friendly hotels include the Medusa (p191), Sullivans (p194) and Medina On Crown (p194).

FURTHER RESOURCES

www.ssonet.com.au Sydney's main gay newspaper.

www.lotl.com Sydney's monthly lesbian magazine.

www.acon.org.au AIDS Council of NSW.

www.pinkboard.com.au Gay bulletin boards and information.

www.gaydar.com.au Sydney's main gay personals site.

lonely planet Hotels and Hostels

Want more Sleeping recommendations than we could ever pack into this little ol' book? Craving more detail – including extended reviews and photographs? Want to read reviews by other travellers and be able to post your own? Just make your way over to **lonelyplanet.com/hotels** and check out our thorough list of independent reviews, then use our *Lonely Planet Hotels and Hostels* booking service to reserve your room simply and securely.

SLEEPING

top picks

- **Park Hyatt** (flash hotel, p188)
- **Establishment Hotel** (glam hotel, p189)
- **Valentine on George** (affordable boutique hotel, p190)
- **Dive Hotel** (beachside boutique hotel, p196)
- **Medina Grand Harbourside** (serviced apartments, p190)
- **Lord Nelson Brewery Hotel** (historic pub digs, p189)
- **Doyles Palace Hotel** (harbourside pub digs, p198)
- **Hart's Homestay** (B&B, p194)
- **Eva's Backpackers** (eastern-suburbs hostel, p192)
- **Billabong Gardens** (inner-west hostel, p196)

SLEEPING

Sydney has a huge quantity and variety of accommodation – from backpackers' hostels to water-side palaces. If you've got limited time and an unlimited budget, the big-ticket hotels around Circular Quay may be the go. If you're hoping to squeeze some pleasure out of a business trip, pick from the numerous city hotels. For a taste of real Sydney life, choose one of the residential suburbs in the city fringes. If you want to fit a little sightseeing around some serious beaching, head for the eastern beaches or Manly. If budget's the driving factor, investigate the hostels around Potts Point/Kings Cross, the beaches or the inner west.

Accommodation listings in this chapter are ordered by neighbourhood, then in price order from most to least expensive based on the price of a standard double in high (but not peak) season. The average double room with bathroom costs about $150, with seasonal variations (lowest in winter and highest around Christmas, New Year's Eve and Mardi Gras). Rooms are also more expensive from Monday to Friday, when business travel is at its peak (outside Sydney, though, weekend rates are often higher because Sydneysiders flee their homes for mini vacations). Generally, we've quoted rack rates for hotels, which tend to be higher than the specials and discounted packages that are often on offer. Always ask a hotel for its 'best rate'. If you're looking for last-minute discounts at higher-end hotels, try www.lastminute.com.au.

THE ROCKS & CIRCULAR QUAY

This neighbourhood ticks a number of boxes: the most attractive part of central Sydney; the most likely to have a harbour view; the most vibrant after dark; the closest to the most sights; the best base for exploring the city by ferry. It should come as no surprise that this glamorous precinct is also the priciest.

This area is tourist central – you won't find much in the way of neighbourhood cafés, affordable restaurants or supermarkets. Yet there is a quiet residential pocket in the Millers Point part of The Rocks, sheltered enough from the hurly-burly of the Quay to be completely charming.

PARK HYATT Map p54   Hotel $$$
☎ 9241 1234; www.sydney.park.hyatt.com; 7 Hickson Rd, The Rocks; d & tw $500-850, ste $1300-6550; 🚇 Circular Quay; 🅿
Commanding the opposite tip of the horseshoe of Circular Quay to the Opera House, the Park Hyatt boasts the best location in Sydney. The graciously low-rise building matches the opulence of its position with sandstone, marble and contemporary design including a particularly groovy mother-of-pearl wall. Absolutely decadent views of the harbour. Around-the-clock butler service. Superluxurious. What more is there to say?

OBSERVATORY HOTEL Map p54   Hotel $$$
☎ 9256 2222; www.observatoryhotel.com.au; 89-113 Kent St, The Rocks; d $429-554, ste $679-754; 🚌 431-434; 🅿
When the owners' other properties include the Orient Express, you expect opulence. That said, the Observatory is remarkably restrained, eschewing excessive gilt in favour of an elegant antique ambience. The building is only 15 years old but in keeping with the surrounding terraced houses in this astoundingly quiet central city nook. The rooms are large with equally spacious marble bathrooms. Some have views and four-poster beds, and bowls of goldfish are available on request for children or lonely executives.

RUSSELL Map p54   Hotel $$
☎ 9241 3543; www.therussell.com.au; 143A George St, The Rocks; d $145-285; 🚇 Circular Quay
Located in The Rocks' main tourist drag, this charming 29-room hotel offers creaky floors, modest flowery rooms (the cheapest sharing bathrooms), pleasant lounge areas and a sunny roof garden. There's an intimate, rambling feel to the turreted 1887 building and plenty of narrow staircases (no elevator).

BED & BREAKFAST SYDNEY HARBOUR Map p54   B&B $$
☎ 9247 1130; www.bedandbreakfastsydney.com; 142 Cumberland St, The Rocks; s $140-214, d $155-260, all incl breakfast; 🚇 Circular Quay

Surrounded by high-rise hotels, this small-scale B&B still manages to squeeze some Opera House views from its superb location on the upper slopes of The Rocks. Each of the nine rooms is charmingly unique, and all come with soft sheets and a hot breakfast, although some share bathrooms.

LORD NELSON BREWERY HOTEL
Map p54   Pub $$

☎ 9251 4044; www.lordnelson.com.au; 19 Kent St, The Rocks; d & tw incl breakfast $120-180, tr incl breakfast $230; 🚇 Circular Quay

Built in 1836 and housing Sydney's oldest continuously licensed pub, the Lord Nelson is well located in the quiet heights of The Rocks. Despite its historic status the friendly owners have resisted the urge to vomit flowers over the walls and drapes, opting instead to highlight the thick sandstone walls with simple, comfortable furnishings. Most of the nine rooms are spacious and have their own bathroom, or you can opt for a cheaper, smaller room with shared facilities.

PALISADE HOTEL Map p54   Pub $$

☎ 9247 2272; www.palisadehotel.com; 35 Bettington St, The Rocks; d $123, tw & tr $128; 🚇 Circular Quay

Standing sentinel-like at peaceful Millers Point, the Palisade Hotel has nine basic rooms with well-kept shared bathrooms. The front rooms open on to a shared balcony with breathtaking views of the Harbour Bridge, while others have windows looking over Walsh Bay. It's a lovely old building with a decent neighbourhood pub downstairs that generally shuts at sleep-friendly hours.

CITY CENTRE

Most hotels here cater to the business brigade – it's easy to splash the cash if the shareholders are picking up the tab. This is not a residential area, so don't expect to gain much insight into how locals live if you base yourself here. Once the hordes vacate the office towers for their commute to the suburbs, this part of the city can be a ghost town. However a train or taxi (hell, chuck that on the charge account as well) will get you to neighbouring suburbs in a jiffy.

SAVILLE 2 BOND ST
Map pp62–3   Serviced Apartments $$$

☎ 1800 222 226; www.savillehotelgroup.com; 2 Bond St; studio apt $414, 1-bedroom apt $449-

PRICE GUIDE

$$$	doubles over $300
$$	doubles $120-300
$	doubles under $120

483, 2-bedroom apt $644, penthouse $990-1550; 🚇 Wynyard; 🚻

The elegant neutral tones may not quite make a home away from home (unless you live in a catalogue), but these spacious apartments sure are comfortable. Those on longer trips will appreciate the joy of having a full kitchen and laundry at your disposal.

WESTIN SYDNEY Map pp62–3   Hotel $$$

☎ 8223 1111; www.westin.com/sydney; 1 Martin Place; d $585-665, ste $1200; 🚇 Martin Place; 🚻

Spreading half of its tentacles into the grand General Post Office building (p65) and the others into a contemporary tower, this is a slick and luxurious address. Choose between the high-ceilinged heritage rooms and the modern tower rooms; all have quality linen, comfy beds and sizable shower heads.

ESTABLISHMENT HOTEL
Map pp62–3   Boutique Hotel $$$

☎ 9240 3100; www.establishmenthotel.com; 5 Bridge Lane; d $350-415, ste $970-1150; 🚇 Wynyard

Hardcore glamour doesn't need to be flashy. In fact, it can lurk behind an inconspicuous entrance off a dark, dank alley – allowing secretive celebrities to slink in, peel back the black shades and head straight to the luxury of the split-level deluxe penthouse. One of Australia's best boutique hotels, Establishment offers 33 beautifully designed rooms sporting fine cotton linen and elegant bathrooms.

MERITON SERVICED APARTMENTS
PITT ST Map pp62–3   Serviced Apartments $$$

☎ 8263 7400; www.meritonapartments.com.au; 329 Pitt St; studio/1-/2-/3-bedroom apt $209/229/305/399; 🚇 Town Hall; 🚻

Forget Wembley Stadium – Meriton is better known in Sydney as the builder of swanky but soulless apartment complexes. This huge tower (42 floors above ground) features Smeg appliances and truly awesome views.

BLACKET Map pp62–3 Boutique Hotel $$

☎ 9279 3030; www.theblacket.com; 70 King St; d & tw $190-260, ste $260-360; ❿ Martin Place

You'll feel very *Sex & the City,* swishing home after cocktails to a loft suite in the heritage-listed Blacket, right at the very centre of Sydney's CBD. The sleek, modern studio rooms are spacious, as are the reasonably priced two-bedroom apartments, which come equipped with CD players and kitchenettes.

HYDE PARK INN

Map pp62–3 Serviced Apartments $$

☎ 9264 6001; www.hydeparkinn.com.au; 271 Elizabeth St; s $165-182, d & tw $182-198, tr $198-215, ste $292; ❿ Museum

Right on the park, this friendly place offers studio apartments with kitchenettes as well as some two-bedroom suites. Renovations in progress at the time of research were modernising the décor and leaving flatscreen TVs and DVD players in their wake.

CASTLEREAGH Map pp62–3 Boutique Hotel $$

☎ 9284 1000; www.thecastlereagh.net.au; 169 Castlereagh St; s $165-210, d $175-220, tw $190-200, tr $205-230, ste $210-270; ❿ Town Hall

Tucked away in a delightful 1920s sandstone building, this Masonic club has plush interiors that recall a swankier time. While secret handshakes may have been replaced by poker machine finger jabs in the main bar, the grand dining room remains the epitome of a gentlemen's club. SThe comfortable rooms have silky bedspreads and fine linen, although some of the bathrooms are tiny. Breakfast and a daily tipple are complimentary.

CENTRAL PARK HOTEL Map pp62–3 Hotel $$

☎ 9283 5000; www.centralpark.com.au; 185 Castlereagh St; d & tw $150-170, ste $195-210; ❿ Town Hall

Blacket's little sister is just as pretty, even if she is cheap. 'Hip on a budget' is the motto, and little touches such as free fruit on reception make this a special place. While the standard rooms are good, it's worth paying the extra $10 for a Park Studio – a much bigger room with a spa bath.

GRAND HOTEL Map pp62–3 Pub $

☎ 9232 3755; www.merivale.com/thegrand; 30 Hunter St; s/d/tw/tr/f with shared bathroom $77/88/100/110/130; ❿ Wynyard

Unusual for the heart of the CBD, this hotel offers 19 cosy, flowery rooms above an unpretentious pub. Some have a balcony.

WYNYARD HOTEL Map pp62–3 Pub $

☎ 9299 1330; www.wynyardhotel.com.au; 107 Clarence St; s/d/tw/f with shared bathroom & breakfast $77/88/100/130; ❿ Wynyard

This modest 1873 three-storey, old-school pub perches on a corner of the CBD, wondering how the youngsters around it got so tall. The rooms are perfectly decent, the self-serve laundry is free and there's access to a kitchen, making this a great deal. In the summer you can enjoy the included light breakfast on the little rooftop terrace.

DARLING HARBOUR & CHINATOWN

This end of town is livelier and the prices cheaper, but it's not the most attractive place to stay – there's little in the way of views or green space. On the upside, this neighbourhood positively sparks with energy and there are plenty of midnight feast or binge options. The area around Central Station has turned into backpacker city.

VALENTINE ON GEORGE

Map p72 Boutique Hotel $$

☎ 9288 9888; www.valentineongeorge.com; 767 George St, Haymarket; d $165-170, ste $290-888; ❿ Central

If valentines are supposed to be secret, this one's playing by the rules. It's a pleasant surprise to find such an upmarket boutique hotel hidden behind a nondescript doorway in this bustling part of town. The rooms are beautifully designed, with king-size beds, Bose stereos, DVD players, marble bathrooms with tiny Italian tiles and glitzy fixtures. There are some two-bedroom suites available, including one with a courtyard.

MEDINA GRAND HARBOURSIDE

Map p72 Serviced Apartments $$$

☎ 9249 7000; 55 Shelley St, King St Wharf; www.medina.com.au; studio apt $222-240, 1-bedroom apt $248-274, 2-bedroom apt $470-514; ❿ Wynyard; ❿

Heaven is a swish, spacious apartment where people clean up after you. Even more so if there are harbour views, as there are in the slightly pricier rooms in this new low-rise development just off King Street Wharf (p74). All have full kitchen and laundry facilities and balconies.

VIBE HOTEL SYDNEY Map p72   Hotel $$
☎ 8272 3300; www.vibehotels.com.au; 111 Goulburn St, city; d & tw $185; 🚇 Museum; 🅿️
The Medina crew have got the vibe right with these smart and funky midrange hotels. Expect clean, sparkling rooms, bright colours and not a shred of stuffiness.

SYDNEY CENTRAL YHA
Map p72   Hostel $
☎ 9218 9000; www.yha.com.au; 11 Rawson Pl, Haymarket; dm $34-39, d & tw $95-107; 🚇 Central; 🅿️
Huge and fancy, Sydney Central YHA houses up to 556 flashpackers in a heritage-listed building near Central Station. It has all you'd expect in a hostel and then some: dorms, private rooms with or without ensuites, lockers, games and movie rooms, large kitchens, laundry facilities, a travel agency, bar, café, shop and even a rooftop swimming pool and sauna.

WAKE UP! Map p72   Hostel $
☎ 9288 7888; www.wakeup.com.au; 509 Pitt St, Haymarket; dm $26-34, d & tw $88-98
Another huge flashpacker hostel near Central Station, Wake Up! is a slightly cheaper version of Sydney Central YHA without the pool or sauna. The rooms are brightly painted and the double glazing is remarkably effective in keeping out the traffic noise in this busy corner site.

RAILWAY SQUARE YHA
Map p72   Hostel $
☎ 9281 9666; www.yha.com.au; 8 Lee St, Haymarket; dm $34-39, d $88-98; 🚇 Central; 🅿️
This hostel's not just central, it's actually in Central Station (p75). It occupies a former parcel shed with its own platform; you can even sleep in comfortable four-bed dorms in converted train carriages, with passenger trains pulling up on tracks just over the fence. The kids will love it, but bring earplugs. Private ensuite rooms are available.

DARLINGHURST TO POTTS POINT

This first belt of eastern suburbs should suit nightclub junkies, gay guys and boozed-up backpackers just fine. The leafy backstreets hide a smattering of boutique hotels and the buzziest backpacker strip in the city (Victoria St). Excellent public transport makes for quick access to the city sights and Bondi.

DARLINGHURST

MEDUSA
Map p78   Boutique Hotel $$$
☎ 9331 1000; www.medusa.com.au; 267 Darlinghurst Rd; d $270-385; 🚇 Kings Cross
This sultry 18-room boutique hotel is pure Sydney – glamorous, flashy, sexy, decadent and gay-friendly. Lose yourself in the curvaceous furniture, and enjoy the chocolates on your pillow, soft linens on your bed and Aveda toiletries in your bathroom.

L'OTEL Map p78   Boutique Hotel $$
☎ 9360 6868; www.lotel.com.au; 114 Darlinghurst Rd; d $150-275; 🚇 Kings Cross
The sheer blinding whiteness of L'otel is a bold style statement but it might have you thinking you've woken up on an operating slab. The rooms are comfortable and reasonably priced, ranging from smallish 'juniors' to spacious 'executives' with huge terraces. The design effort doesn't extend to the bathrooms which are ordinary.

CHELSEA Map p78   B&B $$
☎ 9380 5994; www.chelsea.citysearch.com.au; 49 Womerah Ave; s with shared bathroom $94, d $143-154, ste $165-195; 🚇 Kings Cross

Sydney's Victorian terraces are nearly as iconic as that oversized coat hanger and scrum of nuns down by the harbour. Joining two such beauties together, the friendly Chelsea offers 13 unique, chic rooms in a peaceful street. Some are graced with a balcony; all have luxe cotton sheets and fittings.

WATTLE HOTEL
Map p78   Hotel $$
☎ 9332 4118; www.thewattle.com; 108 Oxford St; d $100-160, tw & f $160; 🚇 Museum

There's no handier place to stay if your Sydney itinerary is largely nocturnal and gay. Consequently the weekend-only rates shoot up by $30-40 per room, while at Mardi Gras be prepared to book a decade in advance and sacrifice your first-born for one of the corner terraces overlooking the parade route.

HOTEL ALTAMONT

Map p78   Boutique Hotel $$

☎ 9360 6000; www.altamont.com.au; 207 Darlinghurst Rd; d incl breakfast $119-135; ☒ Kings Cross
This converted 1830s manor house adopted the name Altamont after several close encounters on the premises with members of the Rolling Stones. It now offers wonderful reasonably priced rooms – some huge and opening on to an internal courtyard. Add to the mix funky modern décor, friendly staff and a free light breakfast and you're sure to get some satisfaction.

ROYAL SOVEREIGN HOTEL

Map p78   Pub $

☎ 9331 3672; www.darlobar.com; 306 Liverpool St; d with shared bathroom $77-88; ☒ Kings Cross
With one of Darlinghurst's favourite drinking dens downstairs, these 19 nifty cheapies are an appealing proposition. They're smartly painted, well-maintained and come with crisp clean white linen.

KINGS CROSS

REGENTS COURT

Map p78   Boutique Hotel $$$

☎ 9358 1533; www.regentscourt.com.au; 18 Springfield Ave; d $250-295; ☒ Kings Cross
In the surprisingly quiet backstreets of Kings Cross, friendly Regents offers stylish apartments fitted with kitchens, dining tables and DVD players. The highlight is the lush and lovely rooftop garden with a city skyline view and harbour glimpses.

SEVENTEEN ELIZABETH BAY ROAD

Map p78   Serviced Apartments $

☎ 9358 8999; www.seventeenapartments.citysearch.com.au; 17 Elizabeth Bay Rd; studio/1-/2-bedroom apt $79/180/230; ☒ Kings Cross
This lovely old deco block offers reasonably priced, self-contained apartments close enough to Kings Cross to be handy but distant enough to escape the din. The studio apartments are small but clean and funky, while some of the one- and two-bedroom apartments have lovely views over Rushcutters Bay.

HOTEL 59 Map p78   B&B $$

☎ 9360 5900; www.hotel59.com.au; 59 Bayswater Rd; s $88, d $110-121, f $132, all with breakfast; ☒ Kings Cross

This small, friendly hotel may be a short skip from the dubious delights of Darlinghurst Rd, but don't expect to bring the party back to yours. Noisy boozers are frowned upon in this quiet family-run place and, besides, the rooms aren't overly big. The café downstairs whips up the great cooked breakfasts.

O'MALLEY'S HOTEL Map p78   Pub $

☎ 9357 2211; www.omalleyshotel.com.au; 228 William St; d $79-113, tr $99; ☒ Kings Cross
This friendly Irish pub comes attached to 15 traditionally decorated, well-furnished rooms with private bathrooms, although not all are ensuite. Two have good harbour views and one has a fully equipped kitchen. It's supercentral, but the traffic on William St doesn't let up, night or day.

EVA'S BACKPACKERS Map p78   Hostel $

☎ 9358 2185; www.evasbackpackers.com.au; 6-8 Orwell St; dm $28, d & tw $80, tr $90; ☒ Kings Cross
Eva's is a class act. This cheerful, brightly painted corner block on a quiet backstreet is kept perfectly spick and span. There's a big sociable kitchen/dining area downstairs and a great rooftop garden. Breakfast and internet access (broadband or wi-fi) are free, as are non-backpackery extras such as shampoo, body wash and laundry powder.

ASYLUM Map p78   Hostel $

☎ 9368 1822; www.asylumsydney.com; 201-203 Brougham St; dm $25, s & d $60-100; ☒ Kings Cross
The friendly nutters at Asylum offer dorm beds or private rooms ranging from prison cells (at the cheaper end) to a harbour view pad with a kitchenette. The craziness continues with free wi-fi, free light breakfasts and free meal vouchers for the nearby Old Fitzroy pub. It's all kept clean and tidy.

POTTS POINT

VICTORIA COURT HOTEL

Map p78   B&B $$

☎ 9357 3200; www.victoriacourt.com.au; 122 Victoria St; d $99-231; ☒ Kings Cross
Lovely, chintzy Victoria Court serves up more than a dash of Victoriana. Marble fireplaces and four-poster beds add to the ambience in many of the rooms, although strict Victorian observances have given way to sensible ensuites. Budgeteers should enquire about the cheaper room with an unattached but private bathroom.

MAISONETTE HOTEL

Map p78   Hotel $$

☎ 9357 3878; maisonettehotel@bigpond.com; 31 Challis Ave; s/d & tw/tr/f $65/120/150/165; 🚇 311

Wake up and smell the coffee on Potts Point's hippest, most caffeinated strip. The rooms range from bright small doubles with ensuites to tiny dark singles with shared bathrooms, but the price is good and gets better the longer you stay.

ORIGINAL BACKPACKERS LODGE

Map p78   Hostel $

☎ 9356 3232; www.originalbackpackers.com.au; 160-162 Victoria St; dm/s/d & tw/tr $28/65/75/95; 🚉 Kings Cross

This long-running hostel meanders through two wonderful historic mansions, offering 176 beds, friendly staff, two kitchens and great outdoor spaces. Rooms have high ceilings, fridges and shared bathrooms, although there is one double with an ensuite ($90). Call from the airport for a free shuttle.

GREAT AUSSIE BACKPACKERS

Map p78   Hostel $

☎ 9356 4551; www.greataussiebackpackers.com.au; 174 Victoria St; dm $22, d & tw $60-70; 🚉 Kings Cross

One of numerous Victoria St hostels, this one has a large central courtyard and an active social programme including pub tours five nights a week, free Friday BBQ and Sunday pancakes. All rooms have TVs and fridges, and the pricier ones have ensuites.

TRAVELLERS REST

Map p78   Hostel $

☎ 9380 2044; www.travellersrest.com.au; 156 Victoria St; dm $20, tw $50, d $60-70; 🚉 Kings Cross

Another old-style hostel on the main backpacker strip; the prices don't come lower than this for your basic bunk bed in a clean four-person dorm. Bathrooms are shared except for in the pricier doubles. You can email Mum from a free internet terminal.

WOOLLOOMOOLOO

BLUE Map p78   Hotel $$$

☎ 9331 9000; www.tajhotels.com/sydney; 6 Cowper Wharf Rdwy; d $280-380, ste $360-900; 🚇 311; 🚉

Fancy being Russell Crowe's neighbour, nearly? Blue occupies the first section of the wonderfully refurbished Woolloomooloo finger wharf, capped by Mr Thighs' penthouse. You're not going to miss out on a water view from either the standard rooms or the ultrachic loft suites. Attention to luxurious detail includes Aveda toiletries, 250 thread-count sheets and goose-down duvets.

WOODDUCK HARBOUR CITY BACKPACKERS Map p78   Hostel $

☎ 9380 2922; www.harbourcityhotel.com.au; 50 Sir John Young Cres; dm $23-25, d & tw $70; 🚉 St James

There's a definite old-school party-hostel vibe to this large, character-filled place, situated on a busy approach road to the harbour tunnel. All of the rooms (except some dorms) have shared bathrooms. Best of all is the large rooftop terrace offering stunning views over the city. If the buzz of the communal areas gets too much, you can easily escape to the Domain, literally across the road.

PADDINGTON TO DOUBLE BAY

Halfway between Bondi and the city, the locale's lovely but accommodation's limited. There's no train service (except for out-of-the-way Edgecliff station) but bus access to the city and beaches is excellent.

PADDINGTON & WOOLLAHRA

HUGHENDEN Map pp84–5   Hotel $$

☎ 9363 4863; www.hughendenhotel.com.au; 14 Queen St, Woollahra; d $148-268, tw $228; 🚇 380

Given its venerable age, considerable size and posh location, you would expect this attractive manor to be luxurious and overpriced. However, the rambling, cluttered Hughenden seems more the preserve of an eccentric Victorian artist than a fusty black-suited gentleman; plenty of charm without much style. The 36 rooms are all different, ranging from tiny to spacious.

KATHRYN'S ON QUEEN

Map pp84–5   B&B $$

☎ 9327 4535; www.kathryns.com.au; 20 Queen St, Woollahra; d $165-209; 🚇 380

There are only three rooms available in this gorgeous grand Victorian terrace, deftly run by a charming hostess. Tastefully decorated in cream and white, with comfortable antique furniture; chose between the attic room with an ensuite or the two first-floor rooms which share a bathroom.

SULLIVANS HOTEL Map pp84–5 · Hotel $$
☎ 9361 0211; www.sullivans.com.au; 21 Oxford St, Paddington; d & tw $165-180; tr & f $180; 🚌 380; 🚇

A popular Mardi Gras stop given its location, friendly Sullivans offers 64 good simple rooms wrapped around a leafy poolside courtyard. The pricier ones face inwards and have a balcony. Family rooms come with bunks for the under eights, or there are interconnecting rooms available ($235). Free extras include internet access, bicycles, in-house movies and a fitness room.

HART'S HOMESTAY Map pp84–5 · B&B $$
☎ 9380 5516; addington91@bigpond.com; 91 Stewart St, Paddington; s $85, d $130-150; 🚌 380

Big on charm *and* style, the Hart family's posh Paddington pad could be described as homeliness personified. There's a small, sunny garden dripping in flowers, while the walls support a staggering number of framed nature portraits (there's a whole room devoted to ducks). One huge bedroom has an ensuite, while the upstairs rooms share a nearby bathroom. The sheets are pure cotton, the duvets unadulterated down, the toiletries French, the bathrobes fluffy and the breakfasts substantial and fruity.

DOUBLE BAY

STAMFORD PLAZA DOUBLE BAY
Map pp84–5 · Hotel $$
☎ 9362 4455; www.stamford.com.au; 33 Cross St, Double Bay; d $180-600; 🚌 323-326; 🚇

Chances are if you're a Double Bay–fancier you'll want to stay at the super-swish Stamford Plaza. It's very old-school grand, with gilt-framed portraits of stuffy Victorian gentlemen, lavish chandeliers and much marble. The smallish rooftop pool has seriously glamorous views, as do the pricier rooms. While its website boasts of playing host to American presidents, it will forever be remembered as the site of INXS star Michael Hutchence's undignified end.

SAVOY HOTEL Map pp84–5 · Hotel $$
☎ 9326 1411; www.savoyhotel.com.au; 41 Knox St, Double Bay; d & tw $119-149, ste $189-260; 🚌 323-326

Unlike the rest of 'Double Pay', the friendly Savoy doesn't seem to have increased its prices in years. The only thing with a whiff of pretension about it is the name. The rooms are pleasant and tidy.

SURRY HILLS TO ALEXANDRIA

If you've got a taste for fine food and designer bars, Surry Hills is a great spot to rest your head, if you can find a pillow. Unfortunately choices are limited.

HOTEL STELLAR
Map pp90–1 · Boutique Hotel $$$
☎ 9264 9754; www.hotelstellar.com; 4 Wentworth Ave, Surry Hills; studio $265-295, 2-/3-bedroom apt $380/495; 🚇 Museum

This Victorian office has been done out apartment-style, with kitchenettes, flat-screen TVs and access to free movies. The result is a series of hip, modern pads you'll wish you lived in – located on the noisy city edge of Surry Hills (earplugs are a good idea). If you're travelling with a posse, the three-bedroom apartment works out to be good value.

MEDINA ON CROWN
Map pp90–1 · Serviced Apartments $$$
☎ 8302 1000; www.medina.com.au; 359 Crown St, Surry Hills; 1-bedroom apt $253-284, 2-bedroom apt $326-356; 🚌 301-303; 🚇

As one of the main pastimes in Surry Hills is eating out, you may find the well-stocked kitchenette of your slick, modern apartment doesn't get a lot of use – the Medina building alone is home to three exalted eateries. The leafy poolside, gym and sauna are plenty popular over Mardi Gras.

MANOR HOUSE Map pp90–1 · Boutique Hotel $$
☎ 9380 6633; www.manorhouse.com.au; 86 Flinders St, Darlinghurst; d $170-220, ste $280; 🚇 Central; 🚇

Step off busy Flinders St and step back in time as you enter this grand 1850s mansion, complete with extravagant chandeliers, moulded ceilings, Victorian tiling and fountains tinkling in the garden. One might say it's a house fit for a queen, and it's certainly popular with the gay community around Mardi Gras time, being right on the parade route and staggering distance from the party.

MACQUARIE BOUTIQUE HOTEL

Map pp90–1   Pub $$

☎ 8262 8844; www.macquariehotel.com; 40-44 Wentworth Ave, Surry Hills; s $88, d $110-125, tr $175; ⊠ Central

This pub represents a good deal on a number of fronts – a supercentral location, low prices, plenty of character and its own microbrewery on the premises! The rooms themselves are in decent shape and have ensuite bathrooms. By the time this book is published, the old girl will have had some work – we're promised double-glazing along with the makeover. The prices may also upgrade.

CITY CROWN MOTEL

Map pp90–1   Hotel $$

☎ 9331 2433; www.citycrownmotel.com.au; 289 Crown St, Surry Hills; d & tw $140-155, tr $155-165; ⊠ 301-3

The location's the clincher for this otherwise run-of-the-mill motel offering simple rooms, some with a balcony or patio. DVD players are a surprising extra. Rates skyrocket for Mardi Gras but drop substantially in the off season.

BIG HOSTEL

Map pp90–1   Hostel $

☎ 9281 6030; www.bighostel.com; 212 Elizabeth St, Surry Hills; dm $27-31, s/tw/d/tr/f $75/89/93/102/125; ⊠ Central

If it weren't for the bunk beds, shared facilities and the strangers sleeping in the same room, you might forget you're in a hostel. Upmarket and stylish, Mr Big has attractive communal areas, including a cute rooftop terrace. All rooms have TVs and video players and wi-fi access is free, as is a light breakfast. Although the dark hollow of Elizabeth St isn't Sydney's most salubrious locale, Central Station's just across the road for a quick escape.

BONDI TO COOGEE

If you'd like some sightseeing with your beach holiday (and not the other way around), plunge into the eastern beaches. Bondi's the most interesting and closest to the city, but you'll find better bang for your buck in Coogee. Buses are frequent but a trip to the city can eat the best part of an hour at busy times.

BONDI

SWISS GRAND Map pp94–5   Hotel $$$

☎ 9365 4422; www.swissgrand.com.au; cnr Campbell Pde & Beach Rd; d & tw $225-300, ste $400-900; ⊠ 380; ⊠

The Swiss Grand is the giant wedding cake at the centre of the Bondi strip; an eyesore or the ultimate in Bondi kitsch depending on your point of view. The rooms are all very pleasant with their own balcony and, of course, the ocean views are superb.

RAVESI'S Map pp94–5   Boutique Hotel $$

☎ 9365 4422; www.ravesis.com.au; 118 Campbell Pde; d $125-295, ste $275-450; ⊠ 380

The 16 contemporary rooms and two-level suites at this posh place with hobbitish curved windows are gorgeous and sleek. Decked out in gun-metal grey or rich chocolate hues, the interiors look good enough to eat. The best rooms have large and luxurious balconies offering five-star peeps at the ocean. Wi-fi access is free.

HOTEL BONDI Map pp94–5   Hotel $$

☎ 9130 3271; www.hotelbondi.com.au; 178 Campbell Pde; s $60-90, tw $130, d $130-175, ste $200-330; ⊠ 380

Continuing the Bondi confectionary analogies, Hotel Bondi is the peach-coloured layer-cake right on the beachfront. It offers small, tidy rooms with only the cheapest singles sharing bathrooms. Note that the hotel is home to three bars and a nightclub – if you want to avoid merry revellers, stay elsewhere. Still, if you have a view of the beach and don't have to get up early, you'll be laughing just as loudly.

COOGEE & RANDWICK

COOGEE SANDS

Map pp94–5   Serviced Apartments $$

☎ 9665 8588; www.coogeesands.com.au; 161 Dolphin St, Coogee; studio $175-460, 1-bedroom apt $190-500; ⊠ 372-374

The sands of Coogee are only a few metres from the front door, making this apartment-style hotel an extremely attractive proposition. Some units have large terraces and impressive views, but if you miss out they all have access to a fabulous rooftop BBQ area. The rooms are pleasant without attempting to be stylish and come with kitchenettes.

DIVE HOTEL Map pp94–5 Boutique Hotel $$
☎ 9665 5538; www.divehotel.com.au; 234 Arden St, Coogee; d $165-280, 3-bedroom apt $350; 🚍 372-374

Plenty of hotels don't live up to their name (the most flagrantly misused epithets being grand, palace and central) and thankfully neither does this one. The 14 modern rooms at this delightful boutique hotel are wonderfully luxurious and come with a kitchenette and small groovy bathroom. There's a separate family-friendly three-room apartment in a nearby street. You can enjoy the complimentary breakfast buffet in the elegant kitchen or on the Asian-flavoured back patio.

AVONMORE ON THE PARK
Map pp94–5 Boutique Hotel $$
☎ 9399 9388; www.avonmoreonthepark.com.au; 34 The Avenue, Randwick; d & tw $145-225; 🚍 374

This elaborate three-storey grand Victorian terrace house is the biggest of its kind in Sydney. The breathtaking entrance has beautiful tiles and a lavish carved wooden staircase that will have you itching to make a movie-star-style descent. The 24 rooms (all with a kitchenette) are divided between the old servants' wing and the spacious heritage rooms – with polished wooden floors, acres of floral fabric and marble fireplaces.

BEACHHOUSE Map pp94–5 Hostel $
☎ 9665 1162; fax 9665 0365; 171 Arden St, Coogee; dm/s/d & tw/tr $30/60/80/100; 🚍 372-374

This friendly, comfortable hostel offers four-person dorms and basic private rooms, all with shared bathrooms. The welcoming hosts maintain scrupulous standards and offer a complimentary light breakfast and an outdoor BBQ for guests' use.

INNER WEST

It's a pleasure to wake up in the inner west, but only Glebe is well served by accommodation options. Transport connections to the city are excellent, but accessing the beaches requires a bit more effort.

TRICKETTS B&B Map pp100–1 B&B $$
☎ 9552 1141; www.tricketts.com.au; 270 Glebe Point Rd, Glebe; s $150, d $176-198, all incl breakfast; 🚍 431

Seven lovely rooms and spacious, antique-filled common areas will make you feel right at home – if your home is a gorgeous 19th-century restored mansion. There's a deck out the back and a beautiful marbled patio overlooking the front garden's fountain.

ALISHAN INTERNATIONAL GUEST HOUSE Map pp100–1 Guesthouse $
☎ 9566 4048; www.alishan.com.au; 100 Glebe Point Rd, Glebe; dm $27-33, s $55-99, d & tw $70-115; 🚍 431-434

Rooms in this lovely old house range from small basic cheapies with shared bathrooms, to larger self-contained ones. All are kept shipshape, as are the common kitchen, lounge, laundry, and garden BBQ area.

BILLABONG GARDENS Map pp100–1 Hostel $
☎ 9550 3236; www.billabonggardens.com.au; 5-11 Egan St, Newtown; dm $23-25, s $50, d & tw $69-89, tr $90-110; 🚍 422-423; 🚳

It you're more impressed by Che Guevara than Paris Hilton, Newtown's your place and this cosy brick-and-tile hostel should be your first choice. Excellent communal facilities open on to a lush central courtyard with a solar-heated pool. Internet access is free and friendly staff can sort out little extras such as snorkelling equipment if asked. The cheaper rooms have shared bathrooms.

GLEBE POINT YHA Map pp100–1 Hostel $
☎ 9692 8418; www.yha.com.au; 262 Glebe Point Rd, Glebe; dm $28-33, d & tw $74; 🚍 431

Well run and pleasant, this friendly, brightly painted hostel has good facilities, lots of activities and simple, clean rooms with sinks. The covered rooftop with picnic tables, hammocks, a BBQ and views is a highlight.

GLEBE VILLAGE Map pp100–1 Hostel $
☎ 9660 8878; www.glebevillage.com; 256 Glebe Point Rd, Glebe; dm $25-27, s/d $60/70; 🚍 431

Sprawled over Victorian houses (capacity 150), Glebe Village resembles nothing more than a collection of grungy student flats. Frank-the-Tank types, less hung up on comfort than good times, should find themselves quite at home. There's a mix of shared bathrooms and ensuites, good communal areas and sunny tables.

NORTH SHORE

Despite the position on the 'other side' of the harbour, staying on the lower North Shore can often mean a quicker commute into town than one from the inner west or eastern suburbs. And the views can be ridiculously sublime. Manly's a relaxing half-hour ferry ride away from the city centre, offering all the beach benefits and a chance to maximise your harbour exposure whenever you hanker to see the sights. With a gentle harbour beach and ocean surf beach only minutes apart, it is a great place for families.

LOWER NORTH SHORE

VIBE HOTEL NORTH SYDNEY
Map p108   Hotel $$$
☎ 9955 1111; www.vibehotels.com.au; 88 Alfred St S, Milsons Point; tw $200, d $200-224, ste $274-300; 🚊 Milsons Point; 🚗
Spunky and bright, this slick hotel sports 165 very stylish, contemporary rooms and 30 suites. Aqua Vibe rooms offer a choice of Lavender Bay or Kirribilli views, while the rooftop pool gives you both. Due to its location it pulls the business crowd – prices fall by around $50 on the weekends.

GLENFERRIE LODGE
Map p108   Guesthouse $
☎ 9955 1685; www.glenferrielodge.com; 12a Carabella St, Kirribilli; dm $40, s $65-79, tw $99, d $99-159, all incl breakfast; 🚊 Kirribilli
This large old house sits on a quiet residential street and has a wonderfully grassy back garden. With a ridiculous statue out front, it's hard to miss. Basic rooms come with a fridge and TV and the shared bathrooms are clean. Cheap dinners are available, but there's no kitchen access. Arriving by ferry is a glamorous option, but hauling your luggage up the stairs from the wharf may be less so.

MANLY

MANLY WATERSIDE
Map p110   Serviced Apartments $$
☎ 9977 4459; www.manlyholidays.com.au; Short St; apt studio $150-170, 1-bedroom apt $190-220, 2-bedroom apt $350-395; 🚊 Manly; 🚗
This place has around 30 apartments available in blocks scattered around the vicinity. All have kitchen and laundry facilities and some have pools and spas. There's quite a range available and prices vary throughout

the year, so check the website for more information. Concorde is the newest block, while the Grant is older but has killer views.

PERIWINKLE
Map p110   B&B $$
☎ 9977 4668; www.periwinkle.citysearch.com.au; 18 East Esplanade; s $110-160, d $135-190, all incl light breakfast; 🚊 Manly
Occupying a blissfully quiet harbourside spot, this large Federation house offers 18 pleasant, well-appointed rooms, some with ensuites and stunning water views. There's a family atmosphere, a shady courtyard and a communal kitchen.

101 ADDISON ROAD Map p110   B&B $$
☎ 9977 6216; www.bb-manly.com; 101 Addison Rd; s/d $130/150; 🚊 Manly
At risk of sounding like a Victorian matron, the only word to describe this 1880 cottage set on a quiet street is 'delightful'. Two rooms are available but the charming hostess accepts only one booking at a time (from one to four people) – meaning you'll have free reign of the main part of the antique-strewn house, including a private

AIRPORT ACCOMMODATION

HOTEL IBIS SYDNEY AIRPORT
Map pp50–1   Hotel $$
☎ 8339 8500; www.ibishotels.com.au; 205 O'Riordan St, Mascot; d & tw $139; 🚊 Mascot
Nobody stays in these could-be-anywhere airport hotels for kicks – they do so because they have an early flight or they missed it altogether. This one fits the bill perfectly, offering clean, comfortable rooms at reasonable rates, as well as regular airport shuttles (free from the airport, $5 back).

OLD RECTORY Map pp50–1   Guesthouse $
☎ 9559 7841; http://oldrectory.idx.com.au; 2 Samuel St, Tempe; s $55-70, d $70-80; 🚊 Sydenham
A little more character is provided at this small guesthouse on the Pacific Hwy. The cheaper rooms don't have ensuites, but there is a communal kitchen and grassy lawn. Traffic noise is intrusive, coming from both the air and ground. Breakfast and airport pick-ups are offered free; drop-offs are $12.

lounge with a grand piano. This is a rare treat and worth booking well in advance.

WINDERMERE COTTAGE
Map p110   B&B $$

☎ 9977 7363; eland@bigpond.net.au; 31 Cliff St; d $140; ⚓ Manly

If you miss out on a room at 101 Addison Road, this pleasant place nearby offers a very similar setup (two bedrooms, but only one booking accepted at a time). While it doesn't have quite the same sumptuous historic charm, it's still a good proposition.

BUNKHOUSE
Map p110   Hostel $

☎ 9976 0472; www.bunkhouse.com.au; 35 Pine St; dm $30, d & tw $80; ⚓ Manly

Surf central, this is the place for advice on all the northside breaks. Set on a quiet street in a two-storey house with a big backyard, it's a 300m walk to the beach and double that to the Corso. Each room comes with its own TV, kitchenette and bathroom, but if you're not the reclusive type there's also a common kitchen, dining area and TV lounge.

UPPER NORTH SHORE

BARRENJOEY HOUSE
Map p113   Guesthouse $$

☎ 9974 4001; www.barrenjoeyhouse.com.au; 1108 Barrenjoey Rd, Palm Beach; d $180-220; 🚌 L90

This lovely 1923 guesthouse might not be on the 'beach' side of Palm Beach (it faces tranquil Pittwater instead), but it still ranks as one of the best escapes on the Northern Beaches. The house is a testament to all things shabby chic, with an easy-going feel, Mod-Oz restaurant, wooden floorboards, white linen, old coffee tables and cushions galore. Rooms are pretty and feminine, some with ensuites, king-sized beds and views.

PITTWATER YHA Map p113   Hostel $

☎ 9999 5748; www.yha.com.au; Ku-ring-gai Chase National Park via Church Point; dm $25-28, d & tw $63-70; 🚌 E86 from Central to Church Point, then ⚓ Hall Wharf

Wake up to marvellous views over Morning Bay at this hostel, one of the best budget sleeps in Sydney. A converted 1920s guesthouse, it is set about 15 minutes' uphill from the wharf (this is a blissfully car-free

zone). The surrounding bushland is dominated by magnificent purple-grey eucalypti, which harbour a welter of cockatoos and wallabies. Book ahead and bring food; demand for this idyllic retreat is high.

OTHER NEIGHBOURHOODS

If staying in the heart of Sydney fails to excite you, the city's outskirts offer a change of pace and often a cheaper deal.

DOYLES PALACE HOTEL Map pp50–1   Pub $$

☎ 9337 5444; www.doyles.com.au; 1 Military Rd, Watsons Bay; d $145-260, tw $200, ste $230-420; ⚓ Watsons Bay

With a ferry jetty at its doorstep, this is an idyllic spot from which to explore the city or to retreat and relax. More boutique hotel than pub accommodation, the impressive Doyles Palace offers smartly renovated rooms with comfy beds, crisp white linen, attractive ensuites and some amazing views. Noise from the ever-popular bar doesn't seem to penetrate.

CRONULLA BEACHOUSE YHA   Hostel $

☎ 9527 7772; www.cronullabeachyha.com; Level 1, 40 Kingsway, Cronulla; dm $25-26, d & tw $75, tr $100; 🚆 Cronulla

Given that 90% of the clientele are hot surfer dudes who rarely bother to wear shirts (hey, it's something less to wash), no-one's going to get too hung up if the showers aren't totally clean or the rooms are a little shabby. This is a great party hostel that is what it is – and has a free pool table. The private rooms are marginally less noisy than the dorms and have ensuites. Electronic safety boxes are provided.

SHIRALEE CARAVAN PARK
Map pp50–1   Camping $

☎ 9567 7161; fax 9798 7059; 88 Bryant St, Rockdale; site unpowered/powered $25/30; 🚆 Rockdale

If you're looking for a place to pitch a tent or park a campervan reasonably handy to the city, Shiralee offers a quiet spot in walking distance of Rockdale station and Brighton-Le-Sands beach, and handy to the airport. It's nothing flash but there is a kitchen, laundry, TV room and BBQ. Many of the guests are permanent stayers.

EXCURSIONS

EXCURSIONS

Sydney might seem like it has it all, but you'll be missing out if you don't tear yourself away to visit one of the fabulous day-trip destinations just a short hop away.

Superb national parks, secluded beaches, historic towns, timeless rivers, dramatic limestone caves and sophisticated wineries are all easily accessible from the centre of the city. Regular public transport links generally exist, although some of the more isolated (and often more rewarding) pockets are harder to reach. Hiring a car (p219) or taking part in an organised tour (p225) are both good options.

A return trip within a day is feasible for each destination but you'll get more out of some areas – especially the Blue Mountains and the Hunter Valley wineries – if you stay at least one night.

NATURE

Nature-loving Sydneysiders are spoilt for choice when it comes to excursions out of their city. If time and transport options are tight, the perennial favourite for residents and visitors alike is the Blue Mountains (right), which has good transport connections, a wealth of tour possibilities and some of the most magnificent scenery in Australia. There are accommodation and dining options to suit any budget. A popular side trip is a visit to the awe-inspiring grottoes of Jenolan Caves (p207). If you prefer serene waterways, then the stunning Hawkesbury River (p213) offers small townships with local charm, along with the chance to sleep on a houseboat and wend your way through untamed bush on the riverbanks. To the south of Sydney, the Royal National Park (p211) is one of the world's oldest protected areas of natural wilderness. Ghostly eucalyptus trees, magnificent coastline and fine trekking are all part of its appeal.

DRIVING

Bells Line of Road (p206) is arguably the most delightful drive in New South Wales (NSW). It winds its way up through the charming historic township of Richmond, passing through the enchanting hamlets of Kurrajong Heights and Bilpin. The route is particularly appealing at sunset in autumn, and the boxes of orchard-fresh fruit along the road add to the appeal.

BEACHES

The Central Coast (p214) has sun, sand, surf and services in one glorious coastal swathe. You can reach most destinations in a day, with good train links between Sydney and Gosford, but an overnight or weekend trip will let you squeeze the most out of the fine weather and many beaches.

To the south of Sydney, dramatic, a rugged coastline and forests are the backdrop for the unspoilt beaches of the Royal National Park (p211).

WINE

Hunter Valley reds are famous, and justifiably so. We've included the Hunter Valley Wineries (p208) here as a day trip, although the region is a 2½-hour drive from Sydney so staying overnight makes more sense. That way, you can really take advantage of the cellar-door tastings and charming scenery.

THE BLUE MOUNTAINS

For a taste of the extraordinary raw beauty of the Australian bush, few places rival the Blue Mountains, just a couple of hours from the skyscrapers of Sydney. The area's 1001 treks and lookouts allow everyone – from pensioners with pacemakers to the downright intrepid – to explore this unspoilt natural wilderness. It is quite simply a must-do trip for anybody with more than a few days in the city. Age-old rock formations, magnificent ghostly ancient gum trees, impossibly steep gorges and majestic views every which way will haunt visitors long after they leave.

Forming part of the Great Dividing Range, the Blue Mountains begin 65km inland from Sydney and rise to more than 1200m above sea level. The formation is in fact a sandstone plateau riddled with spectacular gullies eroded by rivers over millennia. The blue haze, which gave the mountains their name, is actually a

fine mist of evaporated eucalyptus oil from the gumtrees.

Initially thought to be impenetrable, the mountains were first crossed by European explorers in 1813. In an epic journey, Gregory Blaxland, William C Wentworth and William Lawson followed the mountain ridges over the top, their route pretty much the same as that followed by today's Great Western Hwy. Gradually settlers moved into the area, and in the 20th century it developed into a popular getaway for Sydneysiders to escape the summer heat, experience a bit of a winter wonderland, and for honeymooners seeking upmarket rooms with gorgeous views. While more and more crowds flock here each year, there are still huge swathes of untamed land. As you would expect in such rugged terrain, there are hazards. Walkers sometimes get lost, bushfires can flare up in summer and poisonous snakes do bite. These are relatively rare occurrences, but be aware that the dangers exist and seek up-to-date advice from the visitor centres.

Also be prepared for a difference in climate: you can swelter in Sydney but shiver in Katoomba. Autumn mists and drizzle can make bushwalking somewhat less appealing. In winter the days are often clear, and in the valleys it can be almost warm. There is usually some snowfall between June and August, and the region has a Yulefest in July, when many restaurants and guesthouses offer 'Christmas' dinners.

The Blue Mountains National Park protects large areas to the north and south of the Great Western Hwy. It's the most popular and accessible of the national parks in the area, with great bushwalking, scenic lookouts, breathtaking waterfalls and Aboriginal stencils. There are walks lasting from a few minutes to several days, and the two most popular trekking destinations are Jamison Valley, south of Katoomba, and Grose Valley, northeast of Katoomba and east of Blackheath. The area south of Glenbrook is also rewarding walking territory where you will find Red Hands Cave, an old Aboriginal shelter with hand stencils on the walls. It's an easy 7km return walk, southwest of the Glenbrook Visitor Centre.

The famous artist and author Norman Lindsay (1879–1969) lived 6km northeast of Springwood from 1912 until his death. His home is now the Norman Lindsay Gallery & Museum (☎ 4751 1067; www.normanlindsay.com.au; 14 Norman Lindsay Crescent, Faulconbridge; adult/child $9/4; ☽ 10am-4pm). It houses many of his risqué paintings, cartoons, illustrations and sculptures. The grounds are well worth a wander.

Just south of the town of Wentworth Falls, heading west along the Great Western Hwy, there are great views of the Jamison Valley. You can see the spectacular 300m-high Wentworth Falls from Falls Reserve, also the starting point for a network of walking tracks. The tree-lined streets of Wentworth Falls are home to the Falls Gallery (☎ 4757 1139; www.fallsgallery.com.au; 161 Falls Rd, Wentworth Falls; admission $2; ☽ 10am-5pm Wed-Sun), one of the Blue Mountains' best privately run galleries. The paper and ceramic collections are displayed within a lovingly restored clapboard house amid well-manicured gardens.

Leura, 3km east of Katoomba, is a quaint tree-lined town full of country stores and cafés

---

TRANSPORT: THE BLUE MOUNTAINS

Distance from Sydney to Katoomba 109km

Direction West

Travel time Two hours

Car Take Parramatta Rd and head onto the Western Motorway tollway (M4; $2.20) at Strathfield. West of Penrith, the motorway becomes the Great Western Hwy, and continues to Lithgow.

Train These run approximately hourly from Central Station. The trip takes two hours (peak return $23.20) to Katoomba, and there are stops at plenty of Blue Mountains townships on the way. Services run roughly hourly between stations east of Katoomba and approximately every two hours between stations to the west. One excellent option is the ExplorerLink ticket (adult/child $42.20/16.60) which gets you to Katoomba station and gives access to the Explorer Bus, which stops at 30 Blue Mountains attractions. A three-day ExplorerLink ticket is also available (adult/child $57.60/24.30). See www.cityrail.info/fares/link_tickets.jsp. Sit on the left-hand side of the train going from Sydney to the Blue Mountains, as the views are better.

KATOOMBA

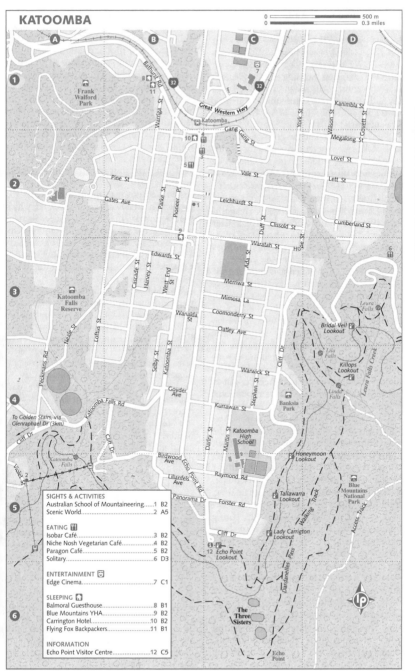

0   500 m
0   0.3 miles

SIGHTS & ACTIVITIES
Australian School of Mountaineering......1 B2
Scenic World...2 A5

EATING 🍴
Isobar Café...3 B2
Niche Nosh Vegetarian Café.....................4 B2
Paragon Café...5 B2
Solitary...6 D3

ENTERTAINMENT 🎭
Edge Cinema...7 C1

SLEEPING 🏠
Balmoral Guesthouse................................8 B1
Blue Mountains YHA.................................9 B2
Carrington Hotel.....................................10 B2
Flying Fox Backpackers...........................11 B1

INFORMATION
Echo Point Visitor Centre.......................12 C5

and home to some of Australia's most beautiful gardens. The NSW Toy and Railway Museum & Leuralla Gardens (☎ 4784 1169; www.toyandrailwaymuseum.com.au; 36 Olympian Pde, Leura; adult/child museum & garden $12/6, garden only $8/4; ☻ 10am-5pm) is an Art Deco mansion, housing a fine collection of 19th-century Australian art, as well as a toy and model-railway museum. The historic house, set in five hectares of lovely gardens, is a memorial to HV 'Doc' Evatt, a former Labor Party leader and first president of the UN. Make sure you cross the road for a stunning valley view. A lookout here includes two statues and an amphitheatre. Also in town is Everglades Garden (☎ 4784 1938; www.evergladesgardens.info; 37 Everglades Ave, Leura; adult/child $7/3; ☻ 10am-5pm spring & summer, 10am-4pm autumn & winter), a magnificent 1930s garden created by Danish 'Master Gardener' Paul Sorenson, with terraces, stone walls, gnarled banksias, waterfalls, grottoes and dramatic views over Jamison Valley.

Sublime Point, south of Leura, is another great cliff-top lookout. Nearby, Gordon Falls Reserve is a popular picnic spot. From here you can take the cliff-top path or Cliff Dr 4km west past Leura Cascades to Katoomba's Echo Point, where there is a visitors centre and the Blue Mountains' most popular sight: the Three Sisters, a trio of rocky pinnacles that draw gasps and launch a thousand photographs. They look particularly attractive when floodlit at night. Katoomba and the adjacent centres of Wentworth Falls and Leura form the tourist centre of the Blue Mountains. Katoomba, which has an excellent hostel, is probably the most convenient base of all. The town itself is Art Deco central, especially at the top end, although it does feel down-at-heel in parts. A cluster of cafés compete for the tourist dollar, particularly at the top of the steep main drag, Katoomba Street. A New Age scene has developed here, mixing peaceably with a strong born-again Christian presence. Several places in town, such as the Australian School of Mountaineering, offer rock climbing, abseiling, canyoning and caving adventure activities.

To the west of Echo Point Lookout, at the junction of Cliff Dr and Violet St, is Scenic World (☎ 4782 2699; www.scenicworld.com.au; round trip on railway & cableway adult/child/family $19/10/48; ☻ 9am-5pm). Imagine Disneyland in the bush and you've almost got it. It's the Blue Mountains, theme-park style, with attractions including a railway, Cableway and Skyway, as well as a scenic walkway. This is great if your time is limited or if the kids are in tow. All rides offer breathtaking views from breathtaking heights. The railway runs to the bottom of the Jamison Valley, where the popular six-hour walk to the Ruined Castle rock formation begins. The railway was built in the 1880s to transport coal miners, and its 45-degree incline is one of the steepest in the world. The Cableway, an enclosed wheelchair-accessible cable car, also descends to the valley floor. The most recently added ride is the Skyway, a cable car that crosses Katoomba Falls gorge. Its 'electro scenic' glass floor gives passengers views of the valley canopies 200m below.

If you have your own transport, you can reach the Golden Stairs walk, a superb, less congested way down to the Ruined Castle. To get there head down Narrow Neck Rd, which soon becomes Cliff Dr. The unsealed Glenraphael Dr is the seventh turn-off on the right. Watch out for the signs to the Golden Stairs a couple of kilometres down on the left. It is a marvellously steep, exhilarating trail down into the canyon.

Should bad weather intervene, you can always catch the views virtually on the giant screen at the Edge Cinema (☎ 4782 8900; www.edgecinema.com.au; 225 Great Western Hwy, Katoomba; admission adult/child $14.50/9.50). It is just outside the town.

Past Katoomba lies the little town of Blackheath, a good base for visiting the Grose and Megalong valleys. Superb lookouts east of town include Govetts Leap (named after a 'daring bushranger'), the adjacent Bridal Veil Falls (the highest in the Blue Mountains) and Evans Lookout (turn off the highway just south of Blackheath). Northeast of the town, via Hat Hill Rd, are Pulpit Rock, Perrys Lookdown and Anvil Rock. This is near the Wind-Eroded Cave where the setting sun can cast an amazing light show. A long cliff-edge track leads from Govetts Leap to Pulpit Rock and there are walks down into the Grose Valley itself. Perrys Lookdown is at the beginning of the shortest route to the beautiful Blue Gum Forest in the bottom of the valley – about four hours return – but you'll want to linger longer. It was damaged by fire in November 2006, but should be reopened to walkers by early 2008.

For updates, and details of other walks, make the very professional and helpful Blue Mountains Heritage Centre your first port of call. It is located on Govetts Leap Rd about 3km off the Great Western Hwy. The centre also has an interesting interpretative display on the natural environment and cultural heritage of the Blue Mountains.

Megalong Valley, south of Blackheath, is largely cleared farmland but it's still a beautiful place,

HARTLEY HISTORIC SITE

About 11km west of Mt Victoria, on the western slopes of the Great Dividing Range, is the tiny, sandstone 'ghost' town of Hartley, which flourished from the 1830s but declined when it was bypassed by the railway in 1887. There are several buildings of historic interest, including the 1837 Greek Revival courthouse (adult $5.50; ☯ tours at 10am, 11am, noon, 2pm, 3pm).

There is a National Parks & Wildlife Service (NPWS) Information Centre (☎ 6355 2117; ☯ 10am-1pm & 2-4:20pm) in the 1845 Farmer's Inn. You can wander around the village for free, but to enter the courthouse you must book a tour (minimum four people); call the visitors centre for information. CountryLink buses meet trains at Mt Victoria station on Tuesday and Friday (both at 10.45am) and Sunday (4.25pm) for the run to Hartley – your own transport is a far better option.

Collits' Inn (☎ 6355 2072/0407 497623; www.collitsinn.com.au; Hartley Vale Rd, Hartley Vale; d from $150) is a lovingly restored 1823 inn with rustic but well-appointed rooms, along with excellent French-influenced food (weekends only). Dinner is the only meal served; reservations are essential. Follow the signs off the Great Western Hwy along a rough unpaved road – or you can go the long way round down a road in better condition.

with awesome sandstone escarpments. The road down from Blackheath passes through pockets of rainforest and you can walk the beautiful 600m Coachwood Glen Nature Trail. A couple of kilometres further on is the small valley settlement of Werriberri, where there are several horse-riding outfits. Werriberri Trail Rides (☎ 4787 9171; www.bluemts.com.au/werriberri; Megalong Rd; rides per hr/4hr from $48/125) can show you the area on a guided horseback ride and, best of all, the horses are well looked after. From Blackheath, it's a 9km winding drive into the Megalong Valley via Shipley and Megalong Rds.

Mt Victoria, the highest settled point in the mountains, is a small, sweet village with a semirural atmosphere, 16km northwest of Katoomba on the Great Western Hwy. It has the cute-as-a-button old-school Mt Vic Flicks (☎ 4787 1577; 2a Harley Ave; admission adult/child $9/7) cinema, which screens interesting, mainly independent films.

At the other end of the beautiful Bells Line of Rd is the Zig Zag Railway (☎ 6355 2955; www.zigzagrailway.com.au; return ticket adult/child $22/11), where you and the kids can experience a ride in an old steam locomotive along a railway trumpeted as a 19th-century engineering masterpiece.

INFORMATION

Australian School of Mountaineering (ASM; ☎ 4782 2014; www.asmguides.com; 166 Katoomba St, Katoomba)

Blue Mountains Heritage Centre (☎ 4787 8877; Govetts Leap Rd, Blackheath; ☯ 9am-4.30pm) The excellent, informative National Parks & Wildlife Services tourist information office in Blackheath. It's stuffed with maps, guides and gifts.

Echo Point Visitor Centre (☎ 1300 653 408; www.visit bluemountains.com.au; Echo Point Rd, Katoomba; ☯ 9am-5pm)

Glenbrook Visitor Centre (☎ 1300 653 408; www.visitbluemountains.com.au; Great Western Hwy at Glenbrook; ☯ 9am-4.30pm Sat & Sun)

EATING

Solitary (☎ 4782 1164; 90 Cliff Dr, Leura Falls; mains $29-35; ☯ 6:30-9pm Wed-Sun, noon-3pm Sat & Sun) 'Views forever' its tagline goes but that doesn't say it all. Along with the supreme location, this understated yet sophisticated restaurant has a refined modern cuisine, with dishes such as Kangaroo Island chicken and roasted barramundi. The Solitary kiosk (open 10am to 4pm) has an informal, less-expensive menu, keeping the great views and cuisine accessible to those on a tighter budget. Book ahead for the restaurant.

Silk's Brasserie (☎ 4784 2534; www.silksleura.com; 128 The Mall, Leura; mains $29-34; ☯ lunch & dinner) The rustic Tuscan-style interior and the Monet-esque drinks bar are lovely, but it's the cuisine that wins the plaudits here. The warm, friendly owners believe in slow food, which is sourced locally and prepared in a way that keeps the most demanding of critics happy.

Conservation Hut (☎ 4757 3827; www.conservationhut .com.au; Fletcher St, Wentworth Falls; mains $19-24, sandwiches $8-10; ☯ 9am-4pm Mon-Fri, 9am-5pm Sat & Sun) You have to put up with inflated prices for the cliff-edge view, but you won't get many finer panoramas with your coffee and cake. It's still a meeting place for a local conservation society and has walking maps and brochures available.

Isobar Café (☎ 4782 4063; 40 Katoomba St, Katoomba; mains $15-22; ☯ breakfast, lunch & dinner) This low-lit

DETOUR: THE BELLS LINE OF ROAD

Quieter and much more scenic (and less congested) than the Great Western Hwy, this is a more northerly route between Sydney and the Blue Mountains. The road, constructed in 1841, runs from near Richmond across the mountains to Lithgow. This is a highly recommended journey if you have your own transport; you can cut across to join the Great Western Hwy near Mt Victoria. There are fine views towards the coast from Kurrajong Heights on the eastern slopes of the range, with orchards around Bilpin, and sandstone cliff and bush scenery all the way to Lithgow. The Bells Line of Rd is flanked by bush, small farms and apple orchards, with abundant fruit stalls.

Midway between Bilpin and Bell, the delightful Mt Tomah Botanic Gardens (☎ 4567 2154; www.rbgsyd.nsw.gov .au; adult/child & concession/family $4.40/2.20/8.80; ⌚ 10am-4pm Mar-Sep, 10am-5pm Oct-Mar) is a cool-climate annexe of Sydney's Royal Botanic Gardens (p57). It specialises in nurturing southern hemisphere flora that might not thrive at the sea-level gardens in the city. The views from the deck of the visitors centre are fabulous; it's a great place to sip an espresso from the café. Parts of the gardens are wheelchair accessible. You can also buy your own piece of botanical history – Wollemi pine cuttings are on sale here.

North of Bells Line of Rd, near the gorgeous little town of Mt Wilson, is a remnant of rainforest known as the Cathedral of Ferns. Settled by people with a penchant for recreating England, the town itself is a tiny, beautiful village of hedgerows, large gardens and rows of European trees, and is particularly lovely in autumn. Near the Post House there's an information board with details of public gardens and some short walks in the area. The township is 8km north of Bells Line of Rd; the turn-off is 7km east of Bell.

Wollemi National Park, north of Bells Line of Rd, is the state's largest forested wilderness area (nearly 500,000 hectares). It stretches as far as Denman in the Hunter Valley, and has good rugged bushwalking and lots of wildlife. Access is limited and the park's centre is so isolated that a new species of tree, named the Wollemi pine, was discovered only in 1994. Don't expect to stumble across them yourself, however. Their location remains strictly under wraps. A more recent and equally thrilling discovery was the July 2003 find of a veritable gallery of Aboriginal rock art, dating back 4000 years.

---

jazzy venue (Art Deco of course) often has live music in the evenings. The staff were overstretched when we were here.

Paragon Café (☎ 4782 2928; 65 Katoomba St, Katoomba; mains $15-22; ⌚ 9am-5pm Mon-Sun) A legendary Art Deco café and restaurant that has seen many a celebrity – from Bob Dylan to Ginger Rogers – snack at one of its dark-wood booths. There is also a fine selection of home-made chocolates for sale.

Leura Gourmet (☎ 4784 1438; 159 The Mall, Leura; mains $15-19, cakes $7-9; ⌚ 8am-5pm) Head to the back of this bustling deli/café to nibble and sip with fine background views.

Niche Nosh Vegetarian Café (☎ 4782 1622; 10 Katoomba St, Katoomba; mains $13.50-16; ⌚ 11am-9pm Mon-Sat, 11am-7pm Sun) The friendly owners realised their dream of setting up a vegetarian café in 2004 with this quirky, left-field and good-value place at the top of the main street. George Harrison would have felt at home with the hippy, New Age vibe. Dairy products are free-range.

SLEEPING

Note that many guesthouses (and even some hostels) require a minimum two-night stay at the weekend. During the week, places tend to be more flexible and cheaper.

Imperial Hotel (☎ 4787 1878; www.hotelimperial .au; 1 Station St, Mt Victoria; tw with shared bathroom $79 Sun-Thu, $89 Fri & Sat; d $139-220) Creaking floorboards in the rambling corridors give away the age of this handsome old hotel on the Great Western Hwy. Bushwalkers can bag a budget room, lovers can sidle into the deluxe ensuite with four-poster bed.

Jemby Rinjah Eco Lodge (☎ 4787 7622; www.jemby rinjahlodge.com.au; 336 Evans Lookout Rd; $170 Mon-Thu; $219 Fri-Sun, extra adult $30) These excellent, secluded, eco-friendly cabins (all with septic tanks, some with rainwater hot tubs) give a real sense of the dramatic bush setting. A purist might argue against the TVs, but that's a minor quibble. There's a daily bird feed at 8:30am. The cabins easily sleep two adults and two children.

Mercure Grand Hydro Majestic (☎ 4788 1002; www .hydromajestic.com.au; Great Western Hwy, Medlow Bath; d from $200) This huge Art Deco sprawl has some magnificent views over the Megalong Valley – although not from all the rooms. Recently it underwent a major facelift – rooms are decorated in Art Deco, Edwardian or French provincial style. Some of the heritage rooms are tight on size.

Broomelea Bed & Breakfast (☎ 4784 2910; www .broomelea.com.au; 273 Leura Mall, Leura; d from $154 Sun-

Thu, $200 Sat & Sun) Leafy Leura gets a bad rap for being hoity toity, but when B&Bs are this comfy, who cares? A manicured garden, cane furniture on the veranda, a cosy roaring fire and a lounge area to sink into are just a few of the charms of this well-appointed Edwardian building. Self-contained accommodation was being refurbished when we passed through.

Victoria & Albert Guesthouse (☎ 4787 1241; www.our guest.com.au/victoria.albert.html; 19 Station St, Mt Victoria; d $140) This guesthouse comes in the grand old style of 1914, with high wood-panelled ceilings. Classically conservative, it will appeal to the slightly older patterned-sweater brigade. Pool and spa are also available. There are also cheaper street-front heritage rooms with shared bathroom.

Balmoral Guesthouse (☎ 4782 2264; www.balmoral house.com.au; 196 Bathurst Rd, Katoomba; d from $120 Sun-Thu, from $135 Fri & Sat, plus Sun where Mon is a public holiday) This historic colonial guesthouse (the oldest in the Blue Mountains, don't you know?) has impeccable period details such as wrought-iron framed beds and classic Victorian décor. There is an outdoor spa and views over the valley out the back, as well as a rather indulgent three-course home-cooked breakfast in the morning. One for romantics.

Carrington Hotel (☎ 4782 1111; www.thecarrington .com.au; 15-47 Katoomba St, Katoomba; d/tw with breakfast and shared bath $119 Sun-Thu, $139 Fri & Sat) Nicknamed the 'Grand Old Lady of the Mountains', this elegant good-time girl still has a sparkle in her eye. A favoured venue for weddings, this huge heritage-listed hotel has rooms that range from affordable (if you are prepared to share a bathroom) to seriously opulent. Dig deep if you want French doors, spas and views.

Kinie-Ger Bush Cabins (☎ 4787 7182; 325 Evans Lookout Rd; cabins $95 Sun-Thu, $110 Sat & Sun; $10 per extra person) These stone-wall bushland cabins, 3km from Blackheath, are more suitable for those on a tighter budget. They can comfortably sleep four and are in a lovely setting. If you are using public transport, you can call in advance to arrange a pick-up.

Blue Mountains YHA (☎ 4782 1416; www.yha.com.au; 207 Katoomba St, Katoomba; dm $26-29, d/tw $73-82) This YHA consistently gets voted one of the best backpacker accommodations in Australia. It's in a fully restored heritage-listed Art Deco building still gleaming from a colourful upgrade. There's a reading area, a BBQ on the terrace, a games room, and an open fire during the winter. On long weekends there is a two-night minimum stay. The hostel's clued-up staff are usually on hand to help you get the best out the Blue Mountains.

Flying Fox Backpackers (☎ 4782 4226; www.theflying fox.com.au; 190 Bathurst Rd; dm including breakfast $24, camping $14) This brightly coloured, sunny and very laid-back hostel has Moroccan-style tapestries draping the walls and loads of information on the region. There is also a chill-out hut, outdoor seating and a BBQ area.

JENOLAN CAVES

Formed hundreds of millions of years ago, the vast, stunningly beautiful Jenolan Caves (☎ 1300 76 3311; www.jenolancaves.org.au; tour adult/child from $22/15; two-hour 'Plughole' adventure tour $58; ☺ tours 9.45am-5pm Mon-Fri, 9.30am-5pm Sat & Sun, ghost tour 8pm Sat) network is still being explored to this day. Lying southwest of Katoomba on the western fringe of Kanangra-Boyd National Park, it is the largest publicly accessible cave system in the world. Clay-dating methods also suggest it is the world's oldest discovered open-cave network, formed millions of years before the demise of the dinosaurs. The caves – pronounced jeh-*noh*-lan – were known as *Binoomur* or 'Dark Places' by the Gundungarra people, to whom they had special significance. White explorers first passed through in 1813. In fact, early European cave enthusiasts were remarkably forward thinking – the Jenolan Caves area was protected from 1866, one of the reasons the translucent crystal formations, giant underground

---

TRANSPORT: JENOLAN CAVES

Distance from Sydney to Jenolan Caves 190km

Direction West

Travel time 45 minutes by car from Hartley

Car Turn off the Great Western Hwy at Hartley – the caves are on Jenolan Caves Rd.

Tours The caves are on plenty of tour itineraries available from Sydney or Katoomba.

Walk The Six Foot Track from Katoomba to Jenolan Caves is a fairly easy three-day walk, but make sure you get information from the NPWS at the Blue Mountain Heritage Centre. The truly hardcore keep-fit fanatic could even attempt the marathon that takes place here every March (see www.sixfoot .com).

caverns and subterranean rivers have been preserved to this day. One cave has been open to the public since 1860, and nine more are open today. Cave snobs will not be disappointed.

Top-notch guided tours, with varying levels of difficulty, leave regularly each day, lasting from two to eight hours. Adventure tours take abseilers and spelunkers to places that are normally off-limits. Be warned, however: the sheer number of visitors can be overwhelming. A quarter of a million visitors troop through the caves each year. If you're visiting at the weekend or in holiday season, it is definitely worth booking in advance. Check times and cave popularity if you would prefer to do a tour without the constant burr of camcorders and 30 other visitors in tow.

Another recent feature is the self-guided audio tour of the enormous, mysterious Devil's Coach House and the open Nettle Cave, where you may hear the haunting screech of roosting sooty owls. It's informative and free if you buy a ticket for any of the guided cave visits.

EATING & SLEEPING

Jenolan Caves Cottages (☎ 6359 3311; www.jenolan caves.org.au; cottages per 6 people Sun-Thu $89, Fri-Sat $121, Bellbird Cottage $143-176) All the mod-cons are to be found in these country-style timber cottages. They are 8km before the caves, but there is also the 1930s Bellbird Cottage just a short stroll from the caves.

Jenolan Caves Resort (☎ 6359 3322; www.jenolancaves house.com.au; Gate House $30 per person, Mountain Lodge Units Sun-Thu $135, Fri-Sat $155, Caves House d Sun-Thu $115, Fri-Sat $125) There are three types of accommodation at this grand old Jenolan Caves institution. There's the classic Caves House with many of the original 19th century furnishings, the motel-style Mountain Lodge and good backpacker beds at the Gate House. There's a restaurant/bistro on site.

Jenolan Cabins (☎ 6335 6239; www.jenolancabins.com .au; 42 Edith Rd, Jenolan Caves; d Mon-Thu $98, Fri-Sun $115; ⬚) These are a comfortably furnished, self-catering cottages with log fires, BBQ facilities and TV. Pull the blinds at night as the sunbeams reach powerfully across the valley in the morning. They are 5km beyond the caves. There's a two-night minimum stay at weekends.

HUNTER VALLEY WINERIES

Nestled serenely at the foot of the Brokenback Range, the Hunter Valley produces enough grapes to keep Bacchus' cup spilling over for eternity. It is the oldest wine-growing country in Australia, with the first vines planted here in 1831. Semillon, Shiraz and, more recently, Chardonnay are the specialties and more than 100 vineyards are dotted about the rolling countryside around Pokolbin, the heart of this wine country. Weirdly, the area is also known for its coal mining – some good-value accommodation is in the mining town of Cessnock – but the Hunter Valley is firmly on the tourist radar for its wineries. A whole bunch of galleries, gourmet food-tasting outfits and golf courses have mushroomed off the vineyards' success. These wineries range from mega-producers to tiny boutique operations that don't even have a cellar door. The vast majority encourage visits and tastings and the bigger and more established players sometimes offer tours. If you can, plan your trip for midweek when the valley is less crowded and the accommodation is cheaper. If you're driving, it's worth taking the scenic route along the old convict-built road that passes through Wollombi, a charming old town in its own right.

Traditionalists grumble that the area has lost its low-key charm since corporate wine and golf packages started creeping in. There is a certain 'wine as theme park' approach in some parts. But with so many cellar doors

---

TRANSPORT: HUNTER VALLEY WINERIES

Distance from Sydney to Cessnock 180km

Direction Northwest

Travel time 2½ hours

Car Take the Sydney–Newcastle Fwy, which starts in Wahroonga on the North Shore, then take Rte 82 to Cessnock.

Bus This is probably your best public-transport option. Rover Coaches (☎ 1800 801 012; www .rovercoaches.com.au) has buses from Sydney (return adult/child $70/35). It departs from Central Station Bay 14.

Train CityRail to Newcastle ($17.40), then Rover Coaches bus service 160 to Cessnock.

HUNTER VALLEY WINERIES

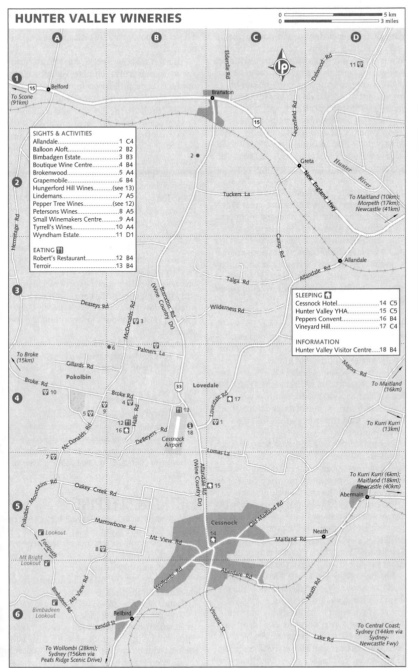

SIGHTS & ACTIVITIES
Allandale	1	C4
Balloon Aloft	2	B2
Bimbadgen Estate	3	B3
Boutique Wine Centre	4	B4
Brokenwood	5	A4
Grapemobile	6	B4
Hungerford Hill Wines	(see 13)	
Lindemans	7	A5
Pepper Tree Wines	(see 12)	
Petersons Wines	8	A5
Small Winemakers Centre	9	A4
Tyrrell's Wines	10	A4
Wyndham Estate	11	D1

EATING 🍴
Robert's Restaurant	12	B4
Terroir	13	B4

SLEEPING 🛏
Cessnock Hotel	14	C5
Hunter Valley YHA	15	C5
Peppers Convent	16	B4
Vineyard Hill	17	C4

INFORMATION
Hunter Valley Visitor Centre	18	B4

dotted around the meandering country roads, it's still easy – and very pleasant – to create your own independent version of the movie *Sideways* (drink-driving excepted, obviously). We mention a few of our favourite wineries below. But perhaps the most fun is to be had by following your nose: dip in and out of the many boutique cellar doors on your own personal quest for the perfect drop.

The most oft-mentioned name to the question, 'Which vineyard *must* I visit?' is Tyrrell's Wines (☎ 4993 7000; www.tyrrells.com.au; 1838 Broke Rd, Pokolbin; tours $4; 🕙 8.30am-5pm Mon-Fri, 8:30am-4:30pm Sat, tours 1.30pm Mon-Sat). It's one of the most established old-school vineyards in the area, and has fiercely defended its independence. There are wine tours and some great views from its cellar door. The vineyard pioneered Chardonnay growing in the valley.

Bimbadgen Estate (☎ 4998 7585; www.bimbadgen.com.au; 790 McDonalds Road, Pokolbin; 🕙 10am-5pm Mon-Sat) is on the crest of a hill, giving its lovely, lunch-only Esca restaurant a spectacular look-out over its vines through the floor to ceiling glass window.

Pepper Tree Wines (☎ 4998 7539; www.peppertreewines.com.au; Halls Rd, Pokolbin; 🕙 9am-5pm Mon-Fri, 9:30am-5pm Sat & Sun) is another upmarket boutique operation in lovely grounds. It produces a wide variety of different grapes.

Over in Lovedale, Allandale (☎ 4990 4526; www.allandalewinery.com.au; Lovedale Rd, Lovedale; 🕙 9am-5pm Mon-Sat, 10am-5pm Sun) produces all its wines on site. Chardonnay is one of its signature wines. Its wine cellar is perched on a hillside with valley panorama.

Brokenwood (☎ 4998 7559; www.brokenwood.com.au; 401-427 McDonalds Rd, Pokolbin; 🕙 9:30am-5pm Mon-Sun) has a low-key, popular cellar door, usually with a line of people clamouring to try the excellent Semillons and Chardonnays.

Petersons Wines (☎ 4990 1704; www.petersonswines.com.au; Mt View Rd, Mount View; 🕙 9am-5pm Mon-Sat, 10am-5pm Sun) has arguably the prettiest location of all the vineyards. It has sparkling wines and Semillons. The staff positively encourage you to set up your own BBQ in the grounds.

Lindemans (☎ 4998 7684; www.lindemans.com.au; McDonalds Rd, Pokolbin; 🕙 10am-5pm Mon-Sun) is the undisputed heavyweight of the area – visit here for a taste of wine as seriously big business.

If you are a real connoisseur, drop into either the Boutique Wine Centre (☎ 4998 7474; www.boutiquewinecentre.com.au; Broke Rd, Pokolbin; 🕙 9am-4:30pm Mon-Sat, 10-4:30pm Sun) or the Small Winemakers Centre (☎ 4998 7668; www.smallwinemakerscentre.com.au; McDonalds Rd, Pokolbin; 🕙 10am-5pm Mon-Sun), which

both have wines from boutique producers so small they don't even have cellar doors. These are bottles you won't find in any supermarket.

The Hunter Vintage Festival, held from January to March in the Hunter Valley, attracts hordes of wine enthusiasts for tastings, grape-picking and grape-treading contests. Other events, such as the Lovedale Long Lunch (www.lovedalelonglunch.com.au) in May are great ways of tasting the best of the area's wines and food. Some of the bigger wineries also hold musical events in their rambling, extensive grounds. They run the gamut from opera to Bryan Adams. They are held most frequently at the long-established Wyndham Estate (☎ 4938 3444; www.wyndhamestate.com; 700 Dalwood Rd, Dalwood; 🕙 10am-5pm Mon-Sun) in its picturesque riverside grounds each year.

Balloon Aloft (☎ 4938 1955; www.balloonaloft.com; 1443 Wine Country Dr, North Rothbury; balloon flights over the valley per adult/child $295/180) is a great – but pricey – adventure travel experience. Apparently marriage proposals are common in the rarefied dawn air above the Hunter Valley. Cheaper, last-minute standby options are also available.

Grapemobile (☎ 0418 404 039; cnr McDonalds Rd & Palmers Lane, Pokolbin; bike hire per day/2 days from $25/35) offers advice on pedalling through the vines.

INFORMATION

Hunter Valley Visitor Centre (☎ 4990 0900; www.winecountry.com.au; 455 Wine Country Drive, Pokolbin; 🕙 9am-5.30pm Mon-Fri, 9am-5pm Sat, 9am-4pm Sun) This visitors centre has a huge stock of leaflets and information on accommodation, attractions and dining in the region.

EATING & SLEEPING

Cessnock Hotel (☎ 4990 1002; 234 Wollombi Rd, Cessnock; d Sun-Thu $60, d incl breakfast Fri & Sat $90) This large, town-centre pub offers maintained rooms with high ceilings and many of their original early 20th-century fittings.

Wright Taste (☎ 4991 4414) The bright, fresh café that adjoins the Cessnock Hotel.

Hunter Valley YHA (☎ 4991 3278; www.yha.com.au; 100 Wine Country Dr, Nulkaba; dm $25, tw $70-90) This is an excellent, small-scale and friendly hostel with very helpful staff. Staying here is easily the best-value way to see the region. Ask for the Grape Escape tour which includes transfers, a wine-tasting tour and accommodation for $159.

Peppers Convent (☎ 4998 7764; www.peppers.com.au; Halls Rd, Pokolbin; d including breakfast from $198 per person) The building, a former nunnery, was transferred in blocks from hundreds of kilometres inland and refurbished in a sumptuous, almost fussy French-provincial style. Nearby is the equally upmarket Robert's Restaurant, part of the adjoining Pepper Tree Wines (opposite).

Terroir (☎ 4990 0711; 1 Broke Rd, Pokolbin; mains $33-39; ✆ noon-3pm Tue-Sun, 6pm-late Wed-Sat) Located at the Hungerford Hill Wines, this is *the* deluxe, refined eating option in the area, with a modern Australian menu rigorously tested to complement fine wines.

Vineyard Hill (☎ 4990 4166; www.vineyardhill.com.au; Lovedale Rd, Lovedale; d $118 Sun-Thu, $170 Fri & Sat) The pleasant self-contained units have decks on which to stretch out and enjoy fine views of the Hunter Valley. There is a BBQ area for guests too. This place usually gets booked up on weekends.

ROYAL NATIONAL PARK

This gem of a park is just 32km south of central Sydney. Formed in 1879, it is the second-oldest national park in the world (the oldest is Yellowstone in the USA). Dramatic coastal cliffs plummet to the Tasman Sea on the eastern side, broken up with the occasional secluded beach. For a relatively small pocket of protected land, the park is home to a surprising range of habitats and fauna – largely due to very careful management by the National Wildlife and Parks Services. Heathlands dominate in the northern sandstone section. Creek gullies and rainforest are further inland. It won't take you long to spot the park's wildlife, whether it's a kookaburra sitting casually on a park sign or a water dragon lizard scuttling off the path. Echidnas, yellow-tailed black cockatoos and swamp wallaby are other notable residents. Be aware too that the park is home to several species of poisonous snake, so watch your step. They are usually just as keen to avoid you as you are them.

The park is also testament to the Australian bush's remarkable powers of recovery. Large swathes of the park were scorched by the 1994 bush fires, but much of the growth has already been regenerated.

Royal National Park begins at Port Hacking, just over 30km south of Sydney, and stretches 20km further south. A road runs through the park with detours to the small township of Bundeena on Port Hacking, to the beautiful swimming beach at Wattamolla, and to the windswept surfers' paradise, Garie Beach.

On the north coast, one excellent walk goes from Bundeena to the Jibbon Aboriginal rock engravings, which are mostly outlines of the animals that the Dharawal people used to hunt and live off. Other Aboriginal sites have been discovered within the park, although they are only accessible by tour (p212).

Right in the heart of the park, Forest Island is a favourite hang-out of lyre-birds. With its picturesque picnic area, this is a particularly recommended stop-off for those with kids.

The spectacular two-day, 26km coastal walking trail running the length of the park is highly recommended. A walking and cycling trail follows the Hacking River south from Audley, and other walking tracks pass tranquil, freshwater swimming holes. You can swim in the upper reaches of Kangaroo Creek but not the Hacking River. To do the coastal walks you'll need a permit (adult/child per night $3/2) from the visitors centre. You can also drive to the campsite at Bonnie Vale.

The Bungoona path near the visitors centre is a 1km wheelchair-friendly section of track that leads to Bungoona Lookout, which has far-reaching views over Hacking River and the rest of the park.

The visitors centre is at the bottom of the hill down from the park's main entrance, off the Princes Hwy near Audley. The friendly and knowledgeable staff sell camping permits and help with any questions about bushwalking or other aspects of the park. You can hire

TRANSPORT: ROYAL NATIONAL PARK

Distance from Sydney to Royal National Park
32km

Direction South

Travel time One hour

Car Leave Sydney via the Princes Hwy and turn left off the highway 2.3km south of Sutherland. Audley is 2km further down the road.

Train Take the Illawarra line to Loftus, Engadine, Heathcote, Waterfall or Otford train stations (adult/child peak return $10.40/5.20), all of which are on the park boundary and have walking trails into the park.

Ferry Access to the coastal walking track can be reached from Bundeena. Take the ferry from Cronulla. This is the best way to get to the park if you're bringing a bike.

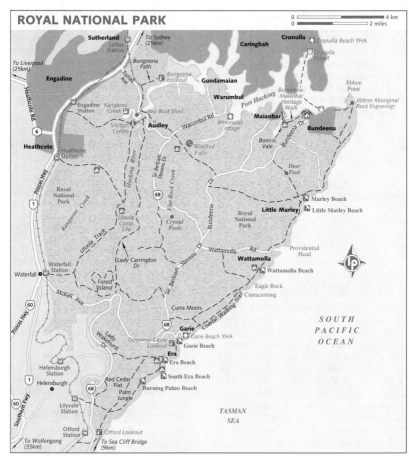

ROYAL NATIONAL PARK

equipment at the Audley Boat Shed just across the lake from the visitors centre.

The road through the park and the off-shoot to Bundeena are permanently open but the detours to the beaches close at 8:30pm. Those coming by car should consider continuing the journey further south to the recently opened Sea Cliff Bridge, a magnificent 665m stretch of raised road between Coalcliff and Clifton.

INFORMATION

Audley Boat Shed (☎ 9545 4967; Farnell Ave; canoes & kayaks per hr/day $16/30, bicycles per hr/day $14/30, aqua bikes per 30min $12; ⏰ 9am-5pm)

Discovery Walks Talks and Tours (☎ 9542 0629, 9542 0666; Royal National Park Visitors Centre) This outfit offers a wide variety of themed Royal National Park tours, ranging from eagle-spotting to Aboriginal survival techniques.

Royal National Park Visitors Centre (☎ 9542 0648; per car per day $11, free for cyclists & pedestrians; ⏰ 9am-4:30pm Mon-Fri, 8:30am-4:30pm Sat & Sun)

SLEEPING

Bonnie Vale Campsite (per night adult/child $10/5) This site is well-equipped with toilets, showers and picnic tables.

Garie Beach YHA (☎ 9261 1111; bookings@yhansw.org .au; dm per person $15) This hostel's remote location by the park's coastal path is delightful. Facilities are basic (cold showers are in the car park) and you will need to bring supplies, including linen, with you. Booking ahead is essential.

Weemalah Cottage (☎ 9542 0632; per night May-Sep $190, Oct-Apr $220) Often booked up a long time in advance at weekends, but worth a shot if you are staying midweek. Within the confines of the national park, the solar-powered cottage has three bedrooms and sleeps eight; features include gas heating, a BBQ, and TV and video.

HAWKESBURY RIVER

The Hawkesbury River weaves for hundreds of kilometres through NSW. A sense of the wild lingers on its shores – much of the riverside is little changed from the time the first European settlers ventured into the bush. Its lower reaches are lined with mangroves, and it meets the sea at Broken Bay, 30km north of Sydney. Before hitting the ocean, the river expands into bays and inlets such as Berowra Creek, Cowan Creek and Pittwater on the southern side, and Brisbane Water on the northern side. The river flows between a number of national parks – Marramarra and Ku-ring-gai Chase (see p112) to the south; and Dharug, Brisbane Water and Bouddi to the north. The town of Windsor is about 120km upstream.

A great way to get a feel for the river is to catch the Riverboat Postman from the sleepy town of Brooklyn. This mail boat does a 40km round trip on weekdays, running as far as Marlow, near Spencer. There are also coffee cruises and all-day outings (bookings are recommended).

The settlements along the river have their own distinct character and life in Brooklyn revolves around boats and the river. The town is on the Sydney–Newcastle railway line, just east of the Pacific Hwy. Berowra Waters is another quaint community further upstream, clustered around a free 24-hour winch ferry that crosses Berowra Creek. There are a couple of cafés overlooking the water, and a marina where you can hire an outboard boat for about $65 for a half-day. Berowra Waters is 5km west of the Pacific Hwy; there's a train station at Berowra, but it's a 7km hike down a very narrow road to the ferry.

The small settlement of Wisemans Ferry overlooks the Hawkesbury River roughly halfway between Windsor and the mouth of the river. It was named after an emancipated convict, Solomon Wiseman, who was granted land in the area and put in place the first ferry in 1826. Winch ferries are still the only means of crossing the river here to this day. Fortunately, they run 24-hours and are free. Mostly tranquil, Wisemans Ferry is getting increasingly used to Sydneysiders out for a rural escape.

An early convict-built road (unsealed, but in good condition) leads north about 21km from Wisemans Ferry to the tiny, delightful settlement of St Albans. It's a pretty drive, with bush on one side, and the flats of Macdonald River, a tributary of the Hawkesbury, on the other. In town it's worth stopping for a drink or meal at the Settlers Arms Inn, a charming inn dating back to 1836.

Yengo National Park, a rugged sandstone area covering the foothills of the Blue Mountains, stretches from Wisemans Ferry to the Hunter Valley. It's a wilderness area with very few facilities and limited road access. There are some trekking trails (plan your water supply), including a stretch along the Old Great North Rd, and a camping area at Mogo Creek. North of

---

TRANSPORT: HAWKESBURY RIVER

Distance from Sydney to Berowra Waters 40km

Direction North and northwest

Travel time One hour

Car To reach Berowra Waters, turn off the Sydney–Newcastle Fwy at Berowra, taking Berowra Waters Rd. To reach Brooklyn, take the Sydney–Newcastle Fwy and follow the signs. A road (signposted) leads to Wisemans Ferry from Pitt Town, near Windsor. You can also get there from Sydney on Old Northern Rd, which branches off Windsor Rd north of Parramatta.

Train There are trains running regularly from Central Station to Brooklyn's Hawkesbury River train station; the 7.40 or 8.15am trains from Central Station ($6.20 one way) gets you to the station in time to meet the morning Riverboat Postman (above).

Ferry Free 24-hour car ferries across the Hawkesbury at Wisemans Ferry put you on the road to St Albans. The Riverboat Postman (☎ 9985 7566; Brooklyn Wharf, Brooklyn; adult/child/family $45/25/115; ☽ departs Brooklyn 9.30am, returns approximately 1.15pm, Mon-Fri) runs a ferry service and a return boat trip from Brooklyn. Bookings are recommended (see above).

the river, a scenic road leads east from Wisemans Ferry to the Central Coast, following the river before veering north through bushland and orange groves.

Dharug National Park, also on the north side of the river, is a wilderness noted for Aboriginal rock carvings that date back nearly 10,000 years. You can also walk along the convict-built Old Great North Rd. There's camping at Mill Creek 8km east of Wisemans Ferry, and Ten Mile Hollow (walk-in track only).

Marramarra National Park, south of the Hawkesbury, has vehicle access from the Old Northern Rd south of Wisemans Ferry. Camping is allowed here.

EATING & SLEEPING

Ripples (☎ 9985 5555, 9985 5534; www.ripples.com.au; 87 Brooklyn Rd, Brooklyn; 4-berth houseboats for 2 nights $500-1200) Prices fluctuate wildly according to seasons and whether you want to travel at the weekend, but if you're in a group, this self-contained floating home with cooking facilities is reasonable value – and there are few finer ways to experience the river.

Settlers Arms Inn (☎ 4568 2111; www.settlersarms .com.au; 1 Wharf St, St Albans; d from $130 during the week) This historic sandstone pub would not look out of place on the banks of the English Avon, besides the corrugated-iron roof and the veranda. The rooms, which are in external log cabins, are very comfortable and much better appointed than the exterior suggests.

Wisemans Ferry Inn (☎ 4566 4301; Old Northern Rd; d/tw $75) This historic hotel is trading somewhat on its past reputation. The bistro is good (although marred by a bystanding army of beeping slot machines) while the accommodation is passable.

THE CENTRAL COAST

The Central Coast has superb surf beaches, lakes and national parks. Once a backwater, it is now developing rapidly and is a very popular weekend escape for Sydneysiders. It is also a popular refuge for retirees seeking stress-free good living. Its beautiful waterways include Broken Bay and Brisbane Water in the south and three contiguous lakes in the north – Tuggerah Lake, Lake Budgewoi near Toukley, and Lake Munmorah. A few kilometres north of Lake Munmorah is Lake Macquarie, which stretches north to Newcastle.

Gosford, the largest town in the area, is 12km inland on the shores of Brisbane Water. On the northern side of the Hawkesbury River, across from Ku-ring-gai Chase National

TRANSPORT: THE CENTRAL COAST

Distance from Sydney to Gosford 85km

Direction North

Travel time One hour 15 minutes

Car The Central Coast is easily accessible from Sydney via the Sydney–Newcastle Fwy.

Train Regular CityRail trains connect Sydney with Gosford ($8.20) and other central coast towns.

Park, Brisbane Water National Park (entry per car $7) is 7km southwest of Gosford. It extends from the Pacific Hwy in the west to Brisbane Water in the east. Made up of rugged sandstone country, the park has mangrove stands and harbours swamp wallabies, platypi and the rare yellow-bellied gliding possum. Head here for the accessible Aboriginal rock engravings at Bulgandry. These were etched by the Gurringai tribe whose territory stretched from Sydney Harbour to Lake Macquarie before European settlers arrived. You can reach the engravings via a short signposted walk off Woy Woy Rd, 3km south of the Pacific Hwy. They are best seen in early morning or late afternoon.

Just off the Pacific Hwy southwest of Gosford is the Australian Reptile Park (☎ 4340 1146, www .reptilepark.com.au, Pacific Hwy; adult/child $22.50/15.00, ☺ 9am-5pm Mon-Sun), famous for Eric, its enormous crocodile, and for milking deadly snakes and its venomous funnelweb spiders.

South of Brisbane Water National Park is Patonga, a small fishing village on Broken Bay, with a large campsite available. A 500m walk off the road to Patonga is Warrah Lookout, which has a lovely panoramic view of Broken Bay.

Bouddi National Park is a smaller protected area, which has some sweet secluded beaches where you are allowed to camp, most notably at Putty Beach.

Upmarket Terrigal, 12km east of Gosford, is the centre of the region's café and restaurant culture. In September 2008, an Australian Navy frigate, the HMAS Adelaide, is set to be sunk just off the town's shore, creating a whole new artificial reef for divers to explore. Terrigal Dive School (☎ 4384 1219; www.terrigaldive.com.au; The Haven), Australia's oldest dive school, can help with diving in the area.

North of Terrigal, Bateau Bay meets the southern section of the small Wyrrabalong National Park. It's popular for surfing.

At Avoca Beach there is a lovely curving surf beach guarded by a string of tall pine trees. It is a low-key little place which also has the charming old-school Avoca Beach Picture Theatre (☎ 4382 1777; www.avocabeachpicturetheatre.com.au; 69 Avoca Beach; admission adult/child $12.50/10).

The Entrance, on the sea inlet of Tuggerah Lake, 15km north of Terrigal, is a slice of sub-urban sprawl set beside a beautiful lake and superb surf beach. It is known as the pelican capital of Australia for its daily beachfront feeding (at 3:30pm) of these charismatic long-beaked birds (interesting fact: the Australian pelican has the longest bill of any bird in the world). You can reach The Entrance either by driving north from Terrigal or by taking the Tuggerah exit off the Sydney–Newcastle Fwy.

North of here are the towns of Toukley and Budgewoi, popular bases for boating and fishing.

INFORMATION

Central Coast Tourism (☎ 1300 132 975, 4385 4430; www.visitcentralcoast.com.au; The Avenue, Mt Penang Parklands, Kariong) Well informed and very helpful main office of the region's tourist authority.

Gosford Visitor Centre (☎ 1300 132 975; 4385 4430; www.visitcentralcoast.com.au; 200 Mann St, Gosford; 🕙 9am-5pm Mon-Fri, 9am-2pm Sat & Sun)

National Parks and Wildlife Services (NPWS office ☎ 4320 4203; www.nationalparks.nsw.gov.au; Suite 36-38, 207 Albany St North, Gosford; 🕙 8.30am-4.30pm Mon-Fri) Call here for info on Brisbane Water and Bouddi National Parks.

The Entrance Visitor Centre (☎ 1300 132 975; 4385 4430; www.visitcentralcoast.com.au; Marine Pde, The Entrance; 🕙 9am-5pm)

EATING & SLEEPING

Crowne Plaza Terrigal (☎ 4384 9111; www.crowneplaza .com.au; Pine Tree La, Terrigal; d from $199) At the hub of Terrigal's tourist business, this monolith has some plush rooms with great views over the beach. There are three restaurants, spas and massage too. Room prices fluctuate radically according to season and availability.

DG's Deli (☎ 4384 3678; 82 Terrigal Drive; mains $17-24; 🕙 7am-8:30pm Mon-Sun) The cuisine at DG's Deli is a notch above most options on the beachfront.

Reef Restaurant and Grill (☎ 4385 3222; The Haven, Terrigal; mains $27-35; 🕙 lunch & dinner Mon-Sun) Expensive, very good restaurant (with a cheaper adjoining café) that scoops major critical plaudits for its modern Australian cuisine. The sweeping ocean panorama from the dining room isn't bad either.

Ye Olde Miami Guesthouse (☎ 4384 1919; www .miamiguesthouse.com.au; 9 Ocean View Dr, Terrigal; s/d with shared bathroom $50/65) These cramped, clean pine-floored rooms are about 10 minutes' walk from the main restaurant and beach zone.

EXCURSIONS THE CENTRAL COAST

TRANSPORT

Sydneysiders love to complain about their public transport system but visitors should find it surprisingly easy to get around. A car is more of a hindrance than an asset to exploring most of the areas covered in this book. Flights, tours and rail tickets can be booked online at www.lonelyplanet.com/travel_services.

AIR
Airlines

Virgin Blue (☎ 13 67 89; www.virginblue.com.au), Qantas and Qantas' budget alternative, Jetstar (☎ 131 538; www.jetstar.com.au), have frequent flights to other capital cities within Australia, while Rex (Regional Express; ☎ 13 17 13; www.regionalexpress .com.au), Air Link (☎ 6884 2435; www.airlinkairlines.com .au) and Aeropelican (☎ 13 13 13; www.aeropelican.com .au) connect smaller centres.

For international flights to Sydney, try the following:

Air New Zealand (Map pp62–3; ☎ 8248 0030; www .airnewzealand.com.au; 18th fl, 264 George St, City)

British Airways (Map pp62–3; ☎ 1300 767 177; www .britishairways.com; 19th fl, 259 George St, City)

Emirates (☎ 1300 303 777; www.emirates.com)

Japan Airlines (Map pp62–3; ☎ 9272 1100; www.jal .co.jp/en; 14th fl, 201 Sussex St, City)

Qantas (Map p54; ☎ 13 13 13; www.qantas.com; 10 Bridge St, City)

Singapore Airlines (Map pp62–3; ☎ 9350 0100; www .singaporeair.com; 17 Bridge St, City)

Thai Airways (☎ 1300 651 960; www.thaiair.com)

United Airlines (Map pp62–3; ☎ 9292 4111; www .united airlines.com.au; 151 Clarence St, City)

Virgin Atlantic (☎ 1300 727 340; www.virgin-atlantic .com)

For other international airlines, see www .sydneyairport.com.au (click on 'Flight Information').

Airport

Sydney's Kingsford Smith Airport (☎ 9667 9111; www.sydneyairport.com.au), 10km south of the city centre, is Australia's busiest airport, taking in flights from all over the country and the world. The international and domestic terminals are a 4km bus trip apart on either side of the runway. Flights cease between 11pm and 5am due to noise restrictions.

Smarte Carte (☎ 9667 0926; suitcase 24hr $11; ☷ 6am-9.30pm) run a left-luggage service in both the domestic and international terminals. There are ATMs and bureaus de change (☷ 6am-11pm) in both terminals.

CLIMATE CHANGE & TRAVEL

Climate change is a serious threat to the ecosystems that humans rely upon, and air travel is the fastest-growing contributor to the problem. Lonely Planet regards travel, overall, as a global benefit, but believes we all have a responsibility to limit our personal impact on global warming.

Flying & Climate Change

Pretty much every form of motor transport generates CO_2 (the main cause of human-induced climate change) but planes are far and away the worst offenders, not just because of the sheer distances they allow us to travel, but because they release greenhouse gases high into the atmosphere. The statistics are frightening: two people taking a return flight between Europe and the US will contribute as much to climate change as an average household's gas and electricity consumption over a whole year.

Carbon Offset Schemes

Climatecare.org and other websites use 'carbon calculators' that allow travellers to offset the greenhouse gases they are responsible for with contributions to energy-saving projects and other climate-friendly initiatives in the developing world – including projects in India, Honduras, Kazakhstan and Uganda.

Lonely Planet, together with Rough Guides and other concerned partners in the travel industry, supports the carbon offset scheme run by climatecare.org. Lonely Planet offsets all of its staff and author travel.

For more information check out our website: www.lonelyplanet.com.

GETTING INTO TOWN

One of the easiest ways to get from the airport into the city centre is with a shuttle company. These take you straight to your hotel or hostel and cost $9 to $12. All go into the city centre; some reach surrounding suburbs and beach destinations. Services include Sydney Airporter (☎ 9666 9988; www.kst.com.au; one-way/return $10/17) and Super Shuttle (☎ 1300 765 685; www.supershuttle.com.au).

Airport Link (www.airportlink.com.au; one-way $13) is a train line which runs to and from city train stations and the domestic and international terminals every 10 to 15 minutes. Trains run from approximately 5am to midnight daily. Tickets can be purchased as part of a TravelPass (p218).

For the cheapest option to Bondi via the cheapest (albeit slowest) route, take the 400 bus ($4.60, one hour) to Bondi Junction, then the 380, 381 or 382 to the beach.

Taxi fares from the airport are approximately $30 to $40 to Circular Quay and $20 to $30 to Central. A slew of car-rental booths will greet you after you exit immigration (see p219).

BICYCLE

From the back of a bike (p174), Sydney's traffic can be scary. The best spots to get some spoke action are Centennial Park (p83), Sydney Olympic Park (p117) and North Head (p109). Helmets are compulsory. Many cycle-hire shops require a hefty deposit on a credit card. See also Skater HQ and Manly Blades (p175).

Centennial Park Cycles (☎ 9398 5027; www.cyclehire .com.au; 50 Clovelly Rd, Randwick; per hour/day/week $12/35/85; ⏰ 8.30am-5.30pm; 🚌 339) Also have a stand in the centre of Centennial Park and at Sydney Olympic Park (both open 9am to 5pm).

Favourite Cycles (Map p110; ☎ 9977 4590; 22 Darley Rd, Manly; ⏰ 9am-6pm Mon-Wed & Fri, 9am-7pm Thu, 9am-5pm Sat, 10am-4pm Sun; per hour/day $9/22; 🚢 Manly)

Inner City Cycles (Map pp100–1; ☎ 9660 6605; 151 Glebe Point Rd, Glebe; per day/week $33/88; ⏰ 9.30am-6pm Mon-Wed & Fri, 9.30am-7pm Thu, 9.00am-4pm Sat, 11am-3pm Sun; 🚌 431-434) Convenient access to the city and to Central Station.

There's no charge for taking a bike on CityRail trains, except for during peak hours (6am to 9am and 3.30pm to 7.30pm Monday to Friday) when you will need to purchase a child's ticket for the bike. Bikes are allowed free on Sydney's ferries, which are equipped with bicycle racks (first come, first served). They're not permitted on buses.

BOAT
Ferries

Sydney's ferries (☎ 131 500; www.sydneyferries.info) provide the most enjoyable way of getting around and have a pretty good reputation as far as reliability, cleanliness and flotation go. Many people use ferries to commute, so there are frequent connecting bus services. Some ferries operate between 6am and midnight, although ferries servicing tourist attractions keep shorter hours. Popular places accessible by ferry include Darling Harbour, Balmain and Parramatta to the west; McMahons Point, Kirribilli, Neutral Bay, Cremorne, Mosman, Taronga Zoo and Manly on the North Shore; and Darling Point, Double Bay, Rose Bay and Watsons Bay in the Eastern Suburbs.

There are three kinds of ferry: regular STA ferries, fast JetCats that go to Manly ($8.20), and RiverCats, which traverse the Parramatta River to Parramatta ($7.70). All ferries depart from Circular Quay. At Wharf 4 you'll find the ferry information office (Map p54; ☎ 9207 3170; ⏰ 7am-5.45pm Mon-Sat, 8am-5.45pm Sun), near the ticket booths. The standard single fare for most regular harbour ferries is $5.20, although making the longer trip to Manly costs $6.40.

If you plan on taking several ferry rides and are keen to save a few bucks, check out the boxed text on p218.

Water Taxis

Watertours (☎ 9211 7730; www.watertours.com.au) has cute yellow water taxis with rates based on zones. A trip to the Shark or Rodd Island (p107) will cost $60 plus $10 per head.

BUS

Sydney's local bus network extends to most suburbs. Fares depend upon the number of 'sections' you pass through; tickets range from $1.70 to $5.60, but most jaunts cost $2.90.

Special discount passes (see below) will save you big bucks. Sydney Buses (☎ 131 500; www .sydneybuses.info) have an excellent website with electronic route planners, route maps and information.

Regular buses run between 5am and midnight, when Nightrider buses take over. During peak hour, buses get hideously crowded and sometimes fail to pick up passengers at major stops if they're full. Bus 380 (going to or coming from Bondi) should be avoided by claustrophobes on sunny weekend days.

The major starting points for bus routes are Circular Quay, Argyle St in Millers Point, Wynyard Park, Queen Victoria Building and Railway Sq (near Central Station). Most buses head out of the city on George or Castlereagh Sts, and take George or Elizabeth Sts coming in. Pay the driver as you enter, or dunk your prepaid ticket in the green ticket machines by the door.

At Circular Quay there's a TransitShop (Map p54; cnr Alfred & Loftus Sts; ☯ 7am-7pm Mon-Fri, 8.30am-5pm Sat & Sun) which sells passes, along with offering bus information. There are other TransitShops at Wynyard Park (on Carrington St), the Queen Victoria Building and Railway Sq.

All long-distance bus services operate from the Sydney Coach Terminal (Map p72; ☎ 9281 9366; Eddy Ave, City; ☯ 6am-10pm), which is located underneath Central Station. Major bus operators include Greyhound (☎ 9212 1500; www.greyhound.com .au), Premier (☎ 13 34 10; www.premierms.com.au) and Murrays (☎ 13 22 59; www.murrays.com.au).

CAR
Automobile Associations

The National Roads & Motorists Association (NRMA; Map pp62–3; ☎ 13 11 22; www.nrma.com.au; 74 King St, City; ☯ 9am-5pm Mon-Fri; ℞ Wynyard) provides 24-hour emergency roadside assistance, road maps, travel advice and insurance, and discounted accommodation. It has reciprocal arrangements with the other state associations and similar organisations overseas – bring proof of membership with you.

Driving & Parking

It's best to avoid driving in central Sydney if you possibly can. The city has an extensive, confusing one-way street system, parking sucks (even at hotels!), parking inspectors are everywhere and tow-away zones are common and have proved to be good revenue raisers. Having a car in Sydney can be like having an expensive anchor around your neck. On the other hand, a car is a great way to get to the far reaches of the city and for day trips (p200).

Australians drive on the left-hand side of the road and the minimum driving age (unassisted) is 18 years of age. Overseas visitors are permitted to drive with their domestic driving licences for up to three months from arriving in the country, but must obtain a New South Wales driving licence after that. Speed limits in Sydney are generally 60km/h (50km/h in some built-up areas), rising to 100km/h or 110km/h on freeways. It is the law that seat

---

TRANSPORT DEALS

There's money to be saved by investigating the confusing array of travel discounts available; try calling ☎ 131 500 or visiting www.131500.com.au.

TravelPasses provide the best value, offering a week's unlimited travel on the regular buses, trains and ferries. There are several colour-coded grades; the Red TravelPass ($33) gets to most tourist destinations, the Green TravelPass ($41) includes Manly and Olympic Park.

The SydneyPass (www.sydneypass.info; adult/child/family three days $110/55/275, five days $145/70/360, seven days $165/80/410) is a pricey option for tourists who want to do it all in a short period of time, offering unlimited travel for a set number of days within an eight-day period on all buses, trains (as far as the Inner West), ferries, Explorer hop on/off buses and three short harbour cruises.

The Daytripper (adult/child $15.40/7.70) covers an unlimited day on all buses, ferries and trains you're likely to need.

Consider the TravelTen or FerryTen tickets if you're likely to be going backwards and forwards between the same stops by bus or ferry.

Several transport-plus-entry tickets are available from Circular Quay, which work out cheaper than catching a ferry and paying entry separately. They include the ZooPass (adult/child $39/21) and the AquariumPass (adult/child $33/17).

belts must be worn, and the use of hand-held mobile phones is prohibited

The blood-alcohol limit of 0.05% is enforced with random breath-checks and severe punishments. If you're in an accident (even if you didn't cause it) and you're over the alcohol limit, your insurance will be invalidated. For more information on road rules see www.rta.nsw.gov.au.

Private car parks are expensive, costing on average around $15 per hour, and even street parking can eat up your coins, at a rate of about $2.20 to $4.40 per hour. Public car parks are signposted: look for the large white 'P' on a blue background. Many maps indicate with a 'P' where you can park your car. See also the *Yellow Pages* under parking stations and the transport section of each area in the Neighbourhoods chapters.

Hire

Car rentals are affordable and relatively consistent with US and European rates. Prices can vary widely depending on time of year and demand, but booking online can sometimes provide savings (as can renting for a longer period). Check the small print on your rental agreement to see exactly where you can take the car (some firms don't allow driving on dirt roads) and what your insurance covers. Also check on any age restrictions.

Avis (☎ 136 333; www.avis.com.au), Budget (☎ 13 27 27; www.budget.com.au), Europcar (☎ 1300 131 390; www.europcar.com.au), Hertz (☎ 133 090; www.hertz.com.au) and Thrifty (☎ 1300 367 227; www.thrifty.com.au) all have desks at the airport, and some have offices in the city centre (mostly on William St). Avis and Hertz also provide hand-controlled cars for disabled travellers. The *Yellow Pages* lists many other car-hire companies, some that specialise in renting near-wrecks at rock-bottom prices – always read the fine print on your rental agreement carefully if you decide on this option. An excellent and reasonably priced local agency is Bayswater Car Rental (Map p78; ☎ 9360 3622; www.nobirds.com.au; 180 Williams St, Kings Cross; ⏰ 8am-6pm Mon-Fri, 8am-noon Sat, 9-11.30am Sun; ⓡ Kings Cross).

For motorbike hire, try Bikescape (p226).

Toll Roads

The Harbour Tunnel and Harbour Bridge both impose a southbound toll of $3; if you're heading from the North Shore to the eastern suburbs, it's much easier to use the tunnel. The bridge still takes cash, but the tunnel requires an RTA E-Toll tag or pass (www.rta.nsw.gov.au) or an E-Way tag (☎ 1300 555 833; www.tollpay.com.au) – electronic payment devices that attach to your windscreen. If you're on a short trip to the city, it's most convenient to buy a pass for each trip rather than going to the trouble of organising a tag.

The Eastern Distributor (cutting from Randwick to Woolloomooloo) imposes a northbound toll of $4.50. The overpriced Cross City tunnel (☎ 9033 3999; www.crosscity.com.au; east or west $3.50) connects Darling Harbour to Rushcutters Bay. You'll need an electronic tag to use it (or you can contact them within 24 hours of crossing to arrange payment).

METRO LIGHT RAIL/ MONORAIL

The Metro Light Rail (MLR; ☎ 8584 5250, www.metrolightrail.com.au; single trip $3-4, day pass $8.50) operates every 10 to 15 minutes (every 30 minutes after midnight) between Central Station and Pyrmont via Darling Harbour and Chinatown. The service continues to Lilyfield via the Fish Market, Wentworth Park, Glebe, Jubilee Park and Rozelle Bay, but only from 6am to midnight. Pay the operator onboard.

The Monorail (☎ 9285 5600; www.monorail.com.au; single/day-pass $4.50/9; ⏰ 7am-10pm Mon-Thu, 7am-midnight Fri & Sat, 8am-10pm Sun) is more of a tourist attraction, circling Darling Harbour and linking it to the bottom half of the city. Shuttles come by every three to five minutes, and the full loop takes about 14 minutes.

TAXI

Taxis are easily flagged down in the city centre and the inner suburbs, except for 'changeover' time (3pm and 3am) when they all vanish. All taxis are metered and Sydney taxi drivers won't usually rip you off, but don't expect them to know where you're going. We've had to direct drivers to the Opera House! If they're unsure get them to turn off the meter while they check the street directory.

Flagfall is $2.90, and the metered fare is $1.68 per kilometre. There's a 20% surcharge between 10pm and 6am, and additional charges for heavy luggage (over 25kg), tolls and a radio booking fee ($1.50). For more

on the taxi system in Sydney check out www
.nswtaxi.org.au.

The four big taxi companies offer a reliable service:

Legion Cabs ☎ 13 14 51

Premier Cabs ☎ 13 10 17

RSL Cabs ☎ 9581 1111

Taxis Combined ☎ 13 33 00

TRAIN

Sydney has a vast suburban rail network
and frequent services, making trains much
quicker than buses. You can reach practically
anywhere within the CBD by train, but lines
do not extend to the northern and eastern
beaches, Balmain or Glebe. Trains run from
around 5am to around 1am (check timetables
for your line for early or late services). As a
rough guide, a short trip on a CityRail (☎ 131
500; www.cityrail.info) train will cost you $2.40.
After 9am Monday to Friday and any time
on Saturday and Sunday, you can buy an off-
peak return ticket for not much more than a
standard one-way fare.

Central Station (p75) has an information kiosk
(🕙 6am-10pm) near platforms four and five.
All long-distance train services arrive and
depart from this station. Book tickets through
the Countrylink Travel Centre (☎ 13 22 32; www.country
link.info; 🕙 6.15am-8.45pm) near platform one.
You can get discounts of up to 50% with two
weeks' notice. Countrylink has another office
at Circular Quay (🕙 9.30am-3.30pm Mon-Fri), and you
can also book online.

BUSINESS HOURS

Most offices and businesses are open weekdays from 9am to 5.30pm. Banking hours are from 9.30am to 4pm Monday to Thursday and until 5pm Friday. Some larger city branches are open from 8am to 6pm weekdays.

Most shops are open 9am or 10am to 5pm or 6pm weekdays, with hours extended to 8pm or 9pm Thursday. Many shops open all day Saturday. On Sunday, many shops close, but on Oxford St and in the city you'll find stores open from about 11am to 5pm.

Restaurants generally open from noon to 3pm and then 6pm to 10pm or 11pm from Monday to Saturday. Cafés are often open for day-long breakfasts. See the Eating chapter (p136) for more details.

CHILDREN

With so many natural attractions, Sydney is a good place to bring the kids. During school holidays many places put on extra children's activities; the Sydney Opera House (p57) has an interesting range of entertainment tailored to juniors, and there are some great arty activities for the little ones at the Art Gallery of NSW (p66).

Look for copies of *Sydney's Child,* a free monthly magazine listing activities and businesses catering for ankle-biters, in newsagents and businesses associated with children. For more general information snag a copy of Lonely Planet's *Travel with Children* by Cathy Lanigan.

See p73 for our top picks of Sydney's sights for children.

Nannies & Helpers (☎ 9363 4221; www.nanniesand helpers.com.au; booking fee $20-33, baby-sitting per hr $15-20) will send a baby-sitter to wherever you're staying for a minimum of three hours. Some of the bigger hotels offer their own services.

CLIMATE

Different Aboriginal nations recognised between six and eight seasons, depending on what part of Australia they lived in. Despite the arbitrary imposition of the European four-season model, Sydney seems to have a few more distinct climactic periods than that.

The calendar year ends and starts in a sweltering tropical summer with many days hitting over 30°C and some over 40°C. During this time the high humidity is often broken by spectacular afternoon thunderstorms and torrential downpours.

Temperatures settle down slightly towards the end of January and into February. Late February and early March tend to be the wettest months, although they still average at least 19 sunny days. Things cool down in April, and by May daily highs average below 20°C. Cool and wet June is as bad as things get – although you'll still strike a mean of 20 sunny days. The Blue Mountains sees snow about once or twice a year.

July through September are cool months, but also the driest – with plenty of crisp, sun-filled days. October to early December have a little more rain, but the temperature is a lot more pleasant, with daily highs back up over 20°C.

You may catch one of Sydney's dramatic hailstorms. The city averages 10 per year, mainly between November and February. In April 1999 a massive storm with tennis-ball-sized hail hit, causing more than $1.5 billion worth of property damage.

At the time of research, Sydney was in the grip of its worst drought in 100 years. There is hope it will lift by the time this book is published.

CONSULATES

Foreign embassies are based in Canberra, but many countries also maintain a consulate in Sydney.

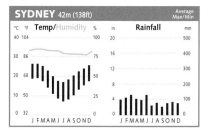

British Consulate General (Map p54; ☎ 9247 7521; 16th fl, Gateway Bldg, 1 Macquarie Pl, City)

Canadian Consulate General (Map p54; ☎ 9364 3000; 5th fl, 111 Harrington St, City)

French Consulate General (Map pp62–3; ☎ 9261 5779; 26th fl, 31 Market St, City)

German Consulate General (Map pp84–5; ☎ 9328 7733; 13 Trelawney St, Woollahra)

Japanese Consulate General (Map pp62–3; ☎ 9231 3455; 34th fl, 52 Martin Pl, City)

New Zealand High Commission (Map pp62–3; ☎ 8256 2005; 10th fl, 55 Hunter St, City)

US Consulate General (Map pp62–3; ☎ 9373 9200; 59th fl, MLC Centre, 19-29 Martin Pl, City)

For others see Consulates & Legations in the Yellow Pages (www.yellowpages.com.au).

CUSTOMS REGULATIONS

When entering Australia you can bring most articles in free of duty, provided that customs is satisfied they're for personal use and that you'll be taking them with you when you leave. There's a duty-free quota per person of 2.25L of alcohol (if you're over 18), 250 cigarettes (ditto) and dutiable goods up to the value of $900 ($450 if you're under 18). Amounts of more than A$10,000 cash must be declared. As these values will change from time to time, it's wise to check current regulations by contacting the Australian Customs Service (☎ 6275 6666; www.customs.gov .au).

Two issues need particular attention: one is illegal drugs – don't bring any in with you; two is animal and plant quarantine – declare all goods of animal or vegetable origin and show them to an official. Authorities are anxious to prevent pests and diseases getting into the country. Fresh food and flowers are also unpopular, and if you've recently visited farmland or rural areas, it might pay to scrub your shoes before you get to the airport.

Weapons and firearms are either prohibited or require a permit and safety testing. Other restricted goods include products made from protected wildlife species, non-approved telecommunications devices and live animals.

When you leave, don't take any protected flora or fauna with you. Customs comes down hard on smugglers.

DISCOUNT CARDS

The See Sydney & Beyond Card (☎ 1300 661 711; www.seesydneycard.com.au) offers admission to a wide range of Sydney's attractions including sightseeing tours, harbour cruises, museums, historic buildings and wildlife parks. One-/two-/three-/seven-day cards cost $65/119/149/209 and are available online or at the Sydney Visitor Centre (p229). The two-/three-/seven-day cards are also available with public transport included for $159/205/275.

The Historic Housing Trust's Ticket Through Time is a must for history buffs; see p65 for details.

There are also a number of transport discounts available in Sydney; see p218 for details.

ELECTRICITY

Standard voltage throughout Australia is 220 to 240 volts AC (50Hz). Plugs are flat three-pin types. Converters for US, European and Asian configurations can be found in airports, outdoors stores, hardware stores, luggage shops and some pharmacies.

EMERGENCY

In the event of an emergency, call ☎ 000 to contact the police, ambulance and fire authorities. Other useful phone numbers and addresses include the following:

Lifeline (☎ 13 11 14) Provides 24-hour phone counselling services, including suicide prevention.

National Roads & Motorists' Association (NRMA; 13 11 11; www.nrma.com.au) Roadside assistance.

Police Stations Bondi (Map pp94–5; ☎ 9365 9699; 77 Gould St); City Centre (Map pp62–3; ☎ 9265 6595; 570 George St); Kings Cross (Map p78; ☎ 8356 0099; Fitzroy Gardens); Surry Hills (Map pp90–1; ☎ 9265 4144; 151-241 Goulburn St)

Rape Crisis Centre (☎ 1800 424 017)

Wayside Chapel (Map p78; ☎ 9358 6577; 29 Hughes St, Kings Cross; ◷ 7am-10pm) Crisis centre.

HOLIDAYS

On public holidays, government departments, banks, offices, large stores and post offices are closed. On Good Friday and Christmas Day, there is limited newspaper circulation and about the only stores you'll find open are convenience stores. Public holidays include the following:

New Year's Day 1 January

Australia Day 26 January

Easter (Good Friday to Easter Monday) March/April

Anzac Day 25 April

Queen's Birthday 2nd Monday in June

Bank Holiday 1st Monday in August

Labour Day 1st Monday in October

Christmas Day 25 December

Boxing Day 26 December

Most public holidays become long weekends (three days), so if a holiday such as New Year's Day falls on a weekend, the following Monday is usually a holiday.

Something else to consider when planning a trip to Sydney is school holidays, when everything gets decidedly more crowded and accommodation rates soar. Sydney students have a long summer break that includes Christmas and most of January. Other school holidays fall around March to April (Easter), late June to mid-July, and late September to early October.

INTERNET ACCESS

Many hostels and midrange hotels have internet access for their guests, and practically all top-end hotels will have internet plugs in rooms. Some offer internet free but others charge a hefty fee (particularly in more expensive hotels). Download the details of your ISP's access numbers before you leave home. It's often cheaper to use an internet café.

Internet cafés have mushroomed all over Sydney, which, happily, means competitive prices for the traveller. Kings Cross has the highest concentration but Chinatown and Bondi are not far behind. As well as allowing you to access the web, many offer word-processing, fax, scanning and printing services too. You can expect to pay around $3 per hour, although night rates are cheaper.

Global Gossip is a reliable local chain of internet cafés, with branches in Kings Cross (Map p78; ☎ 9326 9777; 61 Darlinghurst Rd), Bondi Beach (Map pp94–5; ☎ 9365 4811; 37 Hall St), Haymarket (Map p72; ☎ 9212 4444; 790 George St) and the city (Map p72; ☎ 9365 4811; 415 Pitt St).

Most libraries offer free internet access, but you need to book ahead at busy times. Try Customs House (p58).

Telstra Bigpond (☎ 137 663; www.bigpond.com) is a local provider; the access number is given here.

MAPS

Just about every brochure you pick up includes a map of the city centre, but Lonely Planet's *Sydney City Map* is an exceptional choice. Drivers should pick up Sydney and Blue Mountains street directories by UBD ($42) or Gregory's ($35).

For a great selection of travel maps (and Lonely Planet guidebooks) check out Map World (Map pp62–3; ☎ 9261 3601; www.mapworld .net.au; 280 Pitt St; ⏰ 9am-5.30pm Mon-Wed & Fri, 9am-6.30pm Thu, 10am-3.45pm Sat). For touring maps, particularly of country areas, see the NRMA (p218).

MEDICAL SERVICES

Visitors from Finland, Ireland, Italy, Malta, the Netherlands, New Zealand, Norway, Sweden and the UK have reciprocal health rights, entitling them to treatments that are 'medically necessary', including free treatment in public hospitals and subsidised medicine. In same cases you'll need to pay upfront and then be reimbursed once you've registered at any Medicare (☎ 13 20 11; www.medicare.gov.au) office. Travel insurance is advisable to cover other expenses (such as ambulance and repatriation).

Clinics

If you need to find a dentist in a hurry, call ☎ 9369 7050 (24 hours).

Kings Cross Travellers Clinic (Map p78; ☎ 9358 3066; www.travellersclinic.com.au; 13 Springfield Ave, Kings Cross; ⏰ 9am-1pm & 2-6pm Mon-Fri, 10am-noon Sat; 🚇 Kings Cross) Bookings advised for dive medicals.

Travellers Medical & Vaccination Centre (Map pp62–3; ☎ 9221 7133; www.traveldoctor.com.au; 7th Fl, 428 George St, City; ⏰ 9am-5.30pm Mon, Wed & Fri, 9am-8pm Tue & Thu, 9am-1pm Sat; 🚇 Town Hall) This is the best place to get any travel-related shots and medical advice.

Emergency Rooms

Hospitals with 24-hour accident and emergency departments (sometimes known as casualty wards or emergency rooms) include the following:

Royal North Shore Hospital (☎ 9926 7111; Pacific Hwy, St Leonards)

Royal Prince Alfred Hospital (Map pp100–1; ☎ 9515 6111; Missenden Rd, Camperdown)

St Vincent's Public Hospital (Map p78; ☎ 8382 2520; Victoria St, Darlinghurst)

Sydney Children's Hospital (☎ 9382 1430; High St, Randwick)

Sydney Hospital & Sydney Eye Hospital (Map pp62–3; ☎ 9382 7009; 8 Macquarie St, City)

MONEY

The unit of currency is the Australian dollar, which is divided into 100 cents. There are $100, $50, $20, $10 and $5 notes and $2, $1, 50c, 20c, 10c and 5c coins. The 2c and 1c coins have been taken out of circulation, so shops will round prices up (or down) to the nearest 5c on your total bill.

Notes are plastic (which means they don't disintegrate in the washing machine) and every denomination note is a different colour and size.

Travellers cheques have become something of a dinosaur these days, and they won't be accepted everywhere. It's easier not to bother with them.

ATMS

Central Sydney is chock-full of banks with 24-hour ATMs that will accept all debit and credit cards linked to international network systems, such as Cirrus, Maestro, Barclays Connect and Solo. Most banks place a $1000 limit on the amount you can withdraw daily. You'll also find ATMs in pubs and clubs. Shops and retail outlets will have Eftpos facilities, which allow you to pay for purchases with your debit or credit card.

Changing Money

Both American Express (Map pp62–3; ☎ 1300 139 060; 105 Pitt St, City; ⏲ 8.30am-5pm Mon-Fri; ⊠ Wynyard) and Travelex/Thomas Cook (Map pp62–3; ☎ 9231 2523; 92 King St, City; ⏲ 9am-5pm Mon-Fri, 10am-2pm Sat; ⊠ Martin Place) have branches throughout Sydney.

Exchange bureaus are common in the city centre, but shop around as rates can vary and most charge some sort of commission. Bureaus include the two at Central Station (⏲ 8am-

5pm Mon-Fri, 9am-6pm Sat & Sun) and one opposite Wharf 6 at Circular Quay (⏲ 8am-8.30pm). There are plenty in touristy spots like Kings Cross and Bondi, as well as the airport (where they're open until the last flight comes in; rates here aren't quite as good as in the city centre, however).

Credit Cards

Visa, MasterCard, Diners Club and American Express are widely accepted. For lost cards, contact the organisation:

American Express ☎ 1300 132 639

Diners Club ☎ 1300 360 060

MasterCard ☎ 1800 120 113

Visa ☎ 1800 450 346

NEWSPAPERS & MAGAZINES

The *Sydney Morning Herald* is one of the best newspapers in Australia. It's a serious daily, but also captures some of Sydney's larrikinism. The other big Sydney paper is the Murdoch tabloid, the *Daily Telegraph,* which tends to concentrate on the lowest-common-denominator issues, such as kicking refugees when they're down, 'dole bludger' exposés and Nicole Kidman sightings (an obsession with all papers, actually).

Two national newspapers are available in Sydney: *The Australian,* a relatively conservative daily that has an interesting weekend edition; and the business-oriented *Australian Financial Review.* There are also a healthy number of weekly newspapers for Australia's ethnic communities, some published in English; these can be found in most newsagents.

Magazines worth looking out for include *Delicious,* an excellent Sydney-based foodies' mag with features, reviews and recipes. If it happens to be home-grown Australian political satire you're after, try the Sydney-based newspaper *The Chaser.* Caustically funny, it's probably going to get you up to speed on local politics faster than the broadsheets will. You can purchase a copy at most newsagents.

Sydney has a healthy free street press, available from boutiques, bars and cafés. It includes music publications (*3D World, Revolver, Drum Media*) and gay and lesbian newspapers (*Sydney Star Observer, Lesbians On The Loose, SX*).

ORGANISED TOURS
Harbour Cruises

There's a wide range of harbour cruises available, from paddle steamers to sailing yachts. If you're pinching pennies, take the $12.80 return trip on the ferry to Manly and consider yourself very clever.

CAPTAIN COOK CRUISES
☎ 9206 1111; www.captaincook.com.au; Wharf 6, Circular Quay

As well as harbour highlights and ritzy dinner cruises, this crew offers the aquatic version of a hop-on/hop-off bus tour – with 11 daily departures stopping at Watsons Bay, Shark Island (selected cruises only), Taronga Zoo, Luna Park, Darling Harbour and Circular Quay (adult/child $29/15).

MAGISTIC CRUISES
☎ 8296 7222; www.magisticcruises.com.au; King St, Wharf 5, Darling Harbour or Wharf 6, Circular Quay

The fancy boats of Magistic have a range of cruising options, ranging from CruiseSmart (one hour, adult/child/family $33/18/80, four daily) offering all the harbour icons and a free beer, to a Dinner Cruise (two hours, adult/child $89/49, daily) with a seafood buffet.

MATILDA CRUISES
☎ 9264 7377; www.matilda.com.au; Aquarium Wharf, Darling Harbour

Not waltzing but sailing, Matilda offers eight different cruise options on luxury catamarans, including daily whale-watching trips between June and July (adult/child $75/59).

OZ JET BOATING
☎ 9808 3700; www.ozjetboating.com; East Circular Quay

See the harbour as it whizzes by in a 30-minute (adult/child $55/40) or 45-minute (adult/child $80/55) short, fast, adrenalin-pumping blur. Each trip includes a safety briefing so the actual cruising time is even shorter.

SYDNEY FERRIES HARBOURSIGHTS CRUISES
☎ 131 500; www.sydneyferries.info/attractions /harboursightscruises.php; Circular Quay

These excellent short cruises allow you to take in the sights, sounds and smells of the harbour at a reasonable price. Take your pick from the Morning Cruise (one hour, adult/child $18/9, 10.30am), Afternoon Cruise (2½ hours, adult/child $24/12, 1pm Monday to Friday, 12.30pm Saturday and Sunday) or Evening Harbour Lights Cruise (1½ hours, adult/child $22/11, 8pm Monday to Saturday). You'll need to arrive early as tickets are allocated on a first-in, first-seated basis.

SYDNEY SHOWBOATS
☎ 8296 7200; www.sydneyshowboats.com.au; King St, Wharf 5, Darling Harbour

Settle in for a three-hour, three-course dinner cruise ($125) on these paddlewheelers and you'll get showgirls flashing their knickers Moulin Rougue–style, cabaret singers and a personal magician for your table. Very, very camp.

TRIBAL WARRIOR
☎ 96993491; www.tribalwarrior.org; Pontoon, East Circular Quay

Cruise, learn and experience Aboriginal culture and history on this two-hour boat trip (adult/child $55/45), stopping at Clark Island for a traditional Koori welcome. You'll be contributing to a worthwhile community self-sufficiency project. Bookings essential.

City Bus Tours
BONDI EXPLORER
☎ 131 500; www.sydneypass.info; adult/child/ family $39/19/97; ⏲ 8.45am-4.15pm

The Bondi Explorer runs along a large circuit from Circular Quay to Kings Cross, Double Bay, Rose Bay, Vaucluse, Watsons Bay, Bondi Beach, Coogee, returning to the city via Randwick and Moore Park. Just riding around the circuit takes two hours, so if you want to get off at many of the 19 places of interest along the way, start early. Blue buses depart every 30 minutes, and tickets can be purchased on board or at TransitShops (p218).

SYDNEY EXPLORER
☎ 131 500; www.sydneypass.info; adult/child/ family $39/19/97; ⏲ 8.40am-5.20pm

Red buses navigate the inner city on a route designed to pass most central attractions. A bus departs from Circular Quay every 20 minutes, but you can board at any of the 27 clearly marked red bus stops on the route. Tickets are sold on board and at Transit-Shops (p218) and entitle you to get on and off the bus as often as you like. Commentary is provided, and sights include the Opera House, the Art Gallery of NSW, Kings Cross and the Powerhouse Museum.

Tours on Foot

There are plenty of guided tours for those who prefer to pound the pavement while sightseeing. If you'd prefer to go it alone, we've put together a walking tour for each neighbourhood covered by this book. The City of Sydney (www.cityofsydney.nsw.gov.au) publish a series of walking tour pamphlets, available from information kiosks and downloadable from their website. See also Sydney Architecture Walks (p35).

BRIDGECLIMB Map p54

☎ 8274 7777; www.bridgeclimb.com; 5 Cumberland St, The Rocks; adult $179-295, child $109-195

A once-in-a-lifetime experience and worth the bucks for the unforgettable views and the enthusiastic guides. Even if you're afraid of heights, the scariest part is crossing over the grates while *under* the bridge; on the curved span itself the track is wide enough that you never look straight down. Plus, you're securely attached to a safety cable at all times. Hell, if everyone from Bruce Springsteen to Bette Midler has done it, how bad can it be?

The 3½-hour tour includes safety checks and donning the climbing suit. The Discovery Climb is a new variation, taking you via steep ramps and ladders into the internal workings of the bridge before following the arch to the top.

You'll get a complimentary group photo, but cameras are banned so any other photos must be purchased (at premium prices). The priciest climbs are at dawn and twilight.

SYDNEY ABORIGINAL DISCOVERIES

☎ 9680 3098; www.sydneyaustour.com.au /Abordiscover.html; adult $66-180

This outfit offers a variety of interesting tours focused on indigenous culture and history. Options include a harbour cruise, an enjoyable walkabout tour, a feast of native Australian foods and a Dreamtime cruise.

SYDNEY GUIDED TOURS

☎ 9660 7157; www.ozemail.com.au/~mpfry; 2hr guided walk per person $18, minimum 10 people, or $180 per tour

A one-woman operation, Maureen Fry caters mainly for groups but she can take individuals or perhaps fit you in with another crowd.

THE ROCKS GHOST TOURS

☎ 1300 731 971; www.ghosttours.com.au; tour $34

If you like a good creepy yarn, these two-hour tours depart from Cadman's Cottage (p56) nightly (6.45pm April to October, 7.45pm November to March).

THE ROCKS WALKING TOURS

Map p54

☎ 9247 6678; 23 Playfair St, The Rocks; adult/child $22/11

With regular 90-minute tours, this outfit will lead you through the historical Rocks area, point out details you'd never see on your own and tell you tales of the colourful characters that once lived here. Tours run weekdays at 10.30am, 12.30pm and 2.30pm (January just 10.30am and 2.30pm) and weekends at 11.30am and 2pm.

Other Tours

BIKESCAPE

☎ 9569 4111; www.bikescape.com.au; 183 Parramatta Rd, Annandale; tours from $110

Bikescape offers Harley Davidson tours around town or lengthy road trips. It's also a trustworthy source of motorbikes for hire – from $82 per day for a 125cc Vespa, to $305 for a 1450cc Harley Davidson Road King.

DESTINY TOURS

☎ 9943 0167; www.destinytours.com.au; adult $36-77, child $18-39

Quirky as all hell, this company offers night-time ghost and history tours in a black Cadillac hearse named Elvira. Discover the unwritten side of Sydney while rattling some skeletons in the city's murky closets.

OZ TRAILS

☎ 1300 853 842; www.oztrails.com.au

This reader-recommended tour operator specialises in small-group day tours to the Blue Mountains (adult/child $68/60, departs 8am, returns 6pm), Hunter Valley (boutique wine tour $88) and other choice spots.

You can arrange a charter or join in with another troup.

SYDNEY BY SEAPLANE
☎ 9974 1455; www.sydneybyseaplane.com; Rose Bay Seaplane Base, Lyne Park, Rose Bay; adult $145-475, child $101-330; 🚢 Rose Bay

If you think Sydney looks beautiful from the ground, a scenic flight will knock your socks off. This organisation has a variety of scenic flights (from 15 to 60 minutes) which offer views of Sydney Harbour, the northern beaches and coastline, plus areas further afield such as the Hawkesbury River and Ku-ring-gai Chase National Park. Fly and dine packages are also available, from picnics in obscure places to hard-to-reach posh restaurants.

SYDNEY NIGHT CAT TOURS
☎ 1300 551 608; www.nightcattours.com; adult/child $69/55

Check out some of Sydney's famous quirky nightspots on this night-time bus tour. It offers plenty of opportunities to stop for snacks and drinks, including a complimentary feed. Chartered day trips to the Blue Mountains and Hunter Valley are also available.

PHARMACIES
Every shopping strip and mall has a pharmacy. The following have conveniently long hours:

Blakes Pharmacy (Map p78; ☎ 9358 6712; 20 Darlinghurst Rd, Kings Cross; 🕑 8am-11pm Mon-Fri, 9am-11pm Sat & Sun)

Park Pharmacy (Map pp100–1; ☎ 9552 3372; 321 Glebe Point Rd, Glebe; 🕑 8am-8pm Mon-Sat, 9am-8pm Sun)

Wu's Pharmacy (Map p72; ☎ 9211 1805; 629 George St, City; 🕑 9am-9pm Mon-Sat, 9am-7pm Sun)

POST
There are post office branches everywhere throughout the city centre.

Australia Post (www.auspost.com.au)

General post office (GPO; Map pp62–3; 1 Martin Pl, City; 🕑 8.15am-5.30pm Mon-Fri, 10am-2pm Sat) Original central post office.

Poste restante service (Map pp62–3; ☎ 9244 3732; level 2A, Hunter Connection building, 310 George St, City; 🕑 8.15am-5.30pm Mon-Fri) You'll need identification.

It costs 50c to send a postcard or standard letter within Australia. Airmail letters (weighing up to 50g) cost $1.30 to the Asia/Pacific region and $1.95 to the rest of the world. Mailing postcards anywhere outside Australia costs a flat $1.25.

RADIO
Sydney is not short of radio stations. The Australian Broadcasting Commission (ABC) has the intelligent talk stations Radio National (576AM) and 702 ABC Sydney (702AM), along with the wonderful ABC Classic FM (92.9FM). Triple J (105.7FM) is the ABC's popular alternative rock station. There are also the SBS multilingual stations (1107AM and 97.7FM), the multicultural 2000 FM (98.5FM) and the fabulous subscriber-based 2MBS (102.5FM). The unique Koori Radio broadcasts on 88.9FM.

TAX & REFUNDS
There is a 10% goods and services tax (GST) automatically added to almost anything you buy. If you purchase goods with a total minimum value of $300 from any one store within 30 days of departure from Australia, you are entitled to a refund of any GST paid. Keep your receipts and carry the items on board your flight; you can get a cheque refund at the designated booth located past customs at Sydney airport (see www.customs.gov.au/site/page.cfm?u=4646 for more information).

TELEPHONE
Public telephones, which can be found all over the city, take phonecards, credit cards and occasionally coins. Local calls cost 50c.

Australia's country code is ☎ 61 and Sydney's area code is ☎ 02. Toll-free numbers start with the prefix ☎ 1800, while numbers that start with ☎ 1300 charge only the cost of a local call. Australia's international access code is ☎ 0011 (used when dialling other countries from Australia). Drop the zero from the area code when dialling into Australia.

Most hotels will have services that allow you to send or receive faxes. Global Gossip (see p223) has fax machines as well.

Mobile Phones
Phone numbers with four-digit prefixes beginning with 04 are for mobiles. Australia's

digital network is compatible with GSM 900 and 1800 handsets (used in Europe). Quad-band US phones will work, but to avoid global-roaming charges, you need an unlocked handset that takes prepaid SIM cards from Australian providers such as Telstra, Optus, Virgin or Vodafone.

Mobiles brought from other states of Australia can be used in the Sydney area, but check roaming charges with your carrier. Sydneysiders will seem glued to their mobiles at all times of the day and night. Despite a reasonable grasp of phone etiquette – not in cinemas, not at the opera, not at funerals – many Sydneysiders will still answer handheld mobiles while driving, despite it being illegal. If some idiot nearly runs you down at a pedestrian crossing, chances are they'll be on their mobile.

Phonecards

Local and international phonecards range in value from $5 to $50 – look for the phonecard logo at retail outlets, such as newsagents. There is a bewildering variety of cards available, with all sorts of deals aimed at visitors wanting to get in touch with loved ones in the Europe, Asia and the Americas. Shop around.

TV

Sydney has five free-to-air TV channels. ABC (channel two) is government-funded and relies heavily on BBC material, and also offers good local news and current affairs programs, with the occasional documentary, drama or comedy thrown in. Seven and Nine get the biggest ratings, showing a steady run of popular American shows, shock-and-horror news and endless sports such as cricket and footy. Ten is similar but targeted at the youth market with profitable reality shows, wacky sitcoms and American reruns. SBS invariably has the most intelligent programming, screening plenty of foreign films, multicultural programs, artistic documentaries, occasional soccer finals and the best news around.

TIME

Sydney is on Eastern Standard Time (EST), which is 10 hours ahead of GMT/UTC. That means when it's noon in Sydney it's 9pm the day before in New York, 6pm the day before in Los Angeles, 2am in London, 4am in Johannesburg, 11am in Tokyo and 2pm in Auckland. Daylight savings time is one hour ahead of standard time from late October to March.

TIPPING

Most services don't expect a tip and you shouldn't feel pressured into giving one, even at fancy restaurants. If the service is good, however, it is customary to tip porters (gold coin), waiters and waitresses (10%) and taxi drivers (round up to the nearest dollar).

TOURIST INFORMATION

All hours following vary with the seasons; summer hours tend to be longer.

City Host Information Kiosk Circular Quay (Map p54; 9am-4.45pm); Martin Place (Map pp62–3); Town Hall (Map pp62–3) The Martin Place and Town Hall outlets have sporadic opening hours/days.

Darling Harbour Visitors Centre (Map p72; ☎ 9240 8797; Darling Harbour; 9.30am-5.30pm) Behind the IMAX Theatre; specialising in info about NSW, with lots of pamphlets on tours, hotels and entertainment options.

Manly Visitor Information Centre (Map p110; ☎ 9977 1088; Manly Wharf; 9am-5pm Mon-Fri, 10am-4pm Sat & Sun) This helpful visitors centre, just outside the ferry wharf and alongside the bus interchange, has free pamphlets on the 10km Manly Scenic Walkway (p110) and other Manly attractions, plus loads of local bus information.

Parramatta Heritage & Visitors Centre (☎ 8839 3311; 346A Church St; 9am-5pm) Staff are incredibly knowledgable with loads of brochures and leaflets on hand, and plenty of info on access for visitors with impaired mobility and for those with an interest in Aboriginal sites.

Sydney Coach Terminal (Map p72; ☎ 9281 9366; Eddy Ave, Central Station; 6am-10pm) Bus and hotel bookings, plus luggage storage. Not radically helpful, but then again, it could just be the location, which has extremely bad feng shui.

Sydney Harbour National Parks Information Centre (Map p54; ☎ 9247 5033; Cadman's Cottage, 110 George St, The Rocks; 9.30am-4.30pm Mon-Fri, 10am-4.30pm Sat & Sun) Has maps of walks in different parts of the park and organises tours of the harbour islands.

Sydney Visitor Centre (☎ 9667 6058; Sydney airport; 6am-10.30pm) A good first port of call for travellers flying into Sydney. Book discounted hotel rooms, tours, entertainment tickets and even onward travel.

The Rocks Sydney Visitor Centre (Map p54; ☎ 9240 8788; www.sydneyvisitorcentre.com; cnr Argyle & Playfair Sts, The Rocks; ⏰ 9.30am-5.30pm) Helpful and knowledgable staff, with tons of brochures and information on aspects of Sydney and NSW. Find a hotel, get the lowdown on restaurants with harbour views, book a tour and arrange transport for day trips out of town. Ask about walking around the neighbourhood.

TRAVELLERS WITH DISABILITIES

Compared with many other major cities, Sydney has great disabled access for its citizens and visitors. Most of Sydney's main attractions are accessible by wheelchair, and all new or renovated buildings must, by law, include wheelchair access. Older buildings can pose some problems, however, and some restaurants and entertainment venues aren't quite up to scratch. A number of taxis accommodate wheelchairs – advise the operator when making a telephone booking.

Most of Sydney's major attractions offer hearing loops and sign-language interpreters for hearing-impaired travellers. It's best to make contact with venue staff in advance.

Many new buildings incorporate architectural features that are helpful to the vision impaired, such as textured floor details at the top and bottom of stairs. Sydney's pedestrian crossings feature sound cues.

Sydney also has lots of parking spaces reserved for disabled drivers. The City of Sydney (www.cityofsydney.nsw.gov.au) has information about accessibility on their website.

Organisations

Access Foundation (☎ 9692 9322; www.accessibility .com.au; 56 Bowman St, Pyrmont)

City of Sydney (www.cityofsydney.nsw.gov.au/About Sydney/CBDDisabledAccess/Default.asp) Website lists parking spaces, transport information, CBD access maps and other information.

Deaf Society of NSW (☎ 9893 8555; www.deaf societynsw.org.au; 4th fl, 169 Macquarie St, Parramatta)

Roads and Transport Authority (☎ 13 22 13; www .rta.nsw.gov.au) Supplies temporary parking permits for disabled international drivers.

Spinal Cord Injuries Australia (www.scia.org.au) Publishes the handy Access Sydney ($15.95).

Vision Australia (☎ 1300 84 74 66; www.rbs.org.au; 4 Mitchell St, Enfield)

VISAS

Unless you're a New Zealand citizen you'll require a visa for visiting Australia. Citizens of Canada, the US, Japan, Hong Kong, many European countries and a few others can easily get an Electronic Travel Authority (ETA; www.eta.immi .gov.au) online. It's quick, costs only $20 and is valid for up to three months (and good for one year). You must apply for it from outside Australia. Check the website to see if you are eligible.

If you're not from an eligible country, you'll need to apply for a three- or six-month tourist visa ($70 outside Australia, $204 within the country).

Regular visa application forms are available from either Australian diplomatic missions overseas or travel agents; you can apply by mail or in person. For further details, call the Department of Immigration and Citizenship (DIAC; ☎ 131 881; www.immi.gov.au). For the nearest consulate in your country check www.immi.gov.au /contacts/overseas/index.htm.

WOMEN TRAVELLERS

Sydney is generally safe for women travellers, although you should avoid walking alone late at night. Sexual harassment and discrimination, while uncommon, can occur and shouldn't be tolerated. If you do encounter infantile sexism from drunken louts, the best option is to leave without making any comments. In bars, use good sense and don't accept drinks from people you don't know or leave your drink unattended. Spiking drinks isn't a common practice, but it has occurred in the past.

WORK

Single visitors aged between 18 and 30 from Canada, the UK, the Republic of Ireland, the Netherlands, France, Italy, Germany, Hong Kong, Korea, Japan and most Scandinavian countries may be eligible for a working holiday visa. A few other nationalities are also eligible; see www.immi.gov.au for more information.

A working holiday visa allows for a stay of up to 12 months, but the emphasis is on casual, or incidental, employment rather than a full-time job, so working full-time for longer than three months with any one employer is not allowed.

There are strict regulations governing overseas visitors working in Australia; see the website listed earlier for details. The best place to seek work is in the Saturday employment section of the *Sydney Morning Herald*, but many hostels will help find you work (though it won't be highly paid). Jobs are also available on www.seek.com.au.

BEHIND THE SCENES

THIS BOOK

This guidebook was commissioned in Lonely Planet's Melbourne office, and produced by the following:

Commissioning Editors Meg Worby, Emma Gilmour

Coordinating Editors Brooke Lyons, Jeanette Wall

Coordinating Cartographer Julie Sheridan

Coordinating Layout Designer Pablo Gastar

Managing Editors Geoff Howard, Suzannah Shwer

Managing Cartographer David Connolly

Managing Layout Designer Adam McCrow

Assisting Editors Victoria Harrison, Shawn Lo, Kristin Odijk, Averil Robertson

Assisting Cartographers Corey Hutchison, Sophie Richards

Cover Designer Pepi Bluck

Project Managers Craig Kilburn, Glenn van der Knijff

Talk2Us Coordinator Trent Paton

Thanks to Sin Choo, Mark Germanchis, Lauren Hunt, Laura Jane, Indra Kilfoyle, Adriana Mammarella, Fionnuala Twomey, Celia Wood, Wendy Wright

Cover photographs Sailing Sydney Harbour, Steffan Hill/Alamy (top); a Sydney bar, Daniel New (bottom).

Internal photographs p12 (#3) Simon Bracken; p9 (#2) Chad Ehlers/Alamy; p7 (#5) David Hancock/Alamy; p2, p3, p4 (#1), p6 (#2), p7 (#4), p8 (#3), p12 (#1) Travis Drevers; p6 (#1) Andrew Nisbet/iStockphoto; p10 (#2) Richard Phipps; p11 (#3) Popperfoto/Alamy; p9 (#3) Jan Rihak/iStockphoto; p10 (#3) Jay Valabjee (www.photosbyjay .com.au); p10 (#1) David Wall/Alamy. All other photographs by Lonely Planet Images: p4 (#2), p7 (#3) Ross Barnett; p12 (#2) John Borthwick; p8 (#1, #4), p11 (#1) Greg Elms; p5 (#4) John Hay; p11 (#2) Holger Leue; p5 (#3) Oliver Strewe; p8 (#2), p9 (#1) Gillianne Tedder.

All images are copyright of the photographer unless otherwise indicated. Many of the images in this guide are available for licensing from Lonely Planet Images: www .lonelyplanetimages.com.

LONELY PLANET: TRAVEL WIDELY, TREAD LIGHTLY, GIVE SUSTAINABLY

The Lonely Planet Story

The story begins with a classic travel adventure: Tony and Maureen Wheeler's 1972 journey across Europe and Asia to Australia. There was no useful information about the overland trail then, so Tony and Maureen published the first Lonely Planet guidebook to meet a growing need.

From a kitchen table, Lonely Planet has grown to become the largest independent travel publisher in the world, with offices in Melbourne (Australia), Oakland (USA) and London (UK). Today Lonely Planet guidebooks cover the globe. There is an ever-growing list of books and information in a variety of media. Some things haven't changed. The main aim is still to make it possible for adventurous individuals to get out there – to explore and better understand the world.

The Lonely Planet Foundation

The Lonely Planet Foundation proudly supports nimble nonprofit institutions working for change in the world. Each year the foundation donates 5% of Lonely Planet company profits to projects selected by staff and authors. Our partners range from Kabissa, which provides small nonprofits across Africa with access to technology, to the Foundation for Developing Cambodian Orphans, which supports girls at risk of falling victim to sex traffickers.

Many – such as Louis Sarno who works with BaAka (Pygmy) children in the forested areas of Central African Republic – choose to focus on women and children as one of the most effective ways to support the whole community. Louis is determined to give options to children who are discriminated against by the majority Bantu population.

Sometimes foundation assistance is as simple as restoring a local ruin like the Minaret of Jam in Afghanistan; this incredible monument now draws intrepid tourists to the area and its restoration has greatly improved options for local people.

Just as travel is often about learning to see with new eyes, so many of the groups we work with aim to change the way people see themselves and the future for their children and communities.

THANKS

PETER DRAGICEVICH

I owe a huge debt of gratitude to Jolyon Attwooll, David Mills and Barry Sawtell, and Meg Worby, without whom I couldn't have done it. Thanks to all my Sydney friends and family for advice on everything from hot clubs to hidden boutiques, as well as helping me eat and drink my way around the city: Tony, Daniel, Lauren, Matthew and Linda Dragicevich, Kristen Alexander, Selina Altomonte, Jo Brook, Carly Burgess, Marie Chemney, Mary Cunningham, Liz Davies, Stacy Farrar, James Hedderman & Lorraine Ryan, Drew Lambert, Tim Moyes, Daniel Preston, Jo Stafford, Gary Stocks, Jacqueline Stokes, Kerri Tyler and Sin Won. Back in Auckland, thanks to Phillippa Steel and Scott Judson for the writing retreat, and Dad for your patience. Love always to my Charlie, who never quite escaped Sydney.

JOLYON ATTWOOLL

Covering my birth city and its beautiful surrounds was a revelation – thank you to Meg Worby for giving me the chance. Thanks also to James Thompson and Emma Robson, whose romance brought me back to Australia. Their hospitality was fantastic, as was that of my legendary cousin Ed Thomas in Melbourne. Equally generous were Jane Mundy and Graham Mason, as well as Pam Roberts, whose passion for the Blue Mountains and the North Shore helped me enormously. Sarah Lenthall brought me entertainingly up to speed on the latest Sydney architecture. Main author Peter Dragicevich massively bore the brunt of this complex project – his professionalism and tips were much appreciated. The usual thanks to my family for their back-up. Final mention goes to Hannah Crisford, whose support has been exactly magnificent.

OUR READERS

Many thanks to the travellers who used the last edition and wrote to us with helpful hints, useful advice and interesting anecdotes:

A Kim Ahrend, Alison Anderson, Julia Anten, Helene Apper B Heini Baumgartner, Lachenal Bernard, Bob & Jessica Berryman, Chris Bockisch, Yves Bocquet, Michael Bonnet, G Bowyer-Sidwell, Jen Branigan, Carolyn Brown, Vicky Burling C Andrew Caballero-Reynolds, David Carlin, Dave Cartwright, Joe Cassels, Gina Clark, Natasha Cosby, Lynne Coupethwaite, Greg Crouch D Fe Denton, Heribert Dieter E Tim Evans, Mary Ewen F Joanna Fellows, Tal & Hadas Fuhrer G Emilie Gaboriaud, Anne Glazier, Michelle Godwin, Dorte Gollek, Helen Gordon, Marie-Adele Guicharnaud

SEND US YOUR FEEDBACK

We love to hear from travellers – your comments keep us on our toes and help make our books better. Our well-travelled team reads every word on what you loved or loathed about this book. Although we cannot reply individually to postal submissions, we always guarantee that your feedback goes straight to the appropriate authors, in time for the next edition. Each person who sends us information is thanked in the next edition – and the most useful submissions are rewarded with a free book.

To send us your updates – and find out about Lonely Planet events, newsletters and travel news – visit our award-winning website: www.lonelyplanet.com/contact.

Note: We may edit, reproduce and incorporate your comments in Lonely Planet products such as guidebooks, websites and digital products, so let us know if you don't want your comments reproduced or your name acknowledged. For a copy of our privacy policy visit www.lonelyplanet.com/privacy.

H Liz Hallett, Jim Hamilton, Siobhan Hanbury-Aggs, Monica Hearn, Jamey Heit, Greg Henderson, Josh Heuchan, Ieuan Hopper, Nessa Horewitch, Judith Houlihan, Gemma Hull, Jennifer Hynd J Chris Johnson K Kazuya Kawata, Hilde Keunen L Jan Lane, Gizella Lantai, Simon Lavender, Martin Lerner, Eoghan Lewis, Goff Lucas M Lorna Macgougan, Mark Martelletti, Trevor Mazzucchelli, Maureen McCarthy, Trish McLean, Linda Milward, Erling Moldal, Yasantha Monerawela, T W Mortyn, Maarten Munnik, Phil & Rhonda Murray N Kelly Noyce P S Pathirana, David Patterson, Vikki Peat, Roberta Petri, Kevin Philipson, Scott Phillips, Matt Piper, Iris Plaitakis, Evan Player, Katie Powell, Suzanne Prymek, Dirk Pueschel R Jean Relph, Scott Remnant, Jim Revell, Nathan Reynolds, Monique Rhodes, Julie Richards-Fox, Sue Ring, David Rowe, Noeline Rowe S Pierre Sagrafena, Darren Salter, Kathrin Seyer, Anna Sordo, Stephanie Stevens, Amanda Stillings, Neil Stopforth T George Tam, Andrew Temple, Jamie Textor, Erik Tjernström, Amanda Townsend, Susan Trenholm V Justin Villemin W Jane West, Nick Whyles, Katherine Wilson, Michael Wohl, Alex Wriedt Y Kin Yip, Andrew Young Z Yvonne Zuidam

ACKNOWLEDGMENTS

Many thanks to the following for the use of their content:
Sydney Ferries Corporation Network Map © 2007 Sydney Ferries Corporation
CityRail Sydney Suburban Network Map © 2006 RailCorp

Notes

Notes

Notes

Notes

INDEX

A

Aboriginal people
  art 28
  books 22
  culture 31-2
  history 21-2
  issues 119
  land claims 22, 26
  languages 21
  music 31-2
  rock engravings 95, 110, 112, 214
  rock paintings 109
  sights 58
  stolen generation 24, 25, 26
  voting 25
accommodation 188, *see also* Sleeping *subindex*
  Bondi 195
  Chinatown 190-1
  Circular Quay 188-9
  City Centre 189-90
  Coogee 195-6
  Darling Harbour 190-1
  Darlinghurst 191-2
  Double Bay 194
  Inner West 196
  Kings Cross 192
  Manly 197-8
  Newtown 196
  North Shore 197-8
  Paddington 193-4
  Potts Point 192-3

000 map pages
000 photographs

Randwick 195-6
Rocks, The 188-9
Surry Hills 194-5
Woollahra 193-4
Woolloomooloo 193
activities 174-80, *see also individual activities,* Sports & Activities *subindex*
Adventures of Priscilla, Queen of the Desert, The 27, 104, 126, 184
AFL 178
air travel 216
airport accommodation 197
Alexandria 89, **90-1**
  attractions 89-92
  food 146-7
  shopping 130-1
  transport 89
ambulances 222
animals 39, 41
antiques, *see* Shopping *subindex*
Anzac Bridge 103
Anzac Memorial 67
aquariums 71, 111
architecture 34-7, *see also* buildings & structures
area codes, *see inside front cover*
Argyle Place 59
art galleries, *see* galleries
Art Gallery of NSW 66
Arthouse Hotel 69
arts 18, 26-34, 168-72, *see also individual arts,* Arts *subindex,* Shopping *subindex*
Artspace 80
ATMs 224
Aurora Place 35, 70
Aussie Rules Football 43, 178
Aussie Stadium 85
Australia Day 16
Australia Square 36, 61, 70
Australian Centre for Photography 85
Australian Fashion Week 17
Australian Football League 43

Australian Museum 77
Australian National Maritime Museum 71
Australian Rules Football 43, 178
Avalon 112
Avoca Beach 215

B

baby-sitting 221
Balls Head Reserve 109
Balmain 99, **100-1**
  attractions 103-4
  bars, pubs & clubs 165-6
  food 150
  shopping 134
  transport 103
Balmain Markets 124
Balmoral 106
Balmoral Beach 111, 115
Banks, Joseph 22
Barrenjoey Lighthouse 113
bars, *see* drinking, drinking & Nightlife *subindex*
Bateau Bay 214
bats 57
beaches
  Avalon 112
  Balmoral Beach 111, 115
  Bilgola 112
  Bondi Beach 19, 93, 98, **4**
  Bronte Baths 98
  Bronte Beach 96, 98
  Camp Cove 117, **4**
  Chinaman's Beach 111
  Clontarf Beach 111
  Clovelly Beach 98
  Cobblers Beach 111
  Collaroy 112
  Coogee Beach 96, 97
  Coogee Ocean Pools 96
  Curl Curl 112
  Dee Why 112
  Dolphin Point 97
  Forty Baskets Beach 111
  Freshwater 112
  Lady Bay 117
  Mahon Pool 97, **5**
  Manly Cove 111
  Narrabeen 112
  Northern Beaches 112
  Obelisk 111

Palm Beach 112
Parsley Bay 117
Redleaf Pool 87, 117
Reef Beach 111
Shark Beach 117
Store Beach 111
Tamarama Beach 96, 98
Washaway Beach 111
Whale Beach 112
Bellevue Park 95
Bells Line of Road 206
Ben Buckler Lookout 98
Berowra Waters 213
Bicentennial Park 103
bicycle travel, *see* cycling
Biennale of Sydney 18
Big Day Out 16
Bilgola 112
birds 39
Blue Mountains 200-7, **203**
boat travel 217
Bondi 93, **94-5, 97**
  accommodation 195
  attractions 93-6
  bars, pubs & clubs 163
  food 147-8
  shopping 131-2
  transport 95
  walking tour 97-8
Bondi Beach 19, 93, 98, **4**
Bondi Icebergs Swimming Club 163, 175, **2**
Bondi Markets 124
books 33-4, *see also* Shopping *subindex*
Botanic Gardens 30, 57-8, 60, **9**
Botany Bay National Park 119
Bouddi National Park 214
Boyd, Arthur 29
Brett Whiteley Studio 89
BridgeClimb 226, **12**
Brisbane Water National Park 214
Broken Bay 214
Bronte 93, **94-5, 97**
  attractions 96
  food 148
  transport 95
  walking tour 97-8
Bronte Baths 98

INDEX

000 map pages
000 photographs

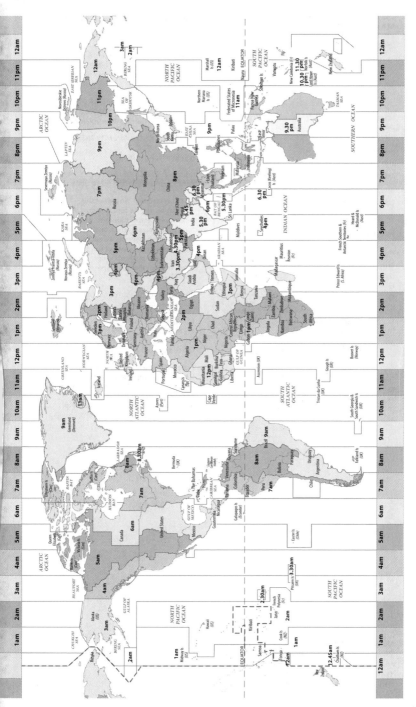

MAP LEGEND

ROUTES

Tollway	Mall/Steps
Freeway	Tunnel
Primary	Pedestrian Overpass
Secondary	Walking Tour
Tertiary	Walking Trail
Lane	Walking Path
Unsealed Road	
One-Way Street	

TRANSPORT

Ferry	Rail
Monorail	Rail (Underground)

HYDROGRAPHY

River, Creek	Water

AREA FEATURES

Airport	Land
Beach	Mall
Building	Market
Campus	Park
Cemetery, Christian	Sports

POPULATION

◉ CAPITAL (STATE)	● **Large City**
● Small City	○ Town

SYMBOLS

Sights
- Beach
- Christian
- Jewish
- Monument
- Museum, Gallery
- Point of Interest
- Winery, Vineyard
- Zoo, Aquarium

Sports & Activities
- Diving, Snorkelling
- Pool

Eating
- Eating

Drinking & Nightlife
- Drinking & Nightlife

The Arts
- The Arts

Shopping
- Shopping

Sleeping
- Sleeping
- Camping

Transport
- Airport, Airfield
- Bus Station

Directory
- Bank, ATM
- Embassy/Consulate
- Hospital, Medical
- Information
- Internet Facilities
- Police Station
- Post Office, GPO
- Toilets

Geographic
- Lighthouse
- Lookout
- Mountain, Volcano
- National Park
- Pass
- Waterfall

Published by Lonely Planet Publications Pty Ltd
ABN 36 005 607 983

Australia Head Office, Locked Bag 1, Footscray, Victoria 3011, ☎ 03 8379 8000, fax 03 8379 8111, talk2us@lonelyplanet .com.au

USA 150 Linden St, Oakland, CA 94607, ☎ 510 893 8555, toll free 800 275 8555, fax 510 893 8572, info@lonelyplanet.com

UK 186 City Rd, London, EC1V 2NT, ☎ 020 7106 2100, go@lonelyplanet.co.uk

Printed through Colorcraft Ltd, Hong Kong. Printed in China.